AF748020

Human–Computer Interaction Series

Editors-in-chief
Desney Tan, Microsoft Research, USA
Jean Vanderdonckt, Université Catholique de Louvain, Belgium

HCI is a multidisciplinary field focused on human aspects of the development of computer technology. As computer-based technology becomes increasingly pervasive – not just in developed countries, but worldwide – the need to take a human-centered approach in the design and development of this technology becomes ever more important. For roughly 30 years now, researchers and practitioners in computational and behavioral sciences have worked to identify theory and practice that influences the direction of these technologies, and this diverse work makes up the field of human-computer interaction. Broadly speaking it includes the study of what technology might be able to do for people and how people might interact with the technology. The HCI series publishes books that advance the science and technology of developing systems which are both effective and satisfying for people in a wide variety of contexts. Titles focus on theoretical perspectives (such as formal approaches drawn from a variety of behavioral sciences), practical approaches (such as the techniques for effectively integrating user needs in system development), and social issues (such as the determinants of utility, usability and acceptability).

Titles published within the Human–Computer Interaction Series are included in Thomson Reuters' Book Citation Index, The DBLP Computer Science Bibliography and The HCI Bibliography.

More information about this series at http://www.springer.com/series/6033

Linda Little • Daniel Fitton
Beth T. Bell • Nicola Toth
Editors

Perspectives on HCI Research with Teenagers

Springer

Editors
Linda Little
PaCT Lab, Department of Psychology, Faculty of Health and Life Sciences
Northumbria University
Newcastle, UK

Beth T. Bell
Faculty of Health and Life Sciences
York St John University
York, UK

Daniel Fitton
Child-Computer Interaction Group, School of Physical Sciences and Computing
University of Central Lancashire
Preston, UK

Nicola Toth
PaCT Lab, Department of Psychology, Faculty of Health and Life Sciences
Northumbria University
Newcastle, UK

ISSN 1571-5035
Human–Computer Interaction Series
ISBN 978-3-319-33448-6 ISBN 978-3-319-33450-9 (eBook)
DOI 10.1007/978-3-319-33450-9

Library of Congress Control Number: 2016947431

© Springer International Publishing Switzerland 2016
This work is subject to copyright. All rights are reserved by the Publisher, whether the whole or part of the material is concerned, specifically the rights of translation, reprinting, reuse of illustrations, recitation, broadcasting, reproduction on microfilms or in any other physical way, and transmission or information storage and retrieval, electronic adaptation, computer software, or by similar or dissimilar methodology now known or hereafter developed.
The use of general descriptive names, registered names, trademarks, service marks, etc. in this publication does not imply, even in the absence of a specific statement, that such names are exempt from the relevant protective laws and regulations and therefore free for general use.
The publisher, the authors and the editors are safe to assume that the advice and information in this book are believed to be true and accurate at the date of publication. Neither the publisher nor the authors or the editors give a warranty, express or implied, with respect to the material contained herein or for any errors or omissions that may have been made.

Printed on acid-free paper

This Springer imprint is published by Springer Nature
The registered company is Springer International Publishing AG Switzerland

Preface

The premise for this book emerged from a 2011 EPSRC grant 'Taking on the Teenagers (TAKEEN)' under the Transforming Energy Demand Through Digital Innovation (TEDDI) scheme. The grant was led by Professor Janet C. Read, director of the Child-Computer Interaction (ChiCI) research group at the University of Central Lancashire (UCLan), in collaboration with four other UK universities: Northumbria, Birmingham, Swansea and the Knowledge Lab, London. 'TAKEEN' was the first energy research project to engage directly with teenagers and involve them as 'co-investigators'. As teenagers acted as both participants and co-investigators, this made the project unique as it educated, informed and empowered teenagers through their active involvement. However, when designing studies for the TAKEEN project, the research teams at Northumbria and UCLan found a distinct gap in the literature with regard to methods and approaches that best suit teenage populations.

Understanding teenagers and developing appropriate methods are key to conducting successful HCI research. Working with teenagers typically presents more challenges than working with adults. Teenagers inhabit a diverse and changeable world that is often unfamiliar to adults. Teenagers are also subject to change through the biological, psychological and physical developments that occur during adolescence. Therefore it is vitally important that researchers understand teenagers' needs and preferences when creating new technologies and products with, and for, them. We need to consider that adults and children have received significant specific attention within the HCI community, whilst teenagers (or adolescents) have to date received comparatively little.

The lack of literature pertaining to appropriate methods was also reflected by the broader HCI community in international workshops held at CHI (2012, 2013, 2014) and IDC (2013). The overall aim of this book is to contribute to the methods and understandings necessary to successfully and sensitively engage teenagers in HCI research by providing (i) examples of robust methods all of the contributors have used when working with teenagers in research and design projects and (ii) a comprehensive reference book describing in detail methods, approaches and examples of how these can been applied to HCI research and teaching.

Finally, thanks are given to the teenagers that participated and to their families and teachers who facilitated the work.

Newcastle, UK — Linda Little
Preston, UK — Daniel Fitton
York, UK — Beth T. Bell
Newcastle, UK — Nicola Toth
March, 2016

Acknowledgement

The editors would like to thank everyone in the TAKEEN research teams based at Northumbria and University of Central Lancashire, UK. The editors would also like to thank all the contributing authors for all their hard work in making this book possible.

The idea for this book emerged from a project funded by the Research Councils UK's Digital Economy and Energy Programmes **EP/I002251/1** and **EP/I000720/1.**

Contents

Contributors

Sarah Atkinson Human Factors Research Group, University of Nottingham, Nottingham, UK

Beth T. Bell Faculty of Health and Life Sciences, York St John University, York, UK

Sue Cobb Human Factors Research Group, University of Nottingham, Nottingham, UK

Antonello Conti Digitaria International SA, Luxembourg, Luxembourg

Michael P. Craven NIHR MindTech Healthcare Technology Co-operative, Institute of Mental Health, University of Nottingham, Nottingham, UK

Alma Culén Department of Informatics, University of Oslo, Oslo, Norway

Daniel Fitton Child-Computer Interaction Group, School of Physical Sciences and Computing, University of Central Lancashire, Preston, UK

Jodi Forlizzi Human Computer Interaction Institute, Carnegie Mellon University, Pittsburgh, PA, USA

Voula Gkatzidou Department of Design, Brunel University, Uxbridge, UK

Peggy Gregory School of Physical Sciences and Computing, University of Central Lancashire, Preston, UK

Matthew Horton Child-Computer Interaction Group, School of Physical Sciences and Computing, University of Central Lancashire, Preston, UK

Alexandra R. Lang Human Factors Research Group, University of Nottingham, Nottingham, UK

Linda Little PaCT Lab, Department of Psychology, Faculty of Health and Life Sciences, Northumbria University, Newcastle, UK

Steve Love Digital Design Studio, The Glasgow School of Art, Glasgow, UK

Marco Mazzola Politecnico di Milano, Design Department, Milan, Italy

Neosperience Spa, Milan, Italy

Kerry McKellar Psychology and Communication Technology (PaCT) Lab, Department of Psychology, Faculty of Health and Life Sciences, Northumbria University, Newcastle, UK

Britt Nakstad Department of Pediatrics and Adolescent Medicine, Akershus University Hospital, Lørenskog, Norway

Institute for Clinical Medicine, University of Oslo, Oslo, Norway

William Odom School of Interactive Arts and Technology, Simon Fraser University, Surrey, BC, Canada

Janet C. Read Child-Computer Interaction Group, School of Physical Sciences and Computing, University of Central Lancashire, Preston, UK

Michelle Rouse Macmillan Cancer Support, London, UK

Lucy Simons NIHR MindTech Healthcare Technology Co-operative, Institute of Mental Health, University of Nottingham, Nottingham, UK

Margaret Machniak Sommervold Department of Informatics, University of Oslo, Oslo, Norway

Nicola Toth PaCT Lab, Department of Psychology, Faculty of Health and Life Sciences, Northumbria University, Newcastle, UK

Maja van der Velden Department of Informatics, University of Oslo, Oslo, Norway

Christopher R. Wilkinson University of Cambridge Research Office, Cambridge, UK

Neil Winterburn Child-Computer Interaction Group, University of Central Lancashire, Preston, UK

John Zimmerman Human-Computer Interaction Institute, Carnegie Mellon University, Pittsburgh, PA, USA

Chapter 1
Introduction: HCI Reaches Adolescence

Daniel Fitton, Linda Little, and Beth T. Bell

Abstract Adults have long been considered in detail in the Human Computer Interaction (HCI) community and children within the Child-Computer Interaction (CCI) community. However, teenagers (adolescents) have received far less specific consideration within the HCI and CCI areas (Fitton and Bell 2014; Fitton et al. 2013a). Teenagers are possibility the most diverse, dynamic, exciting, and technologically-aware user groups that will soon become be the next generation of adults. Working with teenagers can enable researchers to gather valuable insights and opportunities to inform the creation of new technologies. Researchers have now begun to explore this new and emerging area of Teen-Computer Interaction (TeenCI) and this book brings together some of the best work in this field to-date. The book provides the HCI and CCI communities with an inclusive account of methods and examples of best practise to inform those working with teenagers in technology contexts. The chapters recount research with teenagers in many different domains and provide many different contributions to the field of TeenCI including design methods, models, case studies and ethical consideration important for working with this user group. The aim of this book is to provide a solid foundation from which the TeenCI research area can grow alongside providing a valuable resource for those wishing to conduct HCI research with teenagers.

D. Fitton (✉)
Child-Computer Interaction Group, School of Physical Sciences and Computing, University of Central Lancashire, PR1 2HE, Preston, UK
e-mail: DBFitton@uclan.ac.uk

L. Little
PaCT Lab, Department of Psychology, Faculty of Health and Life Sciences, Northumbria University, Newcastle NE1 8ST, UK

B.T. Bell
Faculty of Health and Life Sciences, York St John University, York YO31 7EX, UK

© Springer International Publishing Switzerland 2016

L. Little et al. (eds.), *Perspectives on HCI Research with Teenagers*, Human–Computer Interaction Series, DOI 10.1007/978-3-319-33450-9_1

1.1 Human Computer Interaction

Human-Computer Interaction (HCI) has one of the largest and most diverse research communities in the world today. HCI is defined as a 'discipline concerned with the design, evaluation and implementation of interactive computing systems for human use and with the study of major phenomena surrounding them' (Hewett et al. 1992). The discipline spans across many areas; including Computer Science, Design, Psychology, Ergonomics, Art, Architecture, Sociology, and Music, to name just a few. The need to understand HCI became clear after many serious and sometimes fatal incidents involving computer-based systems (Leveson and Turner 1993). These incidents highlighted the fact that users of systems, user interfaces and associated usage had received frighteningly little consideration by those that created them.

While significant research on important HCI topics had been taking place since the 1960s, it was in 1983 with the formation of ACM SIGCHI (Special Interest Group on Computer-Human Interaction) when the HCI community we know today began to form. This new area sought to bring together academics and practitioners interested in taking an interdisciplinary approach to human factors, human performance, and improving users interfaces, all in the context of creating more useful and usable interactive technology. These areas were covered in the seminal book 'The Psychology of Human Computer Interaction' (Card et al. 1983).

The HCI research community is rich and diverse. This diversity is reflected in the associated academic publications where contributions span all areas from highly experimental and empirical works, to exploring theory and methods, to case studies from both research and industry. The field of HCI is constantly evolving and changing, and initial focus on technology in the workplace has expanded to become much more holistic. HCI as a research area will continue to be shaped by new technologies and possibilities that need to be explored, studied and understood in the context of human users.

1.2 Participatory Design

While the field of HCI encompasses many highly interesting areas one of the most pertinent to this book is that of involving end-users in the creation of interactive technologies. This perspective has its roots in Scandinavian Participatory Design (or Cooperative Design as it was originally known) that emerged in the 1970s. Participatory Design (PD) sought not only to include users in the design of new technology to leverage their expertise and lower barriers to change, but also saw users as having the democratic right to participate in decisions made during the design of technology that would impact their working environment (Bjerknes and Bratteteig 1995). PD does not prescribe a single specific technique that must be used but instead advocates a commitment to taking a user-centred perspective throughout the design of a system to ensure users are able to contribute to decisions made during the design process in an informed and independent way (Gregory 2003). There are many specific PD techniques that enable users to participate in the design process that can be organised along dimensions of making, telling and enacting which are chosen by the design team as they deem appropriate (Sanders et al. 2010). The Participatory Design movement also appreciated the importance of values within the design process and the importance of conflict as being a useful resource (Gregory 2003). As use of PD became more mainstream and gained popularity in the USA it shifted towards the involvement of users for commercial gain (Spinuzzi 2002) and had very little specific focus on democracy, values and conflicts (Muller et al. 1991). This more contemporary form of PD focuses on allowing users a 'voice' in the design process and seeking multiple perspectives, appreciating that successfully solving complex problems with technology requires understandings gathered from different disciplines (Muller 2002).

1.3 User-Centred Design

User-Centred Design, or UCD is another key area of HCI directly relevant to this book that emerged in the 1980s and was pioneered by individuals such as Donald Norman and Jakob Nielsen (e.g. Norman and Draper 1986; Nielsen and Molich 1990). UCD seeks to actively involve users in an iterative development life-cycle of technologies. This comprises of four key activities: (1) understanding the context of use; (2) specifying requirements; (3) creating designs; and (4) evaluating designs. This process is specified in the ISO 9421–210 (International Organization for Standardization 2010). In common with PD, UCD does not prescribe the specific techniques that should be used and the designer is free to make their own choices (Vredenburg et al. 2002). A UCD process is often expected to produce high levels of usability and employs usability inspection techniques during evaluation phases. Usability as a standard is defined in ISO 9241–1 as the effectiveness, efficiency and satisfaction with which specified users achieve specified goals in particular environments. While the differences between PD and UCD may appear rather subtle, the key difference is the approach taken towards users in the design process (Sanders and Stappers 2008). In PD the design is created collectively though an equal partnership between the technology designers and technology users, and this can be termed a co-design process. In UCD the user is the subject and focus of the design process, but the designer decides the extent to which they are involved.

1.4 Child Computer Interaction

Up until the mid 1990s the HCI community focussed almost exclusively on adult users, published PD and UCD research was primarily situated in the workplace context from which the field originally emerged. In the 1980s and 1990s computers were being introduced and used in school classrooms in increasing numbers and in this period publications began to emerge which explored the use of computers in education. Early examples of works that considered HCI issues in the context of children included explorations of designing computers specifically for children (Grover 1986) and studies of input devices (Revelle and Strommen 1990). Interest in specific understandings of children as technology users began to flourish in the 1990s, when researchers began to include children as testers and evaluators (e.g. Kafai 1995; Cypher and Smith 1995). This move also saw increasing involvement of children in the creation of technologies and fuller participation of children in a design process (Oosterholt et al. 1996; Druin and Solomon 1996).

Alison Druin was one of the first researchers to pioneer child-centric techniques for including children in the design of technology and developed the 'Onion Model' framework which considers the role of the child in the creation of technology (Druin 2002). This framework defines these roles as user, tester, informant and design partner. The design partner role aligns with PD, the informant role aligns with UCD (along with the tester role to a lesser extent).

Key events in the development of the Child Computer Interaction community included the publication of the book 'The Design of Children's Technology' (Druin 1998) which embodied efforts at the time to focus specifically on the unique challenges of working with children in the design of technology. The annual Interaction Design and Children (IDC) conference began in 2003 which provided a venue for academics and practitioners from many disciplines interested in the specific challenge of creating purposeful technologies for children. A third key milestone was the publication of the book 'Evaluating Interactive Products with and for Children' (Markopoulos et al. 2008) which provided a valuable resource for academic and practitioners. More recently the field of Child-Computer Interaction has been defined in as 'a discipline concerned with the design, evaluation and implementation of interactive computing systems for children's use and with the study of major phenomena surrounding them' (Read and Bekker 2011). These authors also provide a considered reflection of the history of CCI and its differences in comparison to mainstream HCI with adults, for example highlighting the importance of play and learning in addition to considering the key developmental, physical issues and adult-child influences. The CCI community continues to grow and in 2012 the International Journal of Child-Computer Interaction was launched. However, the CCI community focuses almost exclusively on children under the age of 10 and so in the context adolescents (teenagers) there is still much work to be done.

1.5 Teenagers and HCI

Teenagers are not a homogenous group and inhabit a diverse and changeable world that is often alien to adults. Chapter 2 provides a comprehensive overview of the developmental processes underpinning adolescence, which render teenagers a unique developmental population. Our experience of working with teenagers within

HCI has provided valuable insight in to their attitudes, opinions, values and behaviours. As early adopters and appropriators of technology, these insights can even be used to inform and guide the design of technologies for other populations. Teenagers can combine the creativity of younger children with the articulation of adults, and can even design evaluate of technology for younger children. Teenagers also have increasing spending power and can exhibit 'pester power' influence over parents' consumer behaviour, making them an increasingly buoyant and lucrative market. By understanding teenagers we can gather insights into the behaviours and preferences of the next generation of adults, and influencing teenagers may enable them to have great impact on the world. It is therefore vital that we understand and focus on teenagers in research within the HCI community whether we are engaged in PD, UCD or any other work where teenagers are the target users of technology.

A small but growing number of examples do exist within the field of HCI where researchers have worked with teenage populations. These studies have helped to highlight the value of working with teenagers in HCI research and have spanned several different areas. One of the first papers this century involving teenagers and technology was "y do tngrs luv 2 txt msg?" (Grinter and Eldridge 2001). Using logging as a measure this study was successful in exploring texting behaviour among UK teenagers. The involvement of teenagers was due to their early adoption of SMS on mobile devices, and the authors argued their findings could predict future adult behaviours in the workplace. The social dimensions of teen technology use have evolved quickly with rapid adoption of media such as Facebook, Twitter and SnapChat, which are still of great interest to the HCI community (e.g. Jang et al. 2015). Teenagers have been widely involved in research studies that attempt to replace negative behaviour by encouraging positive behavior and retaining this change through to adulthood. Examples include exergames intended to improve heath and fitness (Macvean and Robertson 2012), games intended to reduce energy use in the home (Gustafsson and Bång 2008) and online interventions to reduce teen energy use (Bell et al. 2015).

Berg et al. (2003) sought to meet the specific needs of teenagers through involving them as participants or informants in a design process. Designers in this study were interested in creating a mobile phone device specifically for teen users. This work included ethnography and iterative user-centred design activities. Other researchers sought to create a SMS application specifically for teenagers and involved teens in design workshops and evaluation of a prototype (Amin et al. 2005a, b). In (Labrune and Mackay 2006) work focused on creating social networking technology for teenagers again involving teenagers in design workshops. In later research disaffected teenagers were involved in the creation of an e-learning product to improve their own emotional intelligence (Mazzone et al. 2008). From this point onwards there was a concerted move to give teenagers involved in HCI research more specific consideration than they had received previously. (Iversen and Smith 2012) used a Scandinavian PD approach to engage teenagers using a range of design techniques in a project that created an interactive museum exhibit. Many researchers are pursuing methods, approaches and techniques that successfully involve and engage teenagers in the design of technology. Some of these methods are highly novel (Read et al. 2013; Fitton et al. 2012) and others more traditional (Poole and Peyton 2013) while some have led to a better understanding of factors associated with the concept of 'cool' (Fitton et al. 2012; Horton et al. 2012) and sharing of music (Lehtinen and Liikkanen 2012). Teenagers have also been involved in empirical evalaution of new mobile interaction techniques (Fitton et al. 2013b).

1.6 Contributions of this Book

In this book we aim to highlight clear examples of best practice when working with teenagers in HCI. Chapter 2 "Understanding Adolescents" by Beth T. Bell reviews literature from the social and behavioural science to describe the developmental processes underpinning adolescence, focussing specifically on the teenage years. The chapter seeks to provide a foundation to help further the understanding of teenage development that HCI researchers should consider when working teenagers.

Chapter 3 "Ethical considerations in face-to-face and Internet-mediated research with teenage populations" by Kerry McKellar and Nicola Toth consider the importance of ethics when working with teenagers in research and design projects, and the specific challenges of research ethics when working with teenagers. The authors provide examples of how they have negotiated complex research ethics in their own research.

Alexandra Lang and colleagues explore the use of multi-techniques for teenage Information Communication Technology (ICT) health research in Chap. 4 "Human factors multi-technique approach to teenage engagement in digital technologies health research". Using four case studies the authors present information about adolescents as users of healthcare services and technologies, adolescent personal development and the human factors approaches through which teenagers have been involved in healthcare research projects.

Health research with teenagers is further discussed in Chap. 5 "Designing interactive technologies with teenagers in a hospital setting" by Maja van der Velden and her coworkers. Their research describes a design process with teenagers with chronic health challenges specifically related to two main themes: the transition from paediatrics to adult healthcare and patient-oriented social networking.

Chapter 6 by Steve Love, Voula Gkatzidou and Antonello Conti entitled "Using a rich piccture approach for gathering students and teachers digital education requirements" describes how workshops were utilised to explore young people's views with regard to the design of cross-platform interactive learning frameworks that allow for ubiquitous, flexible and non-linear learning. The authors adopted a novel co-design workshop method that draws on principles from participatory design, future workshop techniques and rich pictures.

Christopher Wilkinson (Chap. 7- "Involving teenagers today in the design of tomorrows technology") presents work on involving teenagers and young people in research to optimise their influence on product and interaction design, and to maximise the output of ideation and design insight acquisition exercises. This is explored by framing interaction in terms of Rasmussen's (1993) Skill, Rule and Knowledge-based Model of Behaviour to determine how knowledge acquisition is facilitated and to identify instances of interactional complexity that could be overcome by better design with input from real users.

Chapter 8 "Designing Teenage Emotions with a Life of their Own" by Neil Winterburn, Peggy Gregory, and Daniel Fitton explores how teenagers describe and represent their emotions. Through participatory design activities teenagers created lo-fi designs describing emotions using 2D and 3D materials which were then analysed. Using understandings gained from the design activities a mobile app was developed which allowed teenagers represent emotions visually and prescribe their movements. The chapter provides insights on the visual metaphors the teenagers in the study used to describe different emotions.

In Chap. 9 "Engaging Teens in Dialogue on Potential Technological Futures with User Enactments" William Odom, John Zimmerman & Jodi Forlizzi explore the design approach of User Enactments to engage teenagers in experiencing and making sense of future technologies. The work focuses on five different design scenarios explored with within a faux teen bedroom constructed within a lab. The authors reflects on findings from their User Enactments approach and more generally how teenagers can play a role in designing their own future technologies.

In Chap. 10 "Working with Teenagers in HCI Research: A Reflection on Techniques Used in the Taking on Teenagers Project", we describe the various techniques that we (the editors of this book) have used in our own research projects in PaCT and ChiCI along with colleagues Janet C Read and Matthew Horton. We outline the methods used when engaging in HCI research activities with teenagers, providing a brief case study example of each. We then reflect critically upon their practical experiences working with teens and the lessons learned, in order to formulate nine guidelines that inform best practice when working with and for this unique population.

In the final chapter Janet C Read provides her thoughts on important directions in the field of TeenCI.

References

Amin AK, Kersten B, Kulyk OA, Pelgrim E, Wang J, Markopoulos P (2005a) The sensems: enriching the SMS experience for teens by non-verbal means. In: Human-Computer Interaction-INTERACT 2005. Springer, Berlin/Heidelberg, pp 962–965

Amin AK, Kersten BTA, Kulyk OA, Pelgrim PH, Wang CM, Markopoulos P (2005b) SenseMS: a user-centered approach to enrich the messaging experience for teens by non-verbal means. In: Proceedings of the MobileHCI 2005. ACM Press, pp 161–166

Bell BT, Toth N, Little L, Smith MA (2015) Planning to save the planet using an online intervention based on implementation intentions to change adolescent self-reported energy-saving behavior. Environ Behav, 0013916515583550

Berg S, Taylor AS, Harper R (2003) Mobile phones for the next generation: device designs for teenagers. In CHI 2003. ACM Press, Ft Lauderdale

Bjerknes G, Bratteteig T (1995) User participation and democracy: a discussion of Scandinavian research on systems development. Scand J Inf Syst 7(1):73–98

Card SK, Newell A, Moran TP (1983) The psychology of Human-Computer Interaction. L. Erlbaum Assoc. Inc., Hillsdale

Cypher A, Smith DC (1995) KidSim: end user programming of simulations. In: Proceedings of CHI'95, Denver, CO, May 1995. ACM Press, pp 27–34

Druin A (ed) (1998) The design of children's technology. Morgan Kaufmann Publishers Inc., San Francisco. http://dl.acm.org/citation.cfm?id=953536

Druin A (2002) The role of children in the design of new technology. Behav Inf Technol 21(1):1–25

Druin A, Solomon C (1996) Designing multimedia environments for childen: computers, creativity and kids. Wiley & Sons, New York

Fitton D, Bell BT (2014) Working with teenagers within HCI research: understanding teen-computer interaction. In: Proceedings of the 28th international BCS Human Computer Interaction Conference on HCI 2014 – Sand, Sea and Sky – Holiday HCI (BCS-HCI '14). BCS, UK, pp 201–206

Fitton D, Read JC, Horton M, Little L, Toth N, Guo Y (2012) Constructing the cool wall: a tool to explore teen meanings of cool. PsychNology J 10(2):141–162

Fitton D, Read JC, Horton M (2013a) The challenge of working with teens as participants in interaction design. Extended Abstracts CHI 2013. ACM Press, pp 205–210

Fitton D, MacKenzie IS, Read JC, Horton M (2013b) Exploring tilt-based text input for mobile devices with teenagers. In: Proceedings of the 27th International British Computer Society Human-Computer Interaction Conference – HCI 2013. British Computer Society, London

Gregory J (2003) Scandinavian approaches to participatory design. Int J Eng Educ 19(1):62–74

Grinter RE, Eldridge MA (2001) y do tngrs luv 2 txt msg? In: Prinz W, Jarke M, Rogers Y, Schmidt K, Wulf V (eds) Proceedings of the seventh conference on European Conference on Computer Supported Cooperative Work (ECSCW'01). Kluwer Academic Publishers, Norwell, MA, USA, pp 219–238

Grover SC (1986) A field study of the use of cognitive-developmental principles in microcomputer design for young children. J Educ Res 79(6):325

Gustafsson G, Bång M (2008) Evaluation of a pervasive game for domestic energy engagement among teenagers. In: Proceedings of the 2008 international conference on Advances in Computer Entertainment Technology (ACE '08). ACM, New York, NY, USA, pp 232–239

Hewett T et al (1992) ACM curricula for human-computer interaction. http://old.sigchi.org/cdg/index.html

Horton M, Read JC, Fitton D, Toth N, Little L (2012) Too cool at school – understanding cool teenagers. PsychNology J 10(2):73–91

ISO 13407: Human Centred Design Process for Interactive Systems

ISO 9241–1: Ergonomics of human-system interaction

ISO DIS 9241–210 (2010) Ergonomics of human system interaction – part 210: Human-centred design for interactive systems. Technical report, International Organization for Standardization, Switzerland

Iversen OS, Smith RC (2012) Scandinavian participatory design: dialogic curation with teenagers. In Proceedings of the IDC 2012. ACM Press, pp 106–115

Jang JY, Han K, Shih PC, Lee D (2015) Generation like: comparative characteristics in Instagram. In: Proceedings of the 33rd annual ACM Conference on Human Factors in Computing Systems (CHI '15). ACM, New York, NY, USA, pp 4039–4042

Kafai YB (1995) Minds in play: computer game design as a context for learning. Lawrence Erlbaum Associates, Hillsdale

Labrune JB, Mackay W (2006) Telebeads: social network mnemonics for teenagers. In: Proceedings of the IDC 2006. ACM Press, pp 57–64

Lehtinen V, Liikkanen L (2012) The meanings of music sharing in tween life. Ext. Abstracts CHI 2012. ACM Press, pp 1907–1912

Leveson NG, Turner CS (1993) An investigation of the Therac-25 Accidents. Computer 26(7):18–41

Macvean A, Robertson J (2012) iFitQuest: a school based study of a mobile location-aware exergame for adolescents. In: Proceedings of the 14th international conference on Human-computer interaction with mobile devices and services (MobileHCI'). ACM, New York, NY, USA, pp 359–368

Markopoulos P, Read JC, MacFarlane SJ, Hoysniemi J (2008) Evaluating interactive products with and for children. Morgan Kaufmann Publishers, San Francisco

Mazzone M, Read JC, Beale R (2008) Design with and for disaffected teenagers. In: Proceedings of the 5th Nordic conference on Human-computer interaction: building bridges (NordiCHI '08). ACM Press

Muller MJ (2002) Participatory design: the third space in HCI. In: Jacko JA, Sears A (eds) The human-computer interaction handbook. L. Erlbaum Associates Inc., Hillsdale, pp 1051–1068

Muller MJ, Blomberg JL, Carter KA, Dykstra EA, Madsen KH, Greenbaum J (1991) Participatory design in Britain and North America: responses to the "Scandinavian Challenge". In: Robertson SP, Olson GM, Olson JS (eds) Proceedings of the SIGCHI Conference on Human Factors in Computing Systems (CHI '91). ACM, New York, NY, USA, pp 389–392

Nielsen J, Molich R (1990) Heuristic evaluation of user interfaces. In: Chew JC, Whiteside J (eds) Proceedings of the SIGCHI Conference on Human Factors in Computing Systems (CHI '90). ACM, New York, NY, USA, pp 249–256

Norman DA, Draper SW (1986) User centered system design; new perspectives on Human-Computer Interaction. L. Erlbaum Assoc. Inc., Hillsdale

Oosterholt R, Kusano M, de Vries G (1996) Interaction design and human factors support, in the development of a personal communicator for children. In: Proceedings of the CHI'96, Vancouver, BC, April 1996. ACM, pp 450–457

Poole ES, Peyton T (2013) Interaction design research with adolescents: methodological challenges and best practices. In: Proceedings of the IDC 2013. ACM Press, pp 211–217

Rasmussen J (1993) Deciding and doing: decision making in natural contexts. Ablex, Norwood

Read JC, Bekker MM (2011). The nature of child computer interaction. In Proceedings of the 25th BCS Conference on Human-Computer Interaction (BCS-HCI'11). British Computer Society, Swinton, UK, 163–170

Read JC, Fitton D, Horton M (2013) Theatre, playdoh and comic strips: designing organic user interfaces with young adolescent and teenage participants. Interact Comput 25(2):183–198

Revelle GL, Strommen EF (1990) The effects of practice and input device used on young children's computer control. J Comput Child Educ 2(1):33–41

Sanders EB-N, Stappers PJ (2008) Co-creation and the new landscapes of design. CoDesign 4(1):5–18

Sanders EBN, Brandt E, Binder T (2010) A framework for organizing the tools and techniques of participatory design. In: Proceedings of the 11th biennial participatory design conference. ACM, pp 195–198

Spinuzzi C (2002) A Scandinavian challenge, a US response: methodological assumptions in Scandinavian and US prototyping approaches. In: Proceedings of the 20th annual international conference on Computer documentation (SIGDOC '02). ACM, New York, NY, USA, pp 208–215

Vredenburg K, Mao J-Y, Smith PW, Carey T (2002) A survey of user-centered design practice. In: Proceedings of the SIGCHI Conference on Human Factors in Computing Systems (CHI '02). ACM, New York, NY, USA, pp 471–478

Chapter 2
Understanding Adolescents

Beth T. Bell

Abstract Adolescent development is complex; involving the interaction between fundamental biological and cognitive developmental processes, and the unique environment inhabited by the adolescent. This chapter draws on contemporary research from the social and behavioural sciences to outline the key features of the biological and cognitive changes occurring during adolescence, which serve to differentiate adolescents from both children and adults. The contextual factors that influence the developmental trajectory of adolescents will be discussed, with particular emphasis on the role of media and technology, which is becoming an increasingly prominent developmental context and is of particular interest to the readers of this book. The chapter also discusses prominent themes in adolescent development that are product of this interaction between developmental processes and the environment, including identity, sexuality, intimacy, autonomy and achievement. It ends with a discussion of how this knowledge may be utilised by researchers working in the field of TeenCI to inform their approach to working with adolescents.

2.1 Defining Adolescence

Although discussions of adolescence may be traced back to Ancient Greece and the works of prominent philosophers, Plato and Aristotle, it was not until the turn of the twentieth century that adolescence became recognised as a unique developmental period (Petersen 1988). Seminal work by Hall (1904) identified adolescence as a period of "storm and stress", claiming that struggles and difficulties during adolescence were not a normative feature of the adolescent experience, but an essential part of healthy development. However Hall's understandings of adolescence were purely theoretical; the *empirical* study of adolescence did not begin until the latter half of the twentieth century, where a boom in the social and behavioural sciences literature pertaining to adolescent development can be observed (Petersen 1988; Steinberg and Lerner 2004). Early empirical studies of adolescence were heavily influenced by Hall, and tended to focus on the problematic aspects of adolescent

B.T. Bell (✉)
Faculty of Health and Life Sciences, York St John University, York YO31 7EX, UK
e-mail: b.bell@yorksj.ac.uk

© Springer International Publishing Switzerland 2016
L. Little et al. (eds.), *Perspectives on HCI Research with Teenagers*,
Human–Computer Interaction Series, DOI 10.1007/978-3-319-33450-9_2

development. However, the notion that adolescence is inherently a period of storm and stress has been challenged as researchers increasingly recognise the malleability and opportunity created by the developmental processes at work during adolescence (Arnett 1999; Blakemore and Mills 2014; Steinberg 2014b). In 2014, Lawrence Steinberg coined the term "Age of Opportunity" to describe adolescence, and characterise this new approach towards understanding adolescents that is focused on recognising potential, rather than problems (Steinberg 2014b).

Within the HCI literature, the terms "teenager" and "adolescent" are often used interchangeably. Whereas the former may be concretely defined in terms of biological age, specifically referring to individuals aged 13–19 years old, the latter is more difficult to define in terms of age-related boundaries. Instead, adolescence is defined as the developmental period straddling the transition from childhood to adulthood, which may be characterised by the biological, cognitive, psychological and social changes that occur during this time (Steinberg 2014b). Assigning age-related boundaries to adolescence is problematic since the developmental processes underpinning the transition from childhood to adulthood begin and end at different times for different individuals (e.g. Dorn and Biro 2011), and do not always follow the same sequence (e.g. Petersen 1988). There is also increasing evidence that the developmental processes underpinning adolescent development stretch beyond the teenage years. Recent neuroscientific research, for example, has suggested that brain development is not complete until one has reached their mid-20s (Blakemore and Mills 2014). Furthermore, there are also important cultural variations in terms of how adolescence is defined, particularly surrounding societal conceptions of how and when adult status is achieved. Many traditional societies view marriage as the marker signifying the end of adolescence, and many adult privileges are not afforded to an individual until marriage is achieved (Grant and Furstenberg 2007). In contrast in industrialised societies, where marriage typically happens much later (if at all), achieving financial independence is more readily recognised as the defining marker of adulthood (Horowitz and Bromnick 2007). Consistent with the teen-centric focus of this book, this chapter will focus primarily on understanding the aspects of adolescent development occurring during the teenage years, though some aspects of development beyond these years will also be considered.

2.2 Changes in Biology

During adolescence, fundamental biological changes – known as puberty – occur within the body, which transform a child into a biological adult capable of sexual reproduction. Puberty is a gradual and sequential process that spans across the adolescent years, and encapsulates multiple and complex biological processes (Dorn and Biro 2011). Puberty triggers rapid increases in height, size and capacity of the heart and lungs, muscle mass, and body fat. Adolescents become stronger and more physically able than children and gender differences in physicality emerge; males will typically grow taller with larger heart and lung capacities, and develop more muscle mass and less body fat, than their female counterparts (Rogol, Roemmich, and Clark 2002). Male pubertal development also includes the deepening of the voice, changes in male genitalia and increases in androgen hormone production. In contrast, female pubertal development includes the growth of breasts, changes to female genitalia and increases in estrogen hormone production. Thus puberty serves to exacerbate sex differences and make them more visually salient. The dramatic changes in the physical appearance of young people triggered by pubertal development can lead individuals to treat adolescents differently; expecting more adult, and often more gender typical, behaviour from them (Bumpus et al. 2001; Hill and Lynch 1983).

Pubertal hormones have an interesting impact on adolescent behaviour, including sexual behaviour, sleep and mood. In terms of sexual behaviour, first feelings of sexual attraction towards potential romantic partners are triggered by pubertal hormones at the very start of adolescence, normally at the age of 10 (McClintock and Herdt 1996). Adolescents will then progressively engage in sexual behaviour involving others throughout the course of puberty, and by the end of adolescence most will have their first experience of sexual contact and most will have experienced their first romantic relationship (Collins et al. 2009). In terms of sleeping behaviour, melatonin – the hormone which regulates sleep and increases with feelings of sleepiness – has been found to increase later in the day in older adolescents, than younger adolescents (Millman 2005). The result is that adolescents going through puberty display a preference for going to bed later, and waking up later, than children (Carskadon 2011). In terms of mood, rapid increases in hormones at the start of puberty seem to be associated with fluctuations in mood in early adolescence, and as these levels stabilise, so too do mood fluctuations (Buchanan et al. 1992). However research examining the link between puberty and moodiness in adolescence has yielded mixed results, leading researchers to conclude that environmental factors must also play an important role in mood regulation (Schneiders et al. 2006).

Finally, puberty triggers important biological changes in brain development during adolescence. Though the brain reaches adult size around the age of 10 (Dekaban and Sadowsky 1978), it continues to develop throughout adolescence in terms of structure and function (Blakemore and Mills 2014). Biological processes of synaptic pruning (removal of unnecessary brain circuitry) and mylenation (insulation of brain circuitry in myelin) in specific brain areas, lead to changes in the efficiency of these areas (Blakemore 2012). Brain regions affected by these processes include (1) the prefrontal cortex, which is responsible for complex thought processes, such as planning, consideration of risk and reward, and impulse control, (2) the parietal cortex, which is responsible for memory, and (3) the temporal cortex, which is also responsible for memory and thinking about others (Blakemore 2012; Blakemore and Mills 2014; Steinberg 2014a). These changes in brain structure are responsible for many of the changes in thinking patterns that are observed during the adolescent years, which will be outlined in the following sections.

2.3 Changes in Thinking Patterns

The changes in thinking patterns (cognitive development) that occur during the adolescent years have important implications for how TeenCI researchers engage with teenagers at all stages of the research process; informing the nature of their research questions, the types of methods employed when working with this population and the way in which these are communicated to the adolescent. It is important therefore to understand how the ways in which an adolescent thinks – and subsequently behaves – are qualitatively different to the ways in which a child thinks and behaves. These differences include the development of the abilities to:

- Think Logically: Logical reasoning skills begin to develop between the ages of 11 and 13 (Zimmerman 2000). During this time, adolescents develop the ability to engage in hypothetical reasoning (using logical thinking to anticipate possibilities) and deductive reasoning (the ability to draw logical conclusions from a set of premises), which they are unable to perform as a child (Keating 2011). These skills are evidenced in the mathematics classroom, where advanced logical reasoning capabilities are a necessary prerequisite for complex problem-solving tasks (such as algebra), which individuals are typically only able to solve from adolescence (Luna 2004).
- Think Abstractly: A child typically thinks in ways that are concrete and bound to observable real-world objects and events (Inhelder and Piaget 1958). In contrast, an adolescent is much more capable of thinking about abstract concepts such as political issues, social issues, religion and morality (Steinberg 2014a) and independent political and religious beliefs may also emerge during this period (Flanagan and Tucker 1999; Koenig et al. 2008). We can see evidence of this in everyday settings, including the conversations adolescents become capable of maintaining, the arguments they are capable of forming and the school-work tasks they may be expected to complete.
- Think in Complex Ways: The ability to think about things in multidimensional ways is an important dimension of adolescent thinking that sets them apart from children. Sarcasm is an example of complex thought as a sarcastic comment (e.g. "That's a nice dress") has both a literal meaning (that dress is nice) and an inferred meaning (dependent upon tone, this comment could be intended as an insult). It is only during the early – mid teenage years that adolescents are able to appreciate the multidimensionality, or multiple meanings, of such remarks and so find them humorous (Demorest et al. 1984). Adolescents are also likely to practice their new found complex thought abilities: there are few parents who have not been on the receiving end of their teen's sarcastic commentary!
- Think about Thinking: A further skill that adolescents develop is that of metacognition: the ability to think about thinking. Metacognition may also underpin, to an extent, self-consciousness during adolescence, as adolescents are prone to

believing that because they are thinking about their own thinking processes, everyone else must be thinking about them too (Vartanian 2000). The novelty of this ability as experienced by adolescents may explain why some start to believe the uniqueness of their own experiences (Vartanian 2000), which can lead to feelings of isolation (e.g. beliefs such as "no one understands me") and beliefs that the negative possible consequences of risky behaviour won't happen to them (Alberts et al. 2007).

These qualitatively different ways of thinking are likely underpinned, in part, by the development of more efficient information processing skills during the adolescent years. Adolescents have been found to have greater attentional skills than children; they are much more efficient in paying selective attention to one stimuli in the presence of others and are much more efficient at paying attention to multiple sets of stimuli at the same time (Huang-Pollock et al. 2002; Pool et al. 2003). They also display larger working memory capacity (the ability to temporarily retain information) and more efficient long-term memory skills (the ability to recall previously learned information and personal life experiences) (Keating 2011). The speed at which adolescents can perform tasks and process information also improves (Kail and Ferrer 2007). Collectively, these improved information processing skills may underpin the more abstract and complex ways in which adolescents think relative to a child.

In general, research has shown that adolescent information processing skills steadily improve up until the age of 15, after which point they begin to stabilise, suggesting that these basic skills have reached adult status (Luciana et al. 2005). However this does not mean that by age 15, an adolescent thinks in the same way as an adult. More sophisticated cognitive capabilities such as planning ahead and weighing up the costs and benefits of decisions, seem to be linked to the development of the prefrontal cortex in the brain, and continue to develop until an individual has reached their mid-20s (Blakemore and Robbins 2012). Neuroscientific research also suggests that a developmental mismatch occurs during adolescence, where the parts of the brain responsible for sensation seeking (i.e. impulsive behaviour) develop before the parts of the brain responsible for these more sophisticated aspects of cognition (Steinberg 2007; Strang et al. 2013). This may explain the well documented link between adolescence and increased risk-taking behaviour, as the adolescent struggles to engage in logical decision making ("I must drive carefully as I am new a driver") in anticipation of the positive emotive consequences associated with risky behaviour ("Driving fast feels good. It is exciting and I look cool in front of my friends"). This mismatch is not rectified until an individual reaches their mid-20s, when the development of advanced cognitive brain systems 'catches up' with the development of the more impulsive brain systems (Steinberg 2007; Strang et al. 2013).

2.4 Changes in Social Thinking

Adolescents are intensely social creatures. Teens spend a substantial amount of their time in the presence of their peers both in school and out of school – including in the virtual presence of their peers (Boyd 2014) – and also spend an increasing amount of time thinking about peer relationships (Richards et al. 1998). Research has demonstrated that adolescent friendships are more complex than childhood friendships and involve greater intimacy, trust and reciprocity (Laursen and Hartup 2002). The increased complexity and importance of adolescent friendships are likely to be underpinned by changes in social cognition, i.e. the way we think about other people and process social information. This includes changes in adolescents' ability to:

- Understand Others: The ability to understand others (known as *mentalizing* within psychology) becomes more nuanced and sophisticated during adolescence. In particular, adolescents develop a more complex theory of mind; the understanding that others have beliefs, intentions and knowledge that are different from their own. Importantly, adolescents also develop the ability to alter their behaviour in response to their understanding of others (Dumontheil et al. 2010) and further develop their skills to judge the appropriateness of the emotions shown by others (Keulers et al. 2010).
- Understand Relationships: As a consequence of their increased socio-cognitive capacity to understand others, adolescents also begin to think about relationships in similarly nuanced and sophisticated ways, becoming more aware of intragroup and intergroup dynamics. Adolescents develop a more intricate understanding of social group membership (Leets and Wolf 2005) and more complex social networks develop (Brown and Klute 2003). Consider the complex clique structure of your own school experiences during adolescence, compared to during childhood, and think of all the different groups and social hierarchies that existed. Adolescents also develop a more complex understanding of their relationships with authority figures, such as parents and teachers, which may lead them to question some of the decisions these authority figures make (Darling et al. 2008).
- Understand Social Rules & Structure: During the early teen years, adolescents start to realise that many social norms and conventions (such as raising their hand before answering a question in class or keeping their bedroom tidy) are just expected behaviours and so may question whether or not they should comply with them (Smetana and Bitz 1996). This more complex understanding of social rules may explain why teenagers are often perceived as rebellious. Adolescents are more able to understand social concepts such as rights and freedoms (e.g. freedom of speech) and are more likely to express beliefs about their perceived entitlement to them (Steinberg 2014a).

More recently, neuroscientific research has linked changes in social cognition during adolescence to changes in brain structure and functioning; suggesting that adolescents may process social information in their brain differently to both children and adults (Blakemore and Mills 2014). Adolescents also display an increased sensitivity to peer rejection and social exclusion, and again, this seems to be reflected in brain functioning; the areas of the brain activated during social exclusion show increased activation in experiments that aim to trigger feelings of exclusion among adolescents, in comparison to adults (Sebastian et al. 2010). Social information may also impede rationale decision making behaviour during adolescence, and the mere presence of peers in the adolescent years has been demonstrated to increase risky decision making, whereas adults seem unaffected (Chein et al. 2011). Taken in sum, this evidence appears to suggest that the brain is hot-wired to focus on social information during adolescence and try to understand it, in ways that the brains of children and adults are not. This has important implications for the adolescent behaviour in social situations, including their behaviour in group research situations (such as focus groups). TeenCI researchers should be mindful that and adolescents' behaviour in a group environment may not be a reflection of their true self, though this may be a desirable outcome if the focus of the group-based research is to understand teen attitudes and behaviours in social contexts.

2.5 Contextualising Development

The differences between adolescents are as striking as the similarities between them, and the environmental context in which development occurs is at least as important as biological processes in shaping the nature and course of each adolescent's developmental trajectory (Bronfenbrenner 1979; Lloyd 2002; Smetana et al. 2006). According to the ecological model of human development (Bronfenbrenner 1979), there are multiple layers of contextual factors influencing the developmental course of humans. In close proximity to the adolescent, the first layer – the *microsystem* – encompasses relationships and interactions that directly influence the adolescent, including school, family, peer-groups and community. The next layer – the *mesosystem* – encompasses the interactions between different agents in the microsystem that influence the adolescent, such as parent interactions with teachers. The adolescent has no direct contact with the third layer of context – the *exosystem* – which includes factors that influence agents in their microsystem, such as how changing conditions in a parent's workplace may influence their availability in the adolescents life. The final layer, the *macrosystem*, encompasses broader cultural attitudes and ideologies shaping adolescent development, such as government ideology and laws. These developmental contexts influence each other and the adolescent in multiple complex and overlapping ways, leading to the vast individual differences observed amongst adolescents in the world today.

Relevant to the HCI focus of this book, media and technology are becoming increasingly important sociocultural factors shaping adolescent development, at all of Bronfrenbenner's contextual layers. In terms of the microsystem, media and technology have infiltrated many of the relationships and interactions that directly influence adolescent development, changing the nature of adolescents' experiences and interactions within them. For example, the widespread use of the internet and computers in schools has influenced teaching styles, classroom activities, and lesson content, thus changing the nature of adolescents' schooling experiences (Bentley 2012). Alternatively, since media and technology transcend the boundaries of physically distinct everyday environments, such as home and school, they may be conceptualised as creating an important microsystem within their own right. Adolescents increasingly turn to media and technology as a source of socio-cultural information to guide their attitudes, beliefs and behaviours in a variety of domains (Lloyd 2002; Mitchell et al. 2014), much in the same way they may have traditionally turned to family, teachers and peers (Strasburger and Wilson 2002).

Media and technology have also influenced mesosystems. Social media – for example – can facilitate greater communication between parents and an adolescent's peers, including through profile monitoring practices (such as snooping). Media and technology also serve as exosystems that influence microsystems and mesosystems, such as the way in which mobile technologies have impacted upon parents' working patterns allowing more opportunity to work from home and thus potentially impacting upon the nature of the adolescent-parent relationship (Hilbrecht et al. 2008). Lastly, media and technology may also be seen as part of the macrosystem shaping cultural norms and values. In particular, the ability of the Internet to connect diverse and geographically-distant cultures, and facilitate content co-creation across these cultures, has led to the development and proliferation of new cultural norms, values and practices (Reed 2014). Understanding how media and technology influence and interact with adolescent development is an important research question within the TeenCI community and there is a growing body of literature in this area (e.g. Boyd 2014; Lloyd 2002).

2.6 Psychosocial Developmental Challenges

During adolescence, the complex interaction between fundamental bio-cognitive developmental processes and environmental context create issues – or developmental challenges – for adolescents, which are both psychological (internal within each adolescent's individual psyche) and social (bounded by external social constraints) in nature. Adolescents must negotiate, or make sense of, these issues in order to prosper. According to Steinberg (2014a) there are five important psychosocial developmental challenges during adolescence: identity, sexuality, intimacy, autonomy and achievement. In this section, these challenges are briefly described:

- *Identity.* Identity refers to the way we see ourselves. It is our sense of who we are, how we fit into the world, and encompasses our beliefs about ourselves in relation to others (Lloyd 2002; Waterman 1999). Identity formation is widely regarded as the primary psychosocial developmental task faced by adolescents (Erikson 1968) and has been the fixation of many adolescent focused books, films and TV series. The quest for identity may be more salient for some adolescents than others: some adolescents will invest vast amounts of time and energy exploring possible identities, whereas others may adopt an identity (usually one similar to their parents) without much exploration (Waterman 1999). In addition to negotiating a personal identity, adolescents must also negotiate their social identities (i.e. their sense of identity based on the social groups they belong to). Gender and ethnic identity are two very important identities that adolescents must negotiate. For many adolescents, being able to express group membership is as important as being able to express their individuality (Manago et al. 2008). Social media currently provides an excellent tool for the development of both personal and social identities (Boyd 2014; Manago et al. 2008).

- Sexuality. As the adolescent, through the biological processes of puberty, becomes an adult capable of sexual reproduction, they must learn to understand and express their sexual feelings. Sexual behaviour follows a remarkably similar developmental trajectory across cultures: first feelings of sexual attraction generally emerge at the age of 10, engagement in autoerotic sexual behaviours will follow shortly afterwards, and then adolescents will begin to engage in sexual contact with another individual in a gradually intimate manner (e.g. kissing, touching) until they finally engage in oral sex and/or sexual intercourse (Collins et al. 2009; Diamond and Savin-Williams 2009; McClintock and Herdt 1996). Despite the seeming universality of this pathway, gender, ethnic and cultural differences can be observed in the age at which adolescents engage in sexual activity (Browning et al. 2004; Madkour et al. 2010). There are multiple risks associated with sexual behaviour, including sexually transmitted infections and unwanted pregnancy. An adolescent must learn to behave responsibly in sexual encounters to prevent unwanted outcomes; behaviours that may be especially difficult to control, given how the adolescent brain is programmed to behave more riskily in the presence of others (Chein et al. 2011). Recent developments in media and technology may also influence adolescent sexual development in modern society and there are many pressing research questions surrounding the influence of sexting, Internet pornography and dating apps (such as Tinder and Grindr) in this domain. There is also positive potential for technology to improve teen sexual health. A number of digital sexual health interventions have been developed with some success, though more robust evaluation of such interventions is needed (Guse et al. 2012).
- Intimacy: Adolescents are more able to appreciate the complexities and value of intimate relationships – characterised by a sense of closeness and emotional attachment (Montgomery 2005) – than children, due to the development of increasingly sophisticated socio-cognitive skills during this time. Friendships change during adolescence and become more based on mutual values than shared activities, than in childhood (Gifford-Smith and Brownell 2003). Adolescents become more aware of different types of friendships and show greater loyalty, trust and self-disclosure in close friendships than casual friendships (Leets and Wolf 2005). Female adolescents will typically develop intimate relationships earlier than males and typically display more intimacy within these friendships –

though some have argued that girls are more concerned about intimacy or more likely to talk about relationships than boys, rather than more intimate per se (Johnson 2004; Radmacher, and Azmitia 2006). Negotiating intimacy in romantic relationships is also important during adolescence. Research indicates that the quality of adolescent romantic relationships is related to self-esteem, social competence and wellbeing; though it is likely these relationships are bidirectional (Collins et al. 2009). Social technologies that facilitate communication, such as smartphones and social media applications, have been widely adopted by adolescents and may have implications for the development of intimacy during adolescence (Boyd 2014; Peter et al. 2005).

- Autonomy: A child is highly dependent upon adults to guide their decision-making and inform their attitudes, beliefs and behaviours. However, in the adolescent years, individuals gradually move towards becoming autonomous, independent and self-governing adults. This quest for autonomy involves becoming gradually less reliant on parents for practical assistance and emotional support (Rueger et al. 2008; Steinberg 2001). It also involves the establishment of an independent set of values, opinions and beliefs, and as this occurs, adolescents may become more questioning of parental rules and decisions (Darling et al. 2008). Parents can find allowing adolescents to behave autonomously very difficult and many disputes in the teen years stem from an adolescent's desire to become more autonomous, and an authority figure's struggle to accept this (Jensen and Dost-Gözkan 2015). However research has shown that conflict and distancing within parent-adolescent relationships does not necessarily diminish closeness; many adolescents and their parents still report getting along during the teenage years (Laursen and Collins 2009). Developing a sense of morality is also an important component of autonomy, and in late adolescence, individuals are more likely to define morality in terms of their own moral principles, rather than relying on societal norms and rules (Eisenberg et al. 2005; Killen and Smetana 2005). However, as the adolescent brain is susceptible to social influence, it may be that adolescents do not always behave in ways congruent with their beliefs in the presence of peers. Technology has been successfully used to facilitate the development of autonomy during adolescence, including among youths with long-term health conditions (e.g. diabetes) who have traditionally struggled to establish independence as a consequence of the demands of their condition (Harris et al. 2012).
- Achievement: Adolescents, through the performance of positive behaviours and the experience of positive feelings in evaluation settings (Steinberg 2014a, b), begin to develop a sense of achievement during the teen years. Though achievement is valued in school settings throughout childhood, it is only during adolescence that individuals come to appreciate the value and implications of this. This is partially due to cognitive development; the logical, abstract and metacognitive thinking abilities that mature during the teen years enable adolescents to think about their future in more tangible terms. It is also partially due to the looming prospect of adulthood and the changes in social role that adulthood brings, as unlike children, adults must make important decisions about their role within

society, including choosing an occupation, which can be highly dependent upon their achievements (particularly their academic achievements) during the adolescent years (Mello 2008). Thus adolescents generally become more aware of the importance of achievement, though there are large individual differences in the extent to which they are motivated towards achievement (e.g. Accordino et al. 2000), and also begin to cultivate beliefs about their own abilities to achieve (Schunk and Meece 2006). Parents, peers and teachers play an important role in shaping adolescents' achievement-orientated motivation and achievement-related beliefs about the self (Bouchey and Harter 2005; Schunk and Meece 2006). There are many ways in which technologies may be used to facilitate development of achievement in adolescence. For example, technologies have been successfully used to support reading achievement among dyslexic adolescents (Cheung and Slavin 2011). However most research into adolescent achievement (in TeenCI and the social and behavioural sciences more broadly) has centred on educational settings, yet there are other settings in which an adolescent's sense of achievement may be fostered, including in leisure based activities, such as performing with a band for the first time, and in occupational settings, such as achieving promotion in a part-time job. The TeenCI community should consider how it can understand and facilitate adolescent achievement in non-academic domains also.

These five psychosocial challenges should not be regarded as mutually exclusive as considerable overlaps exist between them. For example, sexuality may be an important aspect of identity, particularly among sexual minority youth (Hammack et al. 2009). Sexuality may also intersect with intimacy; research indicates that sexual minority youth report lower levels of companionship than their heterosexual peers (Williams et al. 2005). There are also some complex issues that commonly affect adolescents, which straddle the multiple aspects of adolescents' psychosocial development and further blur the lines between them. For example, the experience of negative body image (defined as the experiences of negative thoughts and feelings towards one's own body) during adolescence may affect sexual behaviour and intimacy within romantic relationships (Woertman and van den Brink 2012). The way in which developmental challenges intersect within each adolescent's own unique experiences should not be overlooked.

It is also important to note that these psycho-social developmental themes do not exclusively manifest during adolescence. That is, individuals will continue to develop their sense of identity, sexuality, intimacy, autonomy and achievement throughout the life span. Consider how important life events, such as motherhood, may affect an individual. A new mother may have to negotiate a renewed sense of identity to incorporate her new social role as a mother, a renewed sense of intimacy as she bonds with the baby, and a renewed sense of sexuality as she re-engages in sexual activity post-partum. Motherhood may also influence her sense of autonomy as her feelings of independence are altered by her new found responsibilities as a mother, and her sense of achievement as her new role encourages her to re-evaluate her sources of self-worth. Thus prominent themes in adolescent development may become salient once again in life, particularly following prominent life events and during periods of transition. However the way in which identity, sexuality, intimacy, autonomy and achievement are experienced in adolescence may be regarded as unique due to the novelty and newness of the experience during these formative years.

2.7 Reflecting on Teen-Computer Interaction (TeenCI)

Teenagers are highly complex and diverse group, which must be considered very carefully in the context of HCI research. Unfortunately many researchers mistakenly believe that they are experts on what it means to be a teenager because they were once teenagers themselves. Instead, this chapter has drawn on contemporary research from the social and behavioural sciences to outline the core developmental processes occurring during adolescence. It has explained the fundamental and universal biological and cognitive processes shaping adolescent development, and how differences in the sociocultural environments of adolescents mould each individual's unique developmental trajectory. Understanding how (and why) adolescents think and behave differently to both children and adults crucially builds a rationale to support the importance of studying teenagers in their own right. In particular, TeenCI researchers may wish to consider:

- <u>The cognitive sophistication of teenagers, relative to children, while acknowledging that teenagers' cognitive capacities are still not as sophisticated as adults.</u> Teenagers think in more abstract, logical and complex ways than children, and these abilities steadily improve with age. However, in situations where emotional impulses must be regulated (such as when controlling impulses to engage in risky behaviour) or situations that simply involve other people, teenagers do not necessarily think and behave in ways that are consistent with their new found cognitive abilities.
- <u>The heightened sensitivity of teenagers to social information</u>. Teenagers spend large amounts of time engaging with peers, both offline and online, and are often pre-occupied with thoughts and concerns about peer relationships. They are typically more susceptible to peer influence and more sensitive to peer rejection, than adults, and these differences seem to be reflected in brain function.
- <u>The self-orientated nature of the teenage experience.</u> Understanding the self in relation to others is a common theme overarching all aspects of psychosocial development (i.e. identity, sexuality, intimacy, achievement and autonomy) during adolescence. The teenage years are characterised by self-orientated cognitions, and teenagers may seem self-conscious – or even self-obsessed – as they focus on understanding who they are and how they fit in.
- <u>The differences amongst teenagers are as striking as the similarities between them</u>. Teenagers are not a homogeneous group. The rich and unique sociocultural environment, in which adolescent development occurs, fosters the

development of unique individuals. The potency and plurality of contextual factors shaping adolescence may explain why participatory research approaches, such as those outlined in the chapters of the present book, are becomingly increasingly used with this age group. Group-based differences (such as age, gender and ethnicity) should also be considered.

- The commonalities between teenagers and other populations. Teenagers are not wholly distinct to other demographic groups and some insights gleaned from research with teenagers may be transferrable to other populations, and vice versa. For example, basic cognitive skills, such as information processing, seem to plateau during the teenage years, suggesting that there is little differences between adults and teenagers in terms of these basic skills. Similarly, concerns about identity, sexuality, intimacy, autonomy and achievement are commonplace amongst adults also.

It is hoped that the brief overview of adolescent development provided in the present chapter will provide useful foundational knowledge to researchers in the TeenCI community. This knowledge should be used to inform research approaches, research questions, and research methods when working with teenagers in TeenCI research, ultimately contributing to a more comprehensive interdisciplinary understanding of teen interactions with technology.

References

Accordino DB, Accordino MP, Slaney RB (2000) An investigation of perfectionism, mental health, achievement, and achievement motivation in adolescents. Psychol Sch 37(6):535–545. doi:10.1002/1520-6807(200011)37:6<535::AID-PITS6>3.0.CO;2-O

Alberts A, Elkind D, Ginsberg S (2007) The personal fable and risk-taking in early adolescence. J Youth Adolesc 36(1):71–76. doi:10.1007/s10964-006-9144-4

Arnett JJ (1999) Adolescent storm and stress, reconsidered. Am Psychol 54(5):317–326. doi:10.1037/0003-066X.54.5.317

Bentley T (2012) Learning beyond the classroom: education for a changing world. Routledge, Oxon

Blakemore SJ (2012) Imaging brain development: the adolescent brain. Neuroimage 61(2):397–406. doi:10.1016/j.neuroimage.2011.11.080

Blakemore SJ, Mills KL (2014) Is adolescence a sensitive period for sociocultural processing? Annu Rev Psychol 65:187–207. doi:10.1146/annurev-psych-010213-115202

Blakemore SJ, Robbins TW (2012) Decision-making in the adolescent brain. Nat Neurosci 15(9):1184–1191. doi:10.1038/nn.3177

Bouchey HA, Harter S (2005) Reflected appraisals, academic self-perceptions, and math/science performance during early adolescence. J Educ Psychol 97(4):673. doi:10.1037/0022-0663.97.4.673

Boyd D (2014) It's complicated: the social lives of networked teens. Yale University Press, New Haven

Bronfenbrenner U (1979) Contexts of child rearing: problems and prospects. Am Psychol 34(10):844–850. doi:10.1037/0003-066X.34.10.844

Brown BB, Klute C (2003) Cliques, crowds, and friendships. In: Adams GR, Berzonsky M (eds) Handbook of adolescent development. Blackwell, London, pp 330–348

Browning CR, Leventhal T, Brooks-Gunn J (2004) Neighborhood context and racial differences in early adolescent sexual activity. Demography 41(4):697–720. doi:10.1353/dem.2004.0029
Buchanan C, Eccles J, Becker J (1992) Are adolescents the victims of raging hormones? Evidence for activational effects of hormones of hormones on mood and behaviour at adolescence. Psychol Bull 111:62–107. doi:10.1037/0033-2909.111.1.62
Bumpus MF, Crouter AC, McHale SM (2001) Parental autonomy granting during adolescence: exploring gender differences in context. Dev Psychol 37(2):163–173. doi:10.1037/0012-1649.37.2.163
Carskadon MA (2011) Sleep in adolescents: the perfect storm. Pediatr Clin N Am 58(3):637–647. doi:10.1016/j.pcl.2011.03.003
Chein J, Albert D, O'Brien L, Uckert K, Steinberg L (2011) Peers increase adolescent risk taking by enhancing activity in the brain's reward circuitry. Dev Sci 14(2):F1–F10. doi:10.1111/j.1467-7687.2010.01035.x
Cheung AC, Slavin RE (2011) The effectiveness of education technology for enhancing reading achievement: a meta-analysis. Center for Research and Reform in Education. Retrieved from: http://eric.ed.gov/?id=ED527572
Collins WA, Welsh DP, Furman W (2009) Adolescent romantic relationships. Annu Rev Psychol 60:631–652. doi:10.1146/annurev.psych.60.110707.163459
Darling N, Cumsille P, Martínez ML (2008) Individual differences in adolescents' beliefs about the legitimacy of parental authority and their own obligation to obey: a longitudinal investigation. Child Dev 79(4):1103–1118. doi:10.1111/j.1467-8624.2008.01178.x
Dekaban AS, Sadowsky D (1978) Changes in brain weights during the span of human life: relation of brain weights to body heights and body weights. Ann Neurol 4:345–356. doi:10.1002/ana.410040410
Demorest A, Meyer C, Phelps E, Gardner H, Winner E (1984) Words speak louder than actions: understanding deliberately false remarks. Child Dev 55:1527–1534. doi:10.2307/1130022
Diamond LM, Savin-Williams RC (2009) Adolescent sexuality. In: Lerner R, Steinberg L (eds) Handbook of adolescent psychology. Wiley, New York. doi:10.1002/9780470479193.adlpsy001015
Dorn LD, Biro FM (2011) Puberty and its measurement: a decade in review. J Res Adolesc 21(1):180–195. doi:10.1111/j.1532-7795.2010.00722.x
Dumontheil I, Apperly IA, Blakemore SJ (2010) Online usage of theory of mind continues to develop in late adolescence. Dev Sci 13(2):331–338. doi:10.1111/j.1467-7687.2009.00888.x
Eisenberg N, Cumberland A, Guthrie IK, Murphy BC, Shepard SA (2005) Age changes in prosocial responding and moral reasoning in adolescence and early adulthood. J Res Adolesc 15(3):235–260. doi:10.1111/j.1532-7795.2005.00095.x
Erikson E (1968) Youth: identity and crisis. Norton, New York
Flanagan C, Tucker C (1999) Adolescents' explanations for political issues: concordance with their views of self and society. Dev Psychol 35:1198–1209. doi:10.1037/0012-1649.35.5.1198
Gifford-Smith ME, Brownell CA (2003) Childhood peer relationships: social acceptance, friendships, and peer networks. J Sch Psychol 41(4):235–284. doi:10.1016/S0022-4405(03)00048-7
Grant M, Furstenberg F (2007) Changes in the transition to adulthood in less developed countries. Eur J Popul 23:415–428. doi:10.1007/2Fs10680-007-9131-9
Guse K, Levine D, Martins S, Lira A, Gaarde J, Westmorland W, Gilliam M (2012) Interventions using new digital media to improve adolescent sexual health: a systematic review. J Adolesc Health 51(6):535–543. doi:10.1016/j.jadohealth.2012.03.014
Hall GS (1904) Adolescence: Its psychology and its relation to physiology, anthropology, sociology, sex, crime, religion and education. Prentice-Hall, Englewood Cliffs
Hammack PL, Thompson EM, Pilecki A (2009) Configurations of identity among sexual minority youth: context, desire, and narrative. J Youth Adolesc 38(7):867–883. doi:10.1007/s10964-008-9342-3
Harris MA, Hood KK, Mulvaney SA (2012) Pumpers, skypers, surfers and texters: technology to improve the management of diabetes in teenagers. Diabetes Obes Metab 14(11):967–972. doi:10.1111/j.1463-1326.2012.01599.x

Hilbrecht M, Shaw SM, Johnson LC, Andrey J (2008) 'I'm Home for the Kids': contradictory implications for work–life balance of teleworking mothers. Gend Work Organ 15(5):454–476. doi:10.1111/j.1468-0432.2008.00413.x
Hill JP, Lynch ME (1983) The intensification of gender-related role expectations during early adolescence. In: Brooks-Gunn J, Peterson AC (eds) Girls at Puberty. Springer, pp 201–228. doi:10.1007/978-1-4899-0354-9_10
Horowitz AD, Bromnick RD (2007) Contestable adulthood: variability and disparity in markers for negotiating the transition to adulthood. Youth Soc 39:209–231. doi:10.1177/0044118X06296692
Huang-Pollock CL, Carr TH, Nigg JT (2002) Development of selective attention: perceptual load influences early versus late attentional selection in children and adults. Dev Psychol 38:363–375. doi:10.1037/0012-1649.38.3.363
Inhelder B, Piaget J (1958) The growth of logical thinking from childhood to adolescence. Basic Books, New York. doi:10.1037/10034-000
Jensen LA, Dost-Gözkan A (2015) Adolescent–parent relations in Asian Indian and Salvadoran immigrant families: a cultural–developmental analysis of autonomy, authority, conflict, and cohesion. J Res Adolesc 25(2):340–351. doi:10.1111/jora.12116
Johnson HD (2004) Gender, grade, and relationship differences in emotional closeness within adolescent friendships. Adolescence 39(154):243–255
Kail RV, Ferrer E (2007) Processing speed in childhood and adolescence: longitudinal models for examining developmental change. Child Dev 78(6):1760–1770
Keating D (2011) Cognitive development. In: Brown B, Prinstein M (eds) Encyclopedia of adolescence, vol 1. Academic Press, New York, pp 106–114
Keulers EH, Evers EA, Stiers P, Jolles J (2010) Age, sex, and pubertal phase influence mentalizing about emotions and actions in adolescents. Dev Neuropsychol 35(5):555–569
Killen M, Smetana J (eds) (2005) Handbook of moral development. Lawrence Erlbaum Associates, New Jersey
Koenig LB, McGue M, Iacono WG (2008) Stability and change in religiousness during emerging adulthood. Dev Psychol 44(2):532–543. doi:10.1111/j.1467-8624.2007.01088.x
Laursen B, Hartup WW (2002) The origins of reciprocity and social exchange in friendships. New Dir Child Adolesc Dev 95:27–40. doi:10.1002/cd.35
Laursen B, Collins WA (2009) Parent–child relationships during adolescence. Handb Adolesc Psychol 2(I):1. doi:10.1002/9780470479193.adlpsy002002
Leets L, Wolf S (2005) Adolescent rules for social exclusion: when is it fair to exclude someone else? J Moral Educ 34:343–362. doi:10.1080/03057240500211618
Lloyd BTN (2002) A conceptual framework for examining adolescent identity, media influence, and social development. Rev Gen Psychol 6(1):73–91. doi:10.1037/1089-2680.6.1.73
Luciana M, Conklin HM, Hooper CJ, Yarger RS (2005) The development of nonverbal working memory and executive control processes in adolescents. Child Dev 76:697–712. doi:10.1111/j.1467-8624.2005.00872.x
Luna B (2004) Algebra and the adolescent brain. Trends Cogn Sci 8:437–439. doi:10.1016/j.tics.2004.08.004
Madkour AS, Farhat T, Halpern CT, Godeau E, Gabhainn SN (2010) Early adolescent sexual initiation as a problem behavior: a comparative study of five nations. J Adolesc Health 47(4):389–398. doi:10.1016/j.jadohealth.2010.02.008
Manago AM, Graham MB, Greenfield PM, Salimkhan G (2008) Self-presentation and gender on MySpace. J Appl Dev Psychol 29(6):446–458. doi:10.1016/j.appdev.2008.07.001
McClintock MK, Herdt G (1996) Rethinking puberty: the development of sexual attraction. Curr Dir Psychol Sci 5(6):178–183. doi:10.1111/1467-8721.ep11512422
Mello ZR (2008) Gender variation in developmental trajectories of educational and occupational expectations and attainment from adolescence to adulthood. Dev Psychol 44(4):1069–1080. doi:10.1037/0012-1649.44.4.1069
Millman RP (2005) Excessive sleepiness in adolescents and young adults: causes, consequences, and treatment strategies. Pediatrics 115(6):1774–1786. doi:10.1542/peds.2005-0772

Mitchell KJ, Ybarra ML, Korchmaros JD, Kosciw JG (2014) Accessing sexual health information online: use, motivations and consequences for youth with different sexual orientations. Health Educ Res 29(1):147–157. doi:10.1093/her/cyt071
Montgomery MJ (2005) Psychosocial intimacy and identity from early adolescence to emerging adulthood. J Adolesc Res 20(3):346–374. doi:10.1177/0743558404273118
Peter J, Valkenburg PM, Schouten AP (2005) Developing a model of adolescent friendship formation on the Internet. CyberPsychology Behav 8(5):423–430. doi:10.1089/cpb.2005.8.423
Petersen AC (1988) Adolescent development. Annu Rev Psychol 39(1):583–607. doi:10.1146/annurev.ps.39.020188.003055
Pool MM, Koolstra CM, van der Voort THA (2003) The impact of background radio and television on high school students' homework performance. J Commun 53:74–87. doi:10.1111/j.1460-2466.2003.tb03006.x
Radmacher K, Azmitia M (2006) Are there gendered pathways to intimacy in early adolescents' and emerging adults' friendships? J Adolesc Res 21(4):415–448. doi:10.1177/0743558406287402
Reed TV (2014) Digitized lives: culture, power, and social change in the internet era. Routledge, New York
Richards MH, Crowe PA, Larson R, Swarr A (1998). Developmental patterns and gender differences in the experience of peer companionship during adolescence. Child Dev:154–163. doi:10.2307/1132077
Rogol AD, Roemmich JN, Clark PA (2002) Growth at puberty. J Adolesc Health 31(6):192–200. doi:10.1016/S1054-139X(02)00485-8
Rueger SY, Malecki CK, Demaray MK (2008) Gender differences in the relationship between perceived social support and student adjustment during early adolescence. Sch Psychol Q 23(4):496
Schneiders J, Nicolson NA, Berkhof J, Feron FJ, van Os J, deVries MW (2006) Mood reactivity to daily negative events in early adolescence: relationship to risk for psychopathology. Dev Psychol 42(3):543–544. doi:10.1037/0012-1649.42.3.543
Schunk DH, Meece JLD (2006) Self-efficacy development in adolescence. In: Pajares F, Urdan TC (eds) Self-efficacy beliefs of adolescents, vol 2. Information Age Publishing, Greenwich, pp 29–52
Sebastian C, Viding E, Williams KD, Blakemore SJ (2010) Social brain development and the affective consequences of ostracism in adolescence. Brain Cogn 72(1):134–145. doi:10.1016/j.bandc.2009.06.008
Smetana JG, Bitz B (1996) Adolescents' conceptions of teachers' authority and their relations to rule violations in school. Child Dev 67:1153–1172. doi:10.1111/1467-8624.ep9704150189
Smetana JG, Campione-Barr N, Metzger A (2006) Adolescent development in interpersonal and societal contexts. Annu Rev Psychol 57:255–284. doi:10.1146/annurev.psych.57.102904.190124
Steinberg L (2001) We know some things: parent-adolescent relationships in retrospect and prospect. J Res Adolesc 11(1):1–19. doi:10.1111/1532-7795.00001
Steinberg L (2007) Risk taking in adolescence new perspectives from brain and behavioral science. Curr Dir Psychol Sci 16(2):55–59. doi:10.1111/j.1467-8721.2007.00475.x
Steinberg L (2014a) Adolescence, 10th edn. McGraw Hill, New York
Steinberg L (2014b) Age of opportunity: lessons from the New science of adolescence. Houghton Mifflin Harcourt, New York
Steinberg L, Lerner RM (2004) The scientific study of adolescence a brief history. J Early Adolesc 24(1):45–54. doi:10.1177/0272431603260879
Strang NM, Chein JM, Steinberg L (2013) The value of the dual systems model of adolescent risk-taking. Front Hum Neurosci 7:223. doi:10.3389/fnhum.2013.00223
Strasburger VC, Wilson BJ (2002) Children, adolescents & the media. Sage Publications, Beverly Hills
Vartanian LR (2000) Revisiting the imaginary audience and personal fable constructs of adolescent egocentrism: a conceptual review. Adolescence 35(140):639–662

Waterman AS (1999) Identity, the identity statuses, and identity status development: a contemporary statement. Dev Rev 19(4):591–621. doi:10.1006/drev.1999.0493
Williams T, Connolly J, Pepler D, Craig W (2005) Peer victimization, social support, and psychosocial adjustment of sexual minority adolescents. J Youth Adolesc 34(5):471–482. doi:10.1007/s10964-005-7264-x
Woertman L, van den Brink F (2012) Body image and female sexual functioning and behavior: a review. J Sex Res 49(2–3):184–211. doi:10.1080/00224499.2012.658586
Zimmerman C (2000) The development of scientific reasoning skills. Dev Rev 20(1):99–149. doi:10.1006/drev.1999.0497

Chapter 3
Ethical Considerations in Face-to-Face and Internet-Mediated Research with Teenage Populations

Kerry McKellar and Nicola Toth

Abstract Research ethics is a critical part of any project but requires special consideration when conducting research with teenagers. Teenagers are deemed a vulnerable group and it is important to thoroughly consider ethical issues when conducting research with teenagers. Due to the proliferation and ease of access of the internet, internet-mediated research has become a beneficial modality for collecting data from teenagers in a HCI research context. Internet-mediated research is the process of gathering data via web-based technologies directly from research participants. Yet, internet-mediated research is still in its early stages and the key ethical issues with internet-mediated research are not immediately obvious. Therefore, this chapter examines key ethical standards for conducting research with teenagers through traditional face-to-face and internet-mediated methods. The key ethical issues are highlighted and discussed in the context of research with teenage populations. Personal experiences of both face-to-face and internet-mediated research with teenagers are discussed and reflected upon. This chapter contributes key understandings of ethical issues within the context of HCI research involving teenage participants.

3.1 Aims of the Chapter

This chapter considers the importance of ethical issues when conducting research with teenagers. The chapter is divided into five sections. This section outlines the aims of the chapter, Sect. 3.2 is a discussion of the importance of ethics and provides a background understanding of ethics and ethical guidelines. Section 3.3 considers ethical issues in traditional face-to-face research and subsequently Sect. 3.4

K. McKellar (✉)
Psychology and Communication Technology (PaCT) Lab, Department of Psychology, Faculty of Health and Life Sciences, Northumbria University,
Northumberland Building, Newcastle upon Tyne, United Kingdom
e-mail: kerry.mckellar@northumbria.ac.uk

N. Toth
PaCT Lab, Department of Psychology, Faculty of Health and Life Sciences, Northumbria University, Newcastle NE1 8ST, UK

© Springer International Publishing Switzerland 2016

L. Little et al. (eds.), *Perspectives on HCI Research with Teenagers*,
Human–Computer Interaction Series, DOI 10.1007/978-3-319-33450-9_3

discusses these in relation to internet-mediated research. A discussion and reflection of our own personal experiences of two different research projects working with teenagers and the ethical issues encountered are described in Sect. 3.5. Section 3.6 is an overall reflection and conclusion of the chapter.

3.2 The Importance of Ethics

Research ethics provides guidelines for the responsible conduct of research to ensure all research is conducted at a high ethical standard. This is especially important to TeenCI researchers when conducting research with teenagers as those under the age of 18 are deemed as vulnerable members of society and special considerations of consent, understandings of the research and anonymity are often legal, if not moral, requirements.

> *... Our primary obligation is always to the people we study, not to our project or to a larger discipline. The lives and stories that we hear and study are given to us under a promise, that promise being that we protect those who have shared them with us.* (Denzin 1989:83)

As Denzin (1989) suggests, the researchers' obligation must be to the participants in the project and it is highly important to ensure they are under no psychological harm or discomfort. A thorough consideration of ethics should always be a critical part of the planning, design and conduct of the research process. This will help the researcher to fully understand what moral principles guide the research, the researcher's responsibility to the participants and how the research will benefit those who participated in the study. Research should be conducted safely and meet agreed principles, standards and codes of practice. Research should also produce knowledge, which benefits participants and society and deepens academic understanding of the subject area. Thus, ethics should be fully considered from the planning stages to ensure good, strong, ethically sound research is being conducted. This chapter will further discuss ethical principles and how these can be achieved when working with teenagers to ensure that the participants are protected and the research is of high moral and ethical standards.

3.2.1 A Brief Background to Ethics

Modern ideas about research ethics began with a desire to protect human subjects involved in research projects. Though there is a set of laws for defining good medical practice and morals – the Hippocratic Oath – however, there is currently no such oath for Scientists. One of the first guidelines for good ethical practice began during the doctors' trial of 1946–1947. The doctors' trials were a segment of the Nuremberg trials for Nazi war criminals and in the trial 23 German Nazi physicians were accused of torturous experiments, including exposing participants to extreme temperatures and altitudes. As a result, the 'Nuremberg code' was created consisting of 10 guidelines (Nuremberg Code 1949):

1. Participants must give their voluntary consent for research participation.
2. The aims of the research study should benefit society.
3. Research studies must be based on prior animal testing and sound theory.
4. Researchers must avoid all unnecessary physical and mental suffering.
5. If serious injury and/or death to human participants are potential outcomes then the research project cannot go forward.
6. The degree of risk to research participants cannot exceed predicted benefits of results.
7. Appropriate environment and protection for research participants is necessary.
8. Experiments must only be conducted by a qualified person.
9. Human subjects have the right to withdraw from their participation at any time.
10. If there is cause to believe that the research project will be harmful or result in injury or death the project must be terminated.

This led to the Helsinki declaration. The declaration of Helsinki was adopted in 1964 by the World Medical Association an asset of ethical principles covering human experimentation. The key ethical articles are (Goodyear et al. 2007):

- Respect for the individual (Article 8)
- The right to self-determination and the right to make informed decisions (Articles 20–22).
- The duty of the researcher is towards the patient or the volunteer (Articles 2,3,10,16,18).
- The welfare of the participant must always take precedence over the research (Article 9).
- Individuals or groups who are deemed to be 'vulnerable' require special vigilance (Article 8).
- Even if consent is granted by someone else legally permitted to give it, the individual must still give their assent (Article 25).

3.2.2 *British Psychological Society Ethical Principles*

These guidelines led to the development of the British Psychological Society's ethical principles, which are followed by Psychologists conducting research in the UK. Psychologists follow strict codes of ethics practise and the BPS principles will be discussed here. The British Psychological Society is regarded as a prominent authority on ethical guidelines involving human participants for social and behavioural science. They may be useful for TeenCI researchers as psychology is an important sub-discipline of human computer interaction and ethical guidelines in the other sub-disciplines, including computer sciences and design are less developed. The BPS outline several ethical principles that cover four main areas; respect, competence, responsibility and integrity. Each area will be discussed below. The BPS Code of Conduct (2009) provides guidelines and therefore, the language used is 'should' rather than 'must' and suggests that researchers reinforce the advisory nature of the code as a framework in support of professional judgement.

3.2.3 Respect

> *Psychologists value the dignity and worth of all persons, with sensitivity to the dynamics of perceived authority or influence over clients, and with particular regard to people's rights including those of privacy and self-determination* (BPS Codes of Ethics and Conduct 2009: p9).

3.2.3.1 Standards of General Respect

TeenCI researchers should always respect participants and avoid any practice that would be unfair or prejudiced. All individuals should be respected, especially their cultural and role differences, including; age, sex, nationality, ethnicity, disability, sexual orientation, marital or family status and socio-economic status (SES). TeenCI researchers must respect the knowledge, insight, experience and expertise of teenagers, third parties (such as schools and youth groups) and the general public.

3.2.3.2 Standards of Informed Consent

TeenCI researchers need to ensure that participants, parents and teachers are given sufficient information and time to understand the nature, purpose, and possible consequences of their research participation. It is particularly important in TeenCI research to gain informed consent from teenagers. Written consent must be obtained and this information must be securely stored. If individual consent cannot be provided because the participant is under the age of 18 or are vulnerable and not able to provide consent then it should be obtained from parents or others in loco parentis (in the place of a parent) who are legally permitted to provide it (e.g. teacher/carer/doctor). If seeking consent from an individual who may be pressured into consent (from their prison, team, school etc.) then extra care should be taken to minimise this pressure. This could be achieved by the researcher presenting the research to teenagers rather than a teacher presenting the research. Teenagers should also be allowed adequate time to consider the research and the researcher should remind them that they are able to withdraw at any stage of the research, without having to provide a reason for this. Consent should always be voluntary, informed and written. Intentional deception must be avoided unless it is necessary to preserve the integrity of the research.

3.2.3.3 Standards of Privacy and Confidentiality

TeenCI researchers must ensure that they maintain appropriate records and restrict the scope of disclosure to that which is consistent with professional purposes. Confidential information must be stored appropriately to ensure disclosure is avoided. All participants must be informed that information might be shared with a third party and that some information might be published and presented in public, however participants would be kept anonymous. All video/audio/photographic recordings of participants must only be made with their informed consent.

3.2.3.4 Standards of Self-Determination

The researcher must ensure that participants are aware of their right to withdraw at any time and without prejudice. TeenCI researchers must comply with the requests of participants who are withdrawing from research participation that their data is withdrawn, and any information that might identify them is destroyed. If a teenager withdraws from the research it must be managed carefully. If the research is taking place at an organisation (for example, a school) the researcher should arrange with the teachers for a space to be provided for any teenagers who decide to withdraw during the study. If the research is happening outside of their organisation (for example, a research institute) there should be space available and an alternative activity arranged for teenagers, until the other participants have completed their participation.

3.2.4 *Competence*

> *Psychologists value the continuing development and maintenance of high standards of competence in their professional work, and the importance of preserving their ability to function optimally within the recognised limits of their knowledge, skill, training, education, and experience* (BPS Codes of Ethics and Conduct 2009: p15).

3.2.4.1 Standard of Awareness of Professional Ethics

Ethical considerations in any research project are an element of continuing professional development; this is because each project will have its own unique ethical issues and different considerations will need to be made. As such, it is vital that TeenCI researchers stay up to date with current ethical procedures and guidelines. TeenCI researchers should gain access to their institutional ethics guides and codes of practise in order to maintain a comprehensive awareness of professional ethics, e.g. from professional bodies. They may also find it useful to attend training courses as institutions may struggle to keep up with the changing nature of technology and the new ethical challenges these technologies pose.

3.2.4.2 Standard of Ethical Decision Making

TeenCI researchers should recognise that ethical dilemmas will inevitably arise in the course of professional practice and attempt to resolve such dilemmas with the appropriate combination of reflection, supervision and consultation. In order to do this researchers should be committed to the requirements of the code of practise they are following, and remain up to date with the current versions. Once researchers have reflected on any ethical dilemmas (preferably as part of a research team) they should seek peer review to ensure they have fully considered the ethical dilemmas and attempted to resolve them. Researchers should be able to justify any action on ethical grounds while meeting ethical principles and legal requirements (for example, safeguarding). Safeguarding is a term that is broader than 'child protection' and relates to the action of promoting welfare of children and teenagers and protecting them from harm (Gov.UK 2014). It is important to safeguard children and teenagers during research. Researchers should check with the organisation where the research is taking place (for example, a university or school) to ensure the organisation's safeguarding policies are being followed. Consulting with research collaborators in other TeenCI disciplines may also be useful in overcoming ethical dilemmas.

3.2.4.3 Standard of Recognising Limits of Competence

TeenCI researchers should practice within the boundaries of their competence. The BPS Codes of Ethics and Conduct (2009) outlines guidelines for this:

1. Researchers should engage in Continued Professional Development.
2. Researchers should keep up to date with Scientific, ethical and legal innovations suitable to their professional activities.
3. Researchers should seek supervision when they are being challenged in their scientific or professional expertise.
4. Researchers should engage in additional professional development, only once they have obtained sufficient knowledge for competent functioning.
5. Researchers should remain aware of and acknowledge the limits of their methods and conclusions.
6. Researchers should ensure that anyone working under their supervision complies with each of the requirements of these standards.

3.2.4.4 Standard of Recognising Impairment

TeenCI researchers should monitor their own personal and professional lifestyle in order to remain alert to signs of impairment and take action against any impairment. For example, if a researcher becomes aware of any health-related or personal problems which may seriously impair their own professional competence when working with participants then they should refrain from practice and seek professional consultation or assistance.

3.2.5 *Responsibility*

> *Psychologists value their responsibilities to clients, to the general public, and to the profession and science of Psychology, including the avoidance of harm and the prevention of misuse or abuse of their contributions to society* (BPS Codes of Ethics and Conduct 2009: p18).

3.2.5.1 Standards of General Responsibility

TeenCI researchers should be mindful to any potential risks to themselves when conducting research, especially when visiting external organisations. For example, if a TeenCI researcher is visiting a school or youth group to recruit teenagers, they should make sure that they have spoken to the school about health and safety issues in advance, and if working alone, arranged for a contact person at the school or youth group. If a problem were to arise, for example a verbal attack on another participant or the researcher it is important to have someone available from the organisation. The contact person would be able to help or remove a participant (if necessary) with minimal disruption.

3.2.5.2 Standards of Termination and Continuity of Care

TeenCI researchers should make sure that the participants understand the conditions in which a research project may be terminated and participants should be made aware of these at the earliest opportunity. For example, in the unlikely circumstances that a research project has to be terminated because the researcher had an illness and another researcher could not take over the study. The participants should be made aware that the research project has ended and be fully debriefed, even if they have not fully completed their participation.

3.2.5.3 Standard of Protection of Research Participants

TeenCI researchers should consider all research from the standpoint of the research participants, for the purpose of eliminating potential risks to psychological well-being, physical health, personal values, or dignity. TeenCI researchers need to consider physical harm to the participant. All procedures should be risk assessed and health and safety checked. However, an issue that is not immediately obvious is psychological wellbeing of the participant. For example, teenagers' well-being may be affected by becoming embarrassed or feeling 'uncool' in front of their peers. This is an issue which is not often considered or noticed by adults, yet it may be extremely important to participants. Therefore, it is vital to try and avoid issues like this. Piloting procedures and getting feedback from teenagers and experts who work with teenagers can be a way of receiving advice on procedures and making any modifications, before implementing them with teenagers. As discussed previously, teenagers should be made aware of their right to withdraw and regularly reminded of this throughout the research.

3.2.5.4 Standard of Debriefing of Research Participants

Participants should be debriefed at the conclusion of their participation; this should include informing them of the outcomes and nature of the research and identifying any unforeseen harm, discomfort, or misconceptions. If any unforeseen harm is identified then assistance (for example, medical attention) should be arranged as necessary. TeenCI researchers should take particular care when discussing outcomes with research participants, as seemingly evaluative statements may carry unintended weight. They also need to phrase the debrief in a teen-centric way, making sure all specialist language is adequately explained.

3.2.6 Integrity

> *Psychologists value honesty, accuracy, clarity, and fairness in their interactions with all persons, and seek to promote integrity in all facets of their scientific and professional endeavours* (BPS Codes of Ethics and Conduct 2009: p21).

3.2.6.1 Standard of Honesty and Accuracy

TeenCI researchers must be honest and accurate in representing their professional affiliations and qualifications, including such matters as knowledge, skill, training, education, and experience. For example, if a researcher is developing an app for forum support for a health condition (for example, diabetes), participants should be informed right at the beginning of the research within both the written information and verbally if the researcher is not an expert in diabetes so that participants do not gain unrealistic expectations or ask questions or advice that the researcher could not answer.

3.2.6.2 Standard of Avoiding Exploitation and Conflicts of Interest

TeenCI researchers must remain aware of the problems that may result from dual or multiple relationships, for example, conducting research with their teenager or their teenager's friends. Problems may include, impairing a researcher's objectivity or exploiting another party, impair judgements or relationships may be exploitive. Therefore, if a potentially harmful multiple relationship has arisen, the researcher should attempt to resolve it with due regard for the best interest of the affected person and maximal compliance with their institution's ethics code.

3.2.6.3 Standard of Maintaining Personal Boundaries

TeenCI researchers must refrain from engaging in any form of sexual or romantic relationship with persons to whom they are providing research participation, or to whom they owe a continuing duty of care, or with whom they have a relationship of trust. This might include a former patient, a student or trainee, or a junior staff member and there may be legal implications of this.

3.2.6.4 Standard of Addressing Ethical Misconduct

TeenCI researchers should challenge colleagues, by bringing it to the attention of their relevant ethics board, who appear to have engaged in any ethical misconduct. This is important as the TeenCI community develops and grows as it is important for the discipline to maintain credibility.

3.3 Existing Ethical Guidelines when Conducting Research with Teenagers

Similar to the BPS code of ethics and conduct (2009) the Society for Research in Child Development has outlined 16 principles of ethical standards in research (SRCD Governing Council 2007). Below is a summary of the principles and how they can be achieved when working with children and teenagers. Direct quotes from the ethical standards are presented and further explained underneath. As with the BPS guidelines, the wording of 'should' is used rather than 'must'.

3.3.1 Principle 1 – Non-harmful Procedures

Principle *The investigator should use no research procedure that may harm the child either physically or psychologically. The investigator is also obligated at all times to use the least stressful research procedure whenever possible. Psychological harm in particular instances may be difficult to define; nevertheless, its definition and means for reducing or eliminating it remain the responsibility of the investigator.* (SRCD Governing Council 2007)

How It Can be Achieved

- All procedures should be piloted, with participants who are knowledgeable of teenagers' capabilities (e.g. teachers) and risk assessed before being implemented with teenagers.
- Consultations should be sought from others who have knowledge of the procedures and/or have expertise in working with children or teenagers (e.g. teachers).
- If harm is inevitable then procedures should be improved to have the least harm possible. For example, in body image research, researchers may aim to trigger body image concerns, but only in the short-term, no permanent harm to participants would be triggered (Bell and Dittmar 2011).

3.3.2 Principle 2 – Informed Consent

Principle *Assent means that the child shows some form of agreement to participate without necessarily comprehending the full significance of the research necessary to give informed consent. Investigators working with infants should take special effort to explain the research procedures to the parents and be especially sensitive to any indicators of discomfort in the infant.* (SRCD Governing Council 2007)

How It Can be Achieved

- TeenCI researchers should inform the teenager of all tasks and requirements of the research, before the research begins and this should be in simplistic language.
- The teenager should have the chance to ask questions and questions should be appropriately answered.
- The teenager should have freedom to take part and to withdraw at any point during the research and should be reminded they can withdraw without prejudice or reason. A space and another activity should be provided for those who withdraw from the research.
- In the unlikely circumstance that consent cannot be sought because it would make the research impossible to carry out (for example, existing data on a public

blog) then the research should be ethically suitable and participant's anonymity protected. However, this would only be acceptable if the researcher had discussed it with an institutional review board.

3.3.3 Principle 3 – Parental Consent

Principle *The informed consent of parents, legal guardians or those who act in loco parentis (e.g., teachers, superintendents of institutions) similarly should be obtained, preferably in writing.* (SRCD Governing Council 2007)

How It Can be Achieved

- Parents or caregivers should be fully informed of the research and have the chance to ask the researcher questions and these should be appropriately answered.
- Any information sheets that are given to parents/carers should include the profession, institution and contact details of the researcher.
- If parents/carers refuse to consent then their decision should be respected.
- Parents and carers should be reminded that they can withdraw at any time without any penalty to them or their child.
- There should be sufficient time for parents/carers to consider the research before consenting.
- Two methods of parental consent are usually sought, either opt-in, parents give permission for their child to take part in the research, or opt-out where parents inform the researcher if they do not want their child to take part in the research. Opt-out consent is suitable when working with an organisation that can give consent for the opt-out procedure (for example, a school). Whereas, opt-in consent is most suitable for sensitive research topics or tasks and when recruiting participants from the general population or recruiting through parents.

3.3.4 Principle 4 – Additional Consent

Principle *The informed consent of any persons, such as schoolteachers for example, whose interaction with the child is the subject of the study should also be obtained.* (SRCD Governing Council 2007)

How It Can be Achieved

- Any teachers who will be involved in the research should be fully informed of all features of the research.
- Any questions teachers have should be appropriately answered.

- Teachers should be reminded that they are free to withdraw themselves, or their pupils from the research at any time without prejudice or reason.
- Written permission should be gained from the school if recruiting teenagers from a school, normally from the Head-teacher.

3.3.5 Principle 5 – Incentives

Principle *Incentives to participate in a research project must be fair and must not unduly exceed the range of incentives that the child normally experiences.* (SRCD Governing Council 2007)

How It Can be Achieved

- Incentives must be considered early in the research stage, be age appropriate and separate from parental incentives. If there are any invasive or additional burdens on the child, then the incentive should be increased but incentives offered should not be coercive (Rice and Broome 2004).
- Incentives could be considered coercive as they are influencing the participant to take part in the research, therefore there should be a clear justification for incentives.
- All incentives should be discussed with the researchers' institutional review board.
- No persuasion or pressure of any kind should be put on participants. Any participants from financially disadvantaged groups should be carefully considered when offering incentives (Alderson and Morrow 2004).
- Participants should know before they start participation in the research project that they can withdraw from the study at any time without losing their payment. Similarly, if there is a 'prize draw' for returning surveys, it should be clear that potential participants can enter the prize draw even if they don't answer the questions in the survey.

3.3.6 Principle 6 – Deception

Principle *Although full disclosure of information during the procedure of obtaining consent is the ethical ideal, a particular study may necessitate withholding certain information or deception.* (SRCD Governing Council 2007)

How It Can be Achieved

- If deception is necessary, employ methods that will have no known effects on the teenagers or their family. For example, if the researcher was investigating behaviour change and needed to compare two groups, they may not fully disclose what groups

teenagers are assigned to in order to not affect the outcome. However, being assigned to either group should not have any known impact on the teenagers. Participants could also be added to a waiting list control group, this is where participants serve as a control group (untreated comparison) during the study, but receive the treatment or intervention at a later date, when the study has concluded.
- All procedures must have scientific validity, avoid and minimise harm, have full parental permission with the parents informed of the deception (Fisher 2005).
- Ethical decisions for using deception must be discussed with the institutional ethics board.

3.3.7 Principle 7 – Anonymity

Principle *To gain access to institutional records, the investigator should obtain permission from responsible authorities in charge of records. Anonymity of the information should be preserved and no information used other than that for which permission was obtained.* (SRCD Governing Council 2007)

How It Can be Achieved

- Anonymity should be explained to teenagers in a way that they can understand. For example, it should be fully explained that names and other identifying information will be removed. It should also be made clear who will have access to the data and what will happen to the data once the research is complete.
- All participants have the right to anonymity. Except where they disclose a risk of harm, for example child protection and safeguarding laws would be more important than anonymity and this should be explained to teenagers and parents in the information sheets.
- The teenager needs to know what action may be taken in the event that they disclose that they are at risk of harm, or where the researcher observes or receives information that is likely to cause harm, arrangements need to be made in advance, following professional advice, on agreed procedures and support for the child. The researcher needs to know where their duty of care ends. The researcher should set up a process with the school for how any disclosures of harm will be managed. For example, researchers may report this to a designated teacher or safeguarding officer, who will then deal with the matter further.

3.3.8 Principle 8 – Mutual Responsibilities

Principle *From the beginning of each research investigation, there should be clear agreement between the investigator and the parents, guardians or those who act in loco parentis, and the child, when appropriate, that defines the responsibilities of each.* (SRCD Governing Council 2007)

How It Can be Achieved

- Responsibilities should be clearly defined at the start of the research project in writing.
- The researchers must honour all promises and commitments made in this agreement.

3.3.9 Principle 9 – Jeopardy

Principle *When, in the course of research, information comes to the investigator's attention that may jeopardize the child's well-being, the investigator has a responsibility to discuss the information with the parents or guardians and with those expert in the field in order that they may arrange the necessary assistance for the child.* (SRCD Governing Council 2007)

How It Can be Achieved

- TeenCI researchers should ensure they have necessary assistance for all participants if there is a chance they will be in jeopardy. For example, if a researcher is evaluating the usability of a health app and the teenager discloses information that suggests to the researcher that they need assistance (For example, a participant with diabetes could report high blood sugar levels), there should be a process in place for who the researcher reports this to, so the teenager can receive the necessary assistance.

3.3.10 Principle 10 – Unforeseen Consequences

Principle *When research procedures result in undesirable consequences for the participant that were previously unforeseen, the investigator should immediately employ appropriate measures to correct these consequences, and should redesign the procedures if they are to be included in subsequent studies.* (SRCD Governing Council 2007)

How It Can be Achieved

- Any procedure that has led to harm or undesirable consequences for participants should be amended before further studies. The new procedure should be checked again by the institutions ethics committee.
- Any support needed for the teenager should be immediately sought, from a relevant person. For example, if any emotional or psychological harm arises, an appropriate professional body, such as the NSPCC should be contacted.

3.3.11 Principle 11 – Confidentiality

Principle *The investigator should keep in confidence all information obtained about research participants. The participants' identity should be concealed in written and verbal reports of the results, as well as in informal discussion with students and colleagues. When a possibility exists that others may gain access to such information, this possibility, together with the plans for protecting confidentiality, should be explained to the participants as part of the procedure of obtaining informed consent.* (SRCD Governing Council 2007)

How It Can be Achieved

- Confidentiality procedures – such as removing names and anonymising data, storage of data and who will have access to the data – should be considered at the very early stages of the research project.
- The researcher may need to report incidents to a teacher or another named safeguarding officer if they believe that the teenager is in jeopardy or at a risk of harm. Therefore, this should be explained clearly to teenagers at the start of the research project, including an explanation of how this will affect their confidentiality if any information is disclosed.
- All paper documents should be kept in a locked filing cupboard separated from the informed consent forms.
- In line with the data protection act, any electronic data should be kept on a password-protected computer.

3.3.12 Principle 12 – Informing Participants

Principle *Immediately after the data are collected, the investigator should clarify for the research participant any misconceptions that may have arisen."*(SRCD Governing Council 2007)

How It Can be Achieved

- TeenCI researchers should fully debrief teenagers once their research participation is completed. The researcher should clearly and in simplistic terms explain the aims of the study and provide time to answer any questions that teenagers might have. Teenagers should also be aware that they will be provided with a summary of the full results and when this summary will be available.
- If any information had to be withheld at the start of the research project, for example the issues discussed in Principle 6, then effort should be made to ensure there are no damaging consequences for the participant.

3.3.13 Principle 13 – Reporting Results

Principle *Because the investigator's words may carry unintended weight with parents and children, caution should be exercised in reporting results, making evaluative statements, or giving advice.*(SRCD Governing Council 2007)

How It Can be Achieved

- The researcher should report the general findings to all participants in terms appropriate to their understanding. For example, using words that are within teenagers' comprehension level and checking the wording with teachers to ensure teenagers in that age group will understand. For example, teenagers aged 16–19 years are likely to understand more complex terms than teenagers aged 13–15 years.
- Special concern should be for the psychological and physical well-being of the children and teenagers in the research, researchers should be careful of failure to report and over reporting suspected problems (Scott-Jones 1994).
- For example, researchers should not give advice that may carry unintended consequences with parents or teenagers. Any evaluative statements used should not over exaggerate the research findings, or provide any worry to parents or teenagers. Therefore, researchers should seek peer review or consult with their research team before making any evaluative statements or giving advice to schools or parents, based on the research findings. For example, if the research was investigating web-based games, the researcher might be seen as an expert in this area, and parents may seek advice on whether their teens should be using these games. Some statements could be seen as harmless but could have unintended implications.

3.3.14 Principle 14 – Implications of Findings

Principle *Investigators should be mindful of the social, political and human implications of their research and should be especially careful in the presentation of findings from the research. This principle, however, in no way denies investigators the right to pursue any area of research or the right to observe proper standards of scientific reporting*. (SRCD Governing Council 2007)

How It Can be Achieved

- TeenCI researchers should be careful in the way they report the implications of their findings and discuss with their research team, before reporting to teenagers or parents.
- The report must be suitable for the audience and the wording and phrasing used must be carefully considered in case the language could be misinterpreted. The

implications should only be reported factually and no judgements should be made. Using the example described above in Principle 13 of web-based game usage, parents may misinterpret the implications and worry about their teen playing web-based games. Therefore, it is important that no personal judgements are included and only factual statements.
- Different versions of the report should be created, for example, reporting the implications to an academic audience should be different to reporting to teenagers or parents. For younger teenagers (aged 13–15 years), it might be more appropriate to use images and present in simplistic language. Whereas, it might be more appropriate to report the implications in a more formal style to older teenagers (aged 16–19 years). However, the wording and style should be checked with a teacher.

3.3.15 Principle 15 – Scientific Misconduct

Principle *Misconduct is defined as the fabrication or falsification of data, plagiarism, misrepresentation, or other practices that seriously deviate from those that are commonly accepted within the scientific community for proposing, conducting, analysing, or reporting research. It does not include unintentional errors or honest differences in interpretation of data.* (SRCD Governing Council 2007)

How It Can be Achieved

- TeenCI researchers should ensure they do not fabricate or falsify data.
- Incomplete data needs consideration about what lead to this and whether it can be used.
- Any data that cannot be interpreted with accuracy should be discussed with the research team and peer reviewed before reporting.
- Any confusion over this should be discussed with the research team, if there is no research team then the researcher should seek peer review or guidance from a professional body.

3.3.16 Principle 16 – Personal Misconduct

Principle *Personal misconduct that results in a criminal conviction of a felony may be sufficient grounds for a member's expulsion from the Society. The relevance of the crime to the purposes of the Society should be considered by the Governing Council in reaching a decision about the matter. It shall be the responsibility of the voting members of Governing Council to reach a decision about the possible expulsion of members found guilty of personal misconduct.*(SRCD Governing Council 2007)

How It Can be Achieved

- Researchers should avoid any misconduct and ensure if they are working with an external organisation (e.g. school or youth group), they receive a copy of their safeguarding and health and safety policies in order to familiarise themselves with the guidelines before the research study begins.

3.4 The Internet and Teenagers

In the United Kingdom teenagers' access to the internet is increasing, both at school and at home (Livingstone and Bober 2004; Office for National Statistics 2011), with approximately 90 % of teenagers aged 12–15 using a PC or laptop at home and 84 % using a smart phone to access the internet (Ofcom 2014). In the United States, 95 % of teenagers aged 12–17 have regular access to the internet (Madden et al. 2013). Though internet use is highest in Western cultures, patterns of increasing internet use can be observed worldwide; 42 % of the world's population in 2015 has access to the internet as opposed to 35 % in January 2014 (Kemp 2015). Also, teenagers are using the internet in different ways. In 2011, only 8 % of teenagers used websites they had not visited before and 51 % only used websites that they had visited before. In comparison in 2014, 18 % used websites they have not visited before and only 35 % only used websites they have visited before. Therefore, teenagers are exploring more of the internet and are more open to exploring novel websites. Teenagers are also communicating more online, with 36 % of 11–15 year olds choosing to communicate through social networking sites compared to phone, email or texting (Ofcom 2014).

Due to the increase in internet use among teenagers, there is scope for TeenCI researchers to make use of Internet-mediated research. It is appropriate and beneficial to conduct IMR with teenagers as it is one of their preferred methods of communication (Pew Research center 2015). Teenagers are familiar with the Internet and have easy access to it (Madden et al. 2013). An advantage of conducting IMR is it allows TeenCI researchers to reach a large number of usually hard-to-reach individuals in a quick and efficient way (Wright 2005), boosting the participation rates and collecting a large amount of data in a short period of time.

3.4.1 Ethics in Online Research

When conducting Internet-mediated research, some ethical issues require special consideration as the complexities with IMR are not always obvious. IMR covers a wide range of both quantitative and qualitative approaches for research that involves human participants; this may be through the Internet or through web-based technologies, such as e-mails, mobile phones, smart devices. Quantitative projects may involve; web-based questionnaires or experiments. Whereas qualitative Internet-mediated research may involve; web-based diary studies, blogs, video blogs and web-based interviews similar to traditional research methods that collect rich, meaningful and elaborate data. There is also scope to collect and evaluate existing data that is publically available, for example; teenage blogs, social networking sites and website hits.

The main ethical issues, according to Ethics Guidelines for Internet-mediated Research (2013: p5) to consider when designing, implementing or assessing an IMR study are:

1. "*Respect for the autonomy and dignity of persons*
2. *Scientific value*
3. *Social responsibility*
4. *Maximising benefits and minimising harm*"

3.4.2 *Principle 1: Respect for the Autonomy and Dignity of Persons*

In IMR contexts, privacy, anonymity and confidentiality are problematic, and needs careful consideration. Different sources of online information may serve as potential research data and the privacy of this information can be unclear. It may also more complex obtaining consent and managing withdrawals.

When Working with Teenagers

- Teenagers may not realise what information is private and public online, especially when looking at online blogs and forums. Even if they have agreed to terms of the web service providers licence agreement, they may not realise that their conversations are publically available.
- TeenCI researchers should take careful consideration of these issues especially if the topic(s) are of a sensitive nature as it could have a damaging effect on participants. Whether written consent is necessary should always be discussed with relevant ethics experts.
- A discussion group moderator or list owner (including any online discussion or forum sites or email lists) may often provide a good point of contact for advice on the best ways to research existing groups online. However, if the moderator or list owner does not respond, then it should be discussed with a relevant ethics expert if the data can be used, and if it is expected that this information is in the public domain.
- Safeguarding of teenagers should always be taken into account, as the information on the web-based site being publically disseminated could have a harmful effect on the participant. For example, if a researcher was examining a health blog containing sensitive information and included direct quotes from the blog within their research publication, these could be traced back to the original

source. Therefore confidentiality would be breached. To avoid this any data taken from the blog should be reworded, and no verbatim quotes should be included in any dissemination. This should be discussed with the research team or the relevant ethics committee when planning the study.

3.4.2.1 Valid Consent

Valid consent should still be obtained when conducting IMR research. However, online data that is considered 'in the public domain' may not need valid consent. For example, the Codes of Ethics and Conduct states that, observations of public behaviour can take place without valid consent when the participants being observed "would expect to be observed by strangers" (p25, 2009). Therefore, participants contributing to a public forum may expect to be observed by strangers. However, each project needs to be taken on a case by case basis and the topic of the public domain taken into account. The terms and conditions of the public forum should also be explored as guidelines on the information being used for research purposes may be included.

When Working with Teenagers

- It can be difficult to verify consent and demographics in research that is not face-to-face. Considerations of this should be accurately reported in describing the work.
- Parental/carer's consent should always be gained first if using opt-in consent methods, this is usually done offline.
- In questionnaire based research participants usually consent online (however offline consent before participation could occur). Detailed information that the participant can print and keep should be provided before consent is sought online. For opt-in consent online, mechanisms should be put in place to ensure a user has given their consent before the data collection part of the web site can be accessed. For consent forms, 'I agree' questions should be counterbalanced to encourage participants to read the information. The questions should not be over complicated and should be at a comprehension level teenagers can understand. The language used should be checked with a relevant teacher, especially for different age groups. Teenagers aged 13–15 years might need more simplistic language than teenagers aged 16–19 years.
- TeenCI researchers need to consider ways in which teenagers are properly informed about how the data they provide will be electronically stored. Participants should be assured that their IP address will not be stored and their information will be stored on a password-protected computer. Teenagers may not know what an IP address is and what the implications of this are, therefore this should be explained to them in simplistic age-appropriate terms.
- It should also be clear to teenagers how they can withdraw from the study with and without their partial data being used. One way to do this would be to include within the information sheets that closing the browser will indicate that partici-

pants do not want their partial data to be used, whereas displaying an exit button but use my partial data should indicate partial data can be used.

3.4.3 *Principle 2: Scientific Value*

In an IMR context the lack of direct physical proximity may impact on levels of control over and knowledge of participant behaviours, characteristics and research procedures. Such lack of control may have an impact on the validity of research, its findings and conclusions for example, particularly in experimental designs where tight control over variables is crucial to validity (Ethics Guidelines for Internet-mediated Research 2013).

When Working with Teenagers

- The lack of face to face contact can cause difficulties in maintaining control over research procedures and environment. Therefore, if a research needs high control over the procedure or environment (e.g. needs to be completed alone in silence) then this needs to be explained to teenagers beforehand. For example, speaking to teenagers face-to-face about how to complete the study. If high control over the procedure or environment is vital for the study then the researcher should reconsider whether IMR is appropriate for the research.
- It may not be clear whether the demographic information is correct for participants. This is particularly important when researching teenagers as if the researcher is unable to physically see the participant, it is difficult to ensure it is a teenager taking part. Therefore it is useful to recruit teenagers through schools, youth groups or parents, to ensure that researchers are actually reaching a teenage population.
- Careful consideration must be taken to ensure that only the teenagers who have had parental consent can take part in the research. To achieve this only teenagers' who have had parental consent should have the link to the research and it should be made clear if the research must be conducted alone or under certain conditions. Parental consent can be gained in advance through face–to-face methods.

3.4.4 *Principle 3: Social Responsibility*

Researchers should have respect for and avoidance of social structures (for example, the dynamics of existing online groups) and should carefully consider the consequences and outcomes of their research. IMR that proposes to make use of existing online social groups (for example, social networking sites, discussion forums, multi-user virtual environments) must bear this in mind (Ethics Guidelines for Internet-mediated Research 2013).

When Working with Teenagers

- TeenCI researchers joining an existing online structure could cause harm. For example, if a researcher joins a group it could change the dynamics or friendships within the group which could affect the participant online and offline. This could potentially have negative consequences on the participants, especially if researching a vulnerable online group (for example, individuals with an eating disorder). Also, it could lead to inaccurate data for the researchers.
- TeenCI researchers should carefully discuss this with their research team or ethics board to decide if the research has potential to cause social harm and whether this type of research is suitable for their research topic.
- Consent to use data may be obtained through the site administrator for the website being targeted for research and participants informed that their data may be used for research purposes and what this means. Participants should be allowed the opportunity to withdraw their data, or not post on the site further.
- Each project should be decided on a case to case basis, and the sensitivity of the information provided should be discussed with the institutional relevant ethics board.

3.4.5 Principle 4: Maximising Benefits and Minimising Harm

This principle embodies many of the key points and issues already raised, including ensuring scientific value (maximising benefits) and taking steps to protect participants from any adverse effects arising from the research. Such steps may include gaining valid consent, ensuring anonymity and confidentiality (to minimise harm), and maintaining appropriate levels of control over the research process (to help maximise benefits and minimise harm) (Ethics Guidelines for Internet-mediated Research 2013).

When Working with Teenagers

- Key ethical considerations must be made to ensure no harm will come to teenage participants. For example, if the researcher is investigating social networking sites, it could potentially make teenagers worry about their own usage, especially if they have had any negative experiences with the site (for example, cyber bullying). This issue has been previously discussed in the chapter with traditional face-to-face research (Sect. 3.3.10). However, in IMR the researcher cannot see the participant in the way they can with traditional face-to-face research, and therefore, it is more difficult to know if any harm has been caused.
- Therefore, this is a further reason why it is important for the aims of the research and the research topic to be clearly explained to teenagers to enable teenagers to decide if they want to take part.
- There should always be sufficient support in place for teenagers, the name and contact details of a person teenagers can contact if they are affected in anyway by

the research should be included in the debrief forms (for example, if researching cyber bullying it would be appropriate to give contact details for a charity working in that area).
- However, if it is a highly sensitive research topic then the researcher should consider if face-to-face research would be more suitable.

3.5 Personal Experience

This next section contains details of our own experiences of negotiating ethics in our research involving teenagers. The research was conducted through both traditional face-to-face research and IMR. The ethical dilemmas faced are described, along with the steps taken to overcome them, in line with the policies outlined in previous sections.

3.5.1 Face to Face Ethical Issues (Study 1)

The first of our own research projects with teenagers that will be discussed was a sexual health study. The study aimed to explore the types of sexual health information teenagers were aware of and whether they had sufficient sexual health intervention programs targeting these issues. This study was part of a larger project involving the creation of an app-based sexual health intervention. Teenagers from low SES backgrounds, aged 13 and 14, were recruited and asked to keep a sexual health diary for 4 weeks. In the diaries, teenagers were asked to record any thoughts to do with sexual health they had on that day and any sexual health information they had encountered.

Thus, this research project was dealing with highly sensitive information with a young age group. In line with Sect. 3.4.5 maximising benefits and minimising harm, it was decided that the diary would be completed offline in paper format. This was to ensure that if teenagers wanted to withdraw from the research they could stop completing the diary and destroy the paper diary, before any data was recorded. The diaries were written confidentially each day, folded and placed into a locked box at their schools reception, a participant code (composed only of numbers) was the only identifying information on the diaries. Before the research began several ethical issues were taken into account. As teenagers would be disclosing sensitive information, in line with standards of privacy and confidentiality (discussed in Sects. 3.2.3.3, 3.11 and 4.2), it was highly important to ensure participants' data would be kept confidential and that participants would remain anonymous. However, due to the sensitive nature of the research topic, participants may have disclosed information that they or someone else was at risk of harm. Therefore, while confidentiality was important, there needed to be a way to identify a participant if they disclosed information that suggested they were at risk of harm as discussed in Sect. 3.2.5.3, it is important to ensure participants are protected during and after the research study.

In order to achieve this, in line with standards of awareness of professional ethics discussed in Sect. 3.2.4.1, the lead researcher contacted the University's law team and met with them to discuss the legal obligations and duty of care of researchers reporting any concern that someone is at risk of harm. After an investigation by the law team, it was finalised that in the UK in 2015 there were no legal obligations. However, child protection and safeguarding legislation states that if a known (not anonymous) young person aged under 18 years discloses any sexual abuse, or any information that they or someone else is at risk of harm, there is a duty of care to report. This should be reported to a relevant safeguarding officer, identified at the start of the study, but not to the child's parents or to the police. Therefore, a structure of safeguarding and reporting was put in place in case any safeguarding issues were to arise. It was decided that the structure would involve safeguarding officers at each school being made aware of the research and contacted if any information arose. It was the responsibility of safeguarding officers' to identify and contact the child. It is important to note that laws change over time and vary between countries. Therefore it is essential that researchers consider the legal safeguarding issues surrounding their research independently.

The lead researcher made contact with each school and asked for the name and contact details of the school safeguarding officer. A face-to-face or telephone meeting was then arranged to discuss each school's individual safeguarding policies and procedures. In line with mutual responsibilities outlined in Sect. 3.3.8, a mutual responsibility of the safeguarding issues that may be encountered in the research was determined between the lead researcher and the safeguarding officers. The information, consent and debrief forms for teenagers and parents were updated, explaining that participants' data will remain confidential, however, if any information was disclosed indicating that they or someone else was at risk of harm, then this information would be disclosed to their school's safeguarding officer. The safeguarding officer would then take this matter further, and identify/contact the pupil(s) involved. This structure ensured research participants were protected and also the researcher knew where their duty of care ended. However, the potential disadvantage of this was that it may have led to less honest responses, as participants may have worried that they would have to speak to their schools safeguarding officer.

In line with standards of general respect discussed in Sects. 3.2.3.2, 3.2.3.3, 3.3.7 and 3.3.11, the lead researcher met with participants twice before the study began, to fully explain the study and safeguarding procedures. The content was delivered through discussions with a group of 10 participants at a time, and typically lasted 30–40 min. The study was explained in terms teenagers could understand and participants had sufficient time to ask questions. It was emphasised that participants could take a break at any time and if they were not comfortable answering a question they could leave it blank. Participants were reminded they could withdraw from the study at any time, without having to give a reason why. It was important that a support structure was in place to ensure any issues arising through participation in the study could be dealt with by appropriate experts. This aligns with jeopardy discussed in Sect. 3.3.9, as researchers need to ensure they have necessary assistance for all participants. To do this, the lead researcher worked closely with each school to confirm there was a school sexual health nurse or counsellor available, in case participants had questions or were affected in anyway by the research. Sexual health practices in the area were also contacted and it was agreed that they could be contacted by participants, should they require further information. The name and contact details of the practice were added to the debrief forms. Therefore, assistance was available for participants in and outside of the school.

3.5.2 Internet-Mediated Research Ethical Issues

In addition to the above offline data collection method, this same research project also included IMR data collection, using an online questionnaire hosted by Qualtrics. The questionnaire was used to determine age, socio-economic background (as determined by parental education) and previous sexual behaviours. This was an important aspect of the research to be able to link participants' demographic background and previous sexual behaviours to their diary entries. Therefore, in line with Sects. 3.3.3 and 3.4.2.1 gaining parental consent online was explored, however, as the researcher was visiting the schools, it was decided consent from parents would be sought offline. The researcher discussed opt-in and opt-out options of gaining consent with the head teachers of each school, and because the schools had previously used opt-out consent in previous research studies it was decided that an opt-out method would be the most appropriate. The head-teacher believed the teachers and parents were familiar with this method because it was a standard practise within the school.

The opt-out consent form was then mailed to parents from the school directly to ensure parents received them, rather than being sent home through the teenagers themselves. Letters given to teenagers to take home does not guarantee that the parent has seen the letter, which is highly important when using an opt-out method. The parents were given a 2 week period to reply if they did not want their child to take part. In line with Sect. 3.2.6.1, standards of honesty and accuracy, the letters included the lead researchers contact details and affiliations so parents were able to contact the researcher with questions. After the 2 week period, teenagers could not take part in the research if their parents had contacted the school or the lead researcher to opt-out of the study. The participants were given full information about the study before the study day, and reminded that they did not have to take part if they did not want to. Participants gave their informed consent on the study day. This was to ensure that teenagers did not feel pressured to take part from their teachers or parents as research participation was voluntary. In line with Sect. 3.2.4, there were no incentives for taking part in this study. Following the policy of valid consent in Sect. 3.4.2.1, participants had a half an hour session explaining how they could withdraw from the questionnaire by closing the browser and their partial data would not be used.

Gaining parental consent through opt-out consent procedures enabled the study to achieve adequate participation rates. During the debrief session, teenagers commented that they enjoyed the online questionnaire as it felt more confidential than completing it in front of people in a classroom, especially as the questions were of a sensitive nature. However, they enjoyed completing the diary in paper format as they could take the diary home and personalise it (by drawing pictures) and writing on it, which was different to the questionnaire which was completed at school. Teenagers believed it was easy to complete the questionnaire at school as they are used to working on computers and liked the opportunity to complete the questionnaire in this way. Participants commented that they enjoyed the combination of offline and online methods, as it avoids boredom. Consequently, as the ethical issues were considered at the start of the research project it allowed participants to feel more confident in terms of the confidentiality of their data and participants enjoyed taking part in the research. In line with Sect. 3.3.13, a general summary of findings was provided to the schools at the end of this study, to publish in their monthly newsletters. A general summary was provided to ensure individual participants were kept anonymous, and outlined the type of sexual health questions teenagers wanted to know and the current information that is available for them. The summary allowed schools to evaluate whether their current sexual health intervention programs were useful for students.

3.5.3 Internet-Mediated Research Ethical Issues (Study 2)

The second research project to be discussed considered a less sensitive topic – energy use – and was part of a multi-disciplinary 3 year research project which utilised multiple methods, both qualitative and quantitative, to explore energy use with teenagers. Online and offline methods were used as part of this research project. This section will focus on reflections of online methods with teenagers. Online data collection was utilised due to the reasons highlighted in Sect. 3.4, most notably their high internet access and familiarity. In addition, the research team felt that the topic being explored, energy use, was suitable for both offline and online methods as it was a less sensitive topic and the combination of offline and online methods allowed the researchers to maintain participants' interest in the research. An online questionnaire and behaviour change intervention were conducted as part of the research project.

As per the previously discussed studies, it was essential to consider ethics at the planning stage of the project. One key aspect to consider is the process of obtaining informed consent from parents and carers using an online method. In this study, issues of consent were discussed in depth by the research team and advice was sought from the BPS via personal communication. The advice received from the

BPS led to the construction of the following possible options for ensuring informed consent from parents/carers:

- Requiring a phone number to be provided online to allow parental consent to be verified verbally
- Requiring a postal address to be provided online to allow parental consent to be verified via post
- Developing a process by which the parents email address is provided and then a password is sent to this email, in order to access the consent form

In addition, an alternative method suggested by the ethics board was to recruit parents/guardians rather than teenagers, and therefore parents/guardians would subsequently ask their child(ren) to participate in the research.

Following careful consideration by the research team, the first option was initially selected. This method would enable consent to verified offline by the research team. This option was selected as it was easier for parents/guardians rather than completing a paper-based form or password. In addition, this method would allow us to recruit teenagers directly rather than recruiting parents/guardians, which may potentially bias the sample.

In practice, this method of verifying consent was not successful. Teenagers did not enter a telephone number online and therefore, their data could not be used since consent could not be verified. Therefore, an alternative method was employed which was the opt-out method. The lead researcher contacted schools to take part in the research study and provided detailed information regarding the project. Head teachers provided informed consent for pupils in their school to take part. Parents/guardians were sent opt-out letters and asked to reply within a set time period if they did not want their child to participate. Teenagers provided their written consent at the beginning of the study and completed the study at school using computers to access the internet-based questionnaire. This method was more successful in participant recruitment in comparison to the initial method.

This experience highlights the importance of considering ethics at the start and throughout research projects. In this experience, it was necessary to adapt the original method of the study to the difficulty encountered when recruiting participants. The opt-out method enabled teenagers to be recruited via schools. The potential disadvantage of this approach is that recruitment was restricted to the participating schools rather than a diverse sample of teenagers. Nevertheless, the recruitment and consent process was successful in completing data and gaining an appropriate amount of participants.

3.6 Refection

We built time into the research plan for considering ethical issues before data collection, as it was a lengthy process. However, it has been highlighted here that it may be necessary to change initial plans if problems are encountered. Our two research projects discussed in this chapter covered different topics (sexual health and energy consumption) using IMR, yet both encountered similar ethical issues. There were no guidelines in place regarding IMR with teenagers when we came across these issues, and therefore we contacted relevant ethics boards and sought guidance from a range of key experts, including ethics practitioners and legal experts. Based on our experiences and reflections, we propose the following guidelines and recommendations for IMR with teenagers:

3.6.1 Research Topic

For research involving sensitive topics or research where high control over the environment is needed, the researchers need to carefully consider if IMR is suitable for their project. In our research projects, this was done by discussing the issues with the research team and other experts and stakeholders (e.g. teachers) where necessary. If the research is dealing with sensitive issues and the researchers agree that IMR is appropriate, then there must be support in place for teenagers. In particular, there should be a procedure in place for how the researcher will deal with any issues that arise. For example, seeking and becoming familiar with the relevant safeguarding procedures as discussed in Sect. 3.2.4.2 standards of ethical decision making. Researchers may also want to seek advice from experts in the topic area, for example if dealing with sexual health issues, safeguarding and support advice would be sought from sexual health professionals who work with teenagers. Therefore, we found that it was worth taking the time to fully consider the research topic and the most appropriate method available, so that we could gain the maximum benefits (increased participation and valuable data) from our research.

3.6.2 Recruiting Teenagers

Though recruiting teenagers can be a lengthy process, it is vital that the appropriate numbers of teenagers are recruited (in order to ensure studies have sufficient power). One problem that could be encountered is that teenagers can feel pressured into taking part by their school or parents, especially if there are school or parental incentives. Teenagers must be able to give their own voluntary consent to take part in the research; if they are pressured into taking part in the research then voluntary consent cannot be achieved. Also, teenagers pressured into taking part may not be as interested in the research, and may not pay sufficient attention to the research questions. It is therefore important that the researcher ensures teenagers are not pressured into taking part in the research. In line with standards of informed consent discussed in Sect. 3.2.3.2, we achieved this by advertising the study to participants in an assembly or in classes, rather than teachers advertising the study to students directly. While this takes longer (and involves more input from the research team), it was valuable to do this, as we knew teenagers had the correct information about the study and were not pressurised to take part. We also used advertisement posters in youth groups and schools. This again ensured that teenagers had the correct information and only took part after showing an initial interest in the study. Though it is impossible to reduce parental and teacher influence entirely.

3.6.3 Parental Consent

One of the main ethical decisions we made in both of the research projects was whether an opt-in or opt-out method for gaining parental consent would be most appropriate. We found that each project required different methods, and every project needs to be considered on a case-by-case basis. As discussed earlier in the chapter in Sect. 3.3.3, opt-in methods are achieved by parents providing their informed consent for their child to take part in the research. This can be a favourable method as the researcher knows they have consent from parents and that parents have read information about the study. However, in opt-out consent methods the parent only contacts the researcher if they do not want their child to take part in the research; therefore it is not always guaranteed the parent has received information about the study. This is particularly an issue if information sheets are given to teenagers to give to their parents. An issue we encountered with opt-in consent was very low recruitment numbers. In previous research we have found parents would not return the forms, or teenagers would lose or forget the forms. It was very difficult to recruit large numbers of teenagers using this consent method. Whereas, a larger number of teenagers could be recruited using an opt-out method. We found that parents were more likely to respond to letters if they had an objection to the research, than if they were happy for their child to take part. However, making sure that parents have seen the letter needs to be carefully considered. We mailed the letters to parents, rather than giving letters to teenagers to give to their parents, as this provided a better chance of the parent seeing the letter. Some schools have electronic mailing lists for parents and this can be a useful means of directly contacting parents to ensure they have read the information sheets. We also found that it is worthwhile checking with schools, as some schools are familiar with an opt-out procedure, and have their own guidelines on how the letters are sent out. For example, holding coffee mornings/evenings and discussing the research with parents or including a summary of the research in their monthly newsletters, so parents know to look out for the letter. There is scope for using a combination of both opt-in and opt-out consent methods. For example, if a researcher needs to recruit a large number of teenagers, they may consider recruiting through schools and recruiting teenagers using posters and web adverts. Therefore, opt-out consent may be most appropriate for the teenagers recruited through schools and opt-in consent may be most appropriate for teenagers recruited outside of schools. This may maximise research participation, by recruiting a larger number of participants.

3.6.4 Explaining Ethics to Teenagers

We found it is important to make sure teenagers have fully understood the research and the ethical considerations (for example, confidentiality and anonymity) before they consent to taking part. It is likely teenagers will understand more than children, however, it needs to be explained to them in a way they can comprehend. As highlighted in Sect. 3.4.2.1 valid consent, teenagers cannot give their voluntary informed consent if they do not fully understand the research and ethical considerations. We piloted our ethical forms with teachers, to ask for their opinions on words teenagers would understand. They recommended that the forms should not be too long, should be bullet pointed and the key information should be highlighted. Also, researchers recruiting through schools have the opportunity to visit the teenagers beforehand and explain the study procedure and ethical procedures face to face and provide participants with the opportunity to ask questions. Researchers who do not have this opportunity could consider creating a video message for teenagers rather than paper forms, to keep them engaged and interested. Copies of the video or paper forms could also be available for teenagers, in case they need to check the information at a later date. By fully considering these issues, there was a better chance teenagers had understood the information and were able to give their informed consent.

3.7 Conclusion and Future Directions

Internet-mediated research is beneficial for TeenCI researchers and participants. As previously discussed, it enables data to be collected through a method frequently used and familiar to teenagers, often allowing the collection of a large amount of data from a usually hard to reach population. Internet-mediated research is also a time-saving method, once data collection has started, as the researcher does not have to be present with the participant so multiple participants may take part at the same time. However, teenagers are a unique population and because there are not adequate ethical guidelines available, it can be a lengthy process to consider the ethical issues. Many ethical issues can be applied to adults, children and teenagers. However, there are key differences, teenagers can understand more about the research and ethical considerations than children but need this information explained to them in a different way to adults. Parental consent issues are very similar in TeenCI research to research involving children. However, we found it was difficult to make sure parents had read the research letters, especially for older teens. Therefore, researchers need to fully consider how to gain parents' attention. Yet, the key difference and the most important for TeenCI researchers, is that teenagers adopt new technologies at a far faster pace than children or adults. The technologies that teenagers favour are expanding and changing, and to collect data using them is potentially very valuable. New ethical issues and challenges will need to be considered carefully. Therefore, there is scope in the future to have teen-specific guidelines and support (e.g. groups) to seek advice and share best practice for those working with teens across disciplines. There are key ethical considerations that have been discussed in this chapter with both face-to-face and Internet-mediated research when conducting research with teenagers. Having additional support and guidelines in place to appropriately address any issues will allow the researcher and the participants to gain the maximum benefits from the study. It is suggested that teen-specific guidelines for IMR are developed so researchers have support in place for ethical issues with teenagers and they can consider the ethical dilemmas right at the start of the research process.

References

Alderson P, Morrow V (2004) Ethics, social research and consulting with children and young people. Barnardos, Barkingside

Bell BT, Dittmar H (2011) Does media type matter? The role of identification in adolescent girls' media consumption and the impact of different thin-ideal media on body image. Sex Roles 65(7–8):478–490

British Psychological Society (2009) Codes of ethics and conduct. Retrieved from http://www.bps.org.uk/system/files/documents/code_of_ethics_and_conduct.pdf

British Psychological Society (2013) Ethics guidelines for Internet-mediated research. Retrieved from http://www.bps.org.uk/system/files/documents/code_of_ethics_and_conduct.pdf

Code N (1949) The Nuremberg Code. Trials of war criminals before the Nuremberg military tribunals under control council law (10):181–182

Denzin NK (1989) Interpretive biography. Sage, London

Fisher CB (2005) Deception research involving children: ethical practices and paradoxes. Ethics & Behavior 15(3):271–287

Goodyear MD, Krleza-Jeric K, Lemmens T (2007) The declaration of Helsinki. BMJ 335(7621):624

Gov.uk (2014) Policy paper, Safeguarding children and young people. Retrieved from https://www.gov.uk/government/publications/safeguarding-children-and-young-people/safeguarding-children-and-young-people

Kemp S (2015) Digital, social & mobile in 2015. Retrieved from http://wearesocial.sg/blog/2015/01/digital-social-mobile-2015/

Livingstone S, Bober M (2004) UK Children Go Online: surveying the experiences of young people and their parents. Retrieved from http://eprints.lse.ac.uk/395/1/UKCGOsurveyreport.pdf

Madden M, Lenhart A, Duggan M, Cortesi S, Gasser U (2013) Teens and technology 2013. Pew Internet & American Life Project

Ofcom A (2014) The communications market report 2014. Retrieved from http://stakeholders.ofcom.org.uk/market-data-research/market-data/communications-market-reports/cmr14/

Office for National statistics (2011) e-Society – statistical bulletin. Available at www.ons.gov.uk/ons/rel/socialtrends-rd/social.../social-trends-41---e-society.pdf

Pew Research Center (2015) Teens, technology and friendships. Retrieved from http://www.pewinternet.org/2015/08/06/teens-technology-and-friendships/

Rice M, Broome ME (2004) Incentives for children in research. J Nurs Scholarsh 36(2):167–172

Scott-Jones D (1994) Ethical issues in reporting and referring in research with low-income minority children. Ethics & Behavior 4(2):97–108

Society for Research in Child Development (2007) Ethical standards in research. Retrieved from http://www.srcd.org/about-us/ethical-standards-research

Wright KB (2005) Researching Internet-based populations: advantages and disadvantages of online survey research, online questionnaire authoring software packages, and web survey services. J Comput-Mediat Commun 10(3):00–00

Chapter 4
Human Factors Multi-technique Approach to Teenage Engagement in Digital Technologies Health Research

Alexandra R. Lang, Michael P. Craven, Sarah Atkinson, Lucy Simons, Sue Cobb, and Marco Mazzola

Abstract This chapter explores the use of multi-techniques for teenage HCI health research. Through four case studies we present information about adolescents as users of healthcare services and technologies, adolescent personal development and the human factors approaches through which teenagers have been involved in healthcare research projects. In each case study comprising of the design or evaluation of a new digital technology for supporting health or well-being, the techniques used by researchers to involve teenagers are explored and analysed. The case studies examine various aspects of technology design and use including but not limited to usability, acceptability and learnability. The penultimate section of the chapter presents a 'Schema for Multi-technique HCI Health Research with Teenagers' and provides the supporting case for a multi-method approach. The conclusions of the chapter reinforce the benefits that are specific to the implementation of multi-technique research with teenage participants. Consideration of the eight factors outlined in the 'Schema' within study designs should serve to unlock the potential of teenagers, ensuring reliable elicitation of their views and needs.

A.R. Lang (✉) • S. Atkinson • S. Cobb
Human Factors Research Group, University of Nottingham,
ITRC Building, University Park, Nottingham NG7 2RD, UK
e-mail: alexandra.lang@nottingham.ac.uk

M.P. Craven • L. Simons
NIHR MindTech Healthcare Technology Co-operative, Institute of Mental Health, University of Nottingham, Jubilee Campus, Triumph Road, Nottingham NG7 2TU, UK

M. Mazzola
Politecnico di Milano, Design Department, Via Durando 38/A, 20158 Milan, Italy

Neosperience Spa, Corso Indipendenza 5, 20125 Milan, Italy

© Springer International Publishing Switzerland 2016

L. Little et al. (eds.), *Perspectives on HCI Research with Teenagers*,
Human–Computer Interaction Series, DOI 10.1007/978-3-319-33450-9_4

4.1 Introduction

As with children, elderly adults and other special populations, teenagers have distinct needs with respect to healthcare so research methods should be designed with that in mind and methods known to work with adults cannot be assumed to work with teenage participants (Lang 2012). To ensure that methods meet the needs of young users, traditional methods can be combined with novel ones or delivered through innovative modes. Techniques can vary due to the opportunities afforded through a collective approach, utilising established methodologies with new ones. To clarify, the term multi-techniques is different to the established term mixed methods (Creswell 1999). Mixed methods refers to the combination of qualitative and quantitative methodologies, whilst the term multi-technique is used here to describe a creative style of study design intended to optimise the process of data collection and, to a greater or lesser extent, engage users in processes of co-production. By combining appropriate and engaging elicitation techniques, we argue that the multi-technique approach should ensure that teenage participants are able to participate fully so that their needs and expectations are understood and fulfilled, and furthermore that this will result in ICT products that meet the needs of users.

The four case study projects presented here demonstrate the use of multi-techniques. These accounts explain why the methods chosen were appropriate for teenage research participants, and reflect on their deployment in practice. They are synthesised to produce a schema to support HCI research study design with teenagers.

The four case studies are:

- PEGASO: The development of a multi-technology ICT platform for teenage personal health promotion and management (PEGASO – Personalised Guidance Services for Optimising lifestyle in Teenagers through Awareness, Motivation and Engagement).
- Innovation Labs evaluation: The evaluation of digital products for young people's mental health, based on two different web and app products and exploring the user and intended value of each service.
- iRAM study, Integrated remote monitoring for Attention Deficit Hyperactivity Disorder (ADHD): A study with young people and their care teams to explore patient, parent and professional views and attitudes towards using digital technology for remote medication monitoring for ADHD.
- Full and Hungry Project: Investigation into the development of location based services for promoting health living in young people and the social dynamics taking place around them (affiliated with the goals of PEGASO).

HCI research with teenagers (TeenCI) is a relatively new sub discipline within HCI generally (Fitton et al. 2013); where adults and children have been involved in participatory research but teenagers as a distinct user population have been less well represented. HCI research associated with teenage health and wellbeing faces increased challenges due to the ethics and sensitivities involved in this kind of research. Some research has begun to emerge in the application of HCI to health and wellbeing with and for teenagers (Ho et al. 2014; Macvean and Robertson 2012) however this is still very much a topic in its infancy and there is great potential for further research in this field.

The chapter begins by presenting the background of teenagers as users of health services and outlines the potential benefits of digital health products with an emphasis on mobile platforms. The second section of the chapter presents four in-depth case studies. In each enquiry, the aims and goals, the selection of multiple techniques and brief results are presented. Personal reflections of the methodological approaches taken by the researchers are included. The last section of the chapter synthesises the experiences from each study and provides discussion and guidance on the benefits and drawbacks of multi-techniques approaches in HCI healthcare research with teenagers. The resulting Schema for Multi-techniques with Teenage Research Participants provides a resource for future research, which is derived from the case studies and supported by the literature.

NB: Throughout this chapter the terms adolescent and teenager are used interchangeably.

4.2 Background

4.2.1 Teenagers as Health Service Users

Involving teenagers in healthcare research has historically been a challenging field of work due to the potential sensitivities involved in health and medical research and the perceived challenges of working with teenagers (Lang et al. 2014). However young people are increasingly becoming users of mobile and online technologies (Hagell et al. 2013; PEW 2013) and these technologies are playing an ever increasing role in healthcare provision (Nasi et al. 2015).

In the UK, the proportion of 10–19 year olds is 12 % of the total population and in the USA adolescents account for 14 % of the total population (USCB 2012). There are trends within the adolescent population that give rise to them as increasing users of healthcare services (Viner and Macfarlane 2005) which has clear implications for service delivery. Therefore, it is important that young people are involved in healthcare research to meet their needs and those of the health service providers.

Viner and Macfarlane (2005) describe five reasons for the need to focus health promotion on young people:

1. Health behaviours in youth continue into adult life – continuity of these behaviours is well documented
2. Immediate effects of adolescent health behaviours – choices made do not just impact immediate behaviours but also long term health state
3. Worrying trends in morbidity and mortality – increasing morbidity trends in adolescence into adulthood argue strongly for urgent attention to adolescent health and the development of targeted adolescent specific interventions
4. Developmental issues – young people have distinct needs in terms of delivery of health promotion messages

5. Clustering of health risk – those who engage in risk taking behaviours are more likely to engage in multiple risk activities

These five points outline the need for general health promotion but do not address the specific reasons for which teenagers as a user group are increasing their consumption of health and social care, some of which are explained below. There are a variety of reasons, many of which are related to social determinants of health – income level, social care, education, youth training and employment, family life, housing and living circumstances and geographical location (area based deprivation) but some are also due to improvements in health and social care resulting in longer life expectancy for those with infant and childhood conditions. Many of these determinants are intertwined, as are the four categories described below which describe the main issues facing healthcare service delivery for teenagers.

Lifestyle Needs and Impact Poor activity and diet leading to detrimental impact on health. In the UK 31 % of young men and 37 % of young women aged 11–18 years old are overweight (Hagell et al. 2013) and in the USA 16.9 % of 12–19 year olds are reported obese and an additional 14.9 % overweight (Fryar et al. 2014). These statistics provide evidence for prevention and proactive management in relation to lifestyle decisions and personal teenage behaviours.

Chronic Conditions The incidence and prevalence of chronic conditions is rising in both developed and developing countries and, especially among adolescents, increased life expectancy from chronic diseases and disabilities are emerging as major health problems (Michaud et al. 2004). It is therefore important that adolescents' requirements are met to improve long-term health outcomes.

Mental Health There is an awareness of increasing mental health problems in young people. In the US it is suggested that 11 % of adolescents have a mood disorder by age 18 and mental illness was the third leading cause of death for youth ages 15–24 (NIMH 1999). In the UK this trend is recognised by the Young Minds charity which reports that 1 in 10 young people have a diagnosable mental health disorder (YM 2015).

Risk Taking Behaviours Neuro-cognitive and developmental psychologists have found evidence of the biological drive for teenagers to take risks (Burnett et al. 2010; Steinberg 2008) and their developmental and biological predisposition mean that they are more prone to exposing themselves to risky behaviour or hazardous external influences.

With consideration for these five issues and Birchers' description of health as "*a dynamic state of well-being characterized by a physical and mental potential, which satisfies the demands of life commensurate with age, culture, and personal responsibility*" (Bircher 2005) there is suggestion of the multi-factorial nature of young people's needs in healthcare. As such, health ICT research should take into account the various influencers on teenage health and wellbeing and ensure that a holistic approach is taken when developing new interventions and technology. The case studies in this chapter demonstrate how a multi-technique approach can assist in tackling the multifaceted issue of researching health and wellbeing with adolescents, where combining methods can facilitate the elicitation of information about their interactions, needs and preferences.

4.2.2 Adolescents as Evolving Individuals

The changes and the development of teenagers into young adults have connotations for their care and affects their involvement in research. Adolescence is the period during which individuals change most rapidly and significantly; other than as an infant (Elliott and Feldman 2010), from a dependent child to independent adult. As such, their needs and requirements are in flux. Adolescence encompasses aspects of physical and cognitive maturity and the accomplishment of tasks such as: establishment of identity; construction of own relationships outside the family, achievement of independence from parents (McDonagh 2000). The egocentricity of teenagers (Elkind 1967) also impacts the way in which they learn and engage with the world and as such should be taken into account when designing research studies involving them.

It is important to appreciate that this process of personal development is not homogenous. There is variation between individuals, as physical and cognitive development will develop at different rates. Kroemer (2005) describes the wide inter-individual variability and rapid intra-individuality of adolescent populations. These attributes are important in their progression and respect for these issues is important in designing research methods, products and services that can be inclusive of adolescent audiences (Lang et al. 2013).

Research involving teenagers should consider the following aspects of personal development that are experienced during the adolescent years;

- *Psychological development*; the development of abstract thinking; appreciation of long term impacts of immediate and short term behaviour; development of identity.
- *Social development*; increasing autonomy away from parents and peer orientation; splitting of peer groups into smaller groups and couples,
- *Physical development*; puberty and development of body image.
- *Risk taking behaviours;* associated with cognitive and social development during adolescence.

These developmental factors underpin the case for multi-techniques use in teenage research, as the use of a single method with teenagers may not adequately cater for the intra-variability of individuals or the inter-variability of a group. Central to the aim of this chapter is the view that research study design and methods need to be age appropriate. As such a multi-techniques approach is advocated to meet those changing needs and capabilities, *"to find methodologies which play to young people's strengths rather than their weaknesses*" (Clark and Moss 2005).

4.2.3 Healthcare and HCI

There have been significant changes over the last 20 years as the rapid evolution of ICT is changing the face of healthcare provision. ICT's have enabled, facilitated and accelerated the development of technologies and systems which alter the role of clinicians and can provide independence and choice to patient users (Bos et al. 2008). This has a double relevance for teenage patients for whom gaining autonomy, identity and independent choice are significant goals in their development while at the same time embracing new technological opportunities. As evidenced by the numbers of teens that have access to mobile phones and engage in social networking e.g., Facebook, Twitter (PEW 2013). Additionally the recent rise in the use of smartphones (Ofcom Communications Market Report 2015) offers potential solutions to reduce burden on the health service providers whilst maintaining quality and safe provision to patients.

The potential of ICT applies to the management of mental health and emotional wellbeing, as well as physical health conditions and healthy behaviours. (Cotton et al. 2014; Hollis et al. 2014; Simons et al. 2015). This is particularly relevant for young people as they turn to online ways of accessing health and wellbeing information and support (YM 2015).

Mobile platforms such as smartphone and tablets offer a number of unique benefits in healthcare education, support, monitoring and social communications. They have an advantage over other ICT devices (desktop, laptop) by being more portable and are more often than not in the owner's possession, allowing the user to stay in touch with other people (whether they be friends, family or healthcare professionals) and to access information via the internet at any time of day or night, from virtually any location.

In clinical use mobile platforms offer two- way communication between patient and clinician (Kazdin and Blase 2011) as well as a wider variety of information gathering and sharing, for example, for rating symptoms, therapy, education, support and advice, treatment progress monitoring (Luxton et al. 2011). Smartphone apps may give more accurate data than paper based questionnaires (Matthews et al. 2008), elicit better adherence and have the potential to save time for both clinician and patient (Clough and Casey 2011). In addition, game applications running on mobile platforms can help initiate and sustain engagement across the healthcare sector (Arnab et al. 2013; Ulicsak 2010). Such games have the potential to reach a large audience and engage players for long periods of time which provides an opportunity for them to be used as a pedagogical tool for awareness and behavior change, where the propensity of an individual to change is seen as a significant factor in promoting positive health behavior.

4.2.4 *Summary of Rationale for a Multi-techniques Approach*

Three important contemporary factors are presented that highlight the importance of healthcare research with teenagers: the need to address health behaviours; adolescents as evolving individuals and the growing importance of HCI/ICT in healthcare. In the following section, the four case studies are presented. Each study focuses on one particular area of HCI and/or the use of ICT related to health and describes novel and creative methods with teenage participants. These case studies provide the context for the schema presented in the final section of the chapter. As will be seen the multiple techniques used in the case studies are mostly within a qualitative methodology with the addition of some rating and some prioritisation elements.

4.3 Teenage HCI Health Research Case Studies

This section will present the four Human Factors (HF) multi-technique case studies, illustrating their implementation in healthcare HCI research with teenagers. To reflect on the methods used in each study, the benefits and challenges encountered are outlined at the end of each case study.

4.3.1 *Case Study 1: PEGASO. Teenage Personal Health Promotion and Management Through the Development and Use of a Mobile Technology Platform*

4.3.1.1 Background

This case study presents the use of multi-techniques workshops with teenagers for eliciting user requirements of an ICT platform for teenage health promotion and management. The workshops explored teenage perceptions about healthy living, the role of technology in health and their use in health and wellness promotion.

This approach was to ensure that the needs of a teenage user population were embedded in the early stages of PEGASO technology development. Figure 4.1 represents the PEGASO system with the individual technology components to be co-developed for teenage use.

PEGASO aims to develop a cross-disciplinary ICT system for teenage health promotion by offering three main functionalities:

- Individual & environmental monitoring,
- Feedback System and personalized healthy modification of lifestyle,
- Social connectivity and engagement through community networks and gaming.

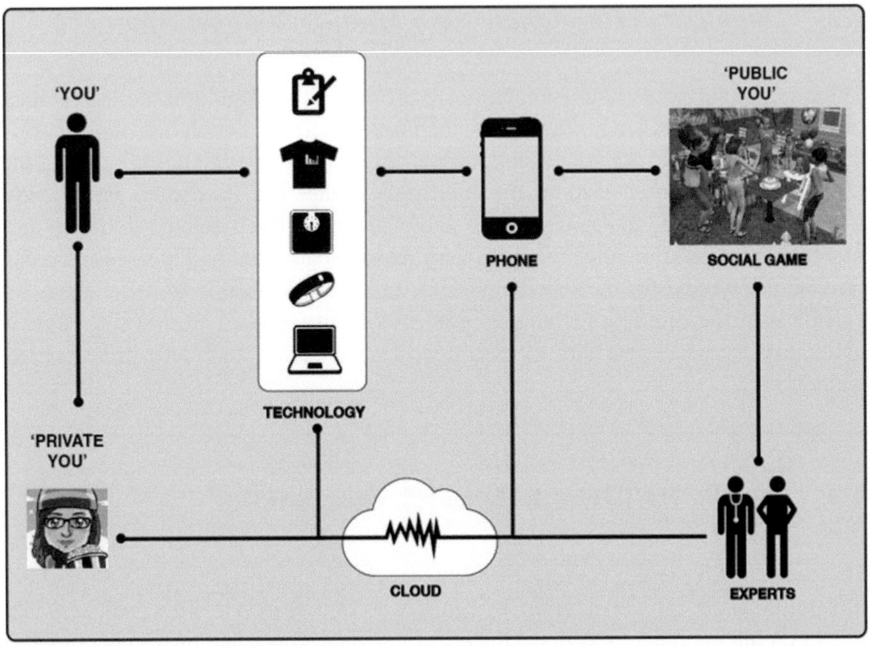

Fig. 4.1 PEGASO system architecture

Furthermore, the project aims to encourage teenagers to become active participants in their wellness, working to improve it through:

- Generating self-awareness,
- Enhancing and sustaining motivation to take care of their health,
- Changing behaviour towards a healthy lifestyle based on healthy diet and adequate physical activity.

The early development of the PEGASO system relied on the implementation of behavioural psychology (Fogg 2009) combined with data from the multi-techniques workshops to provide an evidence-based approach to ICT development based upon the needs, values and priorities of adolescents.

4.3.1.2 Protocol

The study took place in schools across three participating countries: Spain (Catalonia), Italy and UK (England). The teaching staff at each school acted as gatekeepers to the teenage participant population and provided review of the study protocol prior to engaging the researchers in carrying out the study. Participants were aged 13–16 years old and in full time education at the point of recruitment. Adolescents were recruited for the focus group study regardless of any current weight issues or pre-existing medical conditions.

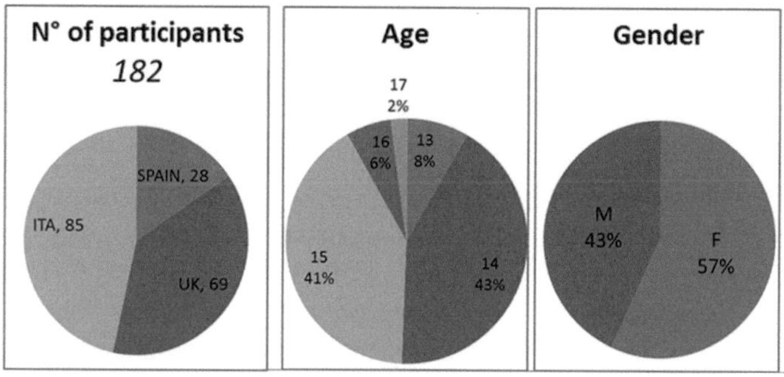

AGE	13	14	15	16	17
SPAIN	0	18	5	4	1
UK	0	28	41	0	0
ITA	15	31	29	7	3

GENDER	F	M
SPAIN	15	13
UK	40	29
ITA	49	36

Fig. 4.2 PEGASO workshop participants

In total 182 participants took part in the multi-techniques workshops. Figure 4.2 provides an overview of the participant details. Each participating site conducted a minimum of 1 male workshop, 1 female workshop and 1 mixed gender workshop.

Ethics approval was sought from local committees in the partner countries. The workshops were conducted on school property and in conjunction with local school timetables and curriculums. Recording equipment was used to capture participant responses and chairs arranged in a circle or semi-circle to facilitate participation. The following description provides details of the multi-techniques workshops.

Introduction Workshop facilitators explained the aims, activities and intended use of the outcomes of the workshop, with emphasis on the importance of the participants' contributions in a real world research study and answering any questions that arose.

Warm Up Activity, Brainstorming Small groups' 2–5 participants took part in rapid ideas generation to explore the topics of health and technology in preparation for the main group discussion. This was done incrementally, firstly unveiling a title of – 'Teenagers & Health' followed by the topics 'Use of Technology for Health Purposes' and 'Use of Gaming for Health Purposes', and lastly 'Use of Social Networks for Health Purposes'.

Focus Group Larger groups of 8–15. The focus group consisted of a discussion of the teenagers general opinions on the PEGASO system. This was introduced through the presentation of a simplified map of the PEGASO system architecture (Fig. 4.2).This enquiry was to investigate the use issues of technology for health in more depth and to discuss the features that teenagers considered the most significant in ensuring system acceptance and motivation.

Post Focus Group Prioritization Carried out in pairs. The objective of this task was to design an advertising campaign for the PEGASO system with the teenagers. Teenagers were asked to determine the three most important elements of the product to adolescent users. Participants had to develop a campaign slogan aimed at adolescents, encompassing the three concepts that they had selected as being the most important to this user group.

Questionnaire Individual questionnaire to provide background information about participant diet, physical activity and their current use of technology.

Summary and Close Up Short briefing at the end of the workshop to provide feedback to the participants and to reiterate the value of their contributions.

Analysis A content analysis was used for comparison and iterative analysis of qualitative data, where the continual development and reassignment of the data throughout the process led to the development of emergent themes. The range of data sources (brainstorms, audio files and transcripts, written questionnaire responses) were examined and coded into tree nodes and sub-nodes, depicting the breakdown of concepts into issues, attitudes and outcomes, awareness and motivations. The development of themes was iterative and the data was reviewed by researchers from different PEGASO partner sites to combat researcher bias, whereby themes elicited in individual countries was presented and reviewed by groups representing a mixture of cultural backgrounds in each of the 3 participating countries and also disciplinary backgrounds – HF, HCI, psychological and technical development.

4.3.1.3 Findings

Thematic analyses were carried out at individual partner sites. Researchers triangulated the data from each of the individual activities to provide insight into the adolescent perspectives and user requirements from individual countries. These reports were then collated centrally to a group of researchers who analysed each of the individual country reports and produced a single deliverable reporting on the commonalities and differences between countries. These were used to identify 'themes' from which practical requirements would be extrapolated by the Human Factors and technical teams to inform the PEGASO technology design.

- *Theme 1*: Technology for healthy living. Impressions on the use of technology for healthy living

- *Theme 2*: Features of Technology. Features which are important and of interest for teenagers and exploring those as incentives/disincentives.
- *Theme 3*: Use of Technology in different contexts.
- *Theme 4*: Information sharing. Exploring who teenagers want to connect with, share information, including notification and feedback system.
- *Theme 5*: Current awareness and use of technologies and state of the art.

The most important domain when asking teenagers about health was the emotional domain (social, well-being, fun and happiness, friendship). Well-being, having fun, happiness, emotions and lifestyle were indicated as influencing factors on health. Teenagers consider friends as a source of happiness, which eventually fosters good health. As a consequence, the social dimension is an important component of the PEGASO system.

Good habits in relation to self-care and nutrition, but also hygiene and diet were of importance to staying healthy, in addition to their awareness of the need for habitual activity and exercise. Teenagers strongly associate the idea of 'being healthy' to the idea of habits and routine but also provided a statement of need for 'routine with diversity'. The need and possibility to build their own habits is in contrast with the fact that they do not feel independent, that routine can sometimes be a constraint within their daily lives, especially when the tools for developing routine and habit can be repetitive or monotonous. The system should facilitate the development of routine and positive habits and behaviours whilst engaging the user through diversity and a dynamic interface. Bad habits were also discussed by teens and were largely related to prohibitions and risk taking behaviours such as drink, drugs and smoking (Fig. 4.3).

With regard to the discussions around health and technology use, teenagers perceived that the two concepts were strongly related, however those perceptions were not always positive as excessive use of technology (mobile phones and gaming) were perceived as detrimental physically and socially. Each of the methods used in the study however did unearth awareness that behaviors and emotion are important factors for them and that they could be influenced by technology in a variety of ways, both positive and negative.

Control and Privacy were significant discussion areas amongst all the teenage groups involved in the study. It was evident that teenagers have an acute awareness of the issues associated with online privacy and some even had concerns about the use of their data in the long term. This was related specifically to the social networking component of PEGASO.

There is a conflict between teenage understanding of health and the importance they place on it and ability to prioritize healthy behaviors. Awareness of health will be influenced by the modes of feedback from the system. This is an important element of PEGASO design which needs further consideration.

More in-depth description of the results from the workshops can be found in PEGASO publications on the project website. (PEGASO 2015).

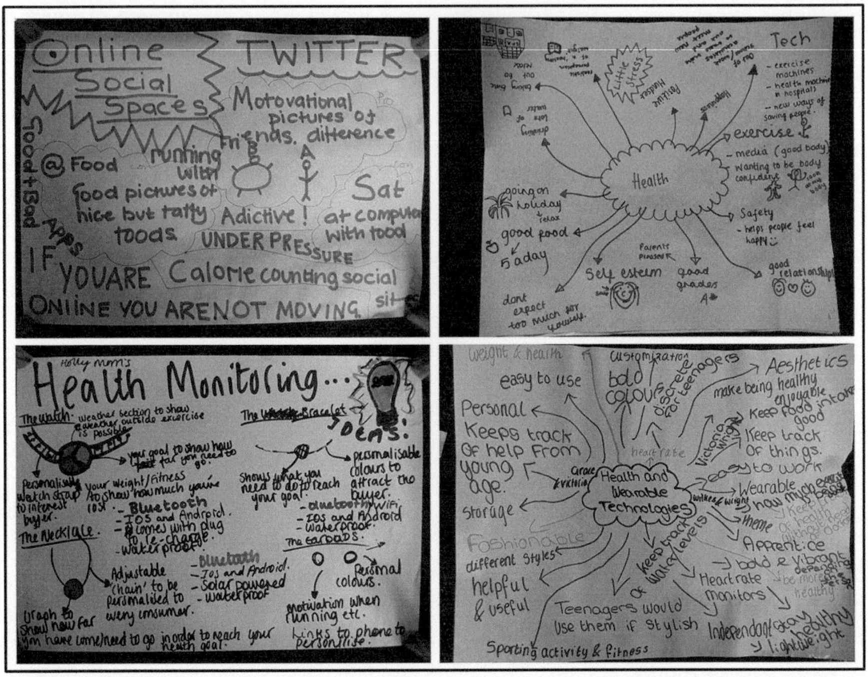

Fig. 4.3 PEGASO workshop ideas generation

4.3.1.4 Reflections

The following reflections are a combination of the informal feedback provided from teaching staff, participating students and additional observations of PEGASO researchers.

Positives: The staff reported that the workshop content provided teenagers with an interesting experience which energised their participation since the perception was that they were not doing ‘real’ school work but were taking part in something ‘wider’ and that their input would have impact. The HCI and technology content was of particular interest to the students as they strongly believed the real world application and believed it enhanced their regular ICT curriculum. The methods used enabled students of all learning abilities to contribute during the workshops as the variety of skills being utilised meant that cognitive and intellectual ability were not the defining factors in participation

The combination of methods offered the teenagers the opportunity to contribute in different sized groups and on their own in an individual questionnaire. This facilitated contributions from teenagers on a variety of levels, on their own, with one person, with a small group of friends, in a larger group. This provided opportunity for inclusion of all participants regardless of classroom dynamics (hierarchies and personalities) and personal confidence levels. The variety of activities also enabled them to express themselves in several different ways e.g. verbal, written both structured and unstructured, prioritisation.

The different methods provided opportunity for individuals to express their own preferences for technology interaction and to discuss their views with others. This was considered important in relation to the health context whereby any potential sensitive issues could be raised but not in the large group forum.

The structure of the workshop and variety of tasks enabled the students to engage with a challenging concept. The planning of the workshop and the way in which multiple techniques built on each other, each time providing more information assisted the students understanding of the technology system being proposed and its eventual use.

The triangulation of large data sets from each individual activity provided an in-depth qualitative account of teenage views of the content and interesting 'examples' of real world use which could be considered by the technical teams which had not been anticipated prior to the workshops.

The participants completed the questionnaire after taking part in the interactive tasks. They were therefore able to reflect on the information presented to them as well as the discussions with other participants – as such their responses provided individual feedback but from a common baseline of knowledge and experience with the topic.

Negatives Participants found the ICT system concept initially difficult to understand and it was felt that more time on each task would have helped to improve the understanding by some participants.

Censorship of responses may have been an issue where quieter teenagers may not have disclosed their needs or preferences in the small and large group activities as much as possible. This may be of significance in relation to the health research context whereby quieter candidates may be the ones with specific needs and who may need specific engagement. Some students contributed less to discussions and this may be because they were not interested in the topic or that it was potentially sensitive. Perhaps another mode of engaging them through anonymous online discussion might have been helpful in discussing ICT solutions for healthcare.

The abstract nature of the ICT system development was a complex idea. Whilst the teenager's comprehension of it was assisted by the incremental nature of the methods, asking adolescents to extrapolate and state user requirements for a system not yet developed was sometimes difficult. Had the multi-techniques approach been possible over a longer period of time a diary study may have been more appropriate as participants garnered use requirements during their everyday lives.

Consideration of acquiescence bias within studies where there is a power dynamic e.g. with young participants and older researchers. This was evident when discussing certain elements about use of the PEGASO system, initial teenage feedback was unanimously positive but then only with continuous probing did the students begin to critically evaluate the prospect of using the system in their everyday lives.

Despite the variety in tasks, concentration levels did drop off towards the end of the workshop, specifically for the completion of the questionnaire. This may be due to the intensity of the workshops or the need to fit in a lot of activity over a short period of time, with limited opportunity for 'breaks' due to the workshop having to fit in with the school academic timetable – leading to participant fatigue. Another possibility is that the ordering of methods could have been different to ensure that the teenagers had sustained engagement whereby they did not end the workshop with a relatively dull activity.

The social desirability of participant responses is another concern of qualitative data collection. In the case of this study it may be that, adolescent participants altered their responses to 'fit in' with the views of their peers. This was especially evident in some of the conversations around gaming.

4.3.1.5 Take Home Points

ICT development processes involving teenagers can benefit from multiple techniques to assist the understanding and communication of HCI requirements by teenagers. By offering different ways in which individuals contribute their views and needs for data capture, the variety of methods provides teenage user populations with a range of ways in which to express themselves at an age when wide disparities will be evident in individual abilities and confidence.

Whilst individual contributions are important in the development of this platform, it is anticipated that one of the key elements in its eventual success is the social networking component. As such, the use of multi- methods to elicit the needs of teenagers as a cohort helps to identify group and social needs and not just those of an individual. The importance of this in the eventual uptake of an ICT platform for health promotion cannot be understated as the teenage emphasis on social and emotional needs means that any interactions designed into the system need to be acceptable from a population perspective.

The triangulation of the data sets from each method has enabled the researchers to 'look beyond' potential acquiescence bias and see where common themes underpin multi-techniques and therefore trust in the validity of the information coming from them.

Where the study took place prior to the development of any technology, the concept of the integrated health platform was quite a difficult one for teenagers to appreciate in its entirety. The incremental way in which they were fed information during each method in the workshop meant that they could gradually build up a working knowledge of the health context and the ICT solution being proposed, something that was considered by the supervising teaching staff to be crucial to participants continued interest in the workshop and its topic.

4.3.2 Case Study 2 Innovation Labs: Evaluating Digital Products for Young People's Mental Health

4.3.2.1 Background

This case study is one part of an independent evaluation (Simons et al. 2015) of a set of 7 apps and websites that had been co-produced with young people, all aimed at supporting young people with mental health and wellness. The entire project was called Innovation Labs (Boardwell and Roberson 2014), and was funded by the Comic Relief charity, the Nominet Trust and the Mental Health Foundation. The evaluation process conducted by a research team from the NIHR MindTech Healthcare Technology Co-operative in Nottingham, UK, was focussed on exploring the user and intended value of the Innovation Labs Initiative, specifically,

- *User Value* – Do intended users engage with the product? Why do they value it? Does it help their mental wellbeing?
- *Intended Value* – Is the product achieving the intended outcomes? What value does it add to existing services, products and sources of support?

Two of the products were evaluated in detail, both having an adolescent population (16–25 years) as a significant target audience. One was a mobile-friendly website Doc Ready, aimed at helping young people feel more confident and get better results when they see their GP about a mental health issue (www.docready.org – launched by FutureGov, London). The website enables the user to create a checklist of issues or concerns that can be selected and saved for discussion at their appointment. The other was a smartphone app called In Hand, described as a digital friend to provide young people with tools, advice and activities when their mental health is at risk (www.inhand.org.uk – launched by FACT, Foundation for Art and Creative Technology, in Liverpool). In Hand consists of four questions about current mood and a set of activities depending on the response, some involving media on the phone such as looking at pictures or reading inspiring quotes, taking photos or jotting down thoughts, others including communication functions such as phoning a friend or accessing professional help (see screenshots below in Figs. 4.4 and 4.5).

4.3.2.2 Protocol

Given that the tools had been publicly launched and were already being used 'in the wild', the research team were interested to observe how and why people (with young people as the target user group) were choosing to engage with them, their level of engagement and the nature of self-reported impact on users' mental wellbeing. A multi-technique observational approach was adopted for the user evaluation which included surveys embedded in the app or website (with a prize draw to encourage engagement) which then contained invites to all respondents to take part in an interview and/or video diary creation to explore their experience in more

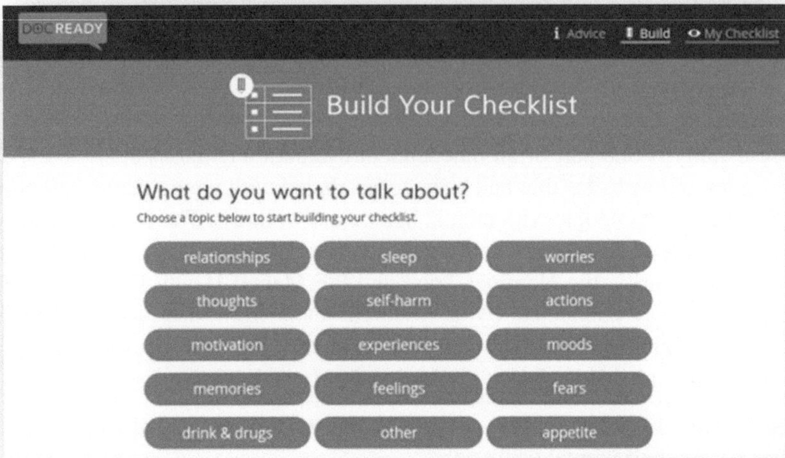

Fig. 4.4 Screen grab 'Doc Ready' website – checklist page and home page with survey link

detail. The evaluation also included interviews with the product teams and anonymous data analytics about the use of each product; although the latter did not provide any information about the age of users so it is not considered further here, (details are reported in Simons et al. 2015).

Ethical Considerations Given the intended population of young people using tools designed to support their mental health, the ethics committee that reviewed the research plan wanted to see that the researchers had thought through how disclosure of distress or risk of harm to self or others would be handled. As survey respondents would remain anonymous and the responses would not be monitored in real time, it was not deemed possible to respond to such disclosures. However, for the one-to-one interviews, a safeguarding protocol was devised. During the study no situation arose where the protocol was required.

Survey Co-Design and Procedure Online surveys (using survey monkey) for Doc Ready and In Hand were designed with some input from young people already involved with Innovation Labs and the development of the individual products. Survey respondents were asked what motivated them to use the tool and which sections of the tools they found most useful. Each survey was designed with plenty of space for free text responses.

A key element of the survey included dimensions from the Short 7-item version of the Warwick-Edinburgh Mental Well-Being Scale (SWEMWBS), designed to measure mental wellbeing in the general population (Stewart-Brown et al. 2009). However, rather than asking survey respondents to rate their wellbeing using this

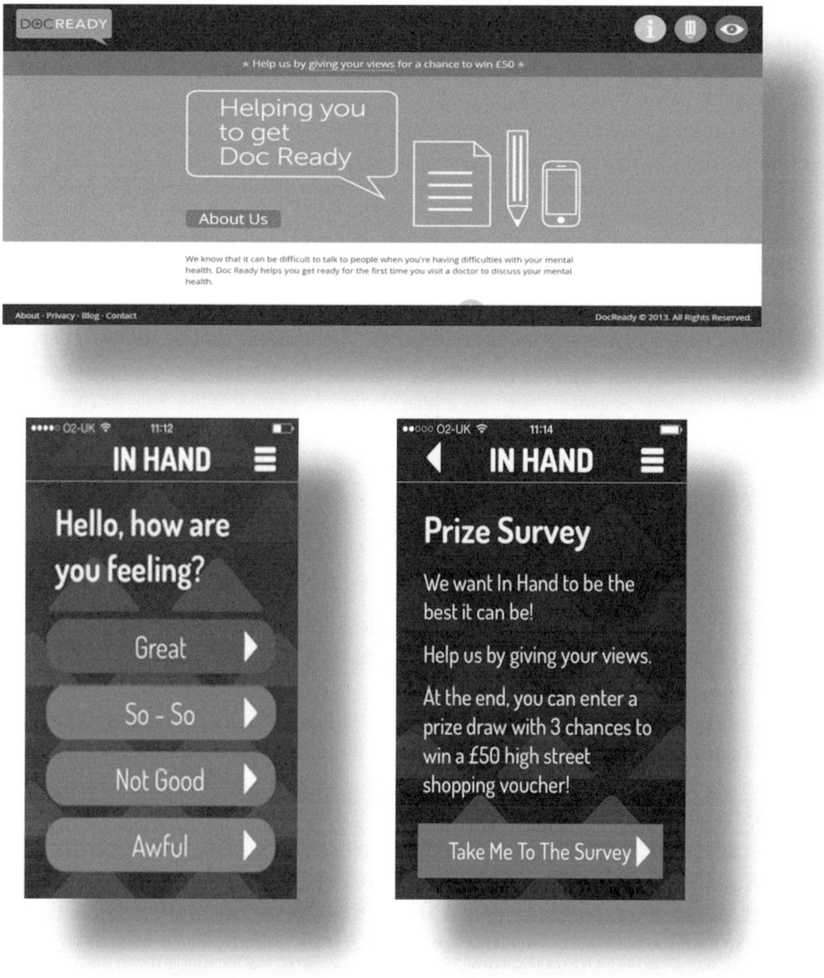

Fig. 4.5 Screen grab 'In Hand' app – home and survey page

measure, they were asked to indicate whether the digital tool had supported this aspects of their mental wellbeing.

Would you say [product] has helped you?:

- Have a positive outlook (Feel optimistic about the future)?
- Feel useful?
- Feel relaxed?
- Deal with problems well?
- Think clearly?
- Feel close to other people?
- Make up my own mind about things?

To this existing list, the young people in the Innovation Labs co-design group added three more dimensions:

- Feel ready to talk to someone else?
- Feel less stressed?
- Feel more able to take control?

Users of both digital products were invited to complete the surveys from links (banner or splash screen) embedded in the digital products (see screen shots, Figs. 4.4 and 4.5).

Once users clicked the links, they were taken to an external website to complete and submit the survey direct to the research team. At the end of the survey, respondents were invited to opt into being contacted by the study team by leaving an email address (this was also required for entry into the prize draw). This was to offer two options for providing further detail about their experiences of using the digital tools – either a telephone/Skype interview with a researcher or submit a 'video diary' of their experiences. This video option was suggested by the young people at the Innovation Labs project board meeting who thought that other young people would be interested in doing this given the wide spread use of YouTube etc. Guidance was drafted to send people if they chose this option. It listed a short set of questions, mirroring the semi-structured interview schedule, to guide their content and included instructions for uploading the video to a secure file sharing website.

4.3.2.3 Findings

The number of participants in the surveys were 56 for the Doc Ready website from which 5 detailed telephone interviews were completed after an expression of interest from 18, and 131 for the In Hand app where 8 interviews were completed after 24 opted in, one of these from the USA asking to write their interview answers by email. No respondent elected to complete a video diary in the end although there had a few opt-ins when responding to the survey (5 for Doc Ready and 9 for In Hand). The majority of survey respondents were aged 16–25 years (67 % Doc Ready and 76 % In Hand).

From the analysis of surveys (of all respondents), Doc Ready was valued by its users because of its core function – the ability to create and use a checklist when seeking help for a health professional for mental wellbeing support. The vast majority of survey respondents were attracted to use the tool to get their thoughts organised for an appointment (91 % of survey respondents rated this as important or very important). Other reasons rated highly were privacy (85 %), and being able to find out about their rights (80 %). Similarly, after the home page, building, seeing and ordering the checklist pages were the top rated sections of Doc Ready. Similarly, the interviewees valued the checklist highly and thought it could be used in a number of ways.

Younger interviewees in particular, thought they would give the list to their GP to read as they felt they might be unable to talk to them directly about how they were feeling. Others thought the value was in keeping them focussed and not forgetting what they wanted to say. They felt this was especially important when feeling anxious, low or having muddled thoughts. The checklist was also valued as a tool to help the user feel in control of their appointment. The topic categories in the checklist function, not only enabled users to prepare a checklist; they also served other important functions such as reassurance that others were feeling similar things and seeking help was valid. Others found that the topics helped them realise what was important to mention to the GP, for example, poor sleep. Feedback from In Hand users via the survey suggested that while people valued the opportunity to think about their mental wellbeing, it was the ability to do this on their own personal mobile device (phone or tablet) that was important. For example, 86 % of respondents thought 'being able to use In Hand wherever I am, whatever I'm doing' as important or very important. Similarly, 'using my phone/tablet to manage things' (79 %) and 'it is private and no one else would see how I'm feeling' (78 %) were highly rated. They talked about In Hand being 'discrete', 'private' and 'it doesn't matter where you are'. The interviewees elaborated on this theme, by describing the importance of the app being anonymous and non-judgemental. It gave them the opportunity to think about how they were feeling without involving others, either personally or professionally. Feedback from the survey and user interviews showed that people were generally using In Hand in one of two ways – to either regularly assess how they were feeling or to use it to give them a boost when feeling low or anxious. 81 % of survey respondents had said they had tried In Hand because they wanted to think about how they were feeling. In free text answers they described how they wanted to increase their awareness, understand their emotions and acknowledge how they were feeling. As a general finding, young people reported that they found these tools valuable because they were helping them develop a level of independence with managing their mental wellbeing (Table 4.1).

4.3.2.4 Reflections

Positives The use of embedded surveys enabled the engagement of young people directly from the digital products remotely and anonymously. Both surveys yielded a good sample.

From the wellbeing scale used in the survey it was seen that In Hand and Doc Ready are being used by relatively large numbers of people, many of whom report the products are making a positive contribution to their mental health in the way that was envisaged by the product teams. We can note that the young people who were invited to review and add questions to the survey added their own values to an existing measure. This represents a degree of involvement in the research process with the caveat that we cannot know if the co-design group was fully representative of the typical users of the product.

Additional product team reflections attributed this positive outcome to three different factors in the development process:

Table 4.1 Mental wellbeing dimension responses

Mental wellbeing dimension	Percentage of users rating *In Hand* as helpful (n = 108)	Percentage of users rating Doc Ready as helpful (n = 44)
Have a positive outlook	82	64
Feel useful	59	66
Feel relaxed	77	70
Deal with problems well	61	66
Think clearly	74	82
Feel close to other people	40	20
Make up my own mind about things	63	77
Feel ready to talk to someone else	51	82
Feel less stressed	78	66
Feel more able to take control	70	77

Simons et al. (2015)

1. the teams' commitment to developing tools that young people wanted,
2. close involvement of young people throughout the development of the product,
3. The approach taken in the projects – being open with each other and communicating well, sharing responsibility for the end product and working hard to meet the project schedule.

By using digital methods, the online survey, the methods should have avoided peer influence as respondents were most likely completing the measures independently. Impersonal methods of contact were used, which on the surface may be considered as a restriction to recruitment; however, the high response rate from young people indicates that method has value.

On the surveys, free text entry was frequently used by respondents (60 % for In Hand respondents and 33 % for Doc Ready), with some thoughtful and detailed responses. In particular, the inclusion of the free text option in the survey enabled a richer understanding of why young people had sought to use each tool and how they understood its value. Capturing this data in the survey as well as the individual interviews helped to build confidence in the findings. The interviews used a semi-structured interview schedule to guide conversations, with primarily open questions so that participants could describe and explain in their own words and in their own way, in addition to referring to the participants' responses to the survey. From this, it was possible to find out how using the tools had supported or helped an individual's mental health, in their own words. Participants were asked if they found feeding back on the product to be a good experience or, as mentioned earlier with respect to ethical approval, if it had raised any concerns or caused any distress. No participant reported any distress at the time of the interview and this was checked with a follow-up email a few days later. Most said that they had valued the opportunity to talk about how they self-managed their mental health and said the interview it was an enjoyable experience.

Lastly, the process of involvement of young people in the Innovation Labs project as a whole, prior to the evaluation, was also seen to be positive by the product teams. The expanded confidence and skills for the young people was seen most strongly with In Hand, culminating in the launch party in May 2014, which was designed and led by the young people. The team captured the co-creation process during the project shown in a short film. One young person had been successful in gaining employment as a web developer, which was attributed to skills learnt in Innovation Labs. While these examples were not part of the post launch evaluation, they show the benefits of co-production in the design part of the project and some of the design team went on to be involved in the evaluation process.

Negatives For the purposes of research with young people as a distinct group, the study was not controlled and the researchers did not know in advance the ages of the respondents. However the digital products were co-designed for and marketed at young people so that there was an expectation of a good sample in the 16–25 range which was realised in practice. Moreover, it was not possible to know in advance which methods of engagement would be most attractive to the target audience. This is a further limitation of a uncontrolled study where respondents are self-selecting and the reasons for their engagement with the survey is not known is that the results may not be generalisable, since the survey sample may not be representative of the whole user population.

The main way that people could have been more creative in their feedback was through choosing to submit a video diary of their experiences, which was suggested by the co-design team, which may have been inspired by the positive experience of producing a video during the design process. In the event no one took up this option, even those who had initially expressed an interest in their survey response. Without further intelligence to understand why this was the case, it can only be concluded that it was a misjudged option that was not attractive to the respondents.

4.3.3 Case Study 3 – Using Mobile Phones for Monitoring and Management of a Long-Term Mental Health Condition, Attention Deficit Hyperactivity Disorder, in Teenagers (iRAM)

4.3.3.1 Background

This study explored using mobile phone technology to assist in the treatment and monitoring of Attention Deficit Hyperactivity Disorder (ADHD). ADHD is a neuro-developmental syndrome that is characterised by three core behaviours; inattention, hyperactivity and impulsivity. It affects 3-5 % of school aged children (NICE 2008) and symptoms typically persist into adulthood. Parental education and psychological treatments are first line treatments, with medication prescribed for those with persistent symptoms. However, an individual's response to medication can be variable, meaning that careful monitoring is required to reach an optimum dose in each case. The aim of this study was to explore patient, parent and health professional views and attitudes towards using digital technology for remote medication monitoring for ADHD (Simons et al. 2016).

The study sought a clearer understanding of the functions all stakeholders (patients, parents and health practitioners) would want to see incorporated into a digital tool for use on smartphones and their design preferences. For example, while prescribing practitioners are likely to be interested in receiving regular reports of symptoms and side effects which are easily integrated into patients' electronic records, additional features such as appointment and medication reminders, information and advice will increase the likelihood that patients and parents will use a tool. The reflection of the multi- techniques used in iRAM user workshops explores the approaches used with teenagers in contrast with those used with adults.

4.3.3.2 Protocol

The study was a cross-sectional focus group study with patients, parents and health professionals. Focus groups were chosen for this study as they facilitate discussion between the participants on a topic of shared interest. The setting was four mental health NHS trusts in the East Midlands region of England. An industrial partner developed an initial prototype system, which was used as a vehicle for exploring the topic with participants. The study received ethical approval from a UK National Research Ethics Service Committee.

The prototype system was developed by an industrial partner following discussions with the research team about what functions might be useful for remote monitoring for medication. Once this prototype was ready, an open day was held to engage with potential end-users of the mobile technology and interested others to elicit initial feedback. It was attended by a young person with ADHD and their parent, two adults with ADHD, one psychiatrist, one psychologist and a medical technology researcher. The insights gained from this open day identified key factors to explore in more detail in the focus groups. However, the experience of demonstrating the prototype system at the open day suggested that demonstrating it in the focus groups would distract from exploring attitudes to and acceptability of the general concept of remote monitoring using smartphones. The prototype system required a lengthy 'on-boarding' process to create personal accounts and would only work if people have access to smartphones with mobile data during the session. Therefore, we decided not to use the digital prototype in the focus groups, but created printed materials from the system to enable a wider range of participants to take part and aid discussion of the concept.

The whole study sample comprised children and young people with ADHD (8), adults with ADHD (11), parents of children and young people with ADHD (9) and health professionals working with people with ADHD (31). There were two avenues for recruitment: ADHD clinics or ADHD support groups. Inclusion criteria for chil-

Table 4.2 Focus groups by type and location

	Staff	Adult	Young people	Parent
Nottinghamshire	N=9	N=4		
Leicestershire	N=7	N=7	N=6	N=7
Derbyshire	N=7		N=2	N=2
Lincolnshire	N=8			
Total (N=59)	31	11	8	9

dren and young people were to be aged 12–17 with a diagnosis of ADHD, for adults to be aged 18 and over with a diagnosis of ADHD, for parents to have a child with a diagnosis of ADHD and for health professionals to be working directly with patients with ADHD (Table 4.2).

Eleven separate focus groups were held with each group limited to one participant type. The focus groups were held in locations convenient to the participants, either NHS premises (7) or support groups (4).

Each focus group was facilitated by one researcher, with another researcher taking field notes and observations. The discussions were guided by a pre-defined topic schedule informed by insights from the user workshop. It covered four key areas:

- using technology for health;
- medication experience/prescribing practice;
- remote monitoring for effects and side effects;
- aspirations for using technology to manage ADHD.

For the children and young people, adult and parent groups' interactive exercises were included to help participants engage with the topics. These included a range of conventional and more interactive elicitation techniques as shown in Table 4.3, which were tailored to the different user groups.

The research was aimed at exploring issues, specifically medication taking, which may be difficult, embarrassing or stigmatising for young people to talk about in a group of peers. It was anticipated that young participants might be reluctant to disclose personal information within a group setting. Therefore, the persona exercise was introduced to the young person's groups as an additional elicitation technique. Personas of two boys with ADHD were sketched out on large sheets of paper and the participants were asked to work in small groups to add detail to these boys' lives (for example, their favourite music, subject at school and food). Different scenarios were allocated to each persona, highlighting different experiences with medication, for example, one of the persona boys found he quickly achieved the optimum dose with few side effects, while the other experienced severe side effects, which affected his behaviour at school. The participants were then asked a series of questions about how each boy might behave and feel when at school and home when taking medication. It was hoped that by asking them about how these fictitious but realistic boys would respond to the medication, they would be able to contribute in non-threatening or exposing way.

Table 4.3 Overview of the activity-orientated questions

Activity	YP	Adults	Parents	HCPs
Warm up rapid fire quiz (about technologies and health)		✓	✓	
Data visualisations (about population technology use in healthcare)	✓	✓	✓	✓
Ideas on sticky notes (to record individual thoughts and ideas before sharing with others)	✓	✓	✓	
Rating personal experience (indicating satisfaction on a visual scale)		✓	✓	
Prototype screen shots (of the digital prototype system)	✓	✓	✓	✓
Personas and scenarios (to explore attitudes towards medication for ADHD with fictitious users in mind)	✓			

Analysis All focus groups were audio recorded and transcribed. Scans and photographs of the outputs from the interactive exercises were also added to the database. Thematic analysis of the data was undertaken to facilitate searching for commonalities and discrepancies across the different participant groups. Working from 4 of the 11 transcripts, an initial coding frame was developed by two researchers, one of whom had not been involved with data collection. This included open coding of the data undertaken independently, followed by discussion to agree a comprehensive coding frame. Through constant comparison, all data were coded into the framework, the appropriateness of which was checked, iterated when required and reapplied to the earlier transcripts. Coding of 35 % of the data set was crosschecked for reliability with 93 % agreement (Kappa=0.922, $p<0.001$) attained by the two researchers. Once all data were coded into a refined and complete coding framework, five overarching, interpretative themes were identified through, larger team discussions and codes assigned to these themes. Theme-level matrixes were created to compare the nature and distribution of the data across the participant groups.

4.3.3.3 Findings

All groups of participants enthusiastically supported the idea of a patient-owned digital platform to support the treatment, monitoring and management of ADHD, which they can choose to share with clinicians and support networks. There was little support for the proposed prototype which was a clinician held digital platform as all groups raised concerns about the burden of clinician-led remote monitoring. Digital technology was fore-fronted as a potential means for better self-monitoring and management in the form of, for example, digital graphs and reminders.

Improving the healthcare consultation concerning communication was another area identified to benefit from a patient held digital platform. Digital communication was also highlighted as a means to address the unmet need of additional support from peers or those "in the know". Furthermore, patient and parent groups emphasised the need for improved access to more personalised information, particularly with regards to drug type and effects. Healthcare professionals also expressed the need for more personalised information to make clinical judgements, such as the context in which self-report assessments are conducted.

Future care pathways for ADHD should capitalise on the receptiveness of patients and healthcare professions towards digital assistance. Research should aim to focus on the development and evaluation of inclusive, engaging and customisable digital tools to meet this need. Peer support and information seeking through the internet is already being used, in the main. Care strategies should also focus on improving access to and the quality of these in order to address the unmet need of additional peer support and personalised information, both of which would contribute to the general wellbeing of patients and parents.

4.3.3.4 Reflections

A range of different techniques for eliciting views and experiences were used in all focus groups, but a different set of interactive exercises were designed for the young person's groups. As described below, the inclusion of the persona exercise achieved a high level of engagement with the topic of medication taking, but was used in different ways by the two different groups of teenagers.

The positives and challenges of the multi-techniques used in this case study are very similar to those found in the PEGASO case study above. However, these are amplified when working with young people with ADHD because they have limited capacity for concentration and maintaining attention on one task.

Positives Even though the young people in the groups had ADHD, increasing the challenge of engaging them successfully in the research, and were at the lower end of the age spectrum for teenagers (12–13), the range of methods employed appears to have achieved the aim to engage them with the topic and enable their participation in the research. For example, feedback from the specialist youth workers at the youth club; where one group took place, was that it was unusual to keep the young people's attention on one topic for the 50 min the session lasted. However, it is also likely that the young people's engagement was facilitated by the topic – using mobile phones and technology for health as they were all regular users of digital devices.

The range of techniques used across the different participant groups in this study emphasizes the need for a multi-techniques approach with teenage participants. For example, in the adult and parent groups, participants often spoken about their personal experiences unprompted and at length, without the use of interactive exercises. They also appeared to value highly the opportunity to share their experiences with each other, gaining some peer support in the process. This occurred when the participants were known to each other through support groups or if they met on the day after being recruited through specialist ADHD clinics.

The range of methods selected for the young people's groups enabled them to contribute individually (post-it note exercises and questionnaire) as well as collectively in the group. In particular, the persona exercise was included to enable a discussion of a potentially sensitive topic – medication taking for ADHD – in a way that would be non-threatening and non-exposing. While both teenage groups engaged with the topic and contributed well, the way in which they responded to the exercise differed across the two groups. It was necessary for the researchers to adapt the techniques in response to this. In the larger group (6 participants), which was drawn from attendees at a specialist youth club for young people with ADHD where the participants were known to each other, they generally stuck to the persona exercise, talking about medication in relation to the persona boys and did not divulge much personal information. Participants did offer different opinions about how the persona boys would respond to medication, giving some confidence that the technique enabled the young people to express divergent views, the extent of this in comparison to adult participation is unknown. Whereas, in the smaller group, with just two participants, who had not met before, they spontaneously started talking about themselves instead of the personas – in fact, after they persisted with talking about their own experiences, it felt more productive to abandon the persona exercise and continue to probe about their own experiences. One factor that probably helped the boys be open with each other and the researchers was that although the boys had not met before, they discovered in the early part of the session that they had a shared interest in playing rugby and both knew other local players –their shared experience of ADHD and sports created a level of trust between them and they felt comfortable talking from their own perspective. Both boys gave interesting and valuable insights into living with ADHD and ways in which technology could support their self-management.

Negatives As with the PEGASO project, the extent of participation in the discussions within the groups was very varied, especially in the larger group, with some participants being very vocal and others much quieter. The researchers tried to carefully encourage the quieter ones to join in the discussion, but at the same time did not want them to feel under the spotlight.

The persona exercise was designed to engage the participants with the topic and access real life experiences, by enabling the participants to project these on to characters designed for the study. While it is possible to assess the level of engagement, it is only possible to speculate how successful the technique was at accessing real life experiences.

4.3.3.5 Take home points

A key take home message from this case study is while the careful planning and design of multi-techniques is critical for successful research with teenagers, researchers also have to flexible when out in the field and confident enough to adapt the methods to suit the participants. The persona exercise, which was included after review and advice from others more experienced in carrying out research with teenagers, was received differently by the two groups. Sticking strictly to this method when the participants were not engaging with it may have been detrimental to their participation in the research.

4.3.4 Case Study 4 – Exploring Social, Environmental and Contextual Influencers on Teenage Health Choices (Full and Hungry Project)

4.3.4.1 Background

The Full and Hungry project aims to document young people's perceptions of healthy food and lifestyles in relation to location, environment and context. This study provides them with training and technology tools to map their local area for triggers associated with healthy and unhealthy behaviours. This will assist their general awareness and help in the development of places and environments that facilitate healthy choices. This case study utilises novel methods of data collection and collaborative analysis with teenage participants including photo and video production and storyboarding. The uses of these technology based research methods are described and commentary is provided about the effectiveness of these multi-methods in research with teenagers and in the development of online and interactive maps and videos as research outputs. The Full & Hungry project is a parallel project of PEGASO (see Case Study 1). Where the PEGASO project approach is user centric; the Full and Hungry project follows a similar ethos but uses technology in a co-design research method.

The research area focuses on the development of location based services, i.e. a set of utilities to enhance individuals' awareness about the opportunities around them in their everyday life for healthier lifestyle choices and the social dynamics that facilitate this. These services aim to highlight 'positive places', food shops, sport infrastructure etc. in the locale where the teenagers live. To design these services, co-design activities with the users represent a fundamental step to understanding their needs, their perception of the messaging services that are built into the online technology resources and the possibilities and services that their territory is able to offer them. The research questions explored within this project are as follows;

- Schools are frequently involved in activities that aim to help teenagers to build their healthy lifestyles; but when they go outside what do they find?
- What are teenager's perceptions about receiving messages with information about food, physical activity and health?
- Do teenagers want the messaging stimulus to be oriented towards personal discernment, accountability and choice, or do stereotypes of teenagers as unengaged, passive users prevail?
- What do teenagers think about these online/technology resources with regards to dependency and autonomy?

From the perspective of the school involved, the Full & Hungry project is part of an educational program named "Educate to Prevent", which is a program involving different high schools in Lombardy, Italy, with the aim of promoting health among the adolescents.

The project was conducted in Milan, at the Liceo Scientifico Vittorini, where, together with the teachers, partners of the PEGASO consortium helped the teenagers to develop the technical and communicative skills to produce a video documentary about their perception of the messages that their territory provides them, directly or indirectly, about nutrition and sports.

The design of this study is strongly related to the need to develop an innovative concept for a location based service for the PEGASO project. The project is based on four keywords: Eat, Move, Play and Share. In particular, the starting point of the Full & Hungry project is the exploration of the gamification approach, where the creation of a social community could be the framework to help raise teenage awareness about physical activity and nutrition.

The proposed technology service was a mobile app presenting local based information and elements of augmented reality which could act as a compass to help teenagers orient themselves in the real world, to find healthy opportunities for sport and food. As such the Full & Hungry project has been designed to elicit a picture of what teenagers perceive from the territory they usually live in, which messages they would like to receive and how they interpret the information.

The technique chosen to reach this objective was the production of a video-documentary where teenage participants present the city of Milan to a generic teenage population attending a global exhibition (EXPO 2015). The aim of which is to make them understand what 'move' and 'eat' means for Milan teenagers, and how to find and explore these concepts in the city.

4.3.4.2 Protocol

Eighteen teenagers aged 13–16 (15 male and 3 female) participated in the Full & Hungry project. Informed consent was prepared and provided to each participant. The consent was prepared to inform parents about the activity, and to obtain authorization for the video recording. In addition, the authorization for the video

Table 4.4 Schedule of Full and Hungry project activities

1st meeting (classroom)	Brief teenagers about PEGASO Project concept and objectives
	PEGASO video teaser and short discussion.
	Brief teenagers about the work schedule of future meetings
	Tutorial on Video Recording Techniques.
	Coordination of the working groups while video recording with the smartphones to document the activities of the teenagers.
	Ask teenagers to start collecting videos and pictures in their living areas, related to the two PEGASO keywords (Eat and Move).
2nd meeting	Comment and discuss the material collected by the students during the week and introduce the story-telling activity. Teenagers are asked to collect videos following a story they want to tell.
	Division of students in two teams one for EAT and one for MOVE. Search the web to find points of interest associated to EAT or MOVE category within the Lombardy region.
3rd/4th/5th meeting	SHARE Teenagers share the recordings made in the city or in the research region
	Discussion and voting of the most interesting videos
6th meeting	Drafting of a storyboard video with the students reviewing the photos and video materials collected as a group.
7th/8th meeting	Students supervised by Neosperience and Polimi operators edit the documentary output with the video and photo material collected during the course

recording for third parties was prepared, to guarantee that all the persons appearing in the final video gave their consents for public reproduction.

The Full & Hungry project has been conducted as a didactical program with schools and comprised of classroom and laboratory activities. Eight meetings with the duration of an hour and a half were held, plus a further two meetings to share feedback and progress (see schedule in Table 4.4).

The final results of the Full & Hungry project are composed of two digital products: a video documentary made by the teenagers under the supervision of the PEGASO partners, and the development of one app that represents one of the services provided with the platform, PEGASO City, developed by NEOSPERIENCE.

The video documentary presents a variety of records of places within the city of Milan, documenting the most interesting food shops and places for sport activities for the participants, together with teenager's interviews about food habits and knowledge.

The PEGASO City app shows places of interests for food and sports through a geo-localised service powered by an augmented reality technology.

Table 4.5 summarizes the main results for students undertaking the study and for the PEGASO project.

Table 4.5 Outcomes of full and hungry project

For students	Increased awareness about healthy lifestyle and food.
	Activities within the protocol not only helped teenagers to express their ideas about this concept but also facilitated their learning from their peers.
	Teenagers were provided with tutorials about video editing and recording techniques
	Skills based learning focusing in co-working and team building
For PEGASO project	Geo mapping of some PEGASO compliant points of interest e.g. places that teenagers relate to healthy living concept
	Video documentary to disseminate PEGASO Project concept and values
	Contact with end users to collect feedback and requirements for the project development over a longer period of time.

4.3.4.3 Reflection on Methods

Positives Schools and teenage participants were attracted to the project by the opportunity to improve their skills whilst taking part in the research, in this case, video recording techniques. This was very important to the study as it helped to overcome a potential limitation of qualitative research with young people, engaging participants and facilitating their active discussion. The use of the technological data collection video and photographic content provided a novel method to ensure their prolonged engagement with the study. Whilst it was a challenge for the participants to learn the new skills and techniques they actively engaged with the tasks and topics assigned to them, leading to the successful production of the PEGASO video narratives.

The teenagers are introduced to the PEGASO topics of interest through a technical assignment. This resulted in an effort by the teenagers to learn, reflect and deepen their knowledge on that topic. As an example, the teenagers attended an exhibition about food and documented their experience; they collected information about food in relation to the seasons and geography to prepare the interview. As a consequence, they reflected on what could be important for them with regard to "Eat" and "Move" and portrayed that through their recording. This study has shown that this combination method can be useful to improve the level of active contribution by each participant. This has in turn led to a positive impact on the research study and the findings generated from the teenage productions.

The peer discussion was confined to the meetings at school, while outside they were free to act as they preferred and consider the topics at their own convenience. This part of the approach was considered important in order to elicit the perspectives of less confident/shy teenagers who are less likely to contribute to public discussion or will acquiesce with the points of view of others e.g. opinion leaders inside the groups etc. This therefore helps to ensure a more representative data set where teenagers of all dispositions are able to contribute.

This technology-facilitated multi-technique demonstrates effectiveness in promoting the teenagers' capability of autonomous thinking. Teenagers were asked to choose independently what to record, and to create their story telling without specific guidelines, with the only request that they had to be related with "Eat" and "Food". Consequently, the participants started to build their own point of view on this health related topics and their opinion, by recording their views in a variety of different ways. This creative approach was welcomed by the teenage participants who felt that their views were listened to and respected in the final outputs of the study.

Negatives A drawback of this approach was its time consuming nature. Despite the enthusiasm for methods and imparting of skills through the research by the teenagers there was attrition to recruitment. The initial enthusiasm demonstrated by adolescents waned over the course of the study and some of the teenagers did not see the process through to the end or produce the video output. This may be due to the fact that participating in a project like this may have incurred too much burden on the teenagers. The research tasks required the participants to record, document and prepare the media that they captured and also their views. This was confirmed by the teacher that followed the project within the Lombardy based school:

> *Additional afternoon commitments are unlikely compatible with the teenager's usual activities, especially if you request the preparation of materials. It seems that respecting deadlines and assignments becomes very hard for them. Over time, the group has changed: a third of recruited abandoned; a third went on to attend, but did not produce much; the rest have been committed to the end, even compensating for the failures of others. Obviously these are the ones most to excited about the experience and results.*

Aside from reducing the burden on participants, another option to overcome this limitation could be to reduce the initial number of participants e.g. selection of participants who demonstrate more interest and investment in the project. With regards the efficacy of the method, this introduces bias, however exploratory co-design activity can elicit useful and meaningful results with a smaller sample population who engage throughout the whole process.

The teacher involved in the project had praise for the approach proposed by the PEGASO partners, especially for the promotion of autonomous thinking within the project:

> *Maybe the final result is not really original, but all the contents are made by the teenagers, and gives an idea of freshness, lightness, naivety, immediacy, that results in a product able to talk to teenagers. [...] The participants' expectation was a technical course, and that they would have worked on predefined contents. [...] They spent a lot of time finding a way, but at the end a leadership of the students has been clear*

4.3.4.4 Take Home Points

The participants demonstrated enthusiasm, particularly for the time they spent testing technologies, working on the video production and recording the speech.

> *We were the best. We recorded the speech in that amazing recording room, and we wrote the contents. We received the compliments for our work, but we also want to thank them [the researchers] for the great experience, really interesting*

Whilst some teenage participants found the multi-techniques and associated tasks a high workload and therefore dropped out of the study the outputs from the remaining students demonstrated insight into the PEGASO topics of 'EAT' and 'MOVE'. The participants were given time to absorb the information given to them and then to explore them creatively in both structured and unstructured ways. The use of technology to achieve this was considered a strength of the method and feedback given suggested that this aspect was partly the reason that some teenagers were able to see the study through from start to finish.

It is important to offer teenage participants something they value in turn for their participation. Where they have little concept of the 'longer term' and have more awareness of the 'here and now' providing incentives which are proportional to their involvement and the overall study can assist engagement in topics and research fields which might otherwise struggle to recruit from this age group.

4.4 Overall Discussion, Best Practice and Guidelines for Designing HF Mixed Methods for Health Research with Teenagers

The case studies describe four different scenarios involving teenage participants in HCI research and the elicitation of their requirements and/or views about health related topics or services. Each case study details how a combination of methods was utilised to involve and engage teenagers in studies ranging in terms of context, temporality, access and contact with the young research participants. The case studies address research into usability, engagement, learnability and acceptability with regard to health related outcomes. Each of the case studies considers, to a greater or lesser extent, the following aspects and is integral to the successful engagement of teenagers in research studies;

- Take into account the sensitivities of working with adolescents and researching health related issues
- Consideration of the inter and intra-variability of the teenage population in terms of skills, competencies and limitations
- Ensure the combination of methods will enable participants to express themselves in a variety of ways providing maximum opportunity for engagement
- Direct benefits – new experiences or opportunities to learn new skills for some.

Our examples are not exhaustive of the multiple techniques that can be used to engage teenagers in HCI healthcare research but provide examples of how to design a study with an appropriate variety of methods and to provide the optimum research experience for teenage participants.

The following section presents the benefits and drawbacks of a multi-techniques approach with this target population. This overview of advantages and disadvantages is supported by literature to provide additional examples of each concept in practice.

4.4.1 Benefits of a Multi-Techniques Approach with Teenagers

The use of multi-techniques provides opportunity for achieving research goals and adds value to the process when involving teenagers (as discussed later in this section and in Table 4.5). For example there was evidence within several of the case studies whereby data from different techniques demonstrated triangulation and complementarity, where information between and within data sets was harmonious and/or cumulative. This benefit has previously been reported by Clarke and Moss who report how multi-technique approaches provide an overall picture of the research enquiry (Clark and Moss 2005).

This approach can provide credibility to findings where they are shaped by the respondents through a variety of modes. This is particularly relevant when trying to prove the reliability of findings and overcome the problem of acquiescence bias on the part of teenage participants. With teenagers (as with other young or vulnerable populations) there is potential for acquiescence bias to the views of – peers, research staff and other adult stakeholders. This means that the mechanisms afforded through multi-techniques are important in providing every opportunity for teenagers to disclose their views without censorship or modification.

The PEGASO and Full and Hungry case studies demonstrate how task-based activities can reduce the 'power relationship' issue between participant and researcher, an aspect also reported by (Punch 2002). Where the workshops were designed to include free thinking and communication, participants were also advised that there were no 'right or wrong' answers and that all of their input was valid and within the scope of the study. The opportunity to creatively produce videos, brainstorm their ideas and produce advertising campaigns led to the teenagers providing sometimes controversial and negative feedback about the system and or topic at hand – suggesting that the tasks developed had successfully broken down the hierarchies that normally lead to participants responding in a manner in which they perceive desirable to the researchers. This is also reinforced by the participatory manner of the tasks which could be said to empower the young participants in their exploration and communication of their needs (Thomas and O'Kane 1998). There is an interesting query as to why the video tasks in Full and Hungry were successful, whilst in the Innovation Labs, the participants did not engage with this type of media for data collection and presentation. Perhaps the collaborative approach taken within Full and Hungry promoted buy-in from the teenagers, which was not feasible in the more remote and unsolicited Labs evaluation.

4.4.2 Drawbacks to a Multi-Techniques Approach with Teenagers

The 'Ladder of Participation' (Hart 1992) provides a framework for the involvement of young people in research, however it is worth noting that as with any population, some individuals will want to take part but may not want to be involved in the higher levels of participation e.g. initiation and direction of research and shared decision making (Punch 2002). Some methods might overcome this by engaging the teenagers so that they are not overtly aware of their participation in terms of directing the research enquiry or establishing creative fields of interest, instead the focus is on their valued input, respect for their views, and needs.

Whilst some methods might appear to offer teenage research participants with attractive and creative ways to engage with the research topics, it may be that the participants bypass these methods. As demonstrated in the iRAM case study and other studies using personas (Lang et al. 2009) sometimes research participants prefer to speak from personal experience and impart their views from a first person perspective. The use of personas to 'distance' the participant responses from potentially sensitive topics (often for ethical reasons) may not provide a satisfactory tool through which teenagers can successfully communicate their views.

The complexity of research enquiries will automatically increase as multiple techniques are employed to elicit information. Careful planning, preparation, piloting and consultation will help to ensure that the approach taken optimises the engagement of young participants, but does not disengage them through burden of the research study or workload within individual tasks. Whilst this is not isolated to teenagers and is applicable to participants of any age range, the tolerance of teenagers for this is lower and is underpinned by the neurobiological development of the brain during these years (Blakemore 2010). Teenage concentration levels and attention spans can be poor and the ability to ignore distractions may not be as developed as in an adult population. Methods employed for teenagers should therefore consider this and 'design for' this type of behaviour. As such, the early work to develop this multi-techniques approaches can be time consuming and relatively complex.

In the planning stages of a research protocol for use with teenagers it is not possible to anticipate the strengths and capabilities of the young people. Consultation with teachers or others used to working with this audience will help to ensure a good balance of methods to get the most out of the teenager's involvement. The variety of methods described in the case studies demonstrate the benefits of planning to ensure that appropriate methods are utilised to ensure inclusive participation of a heterogeneous group in terms of age, maturity, literacy and communication skills.

4.4.3 Multi-Techniques for Teenage Health Research

Figure 4.6 presents the five facets of adolescent health promotion – emotional, physical, intellectual, social and spiritual. The discipline of Human Factors considers the human; whether they are a user of technology or service, or an individual undertaking a task, in a holistic manner. It takes into account the physical, cognitive, social and affective characteristics of users and considers both the tangible and intangible elements of each of these factors at different scales.

Figure 4.6 combines a well-known ergonomics model and adolescent health promotion framework (Viner and Macfarlane 2005), to provide a representation of adolescent health promotion (or research) within the perspective of a human factors

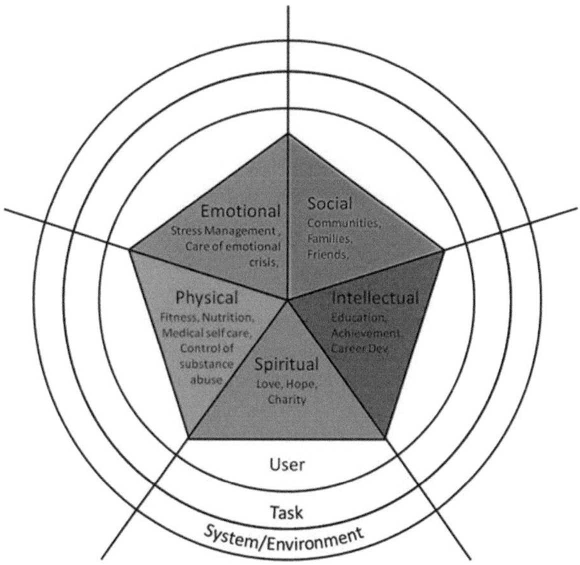

Fig. 4.6 Adolescent health promotion and research through human factors thinking (Lang 2012)

methodological approach and indeed the use of multi-techniques which are designed to tap into all five facets of teenage health. There is a case for the appropriate use of multi-techniques to research teenage requirements, needs and desires within a healthcare context, so that the user voice can be elicited in a multitude of ways to capture the various facets of health promotion.

This model provides a useful tool to assist in planning research enquiries with young people, particularly those associated with health.

4.4.4 Schema for Multi-Techniques HCI Health Research with Teenagers

The multi-techniques approach described in this chapter describe benefits that are specific to the implementation of research with teenagers and are intended to overcome some of the issues normally associated with needs elicitation or research participation from this age group. Eight factors are derived from the research experiences described in the case studies and are supported by literature from HCI, human factors, adolescent development and health. Consideration of these factors in study designs should serve to unlock the potential of teenagers, ensuring reliable elicitation of their views and needs.

The eight factors (AACCEESS) are listed as follows and defined in Table 4.6:

- Avoiding **Acquiescence bias**
- Increasing **Autonomy**
- Making the most of **Capacity**

- Offering opportunity for **Creativity**
- Enhancing **Engagement**
- Providing new **Experience**
- Considering **Social Influence**
- Handling **Sensitivity**

Table 4.7 shows the coverage of the schema from the four case studies. The eight contributors listed in Table 4.7 have been derived from the four case studies and described as key reasons for the various successes experienced in the individual research studies. They have specific pertinence when considered against the backdrop of HCI research, whereby the needs and developmental goals of adolescence (Lang et al. 2014) are now impacted by young people's access to and use of technology. As such, the process that goes into HCI research (and specifically HCI and health research) needs to have an awareness of ways in which research can be

Table 4.6 AACCEESS Schema for teenage research participation

A	Acquiescence bias	The absence of disclosure that is biased towards an assumed desired response.
		The teenage research participant does not provide responses that are not of their own volition.
A	Autonomy	Behaviour within the research context that is free of control or influence.
		The teenage research participant is acting independently
C	Capability	To behave and operate to ones best abilities, taking into account the relative skills, competences and weaknesses within and between people. (For teenagers, this includes growing capacity for abstract rather than concrete thinking).
		The teenagers are able to engage in tasks designed to accommodate their varying and changing abilities.
C	Creativity	To provide opportunity for different and unexpected modes of expression.
		The teenagers are able to use a variety of ways, technology solutions and introduce their own ways of communicating their responses.
E	Engagement	To ensure through the appropriateness and novelty of methods that teenagers are willing and able to engage in a variety of different ways for the duration of the study.
E	Experience	To provide an interesting and enjoyable experience, which taps into teenage developmental goals, behaviours and satisfaction.
S	Social influence	Approach ensures that teenage social and cultural backdrop is considered.
		Understands the importance of teenage awareness of cohort and social standing and the variety of ways this manifests in the current age of social media and online networks.
S	Sensitivity	To provide different modes of data collection to account for the sensitivities associated with teenage participants.
		Consideration of a wide variety of issues including but not limited to personal circumstances, teenage specific anxieties e.g. identity and change, health related concerns, or something as 'innocuous' as embarrassment about hand writing.

Table 4.7 Case study contributions to schema

Schema factor	CS1: PEGASO	CS2: Innovation Labs	CS3: iRAM	CS4: Full and Hungry
Acquiescence bias	✓	✓	✓	✓
Autonomy	✓	✓	✓	✓
Capacity	✓		✓	✓
Creativity			✓	✓
Engagement	✓	✓	✓	✓
Experience	✓		✓	✓
Social influence	✓			✓
Sensitivity	✓	✓	✓	✓

appropriately and inclusively designed to accommodate these changes in society and which have an impact on young people. This new schema is suggested to provide guidance for future research in this area.

4.5 Conclusions

This chapter highlights the importance of using multi-techniques when carrying out HCI health research with teenagers. The case studies described largely make use of qualitative methods for gathering the experiential data of teenage requirements and use of technologies. The proposed schema advocates consideration of the AACCEESS categories when determining what methods to combine and how teenagers might interact with the multiple-techniques being considered. A limitation of the case studies is their lack of co-creation of the research enquiries with teenage research partners. Future HCI research studies should aim to involve the young people at an earlier stage so that they may help to ensure that interaction and user experience research design is not dictated by adult preconceptions.

The case studies address how adolescents can be successfully involved in research studies and demonstrate how with careful planning and inclusive design of the research strategy and methods the challenges associated with adolescent involvement in research can be overcome. They have shown how multi-techniques approaches can benefit research enquiries and the reflections from researchers have provided useful insight into the advantages and disadvantages of this approach.

Future research and novel methodological combinations should be considered against the 'categories' identified within the schema and used in conjunction with knowledge of methods to 'fill any gaps' that are found, whereby the overall protocol may be found wanting in regards to an AACCEESS category. Whilst this schema helps to provide guidance for HCI researchers in this area it is not prescriptive nor a panacea for all research involving young people.

Well co-designed multi-techniques approaches can be used to engage young participants and can work towards breaking down barriers, including hierarchical, cultural and societal, which may impede research enquiries. They can also help to combat assumptions on the part of both the researchers and participants, so that valid requirements gathering and iterative processes can work towards solutions that target what adolescent users want and like and not what society or adults believe adolescents want or like.

Work needs to be carried out to examine the use of multi-techniques with teenagers further, specifically those that make use of novel technology based data collection methods. These opportunities whilst interesting raise a range of ethical and practical issues which to date are not yet fully understood.

This guidance can provide useful insight for not only academic research but also industrial and commercial HCI and healthcare researchers wanting to involve young people in their design and development processes. The AACCEESS schema provides support for those developing studies in this field without being prescriptive about the ways in which young people should be involved. The guidance from a Human Factors perspective and increasingly expected in health research is to (where possible) involve young people in the development of multi-techniques research processes, the selection and creative application of those methods and in piloting and testing prior to formal implementation. This process can provide rigor and reliability in the outcomes, with AACCEESS providing a resource and reference point throughout the process stages.

Acknowledgements The authors acknowledge support of this work through the PEGASO 610727 FP7 project grant. Although the views expressed are entirely their own. The research on iRAM reported in this paper was supported by the NIHR MindTech Healthcare Technology Co-operative. The views represented are the views of the authors alone and do not necessarily represent the views of the Department of Health in England, NHS, or the National Institute for Health Research. The Innovation Labs evaluation was funded by Comic Relief. The contents of this chapter have not been commissioned and have been externally peer reviewed.

References

Arnab S, Dunwell I, Debattista K (2013). Serious games for healthcare: applications and implications. Serious Games for Healthcare: Applications and Implications, 1–295. doi:10.4018/978-1-4666-1903-6

Bircher J (2005) Towards a dynamic definition of health and disease. Med Health Care Philos 8(3):335–341. doi:10.1007/s11019-005-0538-y

Blakemore SJ (2010) The developing social brain: implications for education. Neuron 65(6):744–747. doi:10.1016/j.neuron.2010.03.004

Boardwell J, Roberson J (2014) Learning from the Labs How to fund and deliver social tech for charities and social enterprises. Retrieved from http://www.innovationlabs.org.uk/wp-content/uploads/2014/11/Learning-from-the-Labs-Social-Tech-Ebook.pdf

Bos L, Marsh A, Carroll D, Gupta SMR (2008) Patient 2.0 empowerment. In: Paper presented at the proceedings of the 2008 International Conference on Semantic Web & Web Services (SWWS08). http://members.media-effect.be/P4F/_images/20100408patientempowermenthealth20.pdf

Burnett S, Bault N, Coricelli G, Blakemore SJ (2010) Adolescents' heightened risk-seeking in a probabilistic gambling task. Cogn Dev 25(2):183–196. doi:10.1016/j.cogdev.2009.11.003

Clark A, Moss P (2005) Listening to young children. The mosaic approach. National Children's Bureau, London

Clough BA, Casey LM (2011) Technological adjuncts to enhance current psychotherapy practices: A review. Clin Psychol Rev 31(3):279–292. doi:10.1016/j.cpr.2010.12.008

Cotton R, Irwin J, Wilkins A, Young C (2014). The future's digital Mental health and technology, p 50. Retrieved from http://www.nhsconfed.org/resources/2014/09/the-future-s-digital-mental-health-and-technology

Creswell JW (1999) Mixed-method research: introduction and application. In: Cizek GJ (ed) Handbook of educational policy. Academic, San Diego, pp 455–472

Elkind D (1967) Egocentrism in adolescence. Child Dev 38(4):1025–1034. doi:10.1111/j.1467-8624.1967.tb04378.x

Elliott GR, Feldman SS (2010) At the threshold: the developing adolescent. Harvard University Press, Cambridge MA

EXPO (2015) Giovani Ambasciartori del Cibo. EXPO Milan 2015. European Union Pavillion, Milan. 1st September 2015. Milan, Italy

Fitton D, Read JC, Horton M (2013) The challenge of working with teens as participants in interaction design. In: Paper presented at the In CHI'13 extended abstracts on human factors in computing systems

Fogg BJ (2009). A behavior model for persuasive design. In: Paper presented at the proceedings of the 4th international conference on persuasive technology, Claremont, California, USA

Fryar CD, Carroll MD, Odgen CL (2014) Prevalence of overweight and obesity among children and adolescents: United States, 1963–1965 through 2011–2012. http://www.cdc.gov/nchs/data/hestat/obesity_child_11_12/obesity_child_11_12.pdf

Hagell A, Coleman J, Brookes F (2013) Key data on adolescence 2013. The Association for Young People's Health (AYPH), London

Hart R (1992) Children's participation. From tokenism to citizenship. UNICEF International Child Development Centre, Florence

Ho TC, Yang G, Wu J, Cassey P, Brown SD, Hoang N, … Duncan LG (2014) Functional connectivity of negative emotional processing in adolescent depression. J Affect Disord 155:65–74

Hollis C, Martin J, Amani S, Cotton R, Denis M, Lewis S (2014) Technological innovations in mental healthcare. Annual report of the Chief Medical Officer 2013. Public Mental Health Priorities: Investing in the Evidence. Department of Health, London

Kazdin AE, Blase SL (2011) Rebooting psychotherapy research and practice to reduce the burden of mental illness. Perspect Psychol Sci 6(1):21–37. doi:10.1177/1745691610393527

Kroemer KHE (2005). Design for children and adolescents. 'Extra-Ordinary' ergonomics: how to accommodate small and big persons, the disabled and elderly, expectant mothers, and children. CRC Press, pp 175–198

Lang AR (2012). Medical device design for adolescents. PhD, University of Nottingham, UK

Lang AR, Martin JL, Sharples S, Crowe JA (2009). Enabling adolescents to participate in the design and improvement of medical devices. In: Paper presented at the International Ergonomics Association, 17th World Congress on Ergonomics., Beijing, China

Lang AR, Martin JL, Sharples S, Crowe JA (2013) The effect of design on the usability and real world effectiveness of medical devices: a case study with adolescent users. Appl Ergon 44(5):799–810

Lang AR, Martin JL, Sharples S, Crowe JA (2014) Medical device design for adolescent adherence and developmental goals: a case study of a cystic fibrosis physiotherapy device. Patient Preference Adherence 8:301–309. doi:10.2147/Ppa.S59423

Luxton DD, McCann RA, Bush NE, Mishkind MC, Reger GM (2011) mHealth for mental health: integrating smartphone technology in behavioral healthcare. Prof Psychol Res Pract 42(6):505–512. doi:10.1037/a0024485

Macvean A, Robertson J (2012). iFitQuest: a school based study of a mobile location-aware exergame for adolescents. In: Paper presented at the proceedings of the 14th international conference on Human-computer interaction with mobile devices and services, San Francisco, California, USA

Matthews M, Doherty G, Sharry J, Fitzpatrick C (2008) Mobile phone mood charting for adolescents. Br J Guid Couns 36(2):113–129. doi:10.1080/03069880801926400

McDonagh JE (2000) The adolescent challenge. Nephrol Dial Transplant 15(11):1761–1765. doi:10.1093/ndt/15.11.1761

Michaud PA, Suris JC, Viner R (2004) The adolescent with a chronic condition. Part II: healthcare provision. Arch Dis Child 89(10):943–949. doi:10.1136/adc.2003.045377

Nasi G, Cucciniello M, Guerrazzi C (2015) The role of mobile technologies in health care processes: the case of cancer supportive care. J Med Internet Res 17(2), e26. doi:10.2196/jmir.3757

NICE (2008) Attention deficit hyperactivity disorder: diagnosis and management. NICE Guidelines. Retrieved October, 29, 2015, from https://www.nice.org.uk/guidance/cg72

NIMH (1999) Multimodal Treatment of Attention Deficit Hyperactivity Disorder (MTA) Study. Retrieved October 29, 2015, from http://www.nimh.nih.gov/funding/clinical-research/practical/mta/multimodal-treatment-of-attention-deficit-hyperactivity-disorder-mta-study.shtml

OFCOM (2015) The communications market report 2015. August 6th 2015. Office of Communications, London.

PEGASO (2015) Pegaso fit for future. Retrieved December 4, 2015, from http://pegasof4f.eu/home

PEW (2013) Teens and technology 2013. Retrieved June 5, 2015, from http://www.pewinternet.org/files/old-media//Files/Reports/2013/PIP_TeensandTechnology2013.pdf

Punch S (2002) Research with children – the same or different from research with adults? Childhood 9(3):321–341

Simons L, Craven M, Martin J (2015). Learning from the labs volume 2: evaluating effectiveness, lessons and reflections. Retrieved from http://www.innovationlabs.org.uk/wp-content/uploads/2015/04/Learning-from-the-Labs-Volume-2-Exec-Summary-of-Evaluating-Effectiveness.pdf

Simons L, Valentine AZ, Falconer C, Groom M, Daley D, Craven MP, Young Z, Hall C, Hollis C (2016) Developing mhealth remote monitoring technology for attention deficit hyperactivity disorder: a qualitative study eliciting user priorities and needs. JMIR mHealth uHealth 4(1):e31.

Steinberg L (2008) A social neuroscience perspective on adolescent risk-taking. Dev Rev 28(1):78–106. doi:10.1016/j.dr.2007.08.002

Stewart-Brown S, Tennant A, Tennant R, Platt S, Parkinson J, Weich S (2009) Internal construct validity of the Warwick-Edinburgh Mental Well-being Scale (WEMWBS): a Rasch analysis using data from the Scottish Health Education Population Survey. Health Qual Life Outcom 7. doi:Artn 1510.1186/1477-7525-7-15

Thomas N, O'Kane C (1998) The ethics of participatory research with children. Child Soc 12(5):336–348

Ulicsak M (2010). You can learn your parents are immature: an analysis of what learning can result from family video gaming.In: Proceedings of the 4th European conference on games based learning, pp 403–411

USCB (2012) Age and sex composition in the United States: 2012. Retrieved October 29, 2015, 2015, from https://www.census.gov/population/age/data/2012comp.html

Viner R, Macfarlane A (2005) Health promotion. BMJ 330(7490):527–529. doi:10.1136/bmj.330.7490.527

YM (2015) Mental health statistics. Retrieved October 29, 2015, from http://www.youngminds.org.uk/training_services/policy/mental_health_statistics

Chapter 5
Designing Interactive Technologies with Teenagers in a Hospital Setting

Maja van der Velden, Margaret Machniak Sommervold, Alma Culén, and Britt Nakstad

Abstract This chapter describes a design process with teenagers with chronic health challenges. The design activities were related to two main themes, the transition from paediatrics to adult healthcare and patient-oriented social networking, and were implemented with a group of young patients who were members of the Youth Council, an advisory body to the hospital. We describe two design strategies, Design Stations and Continuous Participation Platform. Design Stations facilitate a design process that uses the time with the teens effectively and caters also to the teens' creativity and attention span. The Continuous Participation Platform contributes to maintaining consistency and continuity between the Design Station meetings. The process consisted of four design workshops, which took place in a hospital, and online activities in between these workshops. Nine small research projects were implemented, using a range of diverse participatory methods and tools. In the chapter we analyse and discuss the results using the SHARM framework, our Participatory Design methodology for designing with and for teenagers with chronic health challenges. SHARM focuses on *situation-based action, having a say, adaptability, respect*, and *mutual learning*. We found that our participants switch between their identity as a patient and as a teenager. Building and strengthening a third identity, namely that of a co-designer, may further improve the design efforts when designing with this particular group of participants.

M. van der Velden (✉) • M.M. Sommervold • A. Culén
Department of Informatics, University of Oslo,
Blindern, N-0316, P.O.Box 1080, Oslo, Norway
e-mail: majava@ifi.uio.no

B. Nakstad
Department of Pediatrics and Adolescent Medicine, Akershus University Hospital, Lørenskog, Norway

Institute for Clinical Medicine, University of Oslo, Oslo, Norway

© Springer International Publishing Switzerland 2016

L. Little et al. (eds.), *Perspectives on HCI Research with Teenagers*,
Human–Computer Interaction Series, DOI 10.1007/978-3-319-33450-9_5

5.1 Introduction

Teenagers[1] with chronic health challenges aren't very different from other teens, but they may experience their teenage years quite differently. During our interviews with teenagers in the Children's Hospital of Eastern Ontario, Canada (van der Velden and El Emam 2013), and Akershus University Hospital in Norway, we learned that teenage patients might spend long periods away from their family, friends, and peers at school because of hospital admissions. Their treatment, especially medication, may affect their bodies, such as weight gain or loss or their cognitive capacities, in undesired ways.

Health-Related Quality of Life (HRQoL) is an assessment of how an individual's well-being may be affected over time by a diagnosis (Khanna and Tsevat 2007). HRQoL is one way to provide insight in the physical, mental, emotional, and social functioning of people and there is ample research on the HRQoL of teenage patients, e.g., (de Wit et al. 2008; Smith et al. 2013). Van der Staa (2012) argues that HRQoL is of limited use if we want to capture the experience of *living with a chronic disease*. How much energy and time do teenagers spend in order to be able to stay on track in school or to 'look good' or establish new friendships and relationships? In general, teenage patients experience wellbeing in a similar way as non-patients. Quoting a Swedish study (Berntsson et al. 2007), van der Staa presents three factors that contribute to teenagers with chronic health challenges feeling 'good': "'a feeling of acceptance if illness/disability as a natural part of life', 'a feeling of support', and 'a feeling of personal growth'" (2012, p.24). Taylor et al. (2008) implemented a literature review and found the following themes that teenagers with chronic health challenges deem important for their wellbeing: (i) developing and maintaining friendships; (ii) being normal/getting on with life; (iii) the importance of family; (iv) attitude to treatment; (v) experiences of school; (vi) relationship with the healthcare professionals; and (vii) the future.

The KULU project, based at the Department of Informatics at the University of Oslo, focuses on the design and use of interactive technologies in support of the independence and self-determination of teenagers and young adults with chronic health challenges. KULU is a Norwegian acronym and stands for *cool technologies for youth with long-term health challenges*. We focus in particular on supporting young patients in living independently and on the transition from paediatric to adult healthcare. This transition is broadly defined as the "purposeful, planned movement of adolescents and young adults with chronic physical and medical conditions from child-centered to adult centered health care systems" (Blum 1993, p. 570. During this process, young patients prepare themselves to take on responsibility for their condition and treatment. Good transitions are needed to ensure a continuum of care

[1] The young people participating in the design workshops discussed in this chapter were between 14 and 20 years old. Teenagers and young adults is a more comprehensive way to address this group of participants. However, the design activities were focusing on the transition of teenage patients to adult healthcare, which takes place around their 18th birthday. In this text, we therefore prefer to use the term teenagers.

and to aid patients in developing skills for being independent and autonomous in the context of health care systems.

KULU consists of a multidisciplinary group of researchers and our objective is to research and design *cool* technologies, using participatory and visual methodologies. We actively involve bachelor and master students in research and design activities with young patients, because they have a more current experience of what is perceived as *cool* by the teenage population. The concept of *cool* represents not only the properties of technologies and designs, but first and foremost a commitment to the interests and needs of the young patients. As a socially constructed concept, *cool* relies on the subjective *knowingness* belonging to the teenage population. In the context of design, *cool* places the young participants in an expert position that is compatible with the values of Participatory Design (van der Velden and Mörtberg 2014).

In December 2012, the Akershus University Hospital (Ahus) in Norway established a Youth Council consisting of 12 young patients between 14 and 20 years old. The purpose of the Youth Council is to advise the hospital on how to improve services to young patients. One of the members expresses her interest to be part of this Council as follows: "*I have stayed in the hospital for a long time and experienced that it isn't so easy for youth, because we are in between children and adults. We can improve on how to keep the patients active while staying in the hospital, share experiences, and engage them a bit more" (girl, 15).* In the Spring of 2013, Ahus and the KULU project discussed the possibility of working together with the Youth Council and in the Fall of 2013 we organised the first of four design workshops.

This chapter will address our design activities with the Ahus Youth Council in the period 2013–2015. The Youth Council participants had expressed several wishes for interactive technologies. Many of those wishes were related to digital communication with their health care providers. The Ahus hospital didn't support such communication, thus this line of inquiry was not explored in our design activities. Another set of wishes related to self-management. The participants mentioned a calendar for consultations, overview of hospital and doctor visits, transition app, and a medical dictionary for young patients. A third set of wishes was related to online communication, such as chat, blogging, and online social networking.

In our research and design project, we organised these wishes into two themes, *Transition* and *Patient-oriented Social Networking* (see also Table 5.1). Each theme consisted of several small design projects and master students implemented the majority of projects. In the *Transition* theme we implemented five design projects and in the *Patient-oriented Social Networking* theme we implemented four design projects.

The nine design projects were implemented in four design workshops, two online prototype evaluations, and three email-based questionnaires. The workshops took place at the hospital and were attended by an average of seven members of the Youth Council. Ten different Youth Council members participated in the workshops, five boys and five girls, between 14 and 21 years old. Their diagnosis varied, such as different types of cancer, Crohn's disease, diabetes, etc. Two hospital staff members, one of which is an author of this chapter, supervised the whole process.

Table 5.1 Methods used during the workshops divided according to main themes and subthemes

Main theme	Subtheme	Methods	Workshop (W)
Transition	Transition app	Brainstorming	W1, W2, W3, W4
		Prototype testing (paper, Axure, InVision)	
	Transition game	Card sorting	W4
	Timelines	Design and drawing session	W3, W4
		Work with prototype (paper)	
	Health rights	Evaluation of paper prototypes	W3, W4
		Mapping interviews using paper-based tools	
	Transition cards	Card sorting	W2
Patient-oriented social networking	User authentication	Future workshop	W3, W4
		User-testing using Leap Motion	
	Privacy settings	Card sorting	W1, W2
		Paper-prototyping	
		Cool arrow	
	Terms and conditions	Cooperative prototyping	W1, W2
		Prototype testing	
	Cool functions of a SNS	Cool Wall	W1

The KULU team consisted of three researchers, three of the authors of this chapter, and seven master students; three to four master students and two researchers attended a workshop. Eight master students have now successfully completed their master studies, submitting a master thesis written on their design activities with the Youth Council (KULU 2015). Besides being useful for the KULU project, we believe that the cooperation with students has also high educational value.

5.1.1 Teenage Patients

The teenage years, or adolescence, are characterised by rapid changes, physically, psychologically, as well as socially (Mulye et al. 2009). These changes include puberty, pubertal growth spurts, changes in body stature and proportions to adult appearance, and changes in the central nervous system and other organ systems. Increases in verbal capacity and improved cognitive ability to more abstract thinking are a prerequisite to assess future consequences of their actions and events. Impulse control and recognition of moral and universal laws gradually increases. Personal identity and independence of parents develop gradually, and lasting friendships and intimate relationships outside the family are established. The adolescent develops to reach a meaningful and responsible life as an adult.

Personal Quality of Life, Life Expectations, and Beliefs Adolescence is a vulnerable time for everyone, especially when it comes to amorous relationships, how one's body is shaped and its proportions, personal appearance, popularity among peers, and performance in school, sports, and social life. Every teenager meets these challenges, but those with chronic disease have additional problems such as pain, restrictions, and concerns because of their disease (Barlow and Ellard 2006). A growing number of children are born prematurely. Some of them develop various chronic diseases and survive into the teenage and adult years (McLaughlin et al. 2008). We know that their quality of life is related to subjective experience in different life situations, which may be more complicated for them than for others.

Young people with chronic illness and/or disabilities often express the needs and wishes for how they should be treated by parents, healthcare providers, and everyone else with statements such as "Treat me like a human being", "Do not treat me like I'm different", and "Do not force me" (Britto et al. 2004; Michaud et al. 2007, p.8). This points out that young people with chronic diagnoses do not feel fully respected and treated as equally as compared to other young people. Self-esteem and a good relationship with parents are associated positively with teenage patients' quality of life and happiness. Lack of these are associated with depression and anxiety (Cheng and Furnham 2003).

Life with a chronic disease may be felt like a constant switching between a struggle against and adaptation to an uncertain daily life and an unpredictable life in the future (Michaud et al. 2007). The perception of the body can be described along a continuum of limitations to freedom governed by the disease. The teens may experience relations with other people varying from being included, feeling closeness, accepted and belonging, to be put off by the lack of precisely these emotional qualities. Life sometimes feels like a fight with or against the disease and a positive or negative self-image. There are also unpredictable variations in the disease itself and often invisible symptoms that could lead to problems being believed and included among their peers.

A key aspect may be a strong desire to be "normal" and care for themselves on an equal footing with the comrades, e.g., (van der Velden and El Emam 2013). A feeling of weakness and being different may vary both individually and over time, but through adolescence, most learn to cope with the disease and comply with the limitations the disease gives them.

The young person's self-esteem and self-worth is affected by the responses from friends, parents, teachers, and recreation leaders, and are linked to what these people define as important or less important to be successful. Physical appearance and being accepted into the circle of friends, or having an intimate relationship, are perceived as important factors for self-esteem. The strong importance of their surroundings, in addition to living with an illness, greatly affects the lives of adolescents and their health and wellbeing (Barlow and Ellard 2006).

Treatment and Responsibility Young people manage disease and treatment very differently. It is not uncommon that teenagers manage their chronic illness worse than during their childhood. Chronic diseases may require complex treatment regimens. Often medications must be taken many times daily, diet and exercise may be required or there are restrictions on activity. Some have painful or difficult medical procedures. Treatment can lead to major disruptions in daily life, with regular appointments with the doctor and hospital, and frequent admissions to hospital meaning absence from school.

During their childhood, parents are responsible, but young people are gradually taking over this responsibility for monitoring their treatment and for dealing with the stress and demands. Also, adolescents with chronic illness, compared to those without, have many additional challenges that require cognitive capacity and personal organisation. The transition to responsibility for treatment should therefore start gradually during the teenage years. In Norway and Canada, the transition to adult health care takes place when the young patient becomes 18 years old.

Young patients can play an important role in advising hospitals on how to support them in the transition from family-oriented paediatric health care to individual-oriented adult health care. For this purpose, advisory bodies consisting of teenage and young adult patients have been established at departments for paediatrics and adolescent medicine in Norway, Canada, and other countries.

5.1.2 Participatory Design with Teenagers

The KULU project is based at the Alma Mater of Kristen Nygaard, one of the founders of participatory design methodology applied in the KULU project. Participatory Design (PD) is based on a set of values and a collection of design practices for involving future users as co-designers in the design process (see Fig. 5.1) (van der Velden and Mörtberg 2014). PD's fundamental values of *having a say*, *mutual learning*, and *situated action*, which first emerged during Nygaard's involvement with the Norwegian Union of Iron and Metal workers in the early 1970s, are central in the KULU project's design perspective (KULU 2015).

Having a say refers to giving the future users of a technological design decision-making power in the design practice. This implies a design practice based on equalising power relations and a commitment to democratic practices (Kensing and Greenbaum 2012). *Having a say* is a process that covers all participatory design activities (see Fig. 5.1). It enables trust among all participants (researcher-designers and-co-designers) and facilitates mutual learning.

"Having a voice does not mean having a say", argue Bratteteig et al. (2012, p. 129). In many design projects involving teenagers, we found that they have a *voice*, but not a *say*. If we locate teens' participation in Druin's (2002) categorisation of the role of children in design, we see that they most often have the role of tester or informant, e.g., (Hingle et al. 2013; Pollock and Amaechi 2013). *Having a say* is based on the recognition that a design project needs different types of knowledge, competences, and expertise, and that these have to be respected. It also addresses the issue of power; it assumes that participants have equal access to the information that is needed to take part in the decision-making processes as the researchers (Bratteteig et al. 2012).

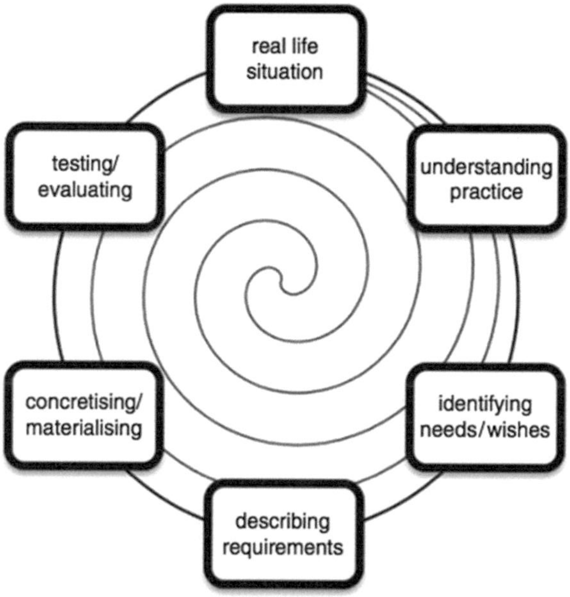

Fig. 5.1 Use-oriented design cycle (Reproduced from van der Velden and Mörtberg 2014)

The principle of *mutual learning* refers to the exchange of skills, competences, and experiences that takes place between researchers and participants. Researchers need to learn about and understand the particular use context in which, and for which, the PD process takes place, as well as the participants' needs and skills. The participants, in Nygaard's days the iron and metal workers, need to learn about design, technologies, and the skills of the researcher. The process of *mutual learning* is also a process of building trust in each other's commitment and skills. It also creates a shared language to support collaboration and consensus building around design decisions.

Situation-based action refers to the understanding that design activities should be located in the participants' particular work environment or other places or situations in which they undertake the activities that are the focus of the design process. *Situation-based action* enables mutual learning, as well as makes the embodiment and situatedness of work and activities visible. It focuses us on human practices within a particular environment, taking the intricate human-technology relations as a starting point for a deeper understanding of the design space (Suchman 2007).

While Nygaard and his colleagues collaborated with workers, we will focus in this review on the design collaboration between researchers and teenage patients. In the 1970s and 1980s, Participatory Design spread to different countries, e.g., the US (Greenbaum and Kyng 1991), and different work environments, e.g., the work of nurses (Bratteteig 2004). By the 1990s, PD also ventured out to non-workplaces and was used as a design methodology in urban planning, architecture, and sustainable development. At our own department, PD was applied to design free and open source District Health Information Systems software. The project started in the early 1990s and now spans a global network of participating universities, institutions, and organisations (Braa and Sahay 2012).

Hart (1987) wrote in 1987 that children and teens' "democratic responsibility can only be acquired through practice and involvement" (p. 217). He called for their inclusion in environmental planning and design, e.g., school yards and schools, in a PD-inspired manner. The first PD projects including non-adults in IT design focused on children (Oosterholt et al. 1996; Druin et al. 1998; Inkpen 1999). The first PD projects with teenagers often focused on the particular needs and interests of teenagers, such as identity and communication, e.g., (Bers 1999; Amin et al. 2005; Kaplan and Chisik 2005). The first Child Computer Interaction Design conferences in 2002 and 2003 played a central role in foregrounding the role of non-adults in design processes, including PD. In those early years, teenagers were seen as older children, not as a particular group of young persons with their own particular needs, skills, behaviour, and physical and cognitive development. This started to change slowly and today we can identify a clear focus on teenagers as specific group of people to design with and for, e.g., (Read et al. 2011; Fitton et al. 2013).

Most Participatory Design projects that engage teenage participants use methods that are also used with adult participants, such as paper prototyping and thinking aloud (Katterfeldt et al. 2012), lab-like environment (Björgvinsson et al. 2010), and future workshop. Hagen et al. (2012) published a list with 12 methods used in PD activities focussing on youth and mental health. All methods are also used in PD activities with adult participants.

Sometimes methods receive mixed appreciation. Katterfeldt et al. (2012) report that role play was an unpopular method among teenage participants, but Sustar et al. (2013) report on positive experiences with role play. The difference may be that this activity had well-known television programmes as setting:

> The *Cool Wall, X-Factor, Dragons' Den* and *Wallace and Gromit* approaches can be understood as efforts to frame the activities of a design process as language games familiar to our young people to serve the design work. The unwritten rules of these games provided participants with models of how they should act within the activities, e.g. rating popular appeal on the '*Cool Wall*', and presenting and defending their ideas in the '*Dragons' Den*'. These references enabled them to easily position themselves into required situations, which would otherwise be difficult to achieve. (p.10)

Also a game-like environment (Mazzone et al. 2008) was very appreciated by teens. This confirms other findings which state that most health interventions for youth are in the form of games, competition frameworks, avatars, and cartoon worlds, e.g., (Gerling et al. 2011; Miller et al. 2013; Khaled and Vasalou 2014).

5.1.3 Designing with Teenagers with Chronic Health Challenges

Our motivation to include young patients as participants in the design of interactive technologies is based on the recognition that young patients have the right to have a say in the decisions that influence their own wellbeing and their own health care.

Involving teenagers with chronic health challenges in the design of these technologies is also an important requirement for patient-centred design (Waller et al. 2006; Berwick 2009; Reis et al. 2011). Designing with young patients is perceived as difficult because of the extra challenges related to ethical issues and consent (Lang et al. 2012). Secondly, they may have self-esteem issues or not associate their personal identity with their diagnosis, or they may not want to participate on the basis of being a patient (Mack et al. 2009; Chira et al. 2010; van der Velden and El Emam 2013).

Kanstrup et al. (2008, p. 7), reporting on PD activities with people with diabetes, mentions that the teenage participants "emphasised the need for technology that is not just designed for illness or medical activities". Similarly, we made the decision not to accentuate in our methodology and methods the fact that they are patients. On the other hand, we needed to take into consideration that some of the participants may have physical or cognitive health challenges that may affect the choice of methods and how we implement the methods.

We organised the workshops on the same weekday, time, and location, as the regular meetings of the Youth Council. During the workshop activities, the participants switched between sharing their own expert knowledge, based on their personal experiences as a patient, and their more generalised knowledge of the experiences of young patients in general and which they felt they were representing in the Youth Council. This dual position strengthened their position as experts as well as gave them the possibility to participate as expert representatives of others, when they didn't want their participation to be solely based on the fact that they were young patients themselves.

In this chapter, we present and evaluate the methodological framework and design methods used in our participatory design activities with teenage patients. In the next section, we introduce the SHARM methodological framework, which guides the selection of methods used in the design activities with the Youth Council. In Sect. 5.3 we present the results of the design activities. In Sect. 5.4 we will discuss these results in the context of SHARM and offer a reflection on how we could have done things differently.

5.2 Methodological Framework for Working with the Youth Council

In this section we will present the SHARM methodological framework and provide an account of how we organised, implemented, and evaluated our research and design activities at the Hospital and its Youth Council. We will present the two design workshop methods we developed for working with this particular group of teenagers: *Design Stations* and the *Continuous Participation Platform*. Design Stations is a design workshop approach in which the participants rotate between different stations. At each station different design activities take place. The Continuous Participation Platform (CPP) is a set of activities that enable participants to be informed of project activities during and after their involvement in the workshops. The Platform consists of a project website, online prototyping, and printed materials. We will also present how we adapted and used existing Participatory Design methods, such as card sorting, future workshop, visualisations, and mapping exercises, in our design activities with the teens.

5.2.1 The SHARM Framework

SHARM presents our overall approach to participatory design activities with and for teenagers with chronic health challenges. The *SHARM* framework is based on five principles and combines insights from the literature and our own experiences in Participatory Design and research with teenagers:

- **Situation-based action**: Base the design activities in the teens' lived experiences and everyday lives
- **Having a say**: Create clear and real opportunities for teens to have decision-making power in the design process
- **Adaptability**: The design situation can change unexpectedly because of the teens' health situation; choose methods and approaches that allow for quick and easy adaptation to the teens' different and changing capabilities and conditions
- **Respect**: Teenagers want to be treated as experts of their own life and as capable of acting in their best interest
- **Mutual learning**: Choose methods and approaches that enable teens to learn as much from us as we do from them

This framework is based on three important Participatory Design principles, *Situation-based action*, *Having a say*, and *Mutual learning*. The principle of *Adaptability* results from our earlier experiences in designing with teenagers in the hospital (van der Velden and El Emam 2013; Sommervold and van der Velden 2015). Doctor rounds, treatment, and visitors can suddenly change what started as a well-planned design activity. There can also be a mismatch between the teen's interest in participation and his or her condition, which can sometimes deteriorate during a design activity. The principle of *Respect* has a particular meaning in our context. Our participants have to manoeuvre in an environment of adults (parents, health care staff), in which they often experience disempowerment. Young patients have expressed their wishes in how they wanted to be treated by adults, e.g., (CHEO 2011; Akershus universitetssykehus 2015). The principle of *Respect* incorporates theses wishes and stresses the fact that we meet the teenage patients as teenagers and young adults with a particular expertise about their own health situation, not as patients that happen to be teenagers.

5.2.2 The Participatory Design Process

Our colleagues Joshi and Bratteteig (2015) described their Participatory Design activities with elderly users as a fragmented process. The participants were not able to participate in all design meetings because of health reasons. The meetings were short because some participants were quickly tired or had reduced capacity to concentrate on different tasks. Certain strategies, such as a particular location of the activities, weekly presence of a researcher, and the visibility of the work made during the design meetings, created continuity. Secondly, the researchers designed small-enough tasks appropriate for the participants' competences and abilities. The researchers assembled the results of these tasks into the larger project.

Building upon these experiences, we evaluated our particular design setting, which consisted of a small group of participants with chronic health challenges and, possibly, limited capacity (energy, physical); a group of master students implementing their master projects; and the hospital location. Based on Joshi and Bratteteig's visualisation of the design process, we developed a design process that would enable task-oriented design meetings (*Design Stations*) and create continuity between the meetings (*Continuous Participation Platform*) (see Fig. 5.2).

Design Stations A Design Station is a stationary place where design activities are implemented. Participants rotate between the different Design Stations and thus participate in several design activities in a short period of time. One researcher (researcher or master student) is responsible for a Design Station and carries out design activities together with the participants. The number of participants in a Design Station can differ, dependent on the activity at hand.

During Workshop 1 (W1) we had four rooms at our disposal. This was convenient for the researchers, because the activities at the different stations did not disturb each other, enabling high quality audio recordings of the activities. This was different for the teenagers in wheelchairs, who needed to manoeuvre between chairs and narrow spaces, which proved to be tiring and time consuming. During the remaining three workshops, the four Design Stations were divided over two large rooms, limiting the amount of times the participants had to move around.

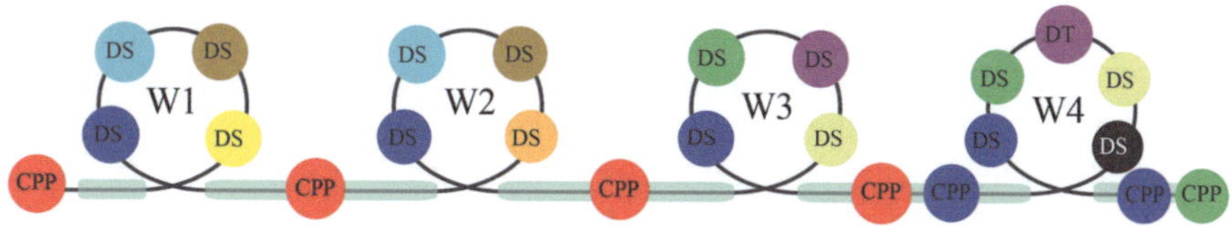

Fig. 5.2 Visualisation of our approach, inspired by Joshi and Bratteteig (2015): Each *circle* represents a workshop with coloured *dots* being the Design Stations (*DS*). The *highlighted line* visualises the Continuous Participation Platform (*CPP*), with each *dot* representing the different activities constituting the CPP. *Dots* with the same colour represent activities within one design project

Each design station presented the participants with a different design challenge. While carrying out the activities, the researcher(s) who had an empty time slot would take pictures and watch the time. Together with the representative from Ahus, we constantly observed and asked about the participants' wellbeing.

Throughout the four workshops, we applied and tested design methods from Participatory Design and user-centered design, which we appropriated and altered to fit our particular research context. The methods were appropriated and designed so that they consisted of short activities with immediate results, as suggested by Mazzone et al. (2008). Because the students would meet the Youth Council twice during their projects, they had to think about continuity in their choice of methods. It was important that the participants could see that their contributions were used in the next iteration of the design proposals and prototypes.

Continuous Participation Platform The Continuous Participation Platform or CPP consisted of a set of digital tools, which were meant to bridge the time between the workshops with the Youth Council. The CPP had three different forms: email correspondence, the KULU project website (kulu.no), and inVision, which would distribute clickable prototypes between all the participants: hospital staff, researchers, master students, and teenagers. The email correspondence functioned not only as means of planning the workshop and provision of information prior to the workshop, but also as a data gathering opportunity. We sent out surveys, invitations to prototype testing, and general questions about the needs of the members of the Youth Council, which we needed to consider in the planning of the workshops.

The KULU project website served as a general information site about the KULU research project, the members of the KULU team, their research interests, and the project results. We updated the site with the published articles, master theses, and reports we wrote about the workshops. In addition to presenting our interests and ourselves to the Youth Council, we wished to promote the principle of *having a say* through the KULU website. As many of the results of our work together with the Youth Council were publications, we wished to make them easily accessible to the Youth Council. We therefore urged them to check the site for updates. In addition we wrote a report to summarise our findings and activities in a more youth-friendly style.

The third component of the CPP was inVision. As the number of workshops with the Youth Council were limited, we intended inVision to become a space where the teens could participate throughout the whole design process and provide their feedback during each step of this process. inVision offers the possibility to leave comments, draw, and click through a prototype on the user's device.

The purpose of the CPP was to widen the spaces for participation for the Youth Council, by involving them in setting the agenda, communicate needs and ideas for design projects, follow their development, give feedback, and see their contribution. The CPP was intended as a tool to ensure that the principles of the SHARM framework were practiced in and beyond the workshops – both in time and in space.

5.2.3 Preparation and Implementation

We considered the opportunity of working with the Youth Council as a unique chance. The teenagers had personal experience in living with a chronic illness as well as a commitment to representing the larger community of teenage patients. In order to respect their restrictions, in terms of time and physical capacity, we carefully prepared the workshops. Prior to each workshop, we had at least two meetings together with the students, in which we tested and fine-tuned the design activities for the Design Stations. We discussed various methods and how they should be appropriated to fit with the research context. We would then decide on a number of design activities, the number of participants per activity, and the amount of time needed for each activity. This resulted in a schedule, which was then produced in several versions, based on different numbers of possible participants, because we never knew in advance how many of the Youth Council members would be able to participate in the workshop.

If needed, we tested the methods on each other and rehearsed the questions and activities. We used considerable amount of time during each of these preparation sessions to discuss the language and how they would ask the questions, as our design vocabulary could be difficult to understand for the teens. We also urged the students to prepare careful and thorough introductions to their design sessions, where they would explain the purpose of their study, why it was important, and why they needed the participation of the Youth Council. In addition, the students, who were preparing for their second workshop, had to explain how they had used the Youth Council's contributions from the first workshop in the development of new prototypes or new design questions.

All tools and materials used during the workshop were laminated, allowing for disinfection. This also contributed to the materials looking nice throughout all the design sessions.

5.2.4 Time Management and Schedule

The workshops coincided with the regular meetings of the Youth Council and had the same duration – a total of three hours. This time slot covered dinner, design activities and the breaks in between the activities.

The participants received nametags with their first name and a number that matched one of the participant numbers on the schedule. This helped the researchers to organise their notes and keep track of the participants when transcribing and coding their recordings, as we did not film the sessions. We used digital equipment to make audio recordings and photos. The storage and use of these data (audio and images) took place in accordance with the requirements of the Privacy Officer of Ahus and the Data Protection Authority for Research in Norway.

After each design session, the coordinator of the workshop (one of the researchers who was not involved in the design activities) would ring a bell to signalise the end of the session upon which the participants would switch stations or researchers would switch places. This proved itself to be very effective and helped us to inform the participants about the end of the session in a fun way.

Due to the short time we had with the Youth Council, we had to make use of each minute we had together. We used the dinner and cake breaks to give an introduction, present progress within the KULU project, and receive feedback on the workshop. At the end of each of the four workshops, we gave the participants a short survey asking questions about time management, their overall impression of the workshop, and any other feedback the youth might have related to our collaboration. Feedback related to time management was very positive. The participants thought it was fun to be able to do a lot of different things and because they had limited time at each station, they reported that they never got the time to get bored or tired of the design activities.

5.2.5 Methods

We used a variety of methods during the workshops. In this section we will briefly present the methods organised by the two main themes of the workshops, *transition* and *patient-oriented social networking* (see Table 5.1). The subthemes represent the projects and research interests of the researchers and master students.

Transition One of the main tasks of the Youth Council is representing young patients in the hospital's efforts toward making the hospital more youth-friendly and facilitating good transition processes. A few members of the Youth Council had already undergone transition and highlighted it as a major life event for young patients with chronic health challenges. Five design projects focused on transition:

Transition App During Workshop 1 (W1), one project focused on identifying functions for a transition app. After a discussion on transition and the challenges related to this particular event in the patients' lives, the participants took part in a brainstorming session in which they were asked to write down their ideas for functions of a mobile application that would support young patients during their transition to adult health care. During the same session, the ideas were organised into two categories: "*Cool to have*" and "*Must have*". This exercise involved all the participants who were present at the workshop. After the workshop, the findings were analysed and a prototype was created using the Axure prototyping tool (see Fig. 5.3). Screenshots of the prototype were printed and laminated. During W2, the participants explored this prototype digitally and on paper. The printed screenshots were used to discuss the various functions and the feedback was used to select the most attractive designs.

Fig. 5.3 First iteration of the Transition app

Fig. 5.4a Transition app: testing with the Youth Council during W3

The design and insights from W1 and W2 were further developed and implemented into a new and high-resolution prototype, which was printed out and presented in W3. The focus was now on the visual design and the look and feel of the transition app (see Fig. 5.4a). The participants explored several visual designs, which allowed them to choose the ones they liked best and also to see the design suggestion as something that could be changed, thus inviting a discussion of new functions and features.

As part of the CPP, the last iteration of the work with the transition app was introduction on inVision (http://www.invisionapp.com/). We implemented the feedback from W3, including new design ideas, into our visual design, which we published in the inVision online prototyping tool. It was then possible to click through the app to get an idea of how it worked and its usability. During W4, we explained the purpose of this prototype to the Youth Council and how they could give us feedback before we would develop it in to an actual app (see Fig. 5.4b). A week after W4, we sent out an email with a link to the online prototype and an online survey containing questions about their experiences with the prototype. This concluded the transition app design project with the Youth Council.

Fig. 5.4b Transition app: the three main functions: calendar, moodLine, and checklists

The Transition Game This project focused on the design of a game to support young patients in transition. During W4, we investigated the purpose and game style of the Transition Game. Three brainstorming sessions with 2–3 participants were implemented, using specially designed inspiration cards to aid the participants in explaining the desired properties and ideas for the game. The participants organised the cards into the components a transition game must have and shouldn't have.

Timeline This project was dedicated to the design of a timeline as a visualisation of different aspects of young patients' lives. The underlying assumption was that such a visualisation might be motivational or informative for the users. Groups of 2–3 teens participated in paper-prototyping sessions; they drew timelines and included aspects of their lives that they would like to be able to track over time. The approach was divergent and hence did not focus on a technology that would mediate the design, but rather on understanding the teens' ideas of a timeline. The analysis of the drawings resulted in a prototype of a mobile application, which was presented at the next workshop, W4 (see Fig. 5.5). During this workshop, the participants worked with paper prototypes and drew on it, thus providing more understanding of the role of timelines in the lives of young patients. The final, high fidelity, prototype was implemented using the inVision. Together with a questionnaire, a link to this downloadable prototype was sent to the Youth Council for evaluation.

Health Rights As young patients grow older, their rights as a patient change. For example, at the age of 16, patients can choose to visit their doctors on their own and make independent decisions related to their treatment. It is important that patients are aware of their legal rights. However documents outlining their rights tend to be a boring and unattractive read for teenagers. This project focused on presenting

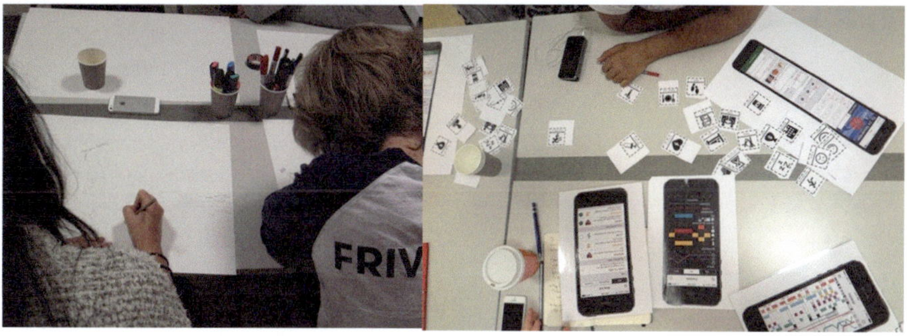

Fig. 5.5 Timelines: paper prototyping (W3) and testing of the prototype (W4)

health rights in such a way that it triggered *curiosity*. The concept of curiosity guided the choice of methods. Two interviewing sessions were implemented with 2–3 participants, using examples of information sites to discuss what triggers curiosity. In W4, the focus was on the teens' information interests and how such information should be presented, using sorting of quotes on pieces of paper and design suggestions containing health rights (see Fig. 5.6).

Transition Cards During W2, we wished to test a card-based method we had developed to investigate the transition process from a patient perspective. In groups of four participants, we asked the teens to explain their expectations and experiences surrounding transition through specifically designed cards covering four themes: *people, things, skills,* and *feelings*. The participants would choose three cards in each theme before giving the cards to the next person (see Fig. 5.6). Each of the cards would be then be placed under each of the time-periods constituting transition: *pediatrics (13–17), 18* (the age for transition in Norway), and *adult medicine* (18–25). We did not have the time for a full discussion of the cards. We were more interested in the Youth Council's opinion on whether this was an appropriate method to encourage talking about transitions with young patients and how it was best implemented. We discussed the method and the teens answered a short survey about what could have been done differently.

Patient-Oriented Social Networking This theme emerged from the Youth Council's interest in online communication and social media and the KULU project's earlier work on patients and social media. Based on the experiences in Canada with Upopolis, a patient Social Networking Site (SNS) for young people between the ages of 6 and 18, we designed a prototype for a *cool* patient-oriented SNS for teenage patients in Norway – Sprinklr (Machniak 2013). Our design activities were related to the design of the different functions and components of Sprinklr. The purpose of these activities was contributing to the body of research on patients and social media by providing research on different aspects of a patient-oriented SNS, which was designed and investigated in a Participatory Design perspective.

Fig. 5.6 Health rights and testing of the transition cards

Cool Functions of a SNS During the first workshop we engaged the members of the Youth Council in short, individual interviews using the Cool Wall (Culén and van der Velden 2013; Machniak 2014). The interviews lasted for ten minutes and added to the data we already had collected in both Norway and Canada. The purpose of this exercise was to map the *coolness* of the social networking site (SNS) functions and their relevance in the design of a closed SNS for teenagers with long-term health challenges. The participants were asked to place icons attached to magnets into five categories on the Cool Wall, which was a magnetic whiteboard (see Fig. 5.7). The categories were *super cool, cool, neutral, not cool,* and *seriously uncool.* Out of the total of 36 magnets, the participants were asked to choose a total of twelve magnets; six magnets representing already existing SNSs, and six magnets representing functions often found on SNSs, and explain their choices.

User Authentication Alternative and *cool* ways for logging in was another SNS-related project. During a Future Workshop in W3, the Youth Council came up with many ideas, the majority suggesting user authentication using behavioural biometrics. As a result, the participants were invited in W4 to further develop the idea of using hand gestures and games to log in on various services with the use of Leap Motion (see Fig. 5.7).

Privacy Settings This project had as a goal to design *cool* privacy settings for the closed, patient-oriented Social Networking Site (SNS). During W1, the participants carried out three activities. The first activity was a card-based method where the participants sorted pictures representing different levels of intimacy (profile pictures, holiday pictures, and pictures from parties) into five categories: *public, friends of friends, friends, close friends,* and *only me.* The next activity was attaching colours to the different contacts on a SNS in order to explore how colours can be utilised in design of privacy settings for teenagers. The third activity was paper prototyping where the participants could design privacy settings by drawing and using ready-made icons. Based on the analysis of the results, several paper-based prototypes were developed, which were evaluated in WP2, using the *Cool Arrow* (see Fig. 5.8). The participants placed the cards containing suggestions on the arrow, which functioned as a scale with *cool* and *uncool* being the outer points on the arrow.

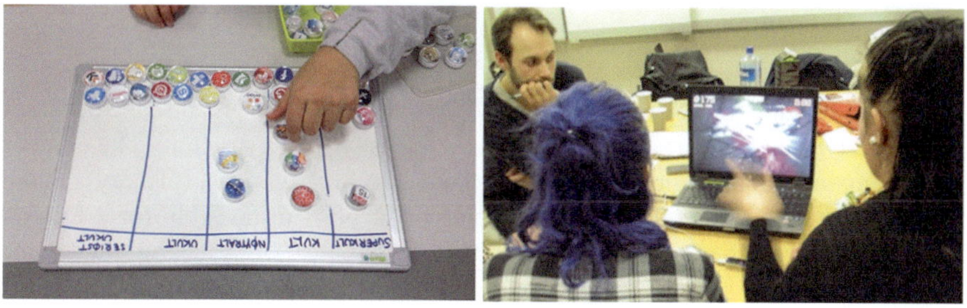

Fig. 5.7 Cool Wall and testing of Leap Motion for user authentication

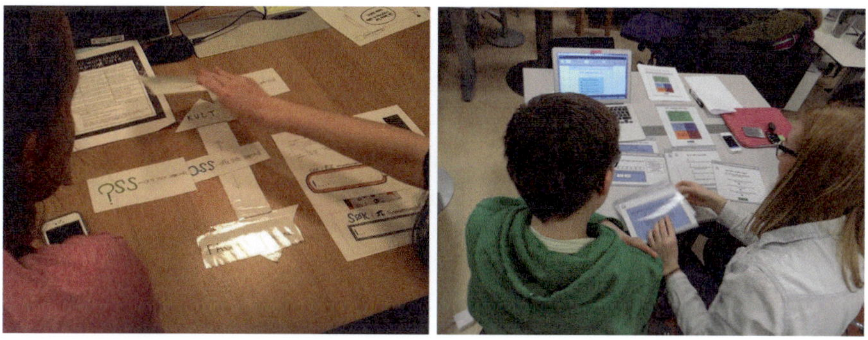

Fig. 5.8 Cool arrow and term and conditions

Terms and Conditions This project explored how playful design could be applied in the design of privacy terms and conditions for a patient-oriented SNS. The participants engaged in semi-structured interviews and cooperative prototyping. They received a set of symbols and textboxes, which they could use to design terms and conditions they would actually read. The analysis of the data resulted in a prototype, which presented the terms and conditions of use of the patient-oriented SNS as a quiz with statements which the users had to mark as true or false. During W2, the participants commented on the prototype, which consisted of paper screen shots and an interactive digital prototype, and contributed with ideas how the prototype could be improved (see Fig. 5.8).

5.3 Results

When we look at the overall production, the cooperation with the Youth Council resulted in eight master theses, several publications, as well as many important insights and findings, which helped us to produce new methods, tools, designs, and prototypes. In this section we will organise the findings according to the two design strategies, *Design Stations* and *Continuous Participation Platform*.

5.3.1 Design Stations

During each of the four workshops we used Design Stations to organise the different design activities. The participants adapted quite easily to this structure. The number of participants per Design Station varied from 1 to 8 participants (plenary). There was always one researcher (master students or faculty) responsible for a Design Station, while other researchers would contribute with taking notes or photographs.

The Design Stations were responsible for almost all design results. These results are organised per theme:

Transition The transition project has elicited the most developed prototype and prepared the ground for our on-going research (see Table 5.2). The project on the transition app alone has resulted in several prototypes of varying fidelity and resolution and is now available as a finished product, the KOOLO app, for both the iOS and Android platform.

Patient-Oriented Social Networking Site The Patient-oriented SNS project has resulted in several insights about teenage patients and their use of social media, two low-fidelity prototypes, and one conceptual prototype (see Table 5.3).

Table 5.2 Findings *transition*

Project	Findings and results
Transition app	(a) The three most needed functions of a transition app are transition checklists, calendar for keeping health related appointments and reminders, and a mood tracker
	(b) A high fidelity prototype published on inVision
	(c) The need for personalisation through colours
	(d) Only three participants evaluated the app on inVision.
Transition game	Card sorting is a productive and appropriate method in game design with teenagers.
Health rights	Set of 14 design principles for *design for curiosity*
Time line	(a) High-fidelity prototype called *Paths* published on inVision. The design focuses on mastery; allowing the user to set their personal goals, add pictures, and track goal completion on a timeline. The participants didn't deem logging pain, activities, socialness, etc. as desirable with regards to mastery.
	(b) A set of design guidelines for design for mastery.
	(c) The participants didn't use inVision to explore, and comment on, the application.
Transition cards	(a) Our Transition Cards, described extensively in (Sommervold and van der Velden 2015), is an effective method for mapping issues related to transition.
	(b) Contrary to findings that card sorting is best performed in groups, card sorting is best performed individually when personal issues, such as coping with health challenges, are involved.

Table 5.3 Findings *patient social networking site*

Project	Findings and results
Cool functions	(a) Chat, calendar, and pictures were rated as the coolest functions for a health-oriented SNS.
	(b) While privacy settings were not rated as the coolest function of a SNS, it was important that they were included.
	(c) Having an overview over different activities they could participate in and possibility of contacting healthcare professionals was also desirable for some of the participants.
	(d) Cool was often connected to functions being desirable or important.
	(e) Youtube, Facebook, Snapchat, Spotify, and Instagram were rated as the coolest social networking sites and apps. Due to the small number of magnets the participants could choose from, they focused on presenting their favourite and most used SNSs, hence leaving the *uncool* and *seriously uncool* categories empty.
User authentication	(a) Login can be cool and fun.
	(b) Teenagers are well aware of the risks related to log-in procedures.
	(c) Hand drawing gestures and drawing in the air are a potential alternative to passwords and codes.
	(d) Behavioural biometrics may inform user-friendly authentication procedures for users with physical or cognitive health challenges.
Privacy settings	(a) Teenagers with health challenges are concerned about their privacy.
	(b) Colours and cool design will help teenagers take care of their online privacy
	(c) The *Cool Arrow*, a new method for evaluation design suggestions.
Terms and conditions	(a) Principles from Playful and Persuasive Design contributed to the design of Terms and Conditions that teenagers were willing to read; they could ensure that the users would actually understand these rules.
	(b) An interactive prototype for web and mobile platforms.

5.3.2 *Continuous Participation Platform*

As presented above, the Continuous Participation Platform (CPP) consisted of the KULU website, emails, and prototypes on inVision. Expressed in numbers, the results are as follows:

- 2 prototypes on inVision
- 14 emails
- 6 respondents on colours-survey
- 3 respondents on the KOOLO app prototype on inVision
- 0 respondents on the Paths-prototype on inVision

These results were obtained in the periods between the workshops and were meant to create continuity in the design efforts when we were not able to meet face-to-face.

5.4 Discussion

The two design strategies, Design Stations and the Continuous Participation Platform (CPP), were central to the success of the project. The Design Stations facilitated a large amount of smaller projects, which produced a large amount of project results, as presented above. The Design Stations were tied together through the Continuous Participation Platform. Together they encompassed all project activities, forming a string of smaller processes (see Fig. 5.2), instead of one all-encompassing process (see Fig. 5.1). The two design strategies enabled us to create continuity and consistency in the research project as a whole and the particular design activities with the teenagers.

The Design Stations enabled smaller work tasks and short activities, allowing the participants to work on diverse tasks within the short time framework we had, and to contribute to various projects within one workshop meeting. Through the CPP we intended to create continuous communication and on-going design activities between the workshop meetings. The advantage of this approach was also that the participants needed to invest less time and energy in design activities than in a regular design process. In what follows, we will structure the discussion of the results according to the SHARM framework:

Situation-Based Action Design activities took form of face-to-face meetings (workshops with Design Stations) and online (Continuous Participation Platform through in-Vision prototypes, email, and questionnaires). While the workshop meetings took place at the hospital, where the teens could easily relate to their lives as patients, we have experienced that it was significantly harder to maintain continuous participation. The latter took place at the teens' homes, outside the workshop context. The participants had busy lives, juggling school and pastime activities. At home, their identity as patient and patient representative is not as dominant as in the hospital environment or during Youth Council meetings, where their identity as patient is part of their lived experience.

Although the members of the Youth Council were fully engaged during the workshops and provided invaluable insights and feedback, only a few members responded to our emails or worked with the prototypes using the in-Vision app. While online prototyping tools are of great value in commercial environments and distributed work places, we believe that for youth with health challenges, accessing these online tools from home is substantially different than it is in diverse work situations where these tools work well. Because of their dedicated participation during the workshops, we don't explain this as a case of *disengaged teenagers,* but rather as a finding supporting the importance of *situation-based action.*

Having a Say Working with prototypes facilitates idea communication and solicitation of new ideas, supporting *having a say* in design matters (Druin et al. 1998; Preece et al. 2015). The majority of the prototypes developed in the KULU projects were clickable and could be presented on either laptops or mobile devices. However, to minimise the risks related to technical difficulties during the workshops, all of the prototypes were printed out and laminated. This proved itself very useful and helpful in several ways. Firstly, even though the participants reported that presenting the prototypes on screen helped them to imagine and see how the design would look and feel like when implemented, the printed screenshots aided them in realising that the prototypes were not final and could be changed. Focusing on one screen at the time on paper allowed them to focus and comment on details and to be more specific in their feedback. Being technologically competent, they had no problems with understanding how the paper-based prototypes related to the ones on screen and could therefore comment on usability aspects. The prototypes were a valuable vessel to communicate that their voices were heard, and the teens expressed their contentment with the fact that their contributions were visible in the next iteration of prototypes. By seeing how important their contributions were, the teens were able to view themselves as experts and establish themselves as co-designers.

The teenagers were invited to have a say outside the workshop arena through the Continuous Participation Platform (CPP). This could also enable further adaptation of our methods to their changing capabilities and conditions. The CPP's online tools were however hardly used.

Adaptability The preparation sessions prior to the workshops ensured implementation of the *Adaptability* principle. Carefully planned time schedules, prepared to deal with a varying number of participants, contributed to the short duration of the design activities, but also allowed for adaptation to the changing conditions and capabilities of the participants. The time schedules also enabled researchers to engage with a varying number of participants at each station. Some stations included all participants at the same time, enabling the researchers to get input from the whole group at once, emulating focus groups, while others had a smaller number of participants (the smallest number of participants was one) enabling in-depth inquiry or walk-throughs.

Respect Both Design Stations and CPP were designed with respect for the participants' time and the realisation that their participation is based on real effort on their part. The CPP was seen as a tool ensuring that the participants could, at any time, have a say, giving them the opportunity to work with prototypes whenever they could. However, we believe that the limited response to this method is due to the fact that the home provides a different context, as explained above, making it harder to get back to being a patient. The Youth Council has expressed their respect for our work in several ways. Most rewarding for us, as researchers, was the fact that they came to our meetings full of eagerness to work and with appreciation for how their ideas were represented through new design suggestions and prototypes.

Mutual Learning Due to the pre-set time constrains, each of the design activities was short and focused. Each of the activities resulted in immediate and often tangible outputs – whether they were paper prototypes, or sorted cards. The participants were able to see the outcome of the activity and we discussed what we would do with these outcomes after the workshop. Hence the participants did not only learn about how designers work, or which methods they use, but in many cases learned and reflected over their own lives and experiences that they shared with the researchers.

When talking about cool technologies, the teens reflected on why they found some technologies cooler than other. When working with health rights, the participants reflected on their own knowledge and what they actually knew about patient rights, but were also made aware of other rights they had. Together we could use this knowledge to inform new ways of presenting information about patient rights. In addition, when we asked the Youth Council to evaluate the transition cards method, they were given a chance to learn about how methods are designed to help other teens to express their knowledge and needs in a meaningful way.

As all the projects were implemented within the KULU research project, the master students learned from their own experience related to designing with teens with health challenges, but also from each other. Sharing each other's experiences and discussing the plans for the design stations, facilitated the design of better methods and tools.

It goes without saying that we have learned a lot from the Youth Council, so we feel confident in proposing that we had achieved *mutual learning* in our workshops with this group of young people.

5.5 Reflections on the Design Strategy

In our design activities with the Youth Council we tried a project approach based on two design strategies that would enable us to create coherence in a design process that was fragmented, both in time as well as because of varying participation of the teenagers. Design Stations and the Continuous Participation Platforms (CPP) formed the basis for this approach. While the Design Stations were a success, we were not able to use the CPP to create the continuity between the workshops in the way that we envisioned it.

Evaluations of the design activities took place at the end of each workshop. The feedback we received from the participants was overwhelmingly positive. We didn't use the CPP for these evaluations. The response on the two invitations for engaging with design proposals on inVision was so minimal, that we weren't convinced that using the CPP for evaluating this lack of engagement would provide us with answers.

Our own evaluation of the CPP has led us believe that it was not the CPP itself that affected the number of responses, but the difference in identity the participants have during a workshop at the hospital and at home. During the workshop, they represented the Ahus Youth Council and, as such, young patients at Ahus. They had a shared identity as a teenager with a chronic health challenge and a member of the Youth Council. At home, they were teenagers who tried to live a life like anyone else – in spite of their particular health situation. Participating in online activities that would stress their identity as a patient, did not seem to have a priority while being at home.

In the literature we found explanations for such "identity switching" (Eschbach and Gómez 1998; Shih et al. 2011). We therefore concluded in our evaluation that we were not able to support the establishment of a new identity among the participants, namely that of a co-designer. This new identity could have encompassed their identity as teenager and as patient and, as such, could have formed a bridge between design activities at the hospital and at home. We realised that we didn't prepare any activities, during the first workshops, which would have enabled the participants to develop and strengthen their role as co-designers. We assume that if we had been more aware of the role identities play during the design process, the participants would have been more willing to take responsibility for the design process at home too.

Teenagers with chronic health challenges that are willing to participate in design processes are never numerous. They form a very heterogeneous group, but issues such as transition and social networking affect them all. Until now, the design community hasn't worked with issues related to transition. We hope that this chapter invites other researchers to look into health-related processes common to all chronically ill teenagers. We intend to continue working in this area of research and will use our design strategy in new KULU design projects. Based on the experiences with the Youth Council, we will need to work more consciously with the roles and identities of teens in the design process.

5.6 Conclusions

Participatory Design with teenagers with chronic health issues provides numerous challenges and opportunities. There is a broad range of challenges, from particular ethical challenges related to patient privacy and hospital security, to possible health risks related to participation in the design process, such as fatigue from the effort to come to the workshop or from activities during participation. The opportunities range from opening new application areas where user participation can help shape new services and products that impact youth, to possibilities that open for creating new design strategies, exemplified in this chapter by Design Stations and the Continuous Participation Platform.

We often visualise a design process as a holistic whole with a clear start and a clear finish, such as the use-oriented design approach we presented above (see Fig. 5.1). We found that a design process with vulnerable users, such as teenagers with chronic health challenges, may benefit from a series of smaller projects. We found that Design Stations were a fun and productive way to run several small projects simultaneously. The possible fragmentation of the design process can be counterbalanced with particular strategies that create continuity and consistency. These strategies need to be appropriate for the particular group of participants or co-designers. In our case, the strategy to continue the design process via email exchanges and an online design platform (inVision), as part of the Continuous Participation Platform, was not successful. A broader understanding of *situation-based action*, which doesn't focus solely on the fact that they are teenagers and patients, but which also looks at their role in the design process, may create a new kind of identity for the participant, namely that of co-designer. This identity may encompass the identities of teenager and patient and can provide the teenage participants with a stable and continuous role in the whole design process.

Acknowledgement We would like to acknowledge the important contribution of the young participants in our research and design projects to our understanding of the design of cool technology with and for teenagers with chronic health challenges. We would like to thank in particular the Youth Council (Ungdomsrådet) of Akershus University Hospital (Ahus) and the teenage patients at the Children's Hospital of Eastern Ontario (CHEO). We also would like to thank the staff of Ahus, CHEO, and the Electronic Health Information Laboratory (EHIL) at the CHEO Research Centre, for their support for our research.

References

Akershus universitetssykehus (2015) Ungdomsrådet på internasjonal HPH-konferanse, juni 2015. https://www.youtube.com/watch?v=izWTk5lqzbM. Accessed 2 Nov 2015

Amin AK, Kersten BTA, Kulyk OA et al (2005) SenseMS: a user-centered approach to enrich the messaging experience for teens by non-verbal means. In: Proceedings of the 7th international conference on human computer interaction with mobile devices & services. ACM, New York, NY, USA, pp 161–166

Barlow JH, Ellard DR (2006) The psychosocial well-being of children with chronic disease, their parents and siblings: an overview of the research evidence base. Child Care Health Dev 32:19–31. doi:10.1111/j.1365-2214.2006.00591.x

Berntsson L, Berg M, Brydolf M, Hellström A-L (2007) Adolescents' experiences of well-being when living with a long-term illness or disability. Scand J Caring Sci 21:419–425. doi:10.1111/j.1471-6712.2006.00490.x

Bers MU (1999) Zora: a graphical multi-user environment to share stories about the self. In: Proceedings of the 1999 conference on computer support for collaborative learning. International Society of the Learning Sciences, Palo Alto, California. http://dl.acm.org/citation.cfm?id=1150240.1150243. Accessed 2 Nov 2015

Berwick DM (2009) What "Patient-Centered" should mean: confessions of an extremist. Health Aff (Millwood) 28:w555–w565. doi:10.1377/hlthaff.28.4.w555

Björgvinsson E, Ehn P, Hillgren P-A (2010) Participatory design and "Democratizing Innovation." In: Proceedings of the 11th biennial participatory design conference. ACM, New York, NY, USA, pp 41–50

Blum RW (1993) Transition from child-centered to adult health-care systems for adolescents with chronic conditions. J Adolesc Health 14:570–576

Braa J, Sahay S (2012) Health information systems programme: participatory design within the HISP network. In: Routledge international handbook of participatory design. Routledge, New York, pp 235–256

Bratteteig T (2004) Making change: dealing with relations between design and use. PhD dissertation, University of Oslo

Bratteteig T, Bødker K, Dittrich Y et al (2012) Methods: organising principles and general guidelines for participatory design projects. In: Routledge international handbook of participatory design. Routledge, New York, pp 117–144

Britto MT, DeVellis RF, Hornung RW et al (2004) Health care preferences and priorities of adolescents with chronic illnesses. Pediatrics 114:1272–1280. doi:10.1542/peds.2003-1134-L

Cheng H, Furnham A (2003) Personality, self-esteem, and demographic predictions of happiness and depression. Personal Individ Differ 34:921–942. doi:10.1016/S0191-8869(02)00078-8

CHEO (2011) CHEO's youth forum – how we want to be treated. http://www.youtube.com/watch?v=NIZVsbfCw8M&feature=youtube_gdata_player. Accessed 2 Nov 2015

Chira P, Nugent L, Miller K et al (2010) Living profiles: design of a health media platform for teens with special healthcare needs. J Biomed Inform 43:S9–S12. doi:10.1016/j.jbi.2010.05.008

Culén AL, van der Velden M (2013) The digital life of vulnerable users: designing with children, patients, and elderly. In: Aanestad M, Bratteteig T (eds) Nordic contributions in IS research. Springer, Berlin/Heidelberg, pp 53–71

de Wit M, de Waal HAD, Bokma JA et al (2008) Monitoring and discussing health-related quality of life in adolescents with type 1 diabetes improve psychosocial well-being a randomized controlled trial. Diabetes Care 31:1521–1526. doi:10.2337/dc08-0394

Druin A (2002) The role of children in the design of new technology. Behav Inf Technol 21:1–25. doi:10.1080/01449290110108659

Druin A, Bederson B, Boltman A et al (1998) Children as our technology design partners. In: Druin A (ed) Morgan Kaufmann Publishers Inc., San Francisco, pp 51–72

Eschbach K, Gómez C (1998) Choosing hispanic identity: ethnic identity switching among respondents to high school and beyond. Soc Sci Q 79:74–90

Fitton D, Read JCC, Horton M (2013) The challenge of working with teens as participants in interaction design. In: CHI '13 extended abstracts on human factors in computing systems. ACM, New York, NY, USA, pp 205–210

Gerling K, Fuchslocher A, Schmidt R et al (2011) Designing and evaluating casual health games for children and teenagers with cancer. In: Anacleto JC, Fels S, Graham N et al (eds) Entertainment computing – ICEC 2011. Springer, Berlin/Heidelberg, pp 198–209

Greenbaum JM, Kyng M (1991) Design at work: cooperative design of computer systems. L. Erlbaum Associates, Hillsdale

Hagen P, Collin P, Metcalf C et al (2012) Participatory design of evidence-based online youth mental health promotion, intervention and treatment

Hart RA (1987) Children's participation in planning and design. In: David TG, Weinstein CS (eds) Spaces for children. Springer, New York, pp 217–239

Hingle M, Nichter M, Medeiros M, Grace S (2013) Texting for health: the use of participatory methods to develop healthy lifestyle messages for teens. J Nutr Educ Behav 45:12–19. doi:10.1016/j.jneb.2012.05.001

Inkpen KM (1999) Designing handheld technologies for kids. Pers Technol 3:81–89. doi:10.1007/BF01305323

Joshi SG, Bratteteig T (2015) Assembling fragments into continuous design: on participatory design with old people. Springer International Publishing, pp 13–29

Kanstrup AM, Bertelsen P, Glasemann M, Boye N (2008) Design for more: an ambient perspective on diabetes. In: Proceedings of the tenth anniversary conference on participatory design 2008. Indiana University, Indianapolis, IN, USA, pp 118–127

Kaplan N, Chisik Y (2005) Reading alone together: creating sociable digital library books. In: Proceedings of the 2005 conference on interaction design and children. ACM, New York, NY, USA, pp 88–94

Katterfeldt E-S, Zeising A, Schelhowe H (2012) Designing digital media for teen-aged apprentices: a participatory approach. In: Proceedings of the 11th international conference on interaction design and children. ACM, New York, NY, USA, pp 196–199

Kensing F, Greenbaum J (2012) Heritage: having a say. In: Routledge international handbook of participatory design. Routledge, New York, pp 21–36

Khaled R, Vasalou A (2014) Bridging serious games and participatory design. Int J Child Comput Interact 2:93–100. doi:10.1016/j.ijcci.2014.03.001

Khanna D, Tsevat J (2007) Health-related quality of life--an introduction. Am J Manag Care 13(Suppl 9):S218–S223

KULU (2015) KULU – cool technologies for youth with long-term health challenges. http://kulu.no/publikasjoner.php?lang=en. Accessed 2 Sept 2015

Lang AR, Martin JL, Sharples S et al (2012) Not a minor problem: involving adolescents in medical device design research. Theor Issues Ergon Sci:1–12. doi:10.1080/1463922X.2012.678910

Machniak M (2013) Sprinklr: Designing a "cool" health-oriented social networking site with and for teenagers

Machniak M (2014) In pursuit of cool and its implications for the design process. In: Strano M, Hrachovec H, Fragoso S, Ess C, van der Velden M (eds) Culture, technology, and communication: celebration, transformation, new directions. Oslo, pp 71–88

Mack R, Giarelli E, Bernhardt BA (2009) The adolescent research participant: strategies for productive and ethical interviewing. J Pediatr Nurs 24:448–457. doi:10.1016/j.pedn.2008.07.009

Mazzone E, Read JC, Beale R (2008) Design with and for disaffected teenagers. In: Proceedings of the 5th Nordic conference on human-computer interaction: building bridges. ACM, New York, NY, USA, pp 290–297

McLaughlin SE, Diener-West M, Indurkhya A et al (2008) Improving transition from pediatric to adult cystic fibrosis care: lessons from a national survey of current practices. Pediatrics 121:e1160–e1166. doi:10.1542/peds.2007-2217

Michaud P-A, Suris J-C, Viner R (2007) The adolescent with a chronic condition: epidemiology, developmental issues and health care provision. http://apps.who.int/iris/handle/10665/43775. Accessed 2 Nov 2015

Miller AD, Pater J, Mynatt ED (2013) Design strategies for youth-focused pervasive social health games. In: 2013 7th international conference on pervasive computing technologies for healthcare (PervasiveHealth). pp 9–16

Mulye TP, Park MJ, Nelson CD et al (2009) Trends in adolescent and young adult health in the United States. J Adolesc Health Off Publ Soc Adolesc Med 45:8–24. doi:10.1016/j.jadohealth.2009.03.013

Oosterholt R, Kusano M, de Vries G (1996) Interaction design and human factors support in the development of a personal communicator for children. In: Proceedings of the SIGCHI conference on Human Factors in Computing Systems. ACM, New York, NY, USA, pp 450–457

Pollock M, Amaechi U (2013) Texting as a channel for personalized youth support: participatory design research by city youth and teachers. Learn Media Technol 38:128–144. doi:10.1080/17439884.2013.756516

Preece J, Sharp H, Rogers Y (2015) Interaction design: beyond human-computer interaction. John Wiley & Sons

Read J, Fitton D, Cowan B et al (2011) Understanding and designing cool technologies for teenagers. In: Proceedings of the 2011 annual conference extended abstracts on Human factors in computing systems. ACM, New York, NY, USA, pp 1567–1572

Reis CI, Freire CS, Fernández J, Monguet JM (2011) Patient centered design: challenges and lessons learned from working with health professionals and schizophrenic patients in e-therapy contexts. In: Cruz-Cunha MM, Varajão J, Powell P, Martinho R (eds) ENTERprise information systems. Springer, Berlin/Heidelberg, pp 1–10

Shih M, Sanchez DT, Ho GC (2011) Costs and benefits of switching among multiple social identities. In: The psychology of social and cultural diversity. Wiley, Chichester, pp 62–84

Smith AW, Bellizzi KM, Keegan THM et al (2013) Health-related quality of life of adolescent and young adult patients with cancer in the United States: the adolescent and young adult health outcomes and patient experience study. J Clin Oncol 31:2136–2145. doi:10.1200/JCO.2012.47.3173

Sommervold MM, van der Velden M (2015) Transition cards: design a method with and for young patients. IADIS 10:2

Suchman L (2007) Human-machine reconfigurations: plans and situated actions, 2nd edn. Cambridge University Press, Cambridge

Sustar H, Bowen S, Dearden A et al (2013) Using popular culture to enable health service co-design with young people. In: EAD. European Academy of Design Conference, Gothenburg, Sweden

Taylor RM, Gibson F, Franck LS (2008) The experience of living with a chronic illness during adolescence: a critical review of the literature. J Clin Nurs 17:3083–3091. doi:10.1111/j.1365-2702.2008.02629.x

van der Velden M, El Emam K (2013) "Not all my friends need to know": a qualitative study of teenage patients, privacy, and social media. J Am Med Inform Assoc JAMIA 20:16–24. doi:10.1136/amiajnl-2012-000949

van der Velden M, Mörtberg C (2014) Participatory design and design for values. In: van den Hoven J, Vermaas PE, Poel I van de (eds) Handbook of ethics, values, and technological design. Springer, Dordrecht, pp 1–22

van Staa AL (2012) On your own feet: preferences and competencies for care of adolescents with chronic conditions. Instituut Beleid en Management Gezondheidszorg (iBMG)

Waller A, Franklin V, Pagliari C, Greene S (2006) Participatory design of a text message scheduling system to support young people with diabetes. Health Inform J 12:304–318. doi:10.1177/1460458206070023

Chapter 6
Using a Rich Pictures Approach for Gathering Students and Teachers Digital Education Requirements

Steve Love, Voula Gkatzidou, and Antonello Conti

Abstract The increasing pervasiveness of mobile technologies and the advent of Web 2.0 technologies such as ubiquitous digital media, networked communications and social media have transformed the way young people access information, create and share knowledge between each other. Twenty four co-design workshops were conducted (290 total participants) with one age-stratified sample (13–17 year olds) of young people from Higher Education establishments in three European countries. These workshops explored young people's views with regard to the design of cross-platform interactive learning frameworks that allow for ubiquitous, flexible and non-linear learning. A novel co-design workshop method was adopted that draws principles from participatory design, future workshop techniques and rich pictures. The data capture from the co-design workshops with young people were analysed using thematic analysis. Four over-arching design domain emerged: in-class interaction, home interaction, content creation and reporting affordances. From these design domains, 14 user design needs for future technology are described.

6.1 Introduction

The continual evolution of modern telecommunications media (e.g. broadband availability over wide area networks, mobile connectivity) has opened up new opportunities for accessing information, especially in relation to ubiquitous

S. Love (✉)
Digital Design Studio, The Glasgow School of Art,
The Hub, Pacific quay, Glasgow G51 1EA, Scotland, UK
e-mail: s.love@gsa.ac.uk

V. Gkatzidou
Department of Design, Brunel University, Michael Sterling 152, Uxbridge UB8 3PH, UK

A. Conti
Digitaria International SA, 16, rue Jean l'Aveugle, Luxembourg L-1148, Luxembourg

© Springer International Publishing Switzerland 2016

L. Little et al. (eds.), *Perspectives on HCI Research with Teenagers*,
Human–Computer Interaction Series, DOI 10.1007/978-3-319-33450-9_6

computing. Technological advances in ICT have allowed for a resource-rich environment and a learner-centred approach that can support different ways of learning, thinking and working across the curriculum, and facilitate new forms of participation. Young people are now often engaged with ICT usage outside the formal educational environment which is more sophisticated than usage inside school. Terms such as "digital natives" (Prensky 2001), "the "millenials" (Howe and Strauss 2003), "Generation Y" (Jorgensen 2003; Weiler 2005; McCrindle 2006), the "net generation" (Tapscott 1998), Google Generation (Rowlands et al. 2008) or the i-Generation (Rosen 2010) have been used to highlight the significance and important of new technologies within the lives of young people (Gibbons 2007).

These new technologies have been such a defining feature in the lives of younger generations and have changed the way young people communicate, socialise, create and learn. This has had profound implication for education and this new generation of pupils are said to prefer receiving information quickly, relying on communication technologies, often multitasking and having a low tolerance for lectures, preferring active rather than passive learning (Oblinger and Oblinger 2005). Research has also highlighted that this generation of technologically advanced pupils would be posing radical questions about the transformation of traditional forms of teaching and learning (Livingstone 2009; Jones and Shao 2011).

The advent of mobile and wireless technology has also led to a shift in technology-enhanced learning research from e-learning to m-learning. Sharples defined m-learning as the process of coming to know through conversations across multiple contexts amongst people and personal interactive technologies (Sharples et al. 2002). This definition encompasses the four central constructs of m-learning (pedagogy, technological devices, context and social interactions). In a review of m-learning Kukulska-Hulme (2009) indicated that research has focused on either the technical, pedagogical or social perspective of mobile learning. Vavoula et al. (2009) state that future work in this area should look at the inter-relationships between the usability, pedagogy and institutional requirements with the help of a formal framework. In addition, Bull et al (2008) state that teachers are currently limited in terms of "best practice" models available on how to effectively integrate social media into their teaching (e.g. how does one ensure that the content meets specific learning outcomes and address the time constraints of certain learning objectives as well addressing usability issues?).

In line with this, the aim of this work is to design a new cross-platform interactive learning framework which will allow students to engage in ubiquitous flexible, non-linear learning. This paper describes the methods and results of a study that examines the digital future of e- and m-learning by exploring the views of pupils from five secondary schools (in England, Luxemburg and Italy) in regards to the contribution of ICT to teaching and learning.

6.2 Background Research

Traditionally, young people's role in the design of new technology has been challenging as young children have a more difficult time verbalising their thoughts than adults, especially when it concerns abstract concepts (Piaget 1971) and much of what they say needs to be interpreted within the context of concrete experiences (Druin 1999). In early days the work was mainly about positioning young people as testers of technologies but more recently much of the focus of the group has shifted towards greater participation including design work with teenagers and longitudinal studies. The participation of teenagers in the research, design, and development of educational new technology has gained popularity in recent years, with methodological approaches ranging from their short-term involvement in the evaluation of near-complete products, to regular and frequent involvement throughout a product's development cycle. (Williamson 2003). A growing body of literature has emerged that discusses teenagers, technology and human computer interaction issues.

Ever since it was promoted by innovators in HCI (Druin 1997; Scaife et al. 1997; Carroll 2003), including children and young people in the design of new technologies, either as informants or design partners has been highlighted as beneficial in order to better understand users, to gather design ideas and to test out new concepts. There are four main roles that young people can play in the technology design process: user, tester, informant and design partner (Nesset and Large 2004) and research methods utilised vary depending on the role. Different traditions of participation evolved with predominant models involving young people in longitudinal co-design practices with adult participants, in an incremental process leading ideas into a design brief (Yip et al. 2013) and models involving them in short bursts of time, in order to capture their ideas and which will then be used as design inspiration by adult designers (Mazzone et al. 2008). Even though there has been considerable effort to address the practical and ethical concerns of children's participation (Read 2015), limited methodological advice has been published to date regarding the adaptation of HCI techniques and methods for children (Markopoulos and Bekker 2003). Therefore, the research work reported in this chapter seeks to add to the HCI methodological research literature by showing the added benefits in terms of design of including young users in the design process from the start of an application and service design project.

6.3 Method

The methodology used for this stage is design-based research (Herrington et al. 2007) that is defined as a 'series of approaches with the intent of producing new theories, artifacts and practices that account for and potentially impact learning and teaching in naturalistic settings' (Barab and Squire 2004, p.2). Design-based research allows one to understand, how, when and why educational innovations work in practice (Kelly 2003; Van den Akker 1999). It seeks to identify the relationship between educational theory, design artefact and educational practice. Many participatory design methods have been developed to involve users in the technology design lifecycle, including informant design (Scaife and Rogers 1999), contextual inquiry (Beyer and Holtzblatt 1998), technology immersion (Druin 1999), and low-tech prototyping (Ehn and Kyng 1991). In regards to methods specific to designing future technologies, the concept of future workshops (Kensing and Madsen 1991) and strategic visioning workshops (Sanders 2000) have been proposed in literature. For the purpose of this work, we required a method that would meet the following criteria:

1. Appropriate for young people (11–18 years old) but also for teachers. We realised that we would have to involve children and young pupils from different European countries in our data collection, hence we needed a method that is not language-specific and would use pictorial representations, to allow young participants to express concepts that would otherwise find difficult to articulate.
2. Suitable for the design of e-learning activities.
3. Minimal participant training. It can be used with adults or children with no prior training to enact and analyse collaborative interaction with technologies that have not yet been envisaged.
4. Collaborative. It can involve group activities to role play the interactions between people and future collaborative technology in order to support the design of novel interactions and technologies.
5. Time efficient and cost-effective. It can be carried out in a classroom, in the young people's environment, with portable equipment, in a half a day workshop (2½h).
6. Relates people and technology. It explores the relations between future learning activities and future technology, providing novel requirements for e-learning systems, not just new pieces of hardware.

Existing workshop formats appear to meet some of the criteria mentioned but none of the ones available in literature meet all of our requirements. For this reason, we developed a novel workshop format that meets the need for a methodical way of developing new technology by envisioning how learners might learn, work or play collaboratively in a future setting. This novel approach is based on an adaptation of future workshops that employs the rich picture-based participatory methods that are specifically tailored to the context of our work. Rich Pictures are a diagramming technique developed by Checkland as part of Soft Systems Methodology (Checkland 1993) which help to capture stakeholder's views non-confrontationally. Rich Pictures are a simple, but powerful, tool for addressing complex problems with diverse stakeholders and can support process improvement especially in the kind of situation where it is difficult even to get a holistic understanding of what the problem actually is let alone begin to identify ways of solving it (Jisc Infonet 2009). Our method builds upon existing participatory design techniques to propose a way of transcending young people's preconceived notions of existing technologies and encourage them to postulate future forms and uses of technology, by emphasising equally on technology interactions and learning activities. The Research Ethics Committee of Brunel University London reviewed and approved the focus group protocols and ethical approval had been granted prior to the study.

6.3.1 Workshop Format

We have used an adaptation of future workshops that is specifically tailored to the context of this work. In our method, participants who are familiar with the domain of interest (but are not generally or necessarily technology experts) are guided through a process of exploring and designing the interactions between current and future technology, and current and future activities. The aim of this method is to enable young people to postulate future use of technology in education and to facilitate a transition from current to future thinking.

The workshop addresses four main questions:

- How your learning activities are currently performed through the use of technology?
- How might these same activities be performed with new technologies in the future?
- What new learning activities might current technologies support?
- What new learning activities could be enabled by future technologies?

Future workshops include three phases: The *Critique* phase (a structured brainstorming session that focuses on existing problems related to the design task), the *Fantasy* phase (where the participants envision a future free of the previously identified problems), and the *Implementation* phase (a group discussion on the feasibility of the vision that resulted in the Fantasy phase and the development of an action plan for the implementation of the vision) (Kensing 1978). In our method, we have also added an additional phase to complement the *Fantasy Phase*, which we call the *Trigger phase*, where possible technological solutions are demonstrated to aid the participants in imagining what might be possible (Arvidsson et al. 2002). The different phases of the workshop with their corresponding design tasks used are described in Table 6.1

For each session participants worked in groups, with six to eight participants per group and a facilitator was available for each group. The workshop was carried out as a half-day event, with 90 min dedicated to the first two phases, and 90 min for the remaining two phases.

In order to facilitate the participants in articulating their views, we have employed the use of rich pictures. To facilitate this process, we provided participants with A0 sheets of paper and a set of laminated symbols to help them with the creation of their rich pictures. These symbols included technological concepts (desktop, tablet,

Table 6.1 Rich picture workshop format

	Phase	Design task
1	Critique	Participants are asked to create a rich picture that describes how their *current* learning is supported by technology.
2	Trigger	A video that defines or facilitate envisioning a desirable future in regards to technology.
3	Fantasy	Participants are asked to create a rich picture describing how their future learning experience might be supported by the new technology.
4	Implementation	Plenary discussion of future scenarios/rich pictures

mobile, printer etc.), learning environments and contexts (home, in classroom etc.), actors (student, teacher) and interactions among those entities.

At the beginning of the workshop, the facilitators drew an example of a rich picture to ensure that all participants would be familiar with this concept. During this example, a number of suggestions of best practice were given to participants by the workshop facilitators that are based upon current relevant literature (Bell and Morse 2010; Armson 2011), such as representing everything they know about the situation, drawing and labelling interconnections and relationships, keep text to a minimum, using colour, and including all objects and processes. It has to be noted that these were not used as directives but as suggestions for best practice to take into consideration.

Participants were then asked to describe their current and future uses of technology in regards to the delivery of the agreed learning scenario for teachers. Participants worked collaborative in groups of 4–6 to create a rich picture of the 'current situation' for 30 min. In order to help participants with the rich picture creation, laminated icons were provided that could be placed onto a blank canvas and teachers were asked to use marker pens to show the various relationships and interactions within the learning model they create. Teachers could also add their own icons.

6.3.1.1 Critique Phase (20–30 min)

The critique phase involves the critical discussion and investigation of the problem by the participants, usually through the means of brainstorming techniques. In our workshop, this phase involves the construction of rich pictures that depict the participants' current learning experience and how this is supported by ICT.

Participants are briefed to select a typical lesson as an example and through the medium of rich picture to describe how learning takes place. The participants are then divided into groups and are provided with a set of low-tech prototyping materials, such as A0 sheets, the set of bespoke icons, coloured pens, post it notes and sticky paper. A facilitator is assigned to each group and encourages participants to use the icons that have been provided to them and to consider key constructs of m-learning such as pedagogy, technological devices, context and social interaction

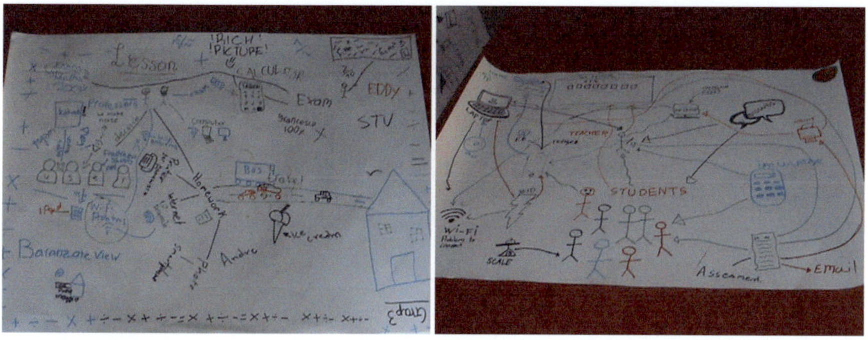

Fig. 6.1 Rich picture examples from the critique phase

(‘How does learning take place outside the classroom? What kind of activities do you do at home on what platforms? How do you collaborate with your fellow pupils outside school? etc). At the end of this phase (20–30 min) each group of participants is asked to present their rich picture to the rest of the workshop in order to help us to understand their model and the various relationships and interactions within it. The outcomes of this phase include the rich pictures that the participants have created (Fig. 6.1), the facilitators’ observation notes during the rich picture creation and the facilitators’ notes during the groups’ presentations.

6.3.1.2 Trigger Phase

After a short break, the second part of the workshop began where participants were shown a short video of the vision of the future, which in this case was a short video of what the new framework could look like. Using the same rich picture procedure, the pupils were asked to create (with the rich picture icons) an interactive learning framework using the new system under design.

6.3.1.3 Fantasy Phase

For this phase, the facilitator asks the groups to confer in order to select one or more of the ideas produced during the first session and to build a model that will demonstrate how the relevant activities are performed. The groups are encouraged to choose different ideas (see Fig. 6.2 below), but this is not compulsory. Asking the workshop participants to work in smaller groups has the advantage that more ideas can be explored; but also gives each participant more chances to influence the designs. The focus during modelling stays on activities: the groups are instructed to avoid producing detailed designs of technology, but rather to create models of

Fig. 6.2 Rich pictures fantasy phase

activity contexts along with any necessary technology props. Hence, the focus is maintained on functionality rather than detailed interface design.

6.3.1.4 Implementation Phase

For this stage of the work, each group presented their rich picture to the other groups and the researchers. The presentation normally lasted for 10 min per group. The aim of this plenary discussion was to get a clear understanding of how each of the groups envisaged their system, how it would work and what were the key requirements needed for it to be used in an effective, efficient and satisfying way. Therefore, the researchers and other participants from other groups could ask questions during this discussion.

6.3.2 Sampling and Recruitment Strategy

An opportunistic sampling approach was adopted for the recruitment of participants in the work reported in this chapter. A key requirement from the project sponsor was to obtain a sample of participants from different European countries. In total, 290 students and 41 teachers took part in the study.

6.3.3 Data Capture Analysis

The rich pictures that were created by the participants were photographed and digitally archived. Facilitators' notes from both critique and implementation phases were also transcribed and a thematic analysis of the textual dataset was carried out by four members of the research team. Given the exploratory nature of this work, coding was conducted inductively, rather than being driven by a priori themes from literature. This particular method has been widely applied within the context of HCI, to inform the design of new technology interfaces (Tanaka et al. 2012; Brown and Stockman 2013), identify key interaction challenges by analysing users experiences with technology prototypes, (Pykhtina et al. 2012) and define the functionality of new technology (Money et al. 2008). Key issues, concepts and design themes were identified by the participants' rich pictures and the facilitators' notes. The author and co-author undertook the analysis and reliability was enhanced by double coding and comparing a subset of transcripts with other two project members (who were also facilitators during the co-design workshops). The next step of the analysis involved identifying a list of high-priority themes and sub-themes against which design recommendations could then be formulated. This was achieved through a group discussion and consensus building process which provides a method for synthesising a range of information (Black et al. 1999) whilst harnessing the insights of multiple researchers involved in the project.

6.4 Results

6.4.1 Participants

Twenty four co-design workshops were conducted in 2014 with samples of young people from three different European countries (United Kingdom, Luxembourg, and Italy). Overall, 290 pupils (n = 290) and 41 teacher from five primary and secondary institutions participated in the co-design workshops and contributed towards design ideas. The participants were recruited using an opportunistic sampling method.

The cohort was split into 24 groups. Participants' median age was 15 years, with 169/290 (58 %) were female and 121 (42 %) were male. Participants were recruited from two high Schools in the UK (39 %), two high schools in Italy (38 %) and one high school in Luxembourg (23 %). All the participants were pupils from maths, technology or science classes as the initial focus of the project was on the teaching of STEM subjects in Europe (Table 6.2).

The different learning scenarios that were covered in the workshops were: The human digestive system, Fractions, Understanding and counting different monetary denominations, Space and the solar system, Understanding pressure, Java Programming, Research methods (during the pilot session of the workshop). The four design themes which emerged were: in-class interaction, home interaction, content creation, and reporting affordances. Within these broad domains a number of user needs and requirements also emerged (Fig. 6.3). The sections that follow describe the results in more detail with illustrative examples from participants' rich pictures.

The following paragraphs report the emerged needs on the basis of the identified domains.

Table 6.2 Participant demographics

Location	No of co-design workshops	No of participants	Age range of pupils	Lesson plans
UK	4	113	School 1: 11–16	The human digestive system
			School 2: 11–18	Space and solar system
Italy	12	110	School 1: 11–16	Java Programming
			School 2: 13–18	Maths (understanding and counting different monetary denominations)
			School 3: 11–16	Physics (understanding pressure)
Luxembourg	8	67	School 1: 11–16	Maths (fractions)

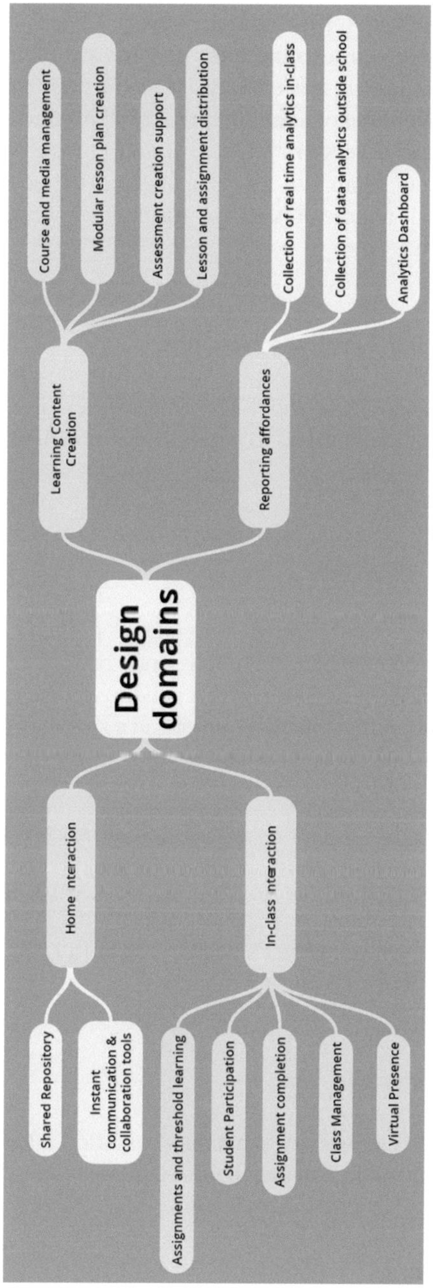

Fig. 6.3 Design domains and user needs that emerged from the co-design workshops

6.4.2 *In-Class Interaction Design Domain*

This domain is concerned with the interaction between students and teachers during class activities and how digital learning tools can support their educational needs and requirements. In this domain it is envisaged that the class will be augmented by technologies, which will consist of a minimum set of tablet devices for each student and each teacher will have access to optional external interactive screens to stimulate pupils' interaction and improve the visualisation of the learning materials. Possible interactions with remote classrooms for cooperative learning approaches have also been considered.

6.4.2.1 Assignments and Threshold Learning

This need stipulates that teachers should be able to present appropriate learning activities and resources or assignments to pupils in real-time within the class according to their competency levels.

6.4.2.2 Assignment Completion

This need ensures that each pupil receives assignments pushed by the teacher. When the assignment has been completed, the pupil sends back their feedback which is stored in their personal learning repository. Depending on the nature of the assignment, the feedback is either immediate or released at a specified date and time. If the pupil meets the learning outcome, they are automatically progressed to the next level of competency for the topic.

6.4.2.3 Class Management

This need can be defined as the teacher's need to retain full control of what the students are doing with their devices during the lesson

6.4.2.4 Student Participation

This allows the student to use a device (i.e. tablet) to follow a lesson (such as watching videos, taking notes) and to manage their assignments.

6.4.2.5 Virtual Presence

Students and teachers should be able to join a lesson from different locations.

6.4.3 *Home Interaction Domain*

This domain is concerned with pupils and teachers ability to access the platform any time, any place and anywhere from multiple devices. Although some schools use Google Drive as a repository to exchange content and upload assessments, participants expressed the need to have a more integrated digital learning environment.

6.4.3.1 Shared Repository

Students require remote access (i.e. from home) to a secure shared learning repository with lessons, learning materials and assignments (homework and assessments). Students also have a notification dashboard.

6.4.3.2 Students Communication and Collaboration

Students need to communicate while at home or out of the classroom for the purpose of assignment collaboration. They are all currently using WhatsApp but they need a more collaborative and integrated tool.

6.4.4 *Learning Content Creation Domain*

Teachers and content creators should have access to an online tool through which they can manage their courses, create lessons, aggregate learning materials and push assignments and activities to the students. These requirements were only obtained from the teachers who took part in the workshops.

6.4.4.1 Course and Media Management

The teacher needs access to a dashboard where they can see all their courses and attach lessons and related assignments to each course. The teacher will then map students to the appropriate courses. In addition, the teacher should be able to create lessons and assignments by assembling existing media or linking them from external sources (e.g. images, texts, pdfs, videos from YouTube, etc).

6.4.4.2 Modular Lesson Plan Creation

The teacher should have the ability to build a lesson or an additional learning material linked to the lesson by creating a sequence of bricks (which is essentially a learning material item such as text, media object etc). Each brick is built by using readymade templates and existing media.

6.4.4.3 Assessment Creation Support (e.g. Assignments, Homework, Learning Activities)

The teacher can build an assignment and specify its properties by creating a sequence of questions or exercises bricks. Each brick is built by filing out ready to use templates.

6.4.4.4 Lesson and Assignment Distribution

This need requires that lessons and assignments created by the teacher should be pushed to all the students associated to the teacher's course, either on the whole group or sub-groups of students.

6.4.5 Reporting Domain

This domain requires the system to collect data about the students' behaviour during their activities and interactions with the system.

6.4.5.1 Collection of Real Time Analytics During a Lesson

The system should collect data about students' behaviour during a lesson.

6.4.5.2 Collection of Data Analytics Outside of the School Environment

Data analytics collected on students use of the new system outside of the school environment will provide vital information on any problems students are having with their homework and assignments. In addition, it will provide information on how they use other learning materials at home and other locations outside the school environment.

6.4.5.3 Analytics Dashboard

The teacher should have access to classroom and personal dashboards for each student in order to produce analytics for each student and grouped data for the classroom. For example, the student dashboard should contain both usage analytics and information on completed assignments.

6.5 Conclusions

The rich picture approach has proven to be, in this instance, a very effective methodological approach for providing salient information for the design of a digital learning interaction framework for school students. This interaction framework is organised on three levels of abstraction.

Design Themes offer perspectives (or viewpoints) and argumentation of an abstract, theoretical level. They define broad research issues and domains

Design Concepts Themes are each concretised with a set of concepts. Concepts provide descriptions of found phenomena and help to summarise generic design issues

Design Guidelines (User requirement): comprehends more directly applicable design guidelines that are easily communicable and comprehensive for entire project team

On reflection, it may have been a better idea to have given participants a "warm up" session to allow them to get used to actually engaging in the rich picture process. This could have been done by giving them 10–15 min to come up with their own versions of the example that was demonstrated to them.

In addition, having a video to record participants as they described their rich pictures would have provided a useful narrative to accompany the images from the rich pictures themselves. Any concerns about participants faces being shown could have been dealt with in the analysis phase by removing them using video editing software. Another approach would have been to set a video camera up on a tripod and have it focussed on the rich picture and excluding the participants as they spoke.

Moving forward, the next planned step of the project is to build a prototype to test and evaluate this interactive learning framework which will be based on a modular growth of the platform. This strategy allows us to control the development of the platform by a step-by-step process which ensures that the interactive learning framework is reliable and valid for the needs of teachers and pupils

The next stage of the development of the platform will focus on the learning environment for school pupils in the 13–14 year old age range. By focussing on this age of pupils we will be able to test the interactive learning framework on the teaching and learning of in-depth STEM (Science, Technology, Engineering and Mathematics) topics through the use of the prototype system both inside and outside the school environment.

References

Armson R (2011) Growing wings on the way. Triarchy Press, Axminster

Arvidsson F, Ihlström C, Lundberg J (2002) Vision of future news – consensus or conflict? In: Proceedings of the 25th information systems research seminar in Scandinavia. CD-ROM. Bautahøj, Denmark, 10–13 August, 2002

Barab S, Squire K (2004) Introduction: design-based research: putting a stake in the ground. J Learn Sci 13(1):1–14

Bell S, Morse S (2010) Rich pictures: a means to explore the 'Sustainable Group Mind'. The 16th annual international sustainable development research conference, Open Research Online, Hong Kong

Beyer H, Holtzblatt K (1998) Contextual design: defining customer-centered systems. Morgan Kaufmann Publishers, San Francisco

Black N, Murphy M, Lamping D, McKee M, Sanderson C, Askham J, Marteau T (1999) Consensus development methods: a review of best practice in creating clinical guidelines. J Health Serv Res Policy 4(4):236–248

Brown N, Stockman T (2013) Examining the use of thematic analysis as a tool for informing design of new family communication technologies. In: Proceedings of the 27th international BCS human computer interaction conference, Brunel University, London

Bull G, Thompson A, Searson M, Garofalo J, Park J, Young C, Lee J (2008) Connecting informal and formal learning: experiences in the age of participatory media. Contemp Issues Technol Teacher Educ 8(2):100–107

Carroll J (2003) HCI models, theories and frameworks: toward a disciplinary science. Published by Morgan Kaufman

Checkland P (1993) Systems thinking, systems practice. Wiley, New York

Druin A (1997) Computers and kids: kids are not adults-in-waiting. SIGCHI Bull (University of New Mexico):1–3

Druin A (1999) Cooperative inquiry: developing new technologies for children with children. In: Proceedings of CHI'99, May 15–20 1999 Pittsburgh. New York: ACM Press, HCIL-99-14, pp 592–599.

Ehn P, Kyng M (1991) Cardboard computers: mocking-it-up or hands-on the future. In: Greenbaum J, Kyng M (eds) Design at work: cooperative design of computer systems. Lawrence Erlbaum Associates, New Jersey, pp 169–196

Gibbons S (2007) Redefining the roles of iprofessionals in Higher education to engage the net generation. Keynote presented at EDUCAUSE conference, Australasia

Herrington J, McKenney S, Reeves T, Oliver R (2007) Design-based research and doctoral students: guidelines for preparing a dissertation proposal. In Montgomerie C, Seale J (eds) Proceedings of the world conference on educational multimedia, hypermedia and telecommunications, 2007. Association for the Advancement of Computing in Education, Chesapeake, pp 4089–4097

Howe N, Strauss W (2003) Millennials go to college: strategies for a new generation on campus. American Association of Collegiate Registrars and Admissions Officers, Washington, D.C.

JISC Infonet (2009) Process review toolkit. Available online https://www.york.ac.uk/admin/po/processreview/JISC%20Infonet%20Process%20Review%20Toolkit.pdf. Accessed Jan 2016

Jones C, Shao B (2011) The net generation and digital natives: implications for higher education. Higher Education Academy, York

Jorgensen B (2003) Baby Boomers, generation X and generation Y? Policy implications for defence forces in the modern era. Foresign 5(4):41–49

Kelly A (2003) Theme issue: the role of design in educational research. Educ Res 32(1):3–4

Kensing F (1978) Generation of vision in systems development, a supplement to the toolbox. In Docherty et al., pp 285–301

Kensing F, Madsen K (1991) Generating visions: future workshops and metaphorical design. In: Greenbaum J, Kyng M (eds) Design at work: cooperative design of computer systems. Lawrence Erlbaum, Hillsdale NJ, pp 155–168

Kukulska-Hulme A (2009) Conclusions: future directions in researching mobile learning. In: Vavoula G, Pachler N, Kukulska-Hulme A (eds) Researching mobile learning: frameworks, tools and research designs. Peter Lang Verlag, Oxford, pp 353–365

Livingstone S (2009) The educational and social impact of new technologies on young people in Britain. ESRC-sponsored seminar series. Report number 4. http://www.lse.ac.uk/media@lse/

WhosWho/AcademicStaff/SoniaLivingstone/Educational%20and%20Social%20Impact%20of%20New%20Technologies%20on%20Young%20People.aspx. Accessed Sept 2016

Markopoulos P, Bekker M (2003) Interaction design and children, editorial for special issue. Interact Comput 15(2):227–243

Mazzone E, Read J, Beale R (2008) Understanding children's contributions during informant design. In: Proceedings of the BCS-HCI'08 BCS, pp 61–64

McCrindle M (2006) New generations at work: attracting, recruiting, retraining and training 'Generation Y': McCrindle Research

Money A, Lines L, Fernando S, Elliman, A (2008) Older adults' experiences of interacting with online forms. Workshop on HCI and the older population. Proceedings of the British HCI group annual conference on people and computers. Liverpool John Moores University, UK

Nesset V, Large A (2004) Children in the information technology design process: a review of theories and their applications

Oblinger D, Oblinger J (2005) Is it age or IT: first steps towards understanding the net generation. In: Oblinger D, Oblinger J (eds) Educating the net generation, pp 2.1–2.20

Piaget J (1971) Psychology and epistemology: towards a theory of knowledge. Viking, New York

Prensky M (2001) Digital natives, digital immigrants. On the Horizon 9(5):1–6

Pykhtina O, Balaam M, Wood G, Pattinson S, Kharuffa A, Olivier P (2012) Magic land: the design and evaluation of an interactive tabletop supporting therapeutic play with children. In: Proceedings of the ACM conference on Designing Interactive Systems (DIS). Newcastle, UK

Read J (2015) Children as participants in design and evaluation. Interactions 22(2):64–66

Rosen L (2010) Rewired: understanding the i-Generation and the way they learn. PalgraveMacmillan, New York

Rowlands I, Nicholas D, Williams P, Huntington P, Fieldhouse M, Gunter B, Withey R, Jamali H, Dobrowolski T, Tenopir C (2008) The Google generation: the information behaviour of the researcher of the future. Aslib Proc 60(4):290–310

Scaife M, Rogers Y (1999) Kids as informants: Telling us what we didn't know or confirming what we already knew? In: Druin A (ed) The design of children's technology. Morgan Kaufmann, San Francisco, pp 27–50

Scaife M, Rogers Y, Aldrich F, Davies M (1997) Designing for or designing with? Informant design for interactive learning environments. In: Pemberton S (ed) Proceedings of the ACM SIGCHI conference on human factors in computing systems Atlanta. ACM, New York, pp 343–350

Sharples M, Corlett D, Westmancott O (2002) The design and implementation of a mobile learning resource. Pers Ubiquit Comput 6:220–234

Tanaka A, Parkinson A, Settel Z, Tahiroglu K (2012) Survey and thematic analysis approach as input to the design of mobile music GUIs. In: Proceedings of theNIME'. University of Michigan, Ann Arbour, USA

Tapscott D (1998) Growing up digital: the rise of the Net generation. McGraw-Hill, New York

Van den Akker J (1999) Principles and methods of development research. Design Methodology and Developmental Research in Education and Training:1–14

Vavoula G, Sharples M, Rudman P, Meek J, Lonsdale P (2009) Myartspace: design and evaluation of support for learning with multimedia phones between classrooms and museums. Comput Educ 53(2):286–299

Weiler A (2005) Information seeking behavior in 'Generation Y' students: motivation, critical thinking, and learning theory. J Acad Librariansh 31(1):46–53

Williamson B (2003) The participation of children in the design of new technology

Yip J, Clegg T, Bonsignore E, Gelderblom H, Rhodes E, Druin A (2013) Brownies or bags-of-stuff? Domain expertise in cooperative inquiry with children. In: Proceedings of the IDC2013. ACM Press, pp 201–210

Chapter 7
Engaging Teens in Dialogue on Potential Technological Futures with User Enactments

William Odom, John Zimmerman, and Jodi Forlizzi

Abstract Teens are a fascinating, dynamic population; they are on the vanguard of emerging technologies, often defining the behaviour and social mores of these products and services. At the same time, teens are still exploring and developing into the person they want to become, making them a terribly sensitive group to work with, and making it all the more crucial to critically and carefully consider how new technologies might shape their lives and practices. There is a clear need for a multiplicity of methods for working with teens in the HCI and interaction design communities. User Enactments has been developed as a design approach that aids design teams in more successfully investigating radical alterations to technologies' roles, forms, and behaviours in uncharted design spaces. In this chapter, we motivate and develop user enactments as a method for moving beyond studies of teen current practices and generatively engaging them in experiencing and making sense of possible technological futures. In this, we describe and reflect on our own experience of putting user enactments into practice through developing five different scenarios within a teen bedroom and, subsequently, conducting a study with 14 teens. Our goal is to surface and reflect on best practices and also potential pitfalls of using the User Enactments approach with teenagers. A higher-level goal of our work is to help better support future research and design practice aimed at engaging teenagers in critically playing a part in determining the roles that technology will play in their lives now and well into the future.

W. Odom (✉)
School of Interactive Arts and Technology, Simon Fraser University, Surrey, BC, Canada
e-mail: wo@willodom.com

J. Zimmerman • J. Forlizzi
Human-Computer Interaction Institute, Carnegie Mellon University, Pittsburgh, PA, USA

© Springer International Publishing Switzerland 2016

L. Little et al. (eds.), *Perspectives on HCI Research with Teenagers*,
Human–Computer Interaction Series, DOI 10.1007/978-3-319-33450-9_7

7.1 Introduction

Most teenagers feel the greatest sense of place attachment—the emotional bond between a person and a place—to their bedroom (Chawla 1992). Here they live with their things, make sense of their lives, and experiment with whom they wish to become (Steele and Brown 1995). The bedroom provides moments for solitude and reflection, a social space to engage parents and peers, and a canvas to experiment with an evolving sense of self (Hodkinson and Lincoln 2008). Teens display and curate their precious material possessions in their bedrooms in order to explore their changing values and aspirations, and to project them to different audiences. Through this process, they construct value with their things, mentally reassigning an individualised sense of worth as they possess and repeatedly use their things over time (Belk 1988). The bedroom provides teens with their first opportunity to author a space, to create their own aesthetic and sense of style in negotiation with their parents (Steele and Brown 1995).

Digital devices and services have become an increasingly large part of teen life (Vetere et al. 2005; Taylor and Harper 2002) and teens commonly alternate their attention and interactions between their material and *virtual possessions* (Odom et al. 2014). Virtual possessions include things that are increasingly immaterial (e.g., books, music, and photos), things that never had a lasting material form (e.g., game avatars, electronic message archives, and social networking profiles), and metadata traces logged during interactions with various systems. In an earlier fieldwork project with teens (Odom et al. 2011), we investigated their value construction activities with material and virtual possessions in their rooms with an emphasis on how these different things shaped their identity construction processes. Observations and interviews from this formative study revealed that teens developed practices to make their virtual things more present, and that they draw on them as critical resources for self-reflection and self-presentation to different social groups.

Findings from this descriptive fieldwork project revealed design opportunities for transforming virtual possessions into more valuable and meaningful resources in teens' everyday lives. However, considering the largely unexplored and unstructured nature of the virtual possessions design space, it was unclear exactly how to proceed. Teen life presents a tricky and sensitive context for HCI and design researchers to operate in, and the potential unintended consequences that could result from new technologies need to be taken very seriously. One's teenage years represents a particularly impressionable time that have a profound impact on ensuing life stages. Additionally, the teen bedroom represents one of the most important, idiosyncratic, and profound places that teen life unfolds. Considering the many tensions and pitfalls that could arise from manifesting virtual possessions in teens' everyday lives, we needed to challenge and explore our fieldwork findings in a generative way to establish a more sensitized and developed understanding of the overall research and design space. We aimed to systematically investigate several possible futures to discover how technology might bring about one that is preferred over teens' present situation.

Fig.7.1 The messy Teen Bedroom created in our design studio that functioned as the scene for our user enactments study

Design, as a form of inquiry and reflective practice, works to intentionally transform current situations into more preferred future states (Nelson and Stolterman 2003; Simon 1996). One issue when designing new interactive products and systems is that they typically involve concepts and technologies with which target users are very unfamiliar (or have point of reference for at all). This makes pursuing new initiatives in emerging design spaces complex and risky; it is difficult to anticipate how people will react to radically new technologies and investigating a large amount of resources into a design direction that is not well understood can have disastrous consequences. We have developed the user enactments design approach to help support design teams in more successfully making this conceptual leap through investigating radical alterations to the forms and behaviours of technologies in new and uncharted design spaces (Odom et al. 2012b). User enactments are part of the broader speed dating methodology (Davidoff et al. 2007). At the end of each enactment, after experiencing a possible future through simulated content, participants reflect on what may have complicated or supported their desires, or led to unexpected experiences.

In order to generatively move from fieldwork findings with teens centering on their use of virtual possessions as resources to support self-reflection and self-presentation [see (Odom et al. 2011) for more details], we conducted a user enactments study where we prototyped a teen bedroom in our design research studio and iteratively developed five user enactment scenarios (see Fig. 7.1). On a high level, the study focused on investigating radically new forms and behaviours of virtual possessions that might better support practices like curation, self-reflection, and presentation of self to different audiences. Specifically, we wanted to understand how making virtual possessions more present in the bedroom and giving them new forms and behaviours influence teens' perceived value for these things. To do this, we generated five design concepts: an auto-redecorating bedroom, a virtual possession 'status' quilt, postcards sent from a teen's digital past, an electronic gift giving application, and a system for curation of multiple digital presentations of self. We then conducted the user enactments study with 14 teens in the prototype bedroom. This approach provided a prism for investigating aspects of several potential futures that teens may or, crucially, may not want.

User enactment sessions revealed that teens desire to have their virtual possessions more present as long as they can control this presence, to curate multiple presentations of self while retaining a sense of authenticity, and to have new forms and behaviours that better support reflection on past self and on the relationship they have with another. These findings suggested significant opportunities for the HCI and interaction design communities to create new forms and behaviours for virtual things in order to modify people's perceived value of them, particularly in terms of *ability to investigate one-on-one relationships* and *supporting reflection on the past*. They also reveal an opportunity to develop richer forms of metadata, and the infrastructure required for its capture, storage, retrieval, and sensitive treatment.[1]

While in this chapter we provide a synopsis of empirical findings, we aim to describe and unpack details and insights beyond the core research questions in the user enactment study itself. In line with the theme of this book, we want to reflect on how user enactments worked (and didn't work) to engage teens in experiencing glimpses of several potential futures and to relate phenomena their encountered back to their own lived experiences, values, and desires. While user enactments as a research method is growing in use and interest, to date only handful of publications illustrate its use, and there is a need for documentation and reflection on experiences of putting user enactments into practice to engage populations, like teenagers, in critical dialogue about the future.

In what immediately follows, we review related work that provided impetus and inspiration for the Teen User Enactments study itself. We then provide an in depth account of the process of designing and constructing the teen bedroom user enactments, which is followed by a synopsis of findings, a critical discussion of our user enactments process, and a conclusion with implications for future research and practice.

[1] See (Odom et al. 2012a) for in depth reporting and interpretation of empirical findings and discussion of suggested design opportunities for the HCI community.

7.2 Background and Related Work

7.2.1 Technology Use in and Around the Home

The ways in which technology affects the social and moral order of the home, and how it might be better designed to improve domestic life continues to be major areas of concern in HCI. Edwards and Grinter (Edwards and Grinter 2001) discuss how even relatively simple technologies can disrupt domestic routines and practices. Subsequent work has emphasised developing technologies that make people feel more in control of their lives, rather than focusing on control of devices and services (Davidoff et al. 2006). Building on the issue of control, Woodruff et al. (2007) illustrated how ceding control to a smart home can help families focus on building social relationships. More generally, Vetere et al. (2005) describe the complex ways technologies mediate intimate relationships and the need to make new designs more rich, nuanced and expressive.

Teenagers and their domestic places have received less attention in the HCI community. March and Fleuriot (2006) explored how technology mediates teens' need for private space within their parents' home. Durrant et al. (2009) proposed ways that teenagers' curation of digital photos opens up opportunities for intergenerational interaction and identity construction. Hodkinson and Lincoln (2008) suggest teens increasingly use social media technologies to extend boundaries beyond the bedroom. Additional research has investigated how teens maintain offline relationships through interactive technology (Taylor and Harper 2002) and their capacity to define new social mores through their use and appropriation of social computing technologies (Boyd Danah 2007). On a broader level, teens present an important population for the HCI community to engage with—they are deeply occupied in the process of constructing their identities (Steele and Brown 1995) and often on the vanguard of digital media and interactive technologies (Ito et al. 2009). While research on teens is beginning to gain purchase in HCI (Fitton et al. 2013; Read et al. 2013b), this audience presents different kinds of challenges to engage with compared to older generations, and there is a clear need for a multiplicity of methods to engage with them (Read et al. 2013a).

7.2.2 Privacy and Self-Disclosure

As everyday technologies have become networked, a wealth of literature has emerged concerning privacy and unwanted disclosure. Palen and Dourish (2003) unpack the multi-dimensional nature of privacy practices, drawing attention to how they are not limited to tensions between people, but also involve a person's internal conflicts over how disclosure shapes their self-concept. Many important works too numerous to mention here have since built on this seminal article, working to reduce unwanted disclosure across mobile platforms and networked services (see

(Ackerman and Mainwaring 2005) for an in depth review). Outside of HCI, Goffman's (1959) sociological work reveals a range of performative practices people engage in to manage self-impression and disclosure to different social audiences. Giddens (1991) later argues that the act of managing presentations of self across different settings can lead to an integrated, holistic life narrative.

Additionally, within HCI there is growing interest in how to support designers in considering user values, such as privacy, throughout the design process (Friedman 2006). Much of this work helps illustrate how designing technologies reflective of users' values can productively open the space for people to construct a deeper sense of value or 'worth' with these things (Cockton 2006).

7.2.3 Personal Digital Content and Archives

Recently, researchers have begun to explore the implications surrounding the design of meaningful and worthwhile interactions with digital artifacts, such as photos (Kirk et al. 2006), music (Voida et al. 2005), and familial possessions (Kirk and Sellen 2010). More generally, the issue of how to design digital artifacts largely characterised by immaterial qualities has been an area of ongoing interest in HCI (Hallnas and Redstrom 2001; Wright et al. 2008). There is also emerging HCI research describing how people develop sentimental attachments to digital artifacts.

Kirk and others (2010) present a values-oriented approach to designing tools to support archiving of cherished digital artifacts. Kaye et al. (2006) describe how digital archives can function as rich resources for identity construction and presentation. Van House (2009) details how digital photos presented online can support curation of identity to different groups. Others have explored how physical mementos can inform the design of systems aimed at creating digital mementos capable of triggering reflection on past experience (Nunes et al. 2008; Petrelli et al. 2008). Finally, Pessapati et al. (2010) designed and implemented a system re-presenting social networking content back to users specifically to evoke reminiscences.

7.2.4 Design-Oriented HCI Methods for Exploring Potential Technological Futures

User enactments builds on several existing HCI design methods, including scenario-based design (Carroll 2000) and experience prototyping (Buchenau and Suri 2000), in addition to the range of methods that embrace role-playing and performance as a critical means to engage users in exploration of potential technological futures (Burns et al. 1994; Iacucci et al. 2000; Kurvinen et al. 2008; Mancini et al. 2010). Similar to these methods, User enactments aim to tap into users' felt experiences of the present and past to open up critical dialogues about what the future could, or should, be. User Enactments shares similar ambitions to other methods like Wizard-of-Oz (Hartmann et al. 2006) and video sketches (Zimmerman 2005) that aim to understand the promise and potential pitfalls of technology in an uncertain future.

On a broader level, there has been an ongoing interest in developing effective methods to support designers in understanding and empathising with user values throughout the design process. The Scandinavian tradition of participatory design has long been invested in engaging potential users in the design of new systems and technologies in the service of supporting their practices, desires and values (Iversen et al. 2010; Kensing and Blomberg 1998). User enactments share some of the same ambitions and interests in that it aims to surface where value tensions may exist around future technologies and embrace them in moving from ideation to iteration. However, it differs by requiring design teams to first create concepts embedded in scenarios, and then asking users to enact them to explore tensions and opportunities around potential near future technologies.

A final important difference is that methods such as experience prototyping (Buchenau and Suri 2000) or technology probes (Hutchinson et al. 2003) tend to focus on developing one concept, whereas user enactments emphasise bringing several visions of the future forward to develop a better overall understanding of a design space. This approach is parallel to ongoing work describing the benefits of variety in ideation (Buxton 2007; Tohidi et al. 2006).

Collectively, our work picks up on these four threads of domestic technology use, privacy and self-disclosure, personal digital content, and design-oriented HCI methods for investigating potential technological futures. The user enactments study we describe in this chapter aimed to advance the HCI community's understanding of how teens currently control and might better control technologies within their bedroom. Our study investigated various ways virtual possession could potentially be manifested in teens' everyday lives in the future and how forms of new technology might better support intimate experiences tied to the development of social relationships and one's self-concept. The user enactments we developed are intended to probe and open up dialog with teens on issues around privacy, disclosure, self-presentation, and self-reflection. On a higher level, our work offers a case example of how user enactments can work to investigate potential technological futures with teenagers.

7.3 The Teen Bedroom: Constructing the Scene and Setting the Stage

Previously we conducted ethnographic interviews with 21 teens in their bedrooms to investigate their perceived value of virtual and material possessions, and how these materials shaped teens' identity construction practices (Odom et al. 2011). Our teen participants in this study were aged between 12 and 17 years old and consisted of 9 female and 12 male. This fieldwork study was conducted in the Pittsburgh, Pennsylvania geographic area in the United States. Our findings detailed design opportunities for value construction activities with immaterial things. These include:

Value in presence—Teens worked to make their virtual possessions more present. We observed teens constantly changing backgrounds on personal devices, printing status updates and comments from friends to display in their rooms, and maintaining a persistent, online connection in order to monitor the virtual world.

Value in self-reflection—Teens used their virtual possessions to reflect on their past. We found teens investigated how many times they listened to a song in their music collection, stored printed status updates, and reflected on popular culture and other images featured on their computer previously. They used both system logs and human constructed metadata to understand and reflect on their past experiences.

Value in curation of multiple presentations of self—Teens used virtual possessions to 'curate' different selves to different audiences. These actions included applying interface 'skins' on gaming consoles, encoding photos of a shared experience into the metadata of songs in playlists given as gifts, and tagging or un-tagging of photos as well as restricting/granting access to photos and other social media content.

The goal of our user enactments study was to advance our understanding of how the design of virtual possessions that were intended to support identity construction activities might influence teens' perceptions of value and meaning, and also where possible tensions or complications might emerge. We chose to conduct speed-dating sessions with user enactments (Davidoff et al. 2007; Odom et al. 2012b) to help better understand our target audience as well as potential opportunities and risks in the design space. In real-life speed dating, people have dating props such as a wine glass, café table and candle. They go on many very short dates in a single evening. At the end, they know very little about any of the people they have met. However, they have developed a much better and more realistic vision of what they want in a partner.

Speed dating with user enactments follows the same approach. Design teams create provocative scenes of possible futures; scenes meant to stimulate discussion on futures people desire or fear. Teams bring in representative participants, place them in a familiar situation, and then provide them with a "sip" of what the future might be like. This allows participants to connect with their felt-life experience as they reflect on what the future might be. Prior to each enactment, participants reflect on their current practices and desires for the future. At the conclusion of an enactment, they reflect on how the technology may have complicated or supported these desires, or led to unexpected experiences. By combining wide exploration across multiple structured engagements, user enactments provide a broad perspective for discovering new design opportunities and for revealing invisible social tensions around potential new technologies.

Fig.7.2 We printed and hung over 50 images in our studio from our prior fieldwork in teen bedrooms (a sample shown above). These images helped us isolate key details of teen bedrooms and develop a sensibility for when we had gotten the UE bedroom to the 'right' level of fidelity. We also sketched, clustered, and hung 94 design concept sketches, which helped better structure the design space and get a sense of what the bedroom would spatially and practically have to look like

Our process in the teen bedroom user enactment study followed a series of steps. First, we began with in-depth review sessions of our field data, related research and design opportunity areas (i.e. the three main value construction activities emerging from our fieldwork study summarised above). During these sessions we made affinity diagrams and free form diagrams to gain a perspective on the overall design space. We then held several concept generation sessions, resulting in 94 concepts. We clustered these thematically to further refine our understanding of the overall design space and to more clearly articulate visions of preferred and undesirable futures. We iteratively filtered these clusters based on their fit to three main criteria: (i) the extent to which the enactment builds on the aforementioned design opportunity areas, (ii) the importance of the issue probed by the concept, and (iii) the feasibility of realising the concept through a user enactment. We then more fully realised 12 remaining concepts by making detailed scenarios and through body storming (Buchenau and Suri 2000). Again, we filtered these concepts resulting in the final set we developed into user enactments.

Our scenarios required us to create a 'teenager's bedroom' within our studio that could effectively function as the set for the user enactments study. Our design process for this began with printing photos of teen rooms we collected in our previous study and placing them on the wall (see Fig. 7.2). We wanted to explore design patterns, exemplars, and outliers to develop a rough design aesthetic and language for

Fig.7.3 The messy teen bedroom featured a 12-screen overlapping display constructed from foamcore and blackboard. An HD projector was used to populate the display screens with high-fidelity interfaces controlled via an Adobe Flash application we custom designed

a place as idiosyncratic as a teen bedroom. Using these images as a resource, we then constructed a bedroom space, where we continually tweaked and augmented it until it "felt" like the rooms we had visited. A major addition to the room included 12 overlapping displays that filled the wall above the teen's desk. These were made from black and white foam-core, and we used a high definition projector to create the illusion that they functioned as independent screens (see Fig. 7.3). We intentionally created a set of displays that could be easily integrated into the bedroom, while at the same time might be perceived as overwhelming. We hoped this tension might provoke teens to critically reflect on the amplified presence of technology in their personal space.

Through repeated meetings to critique scenarios, we iteratively refined the user enactments, often increasing the fidelity by using props and acting out scenes in order to developed a consistent narrative flow. We then repeatedly piloted the enactments. Piloting helped refine our design of the physical bedroom. It also revealed unanticipated narrative problems, which we addressed by developing a specific order for enactments. Finally, piloting helped to find the harmony between giving participants too much freedom and making the scenario mostly exposition. During the piloting stages, we first began with graduate and undergraduate students at our university to obtain a very general sense of where major problems were emerging in the flow, sequencing, and narrative structure of the enactments. We then moved on to using teens during piloting; these sessions helped us better understand not only how to engage with teens within the enactment, they also enabled to probe teens on different material choices in constructing the bedroom. A key finding from this is that some of our teen popular culture references had become outdated in the time that had elapsed (approximately 1 year) since conducting our formative fieldwork project. We made updated bedroom materials such as music and movie posters within the bedroom based on this feedback.

We crafted the scenarios around a fixed set of digital content provided by two teenagers (male and female, respectively). While we were informed by extensive, first-hand experience of teens' lives through our prior fieldwork and we aimed to bring a high degree of sensitivity to constructing the set and user enactments. Clearly this decision is not without its limitations. Yet, we chose to use stock content for two reasons. First, participants have different sets of virtual possessions (e.g., some have large music collections, while some listen to music online; some archive text messages, while others are less meticulous; etc.). Reliance on participants' personal collections would have removed an important control: making sure participants reactions were based on the same stimuli. Additionally, it would make the enactments only as rich as the collections teens keep *now*. Second, acquiring teens' personal collections and building personalised versions of the room would have significantly increased our efforts. One of the key challenges with designing new technology is to reduce the risk of development for things people do not ultimately desire. Thus, we aimed to ground our intuitions and avoid making an over commitment to a specific design direction. We needed to conduct user enactments to help reduce the risk associated with taking a conceptual leap to an emerging design space that has few existing conventions to draw on. Next, we turn to describing each of the five enactments to unpack factors shaping how effective they were in engaging teens in dialog about potential technological futures.

7.4 Unpacking the User Enactments Teen Bedroom Study

For the teen bedroom project we recruited 14 teenagers ranging in age from 14 to 17 (eight female, six male) through word of mouth and through flyers posted in several different areas in and around the city of Pittsburgh, Pennsylvania, USA. Before the user enactments began, we would give participants a tour of 'their' bedroom, introducing them to 'their' digital and physical belongings. Interestingly, upon first entering our bedroom, many teens noted similarities between it and their own room in terms of objects and messiness (Fig. 7.4). During this time, we primed participants with brief explanations of unfamiliar elements in the room (e.g., the 12 screen display) and also made them aware that they would be asked to play the role of 'themselves' during short scenarios. We also noted that for each scenario, there would be a simple task that they will be asked to do (e.g., finishing reading a chapter in a schoolbook), but that there is no 'right' or 'wrong' way of doing this. Participants were also asked to reflect on their own everyday activities and experiences in and outside of their own actual bedroom. This proved to be an important technique in helping us surface additional insights about participants' lives and practices. It also

Fig.7.4 Domestic objects and teen high school materials were acquired from thrift stores for the set. We decorated the room to be messy to reflect the composition of many rooms we had observed in the field

helped further prime primed teens for drawing connections between their own lives and the possible future presented in each enactment.

Another technique that contributed to the viability and success of our enactments centered on playing popular contemporary music in the background throughout nearly the entire session with each participant. While on the surface this may seem trivial, this subtle tweak was highly effective at dissipating tensions emerging from teens being in an unfamiliar and somewhat contrived environment. It enabled the teens and our research team to relax and engage with the user enactments. Importantly, playing background music was highly effective at drawing attention away from the fact that we were in our studio and re-focusing attention on the narratives and dialogues we aimed to open up with our participants. We developed our background playlist after consulting several teens that the research team had personal contact with about their own contemporary musical tastes and listening habits.

Following each enactment we conducted semi-structured interviews, asking participants to reflect on their experience. We began by asking about their everyday practices or activities touched on themes or experiences in the enactment. We then transitioned to talking about the specific enactment. This technique appeared to help participants fluidly make connections between their daily experience and the potential futures; again, supporting this perceptual bridge is essential to conducting a successful user enactments study. Sessions with each participant lasted between 75 and 90 min. We video recorded these sessions, in addition to taking notes. These notes were reviewed immediately following each interview, and tentative insights were logged in reflective memos (Glaser and Strauss 1967). Analysis of the data was an ongoing process. The research team then met weekly over the course of 4 months to repeatedly review the video and notes in order to draw out underlying themes (Miles and Huberman 1994). Affinity diagrams were also created to reveal connections across participants and across enactments. Textual documents were then coded using themes. Data were then organised into concrete themes.

7.5 User Enactment 1: The Socially Reactive Bedroom

In the first user enactment, the teen enters the bedroom after dinner to read an Act from Romeo & Juliet to prepare for an upcoming exam (see Fig. 7.5). 12-displays show various collections, including: a visualisation of messages exchanged with friends over the last 2 weeks, favourite music, photos of a wild party with comments, provocative pop-culture images, and personal photos related to sports and family. A confederate of the same gender plays the participant's friend. She or he shows up and enters the room, triggering five of the screens to automatically re-decorate; presenting new information of shared activities and interests between the two friends. The screens highlight events both had attended—images from parties, a visualisation of communication patterns, and images of the two friends in Halloween costumes from a time *before* they knew each other. The confederate alludes to the meaning and function of the displays through a semi-structured conversation. After a few minutes of discussion, another confederate, in the role of a parent, knocks. The participant presses a remote to change the displays to "parent approved," masking the provocative image and party photos. The participant then allows the parent to enter and drop off folded laundry.

This enactment explored issues surrounding the control of virtual possession displays against the backdrop of different social audiences entering and exiting the room. We wanted to explore questions including, do teens value a system that automatically presents digital content relevant to particular people in the room? Will virtual possessions from a teen's past (i.e. Halloween photos) conflict with their current perception of self?

The socially reactive bedroom was one of the most complex user enactments in our study. It involved two confederates and a researcher triggering the screen transitions—all of which helped collectively guide the enactment's narrative flow. Despite its complexity, we found that the choice to have this enactment come first in the serial order of all enacted scenarios was widely effective at supporting our teen participants in suspending belief and becoming comfortable with engaging with what was immediately happening in the narrative. As we continued to run sessions with participants, it became clear that the combination of a relatively structured initial scenario with free-form spaces for dialog with multiple confederates was effective in leading teens to react in visceral and embodied ways. Our experiences with this enactment and user enactment 3 both illustrated that using confederates to help probe particular aspects of the scenario can be very useful if their role is crafted

Fig.7.5 The teen encounters a visual breakdown of different virtual possessions on the displays, from phone call logs to facebook photos to social ratings of current music tastes (*top row*). When a friend arrives, the screens automatically change to depict representations of information exchanged between the two over time (*middle row*). A parent arrives and the screens change to show a 'parental friendly' digital representation of self (*bottom row*)

to loosely guide the flow of the scenario with planned points for participant engagement. These points need to be fluid enough to move on immediately if needed. In other words, we crafted a situation where a space was opened to elicit reactions from teens without forcing an answer, which appeared to engender a sense of comfort and familiarity with performing the enactments.

Interestingly, teens' reactions to this enactment led to a range of insights. It revealed that teens did not desire bedroom technology that was socially reactive and would curate their virtual possessions depending on who was present (even if it was the teen by her or himself). Teens often viscerally reacted to the simulated experience of having their self-presentation activities regulated or even superseded by a computational system, even if well-intentioned. When confronted with this kind of technology, they felt like it generated contrived, inauthentic representations of who they might be at any given moment, no matter the people present or absent in their bedroom. Even though their virtual possessions are immaterial, out of sight, and, thus, may have less of a capacity for causal or serendipitous encounters, teens wanted to have direct control over what was present and when. From a design perspective, this was an interesting finding as social reactivity presents a behaviour that material possessions could never exhibit. Nonetheless, with this novelty clearly comes huge potential for complications and unintended consequences.

This enactment did unexpectedly lead to several teens remarking on how materials taken down from their bedroom walls are rarely captured and they expressed desires to 'save' the state of their virtual possession wall displays. Here, teens commonly remarked on how revisiting the spatial layout of virtual possessions decorating their bedroom from different eras of their adolescence could stimulate different kinds of memory experiences—experiences tied to how these virtual compositions offer a holistic representation of self form a particular time period in the life than they currently have access to now. Additionally, we anticipated that the Halloween pictures would trigger a range of negative reactions. However, this aspect of the enactment often led teens to describe desires to go even further back into their pasts to explore what was happening in their life during times they were too young to remember; a theme that continued to emerge in reactions to later enactments.

7.6 User Enactment 2: Waking up Under Your Online Updates

The second user enactment was considerably shorter and less complex compared to the socially reactive bedroom. Here, the teen arrives home late in the evening on a school night and goes to bed. The bed that the teen gets into is covered in a 'status quilt.' The bars of the 'status quilt' indicate that the teen has no new or unchecked digital content (which is displayed on the bed quilt via an overhead projector). As the teen lies in bed 'overnight' (which lasts about 30 s as the background music and lights are dimmed), the information on their quilt changes, indicating they have an assortment of new wall posts, photos and emails to check. The enactment concludes as a parent knocks on the door to let the teen know that their school bus will be arriving soon and they must get up and prepare to leave.

During the field study with teens, teens expressed a desire for a persistent connection to their online lives. For example, we often found that they left their personal computers and personal devices perpetually logged in to social networking sites like Facebook, even when engaging in other activities in the bedroom (e.g., reading, playing video games, doing homework). We wanted to push this idea, to see how far they might go. We wanted to force them across a social barrier in order to discover where this barrier might be. So we designed an enactment where teens literally wake up lying under the Internet; where their virtual possessions immediately vie for their attention. As featured in Fig. 7.6, we used a projector mounted above the bed to visualise a changing interface as the core design material in this

Fig.7.6 The teen returns to her bedroom late at night and gets into bed to go to sleep (*top row*). An overheard projector mounted in the bedroom ceiling projected onto the bed to create the 'status quilt' (*middle row*). An illustration of the teen's unchecked virtual possessions that grow while they sleep (*bottom row*)

concept. Our aim in using this technique was to amplify the presence of this potentially unsettling technology and engage teens in exploring what might be a more viable future approachto balancing technology use in the increasingly always-on and connected world they are growing up in.

However, this often produced tepid reactions from teens, and strongly contrasted the visceral engagement participants typically exhibited with the socially reactive bedroom enactment. Teens went through the motions of the status quilt enactment, but were largely ambivalent about their experience and, when prompted, rarely found the quilt to be subtle or peripheral. We expected teens to react strongly against the presence of the quilt, particularly after "waking up" in the updated statuses of their virtual things. Yet, teens were typically unsure of what they were supposed to take away from the scenario, and quickly went through the motions to complete it. Here, having the enactment grounded in an ambient technology that teens were not supposed to focus their full attention on at any key point made it difficult to have enough focus and structure necessary to run an effective enactment. The ambiguity over the structure and flow of the enactment that resulted ultimately complicated our ability to generate an experience that teen participants could relate to.

Despite these issues, brief interviews following this enactment did commonly result in useful dialogues with teens about the creeping distractive potential that digital notifications and nudges to check one's virtual possessions. This supported the broader theme we saw emerging across enactments that centered on teens desire to have more control over the presence (and absence) of their virtual possessions. Nonetheless, after several rounds of iterative piloting and attempting to make changes to this enactment, it still seemed to fall short of generating compelling experiences when compared to the other four enactments in our study. This made clear how complex it is to explore the potential role of ambient technology in teen life through the form of a user enactment. While status quilt enactment did not live up to its expected potential, it offers a useful example of how delicate it can be to strike the balance between exerting enough constraints to effectively guide teens and the ability to improvise freely within an enactment.

7.7 User Enactment 3: The Gift of an Experience-Oriented Assemblage

The third user enactment begins with the teen sitting in the bedroom listening to music, while waiting for a friend to arrive. The song she or he is listening to is from a playlist given as a gift to them by their significant other. A 12-screen display presents machine and human-produced metadata for the current song as well as a collection of annotated photographs assembled by the girl/boyfriend from visit to an amusement park together (see Fig. 7.7). Metadata for the photos lists the time, day, and weather information as well as a topographical map. Other screens display a set of gifted playlists, information about listening habits between girl/boyfriend and participant, and wordclouds of lyrics. After spending a few minutes in the room, a confederate friend arrives, notices the screens, and engages the teen in a semi-structured conversation exploring and prompting reflection on the meaning and function of the displayed information.

In the material world, people commonly craft unique, personalised gifts for loved ones. As an example, for many years teens exchanged personalised mix tapes and CDs, and digital playlists they can currently exchange lack the rich expressiveness and the uniqueness found in these disappearing artifacts. We designed this enactment's interfaces to explore how different kinds of digital materials related to a shared social experience could be combined into an assemblage of multiple kinds of virtual possessions. We wanted to explore how teens might react to this new form of a virtual possession. If teens had the tools to enable this kind of interaction, would it be a viable future design space to explore? To what extent could social or machine-logged metadata help support the work of crafting a digital thing expressive of a social relationship between two people?

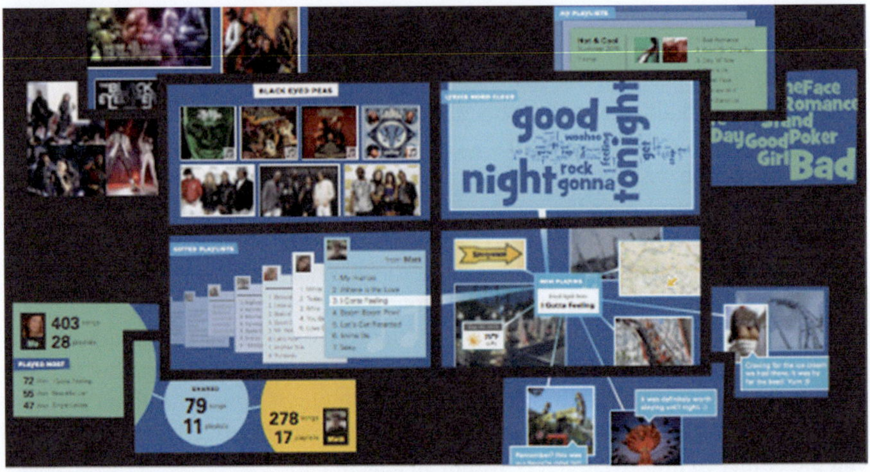

Fig.7.7 The 12-screen display visualising human and machine-produced metadata related to a gifted playlist from the teen's significant other. The *top left* quadrant depicts album art associated with the songs; *top right* is a wordcloud of song lyrics; *bottom right* is the current song being played that is mapped to annotated images of shared experiences associated with the song; *bottom left* is a visualisation of various gifted playlists and stats of favorite songs shared and listened to

In this enactment we returned to using a confederate to introduce social interaction directly within the scenario itself and also to help effectively manage its flow (Fig. 7.8). Our choice to include another enactment with a confederate in the middle of the serial order of all five enactments proved to be an important decision for two reasons. First, as noted, in the preceding status quilt enactment we continually struggled with developing compelling experiences due to the lack of focus that came with introducing an ambient technology as the central point of the scenario. The gifted assemblage enactment was more structured but also had clear open-ended points for teens to improvise. Additionally, we had carefully scripted points where the confederate could speed up or slow down the tempo of the social interaction based on the reaction of each particular teen participant. This helped teens maintain their willing suspension of disbelief needed to be present in the narrative scene, and it helped teens participate in the improvisation in embodied and visceral ways. Second, on a broader level, it provided a turning point in the dramatic arc across all five enactments. The renewed comfort and familiarity that emerged across teen participants in this scenario constructed an important foundation for transitioning to the final two enactments, which were shorter, did not involve confederates, and had primary activities that involved teens simply contemplating phenomena they encountered during the enactments themselves.

Teens' reactions to this enactment both reaffirmed growing themes across the enactments and also lead to new insights. Similar to many aspects of the design of the socially reactive bedroom displays, the gift assemblage even more explicitly projects new forms of virtual possessions that represent 'evidence of action' that reinforce a social relationship. This came in the form of a detailed, annotated music

Fig.7.8 The third enactment returned to the use of a confederate to help guide the flow, structure, and points of open-endedness in the scenario. This proved to be a viable technique that set the stage for making teens comfortable with more the open-ended and less structured enactments that followed

playlist and also information about the number of times a song has been listened to collectively among teens in a relationship. We found the gifted playlist strongly resonated with teens and in many cases they remarked on how different kinds of metadata could be used to explicitly convey the work that went into crafting a unique digital thing that could be symbolic of a valued relationship. Across these instances, teens commonly speculated on the value in self expression that a digital assemblage in the future could offer when compared to the much less expressive qualities of current digital gifts they had experiences with (e.g., the most common being e-cards).

These discussions helped us better understand that a common factor that shaped teens' perceived value of virtual possessions centered on how they could provide resources for investigating *one-on-one* relationships with a friend. While social computing systems and social network visualisation tools typically emphasise a view of a person's complete network, teens' reactions highly resonated with virtual possessions that provided windows into individual relationships. Teens reacted positively to the digital assemblage and aspects of the socially reactive bedroom displays, and often described how these new kinds of virtual possessions could become aesthetically integrated into their bedroom practices and provide mechanisms for actively expressing the social bond shared with another person. Teens communicated strong desires to see the evidence of the actions taken by themselves and others as a way of understanding who they are with that person and possibly where their future social relationship will go with them. These findings made clear that there is a need for new interactive tools, applications, and services to support teens in crafting new kinds of virtual possessions to explore, nurture, and support the social processes of developing and sustaining intimate relationships—a crucial part of teen life and one's development into young adulthood.

7.8 User Enactment 4: Postcards from Your Past Self

In this relatively brief user enactment, the teen simply sits in the bedroom when a parent arrives with two postcards mailed to her or him (see the top row in Fig. 7.9). The postcards present information and metadata scraped from a teen's social networking account from 2 years ago. One summarises personal stats, including the number of: friends on Facebook, people they most frequently tagged in photos, untaggings of self in photos, etc. (bottom right in Fig. 7.9). The other (bottom left in Fig. 7.9) shows an amusement park trip shared with friends, including both social information (e.g. friends that attended, comments about the event) as well as other metadata (e.g. weather and temperature, other events happening that day, celebrities visiting the park that year). After a few minutes, the parent confederate returns to say dinner is ready and the enactment comes to a close.

A core part of teens' lives is the struggle to find out who they are and who they want to become. We wanted teens to confront the material reality of receiving information from their 'past' and probe whether this would be seen as a resource for reflection or a tense reminder of who they once were. In parallel to the unseen record keeping of online interactions (Khovanskaya et al. 2013), we also wanted to probe teens' perceptions of their online personal information being collected. We aimed to provoke discussion on teens' technological practices, issues of self-disclosure, and the need to keep these concerns in mind when creating technologies for self-reflection that incorporate new digital materials. We wanted to explore the question of would receiving a physical postcard constructed from old metadata be perceived to support or conflict with self-reflection? And, how far is 'too far' for teens to look into their past?

This form, content, and duration of this enactment departed substantially from the one preceding it. There were no confederates involved, the main 'task' was to encounter and make sense of postcards from the teen's past, and, as such, it was a much less structured enactment. Our decision to migrate from the 12-screen display at this point in the study was helped provoke teens to think critically about not only the presence of bedroom technology, but also about their more general technological practices and the potential for unintended consequences to emerge over time (e.g., such as unwanted self-disclosure). Additionally, by the fourth enactment, teen participants were making connections across all of the enactments that they had experienced during the post-enactment interview. These kinds of discussions were particularly valuable as they illustrated teens' ability to exercise critical judgment in making sense of the distinct yet related potential technological futures they had

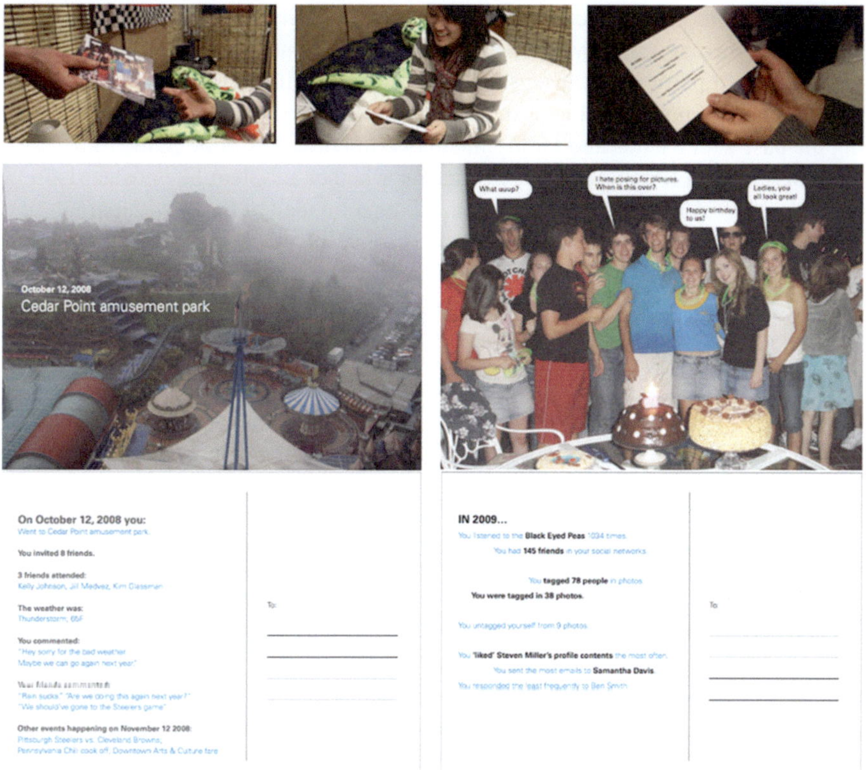

Fig.7.9 The teen receives two postcards from the past while sitting on her bed in the bedroom (*top row of three images*). Each postcard image has the corresponding information on its back directly below it in the figure. The *left* postcard column depicts information related to an amusement part trip 2 years earlier; The *right* column depicts information on a postcard that summarizes personal stats collected and summarized from the teen's usage of social media services from 2 years ago

experienced. The slower pacing and time for personal meaning-making directly in the enactment, where the participant's attention wasn't heavily structured, emerged as being highly effective at setting the tone for these more in depth and nuanced discussions with teens to emerge.

Despite its simplicity, the postcards from the past enactment was successful at provoking teens to consider how technical systems keep traces of their interactions as metadata and how access to this data could shape their perceptions of virtual possessions. While teens frequently brought up the desire to have more transparency over when traces of their digital interactions are recorded and where they are stored, the content itself on the postcard was largely not regarded as overly contentious. We suspected the personal behaviour summary postcard, which presented machine-captured metadata summarising a teen's behavior from 2 years ago, would cause conflicts by prying 'too far back' into the past to their 'pre-teen' days. Surprisingly, this was often not the case and most teens desired to go much deeper into their past to understand and explore times in their lives in which they were too young to remember. Somewhat echoing unexpected findings from the first enactment in which participants discussed the Halloween photos from deep in a teen's past, some teens perceived the postcards could stimulate valued ways for co-exploring the past with friends and family members. Importantly, while in the minority, a handful of teens brought up the concern over whether a system like postcards from the past might also introduce the potential to be reminded of fights with parents and friends, which could unsettle events that had been resolved or forgotten. Collectively, these findings suggested teens have a critical need for more sophisticated and value-sensitive tools that could support activities of reflections and reminiscence on the past through new digital materials.

7.9 User Enactment 5: Managing Your Multiple Digital Selves

In our final user enactment, the teen is sitting in the bedroom after school and viewing four different versions of their social networking profile targeted at four different audiences: family, school friends, sports team, and church (see Fig. 7.10). These are linked to incoming and outgoing digital communication. They enable the teen to post status updates, comments and other content to each group individually. After a few moments she or he receives a text message from a member of the sports team, and this quadrant highlights. She or he reads the text message (on a phone provided to them). A few moments later a different quadrant indicates another text message has arrived from a school friend. The corresponding quadrant highlights and she or he reads that message. The enactment concludes when a parent knocks and asks the teen to get ready for sports practice.

Across our fieldwork, we found teens had developed sophisticated practices for managing multiple digital presentations of self. We tailored the design of this interface to explore how teens would react when confronted with an application that would directly support these behaviours. This interface leveraged the segmented design of the layered panel displays to provoke discussion on the tension teens experience in resolving fragmented identities over time and the role technologies will play in supporting or complicating these practices. We wanted to understand how teens would perceive the ability to explicitly manage different presentations of self to different groups valuable. Are teens disturbed by the explicit fragmentations of their social groups, and the presence of this information in their room?

While its form and content migrated back to focus on the 12-screen display, this enactment exhibited similar overall qualities to postcards from the past. We wanted it to similarly be less structured and place emphasis on teens making sense of phenomena they encountered, and then bring it to a close. Again, this technique was effective at opening a productive space for teens to make connections across enactments and nearly always led to extended post-enactment interviews where teens

Fig.7.10 The teen receives a text message from a sports team member, which associated with the top right quadrant of the 12-screen display and then checks the text message on their simulated foamcore mobile phone (*top row of images*); The 12-screen display with depicting four different versions of their social networking profile targeted at four different social audiences

commented at length on their encounters in this specific scenario and more broadly on connected experiences and reflection across enactments. This proved to be an ideal way of drawing the dramatic arc across all five enactments to a close.

We expected that, similar to the socially reactive bedroom, teens would find the multiple digital selves application to be contentious, particularly in terms of its explicit segmentation and mediation of their digital presentations of self. During our iterative piloting of this enactment during our prototyping phase prior to the study, we used university graduate students as stand-ins for teens. These students often reacted negatively to the idea of displaying different representations of self to different social groups. Interestingly, when we eventually ran our study with teens, they had entirely different reactions. Teens did have concerns over unwanted self-disclosure (e.g., if someone were to walk into the room and see the displays). However, to our surprise, most teens were entirely comfortable with having multiple digital presentations of self clearly segmented and manageable; they felt like this fragmentation could somehow make their lives seem more manageable. In some cases, they even envisioned how saved records of these fragmentations could provide resources for reflecting on personal growth across life transitions and stages.

One reason for this could be that teens have more segmented lives than other people. They move between their home and bedroom, partially controlled by their parents, and their high school, controlled by both peers and school rules. As they work to construct a self-identity, they have the experience of being at least two people much more than young adults who create a separate life when they leave their parents' home and begin to control their own space. This finding helped us better understand and empathise with how this surface-level fragmentation can be crucial to teens' work to construct a unified life narrative and, in essence, develop a concrete sense of self. These issues also further brought into focus just how different the teen world is from other populations, and that designing for teenagers brings the added complexity of supporting practices, desires, and values that are shifting and evolving at accelerated and unpredictable rates.

7.10 Discussion and Reflection

User enactments provided a generative research method for co-exploring with teens how a future teenager's bedroom might support (or complicate) their identity construction practices. However, running a user enactments study can be a complex process that requires careful attention to several factors through iterations of prototyping and piloting—particularly when working with a population as sensitive, dynamic, and unpredictable as teens. In line with the goals of this book, the core contribution of this chapter is to articulate our experiences of putting this method to use with teens in the service of surfacing best practices and potential pitfalls. In what follows, we turn attention towards details outside of our direct application of user enactments in summarising what teens reported about participating in this study and reflecting on our studio as the site for conducting the user enactments study.

While teens can be an unpredictable and diverse population to study, our approach was successful at providing a setting for them to draw on their own experiences in making sense of the phenomena they encountered. We followed the last post-enactment interview by posing a final open-ended question to teens about their overall experience of being a study participant. In many cases, teens reported that the moments transpiring just after their parents had dropped them off in our studio at times felt foreign and awkward, if not uncomfortable. However, after the enactments study started, most teens exhibited a sense of relief upon realising they had a private, open forum to convey their frustrations, emotions, insights and speculations on the future-oriented scenarios they encountered. While moments in over the course of the user enactments could at times falter (e.g., the confusing ambiguities often arising from the status quilt enactment), in general the method created a constructive forum for us to invite teens to explore and critically consider their perspectives about what technology ought to be in their lives in the face of an uncertain future.

Interestingly, the candidness that teens exhibited in our studio at times contrasted our prior experiences of conducting qualitative fieldwork in teenagers' actual bedrooms. In our fieldwork there were instances where the looming presence (or potential presence) of another family member prevented teens from feeling fully comfortable with disclosing certain kinds of personal or sensitive information to us. It became clear that the combination of our study engaging with issues that teens could relate to, while occurring within a setting that operated outside of the social structures of their domestic environment created a context where they felt comfortable with openly expressing themselves.

This finding suggests interesting implications for the use of methods like user enactments with teens, which take place within a studio or lab setting. Clearly, conducting a user enactment study is not aimed at achieving ecological validity in that it operates outside of teens' lived-in domestic spaces. Rather, user enactments ask teens to creatively engage with speculative technologies that could exist in a possible future. On the surface, it seems like this more speculative approach could help avoid or reduce ethical issues associated with recording teen behaviors in their homes and being held accountable for unintended disclosure information from these very sensitive settings. Yet, we found teens often exhibited a greater sense of openness in describing their current and past experiences and, especially, their desires, aspirations, and anxieties bound to their undetermined next steps into the future and the role technology might play in this journey. This makes clear that whether in the field or, perhaps especially, in contexts in which teens are invited to engage in generative explorations of the future, it is of paramount importance that the data, observations, and insights collected from teens are treated in sensitive and ethical ways.

7.11 Conclusion

Teens are a fascinating, dynamic population; they are on the vanguard of emerging technologies, often defining the behaviour and social mores of these products and services. At the same time, teens are still exploring and developing into the person they want to become, making them a terribly sensitive group to work with, and making it all the more crucial to critically and carefully consider how new technologies might shape their lives and practices. We need a multiplicity of methods for working with teens in the HCI and interaction design communities. The core contribution of this chapter is to motivate and develop user enactments as a method for moving beyond studies of teens' current practices and generatively engaging them in experiencing and making sense of possible technological futures. In this, we have described and reflected on our own experience of putting user enactments into practice with teens in the service of surfacing best practices and potential pitfalls. Ultimately, we hope this chapter will help better support future research and design practice aimed at engaging teenagers in critically playing a part in determining the roles that technology will play in their lives now and well into the future.

Acknowledgments This work was supported by NSF grant IIS-1017429 and by Google. We thank the teens (and their parents) that took part in the study. We also thank Hajin Choi, Stephanie Meier, Angela Park, and Alena Tesone for their help in developing the teen bedroom user enactments, Pablo Bariola and Haakon Faste for their photographic assistance, and Scott Davidoff for his foundational work on the Speed Dating methodology.

References

Ackerman M, Mainwaring S (2005) Privacy issues and human-computer interaction. In: Garfinkel S, Cranor L (eds) Security and usability. O'Reilly, Beijing/Farnham/Sebastopol, pp 381–400

Belk R (1988) Possessions and the extended self. J Consum Res 15(2):139–168

Boyd Danah (2007) Why youth (heart) social network sites: the role of networked publics in teenage social life. Youth, Identity, and Digital Media Volume, pp 1–26

Buchenau M, Suri JF (2000) Experience prototyping. In Proceedings of the DIS, (2000), ACM Press, pp 424–433

Burns C, Dishman E, Verplank W, Lassiter B (1994) Actors, hairdos & videotape—informance design. In Conference companion of CHI'94, pp 119–120

Buxton B (2007) Sketching user experiences: getting the design right and the right design. Morgan Kaufmann, Amsterdam/Boston

Carroll J (2000) Making use: scenario-based design of human-computer interaction. MIT Press, Cambridge

Chawla L (1992) Childhood place attachments. In: Altman I (ed) Place attachment. Plenum, New York, pp 63–86

Cockton G (2006) Designing worth is worth designing. In: Proceedings of the NordiCHI'06, pp 165–174

Davidoff S, Lee M, Yui C, Zimmerman J, Dey A (2006) Principles of smart home control. Proceedings of the UbiComp '06, pp 19–34.

Davidoff S, Lee M, Dey A, Zimmerman J 2007 Rapidly exploring application design through speed dating. In Proceedings of the 9th international conference on Ubiquitous computing (UbiComp'07), pp 429–446

Durrant A, Frohlich D, Sellen A, Lyons E (2009) Home curation versus teenage photography: photo displays in the family home. Int J Hum-Comput Stud 67(12):1005–1023

Edwards K, Grinter R (2001) At home with Ubiquitous computing: seven challenges. Ubicomp'01, pp 256–272

Fitton D, Read J, Horton M (2013) The challenge of working with teens as participants in interaction design. In CHI '13 Extended Abstracts on Human Factors in Computing Systems (CHI EA'13). ACM, New York, pp 205–210

Friedman B (2006) Value sensitive design. Interactions 3(6):16–23. ACM Press

Giddens A (1991) Modernity and self-identity: self and society in the late modern Age. Stanford University Press, Stanford, pp 187–201

Glaser B, Strauss A (1967) Discovery of grounded theory: strategies for qualitative research. Sociology press, Mill Valley

Goffman E (1959) The Presentation of self in everyday llife. Double Day, New York

Hallnas L, Redstrom J (2001) Slow technology: designing for reflection. Pers Ubiquit Comput 5(3):201–212

Hartmann B, Doorley S, Kim S, Vora P (2006) Wizard of Oz sketch animation for experience prototyping. Adjunct proceedings of the Ubicomp 2006

Hodkinson P, Lincoln S (2008) Online journals as virtual bedrooms? young people, identity, and personal space. Young 16(1):27–46

Hutchinson H, Mackay W, Westerlund B, Bederson B, Druin A, Plaisant C, Beaudouin-Lafon, Conversy S, Evans H, Hansen H, Roussel N, Eiderbäck B (2003) Technology probes: inspiring design for and with families. In: Proceedings of the SIGCHI conference on human factors in computing systems (CHI '03). ACM, New York, pp 17–24

Iacucci G, Kuutti K, Ranta M (2000) On the move with a magic thing: role playing in concept design of mobile services and devices. In: Proceedings of the 3rd conference on designing interactive systems: processes, practices, methods, and techniques (DIS '00), pp 193–202

Ito M, Antin J, Finn M, Law A, Manion A, Mitnick S, Horst HA (2009) Hanging out, messing around, and geeking out: kids living and learning with new media. MIT Press, Cambridge, MA

Iversen O, Halskov K, Leong T (2010) Rekindling values in participatory design. In: Proceedings. of the PDC'10, pp 91–100.

Kaye J, et al. (2006) To have and to hold: exploring the personal archive. In: Proceedings. of the CHI '06, pp 275–284.

Kensing F, Blomberg J (1998) Participatory design: issues and concerns. Computer Support Collaborative Work 7:167–185. Kluwer Press

Khovanskaya V, Baumer E, Cosley D, Voida S, Gay G (2013) "Everybody knows what you're doing": a critical design approach to personal informatics. In: Proceedings of the SIGCHI conference on human factors in computing systems (CHI '13). ACM, New York, pp 3403–3412

Kirk DS, Sellen A (2010) On human remains: values and practice in the home archiving of cherished objects. ACM Trans Comput-Hum Interact (TOCHI) 17(3):10

Kirk D, Sellen A, Rother C, Wood K (2006) Understanding photowork. In: Proceedings of the SIGCHI conference on human factors in computing systems pp 761–770, ACM

Kirk D, Izadi S, Sellen A, et al. (2010) Opening up the family archive. In: Proceedings of the CSCW '10, pp 261–270.

Kurvinen E, Koskinen I, Battarbee K (2008) Prototyping social interaction. Des Issues 24:46–57

Mancini C, Rogers Y, Bandara A, Coe T, Jedrzejczyk L, et al. (2010) Contravision: exploring users' reactions to futuristic technology. In: Proceedings of the CHI '10, pp 153–162

March W, Fleuriot C (2006) Girls, technology and privacy: "is my mother listening?" In: Proceedings of the CHI'06

Miles MB, Huberman AM (1994) Qualitative data analysis. Sage, Thousand Oaks

Nelson HG, Stolterman E (2003) The design way: intentional change in an unpredictable world: foundations and fundamentals of design competence. Educational Technology, Englewood Cliffs

Nunes M, Greenberg S, Neustaedter C (2008) Sharing digital photographs in the home through physical mementos, souvenirs, and keepsakes. In: Proceedings of the 7th ACM conference on designing interactive systems, pp 250–260, ACM

Odom W, Zimmerman J, Forlizzi J (2011) Teenagers and their virtual possessions: design opportunities and issues. In: Proceedings of the SIGCHI conference on human factors in computing systems (CHI '11). ACM, New York, pp 1491–1500

Odom W, Zimmerman J, Forlizzi J, Choi H, Meier S, Park A (2012) Investigating the presence, form and behavior of virtual possessions in the context of a teen bedroom. In: Proceedings of the SIGCHI conference on human factors in computing systems (CHI '12). ACM, New York, pp 327–336

Odom W, Zimmerman J, Davidoff S, Forlizzi J, Dey A, Lee M (2012) A fieldwork of the future with user enactments. In: Proceedings of the designing interactive systems conference (DIS '12). ACM, New York, pp 338–347

Odom W, Zimmerman J, Forlizzi J (2014) Placelessness, spacelessness, and formlessness: experiential qualities of virtual possessions. In: Proceedings of the 2014 conference on designing interactive systems (DIS '14). ACM, New York, pp 985–994

Palen L, Dourish P (2003) Unpacking "privacy" for a networked world. In: Proceedings of the CHI' 03, pp 129–136

Peesapati S, Schwanda V, Schultz J, Lepage M, Jeong S, Cosley D (2010) Pensive: supporting everyday reminiscence. In: Proceedings of the CHI '10, pp 2027–2036

Petrelli D, Whittaker S, Brockmeier J (2008) AutoTopography: what can physical mementos tell us about digital memories? In: Proceedings of the SIGCHI conference on human factors in computing systems (CHI '08). ACM, New York, pp 53–62.

Read J, Horton M, Iversen O, Fitton D, Little L (2013) Methods of working with teenagers in interaction design. In: Proceedings of the CHI '13 extended abstracts on human factors in computing systems (CHI EA '13). ACM, New York, pp 3243–3246

Read J, Horton M, Fitton D, Little L, Beale R, Toth N (2013) On being cool: exploring interaction design for teenagers. In: Proceedings of the 27th international BCS human computer interaction conference (BCS-HCI '13), Steve Love, Kate Hone, Tom McEwan (eds) British Computer Society, Swinton, Article 10, 10 p

Simon HA (1996) The sciences of the artificial. MIT Press, Cambridge, MA

Steele J, Brown J (1995) Adolescent room culture: studying media in the context of everyday life. J Youth Adolesc 24(5):551–576

Taylor A, Harper R (2002) Age-old practices in the 'new world': a study of gift-giving between teenage mobile phone users. In: Proceedings of the CHI '02, pp 439–446

Tohidi M, Buxton W, Baecker R, Sellen A (2006) Getting the right design and the design right: testing many is better than one. In: Proceedings of the CHI'06

Van House N (2009) Collocated photo sharing, storytelling, and the performance of self. Int. J. Hum.- Comput. Stud. 67(12):1073–1086. Vetere F et al. 2005 Mediating intimacy: designing technologies to support strong-tie relationships. In: Proceedings of the CHI '05, pp 471–480

Vetere F, Gibbs M, Kjeldskov J, Howard S, Mueller F, Pedell S, Mecoles K, Bunyan M (2005) Mediating intimacy: designing technologies to support strong-tie relationships. In Proceedings of the SIGCHI conference on human factors in computing systems (CHI '05). ACM, New York, pp 471–480

Voida A, Grinter RE, Ducheneaut N, Edwards WK, Newman MW (2005) Listening in: practices surrounding iTunes music sharing. In Proceedings of the SIGCHI conference on human factors in computing systems, pp 191–200. ACM Press

Woodruff A, Augustin S, Foucault B (2007) Sabbath day home automation: "it's like mixing technology and religion". In Proceedings of the CHI'07, pp 527–536

Wright P, Wallace J, McCarthy J (2008) Aesthetics and experience-centered design. ACM Trans Comput Hum Interact 15(4):Article 18

Zimmerman J (2005) Video sketches: exploring pervasive computing interaction designs. IEEE Comput 4:91–94

Chapter 8
Involving Teenagers Today in the Design of Tomorrow's Technology

Christopher R. Wilkinson

Abstract Younger people appear adept at creating accurate mental models of product interaction and acquiring new and relevant knowledge through experiential learning. This chapter highlights and explains some of the differences in interaction and learning that occur according to age. This is achieved by revealing the existence of age-effects regarding prior experience and their effect upon interaction with a novel contemporary product, chosen at random for its newness to market, and by investigating if young people, based on their experience of contemporary technology, are able to create more accurate mental models of engagement that facilitate superior interaction. The overall aim is to present best practice when involving teenagers and young people in research to optimise their influence on product and interaction design, and to maximise the output of ideation and design insight acquisition exercises. This is explored by framing interaction in terms of Rasmussen's (1993) Skill, Rule and Knowledge-based Model of Behaviour to determine how knowledge acquisition is facilitated and to identify instances of interactional complexity that could be overcome by better design with input from real users. The work illustrates how insight acquisition activity can drive better and more effective design research in the real world with a greater likelihood of adoption and increased commercial success; designing engaging products for a teenage demographic necessitates their close involvement throughout the design process. This chapter provides examples of how this might be achieved by focussing upon how to better include, motivate and involve teenagers within empirical and commercial research activity.

8.1 Introduction

The purpose of this article is to highlight and present best practice when involving teenagers and young people in product interaction and design insight acquisition exercises. This draws on research conducted at the University of Cambridge that

C.R. Wilkinson (✉)
University of Cambridge Research Office, Greenwich House, Cambridge CB3 0TX, UK
e-mail: crwilkinson@cantab.net

© Springer International Publishing Switzerland 2016

L. Little et al. (eds.), *Perspectives on HCI Research with Teenagers*,
Human–Computer Interaction Series, DOI 10.1007/978-3-319-33450-9_8

investigated the extent to which prior technological experience of products is related to age, to determine if this has implications for the success of subsequent product interaction.

The intention of this chapter is to provide the design community with new knowledge and a greater awareness of the diversity of user needs, both in research and in product design and manufacture. It achieves this by focussing upon how to better include, motivate, and involve a broader subset of the population – and particularly teenagers – within empirical research.

The author has written extensively about Inclusive Design for older groups including the elderly (Wilkinson 2011; Wilkinson et al. 2011; Wilkinson et al. 2013; Wilkinson and De Angeli 2014; Wilkinson and Gandhi 2015), and whilst designing for this group remains highly commendable and should be encouraged, it is also important not to neglect those at the other end of the spectrum.

Literature suggests that the way in which young people interact with technology differs from those over the age of 25 (Docampo-Rama 2001; Weiss 2002). This *generational effect* (Freudenthal 2001) refers to these individuals being optimally receptive to interacting more effectively with new technology. Indeed, younger people appear more adept at creating accurate mental models of product interaction and acquiring new and relevant knowledge through experiential learning (Wilkinson et al. 2013).

The design community has, in the past, been accused of failing to understand and engage with distinct user groups, preferring to design from their personal experience and capability. This risks alienating and excluding significant proportions of the population, as a lack of user understanding is transferred into products that become unsatisfactory, unappealing, and unusable for significant groups of users and subsequently limits uptake and adoption.

However, today we are more attuned to employing User-Centred Design (UCD) techniques and understanding the importance of User Experience (UX) in design than ever before. Although we may recognise that it is important, ensuring it's uptake in commercial contexts can still be problematic. Regardless, the notion that user centred and participatory design can produce a better end-product-fit resulting in greater adoption and engagement, out-of-the-box, continues to gain momentum. That strategically involving users within the design process has the additional advantage of reducing subsequent development costs is a factor that is also beginning to be accepted by mainstream industry.

In communication-based models of design, the user's and designer's interpretation of products and their interaction are considered as mental models. These mental models are based, in part, upon user expectation and perception. Expectation in terms of users existing knowledge, and prior experience about how the product might behave and their perception of how further interaction might occur. These factors are influenced by the feedback and messages received from product features and their tactile and visual cues – form dictating function – and the context within which interaction occurs.

Furthermore, experience is not limited to mere prior *product* experience, but is also heavily influenced by individuals' personal experience of the world, their place within it, and the interactions that occur therein. Thus, it differs according to a multitude of factors but, perhaps most notably, according to age. For example, speed of interaction, the ability to acquire iconic information, and feature recognition, were all found to differ as a function of age. Younger individuals recalled greater numbers of similar products than older individuals and there was a significant effect of age upon awareness and use of contemporary technology (Wilkinson et al. 2013). If the user and context of interaction, then, are not understood sufficiently, the danger remains that designers may not truly appreciate differences in personal capability between themselves and the intended users of technology.

The intention here is to focus more on the teenage population and portray the robust, methodological, approaches that can and should be adopted when conducting research with a younger demographic. From an inclusive design perspective, the aim of this article is to highlight how humans learn and interact with products differently according to age and how best research practice can induce the best design. By increasing our understanding of how learning and mental model development occurs and differs through direct interaction with products, the output of research can help us design more effectively for the teenagers of tomorrow and also improve access to future technology for all.

8.1.1 Background

Historically, the views of individual users were not always sought to inform the design process (Hansen et al. 2007). This lack of involvement in the design and evaluation stages of product development may be responsible for causing some of the generational and age-related issues that preclude large proportions of the populous interacting with products. Further, it may explain many peoples' reluctance and difficulty in engaging with new and contemporary technology; if individuals' views are not sought, then designers will fail to realise and cater effectively for their specific needs. This, in turn, may manifest itself in reluctance on behalf of users and market sectors to purchase or interact with many forms of modern technology (Fig. 8.1).

Almost 10 years ago, Lewis et al. (2006) observed that designers were typically male and able-bodied. More recently, a survey of the UK design industry reinforced concerns regarding a lack of diversity within the design community itself. The survey revealed that the average UK designer is male, white, and 38 years old, with only 7 % of UK designers coming from ethnic minority backgrounds (Design Council 2010). Although designers were found to be typically young and healthy (Zitkus et al. 2011), the concern remains that designers may assume that all users possess the same abilities, needs, and desires in a product as themselves. Such a failure to connect with potential users – the young, old, and those in between – risks alienating significant proportions of the population, and may result in the development of products that perform poorly in both a physical and commercial sense, and suffer from lower rates of uptake and adoption.

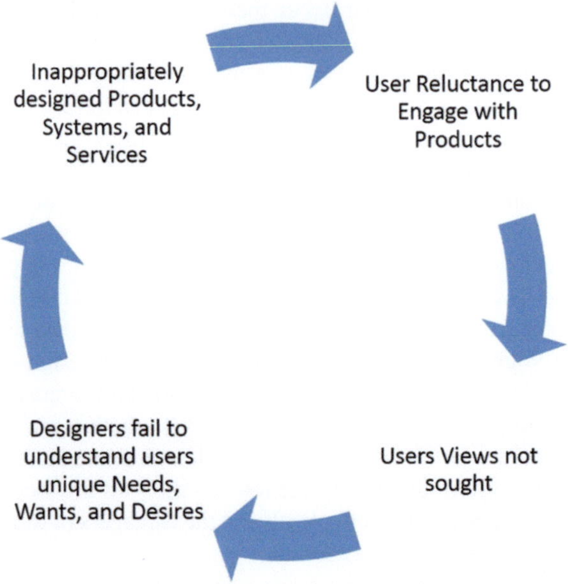

Fig. 8.1 Cycle of design oversight influencing the uptake and engagement of technology (Adapted from Wilkinson 2011)

Developing products that cater more effectively for a larger demographic widens the commercial market, benefits a larger cross-section of society, and makes both commercial and ethical sense. User involvement within the design process is the key solution to effect such an outcome. Including a wider and more representative sample of end-users – able-bodied and less-able bodied users, children, and the elderly – at early stages and throughout the design process, removes the need of designers to rely on their own knowledge or skill sets as personal points of reference. Indeed, catering for diversity within the target market should not be a unique approach; it should be prerequisite for all design and a natural component within requirements specification. Design should consider the user as an individual, possessing individual aptitudes, experiences, and other human characteristics, and account for the abilities and limitations of all potential users. Products designed in this way will be capable of being used by people with the widest possible range of abilities, within the widest range of situations, reaching most, if not all, potential end users.

8.1.1.1 User Centred and Participatory Design

User-Centred Design (UCD) has become an umbrella term for a number of related approaches that aim to involve users in the design process. Inclusive Design is one such approach that aims to create interfaces, artefacts, products, and services that are applicable to as many users as possible within the constraints of the design

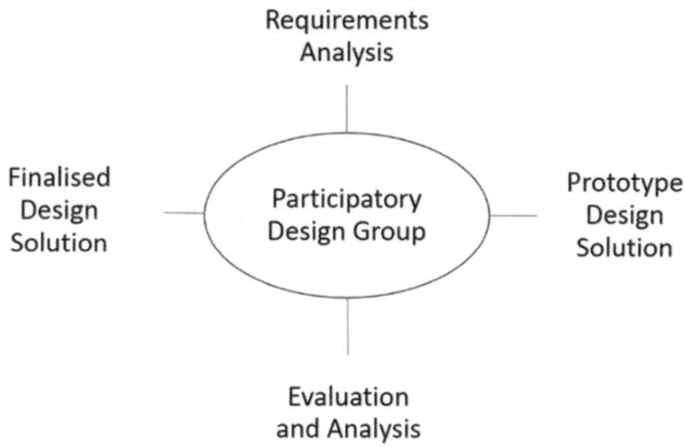

Fig. 8.2 Participatory design group user interaction within the design process (Wilkinson and De Angeli 2014)

specification, and attempts to address the needs of the widest possible audience, irrespective of age or ability (Keates and Clarkson 2003, Design Council 2008). Similarly, Universal Design attempts to optimise product and service design for maximum accessibility and make '*...mainstream design accessible to everyone*' (Pullin 2011, p 2). Participatory Design, too, aims to develop solutions with the close involvement of stakeholders and end-users through cycles of requirements gathering, prototype development, implementation, and evaluation (Sharma et al. 2008).

To inform the design process, it is important to capture user information and feedback ideally at every stage, with input from everyone involved. User Centred and Participatory design approaches can be seen as attempts to better understand and involve real users, and as imperative and important in creating user friendly products or services (Muller 2002; Lindgaard et al. 2006). The importance of individual input is also reflected in Sanders (2002) notion of Participatory Design as a belief that *all* people have something to offer *at every stage* of the design process and that when given the appropriate tools with which to express themselves, they can be both articulate, creative, and inspirational, in terms of generating new ideas and in developing current thinking (Fig. 8.2).

These common notions of placing the user at the centre of the design process are at the core of the research approaches presented within this chapter to appreciate the diverse needs, requirements, and prior experience of users. This creates an environment that fosters effective ideation and insight acquisition, and the techniques proposed can be used to develop products that are more immediately accessible and usable, and to develop products that enjoy greater rates of adoption and engagement 'out-of-the-box'.

Within user centred and participatory design, consideration of individuals' prior experience and other factors such as the context of use and environment of interaction are required to create truly usable and inclusive products, and are key considerations in the performance of usability evaluations (Nielsen 1993). The fact that commercial design practice is resource constrained in terms of time, financial investment, and professional expertise, causes user involvement to often be seen as an unnecessary and expensive luxury (Grudin 1991). However, involving users within the process can enhance the applicability, acceptance, and adoption of the end design, and consequently has the potential to reduce development risk. Mayhew (1999) advocated consideration of users' physical characteristics, knowledge and experience, widening this to include users' psychological characteristics. By understanding these factors, and applying them within design, the potential exists to increase the long-term profitability of product manufacturers and enhance the competitive edge of companies, whilst assisting in the production of better products for all users. One approach to achieve product differentiation is to examine how humans learn and interact with interfaces and designs, and by understanding more about how learning occurs, use this knowledge to influence future design in terms of ease of learning, use, and access to all. The project hereby presented aimed to involve, consider, and understand the effects of age and experience on product interaction and to derive design insights that might drive future product development initiatives.

8.1.2 Research Aims

The primary goal of UCD being to gain insight into human behaviour, attitudes, experience and knowledge applied during interaction, it is felt a combination of both a quantitative, scientific, approach and the application of more qualitative, ethnographic, techniques have the potential to yield the most valuable data (Wilkinson 2011).

The methodology thus involved the use of:

- Verbal/talk aloud/concurrent protocol
- Semi-structured interviews
- Questionnaire administration
- Video-recorded Product Interaction Exercises
- Observational and thematic Analysis

These approaches, in conjunction with analysis of the products icons and features, was used to determine individuals' experience of specific contemporary products and to investigate if there may be factors that facilitate intuitive interaction. The features and icons used on the product itself were examined to determine if age-related differences existed in terms of recognition. If it is possible to identify icons and features that will be optimally recognised by a teenage population, it is important that designers are made aware that every aspect of their design has implications for intuitive use that also have a knock-on effect upon ease-of-use, product uptake and adoption.

The main research aims this approach was intended to address were:

1. To investigate the existence of age-effects regarding prior experience and any associated effects upon interaction with a novel contemporary household product, chosen at random for its newness to market.
2. To investigate if young people, based on their experience of contemporary technology, are able to create more accurate mental models of engagement that facilitate superior interaction with novel products.
3. To investigate the efficacy of framing interaction in terms of Rasmussen's (1993) Skill, Rule and Knowledge-based Model of behaviour and thereby determine how knowledge acquisition is facilitated and identify instances of interactional complexity that could be overcome by better design with input from real users.

8.1.2.1 How Does Classifying Human Behaviour Teach Us About Mental Model Development?

In Crilly et al. (2008) communication-based model of design, the user's and designer's interpretations of artefacts are considered as a form of mental model, based in part upon user expectation – the existing knowledge and prior experience of how the product or interface may behave, and their perception of how further interaction is likely to occur. This perception can be influenced by the messages received from product features, visual and tactile cues, and the context within which interaction occurs. The aspect of mental models that this study investigates is the specific product knowledge acquired that contributes to overall understanding and influences successful interaction. The findings indicate how product features, both functional and aesthetic, can contribute toward successful interaction. The results also indicate how specific product features can adversely affect interaction, either in terms of physical manipulation or in terms of impacting learning and the development of correct and appropriate mental models.

Mental models are constantly matched against situational feedback. This feedback, both pursuant to and discrepant from a person's expectation, leads to the build-up of experience. Prior experience is probably best summarised in Rasmussen's (1993) Skill-Rule-Knowledge (SRK) model, where the increase in experience with a given product allows the user to move from predominately conscious knowledge-based behaviour that requires slow planned reasoning and prediction of outcomes to rule-based behaviour governed by information processing using the 'if (precondition) then (action)' rule, then to skilled, automatic, and non-conscious behaviour.

Research into the effect of prior experience has also uncovered significant effects of age, cognitive capability and ageing (Wilkinson et al. 2013). In particular, different generations of users have been proven to have a varied frequency and level of exposure to technology and range of skills available to deploy (Lim 2010).

8.1.2.2 Rasmussen's Skill, Rule, Knowledge-Based Model

Rasmussen's (1993) SRK model accounted for fluctuations in the level of consciousness required during interaction, based on the assumption that individuals operate at a level appropriate to the familiarity of the situation (Thomas and van Leeuwen 1999). The model was developed by Wickens et al. (1998) to incorporate the type of cognitive processing that occurs. In this context, it was used to classify human behaviour during interaction and simultaneously assess the extent of interactional complexity users experience as a consequence of product design.

Skill-based activities are often highly rehearsed procedures of behaviour: increasing the automaticity of behaviour through repetition (making a cup of tea for example) reduces cognitive loading and allows attentional and cognitive resources to be directed toward other aspects of interaction (Wickens and Hollands 2000). Such actions can be identified as being highly practiced and fluently executed, requiring a minimal amount of conscious effort in their implementation. Considered almost automatic, these actions are often swiftly repeated or repeatable (Embrey 2003; Sicart 2008). Skill-based activity is susceptible however, to attentional errors – skipping or repeating steps in well-rehearsed action sequences, or when stimuli trigger an inappropriate automatic response.

The application of rules in the scenario to achieve the desired outcome is indicative of Rule-based behaviour – the scenario may be familiar but to achieve task completion may require the application of conscious attention to execute the associated rule-based response (Rasmussen 1993). Rule-based mistakes refer to the application of ineffectual rules or rules that are no longer appropriate. These are often short-cuts developed from experience that work most of the time (Wogalter 2006).

Knowledge-based behaviour is characterised by the exhibition of advanced reasoning (Wirstad 1988; Reason 1990). This approach often occurs in novel scenarios, where the situation is unfamiliar: cognitive effort and resources are deployed in understanding the current situation and developing pathways to the desired end-goal scenario which must also be conceptualised. A consequence of exhausting all the options or behaviours at the skill or rule-based level is increased cognitive and situational demand. Resultant interactional response times are usually greater than either skill or rule based interaction activity (Reason 1990). Thus, interaction typically requires greater attention and situational awareness, and is often prone to error (Alario and Ferrand 1999). Knowledge-based errors are failures in the mental models people use or manipulate, or are based on erroneous perception of current stimuli (Reason 1990, p 61).

Langdon et al. (2010) investigated the effect of prior experience on consumer products, finding that the age and technological generation of the user would affect both their expectations of the product or its required method of interaction. This research, then, sets out in some way to replicate these findings that the age and technological generation of the user affects expectations of the product or its required method of interaction. This work goes further by not only examining age and generationally related differences in product interaction, but also investigates ease of learning and knowledge acquisition and the effects of interactional complexity upon these processes.

The analysis in this chapter focusses upon differences between age groups in terms of the Skill, Rule, and Knowledge-based activity participants were engaged in during interaction. It also examines how feature and icon recognition vary according to age, and investigates differences in the level of awareness and familiarity with current technology. It then seeks to determine how all these factors contribute toward more unconscious and intuitive product interaction and use.

8.2 Method: Investigating Age-Effects on Interaction

As mentioned, the consideration of prior experience, context of use, and environment of interaction are important to create truly usable and inclusive products, as is the consideration of users' psychological and physical characteristics, knowledge, and experience. By increasing understanding of these factors and applying them within inclusive design, the potential exists to increase the long-term profitability of product manufacturers and enhance the competitive edge of such companies whilst concurrently assisting in the production of better products for all end users (Dong et al. 2006).

One approach to achieve this is to examine how humans learn and interact with interfaces and designs, and by understanding more about how learning occurs, use this knowledge to influence future design in terms of ease of learning, use, and access to all (Inclusive Design Group 2011).

The research conducted at the University of Cambridge aimed to investigate learning and the effect of prior experience, whilst capturing further information regarding what occurs during interaction with products. This utilised a new-to-market, novel product to ensure users possessed limited or non-existent mental models of interaction, with a focus upon generational effects and the effects of ageing upon interaction.

As humans age, cognitive and physical capabilities decrease as a factor of natural human atrophy (Rabbit 1993, Tarakanov-Plaz 2005). Cognitive processing speed, the ability to switch attention, engage selective attention and working memory, textual comprehension and response time to complex motor tasks all affect behaviour and task performance (Chan et al. 2009; Nichols et al. 2006). Although older individuals may have larger memory banks of interface and interaction knowledge upon which to rely, they may experience difficulty retrieving useful chunks of memory that help them interact with familiar or non-familiar interfaces, and this may be linked to the knowledge that older individuals are required to exert greater effort in learning new tasks (Howard and Howard 1997). Docampo-Rama (2001) and Freudenthal (2001) refer to such differences in age and experience as the Generational Effect, identifying particular stages in life during which individuals are optimally receptive to interacting effectively with new technology; seen typically in those under 25 years of age.

These generational differences are considered symptomatic of exposure to technology at a particular stage in life. In this work, the author presents an approach designed to verify if younger individuals complete product interaction tasks quicker than older individuals' and if they possess a greater awareness and level of interaction with contemporary technology. The study also examines the efficiency, effectiveness, and accuracy of mental model development to determine if it is adversely affected with increasing age. It is possible that in combination with being able to draw on more relevant prior experience, younger people exhibit a greater ability to acquire and consolidate new information and integrate this knowledge in enhanced mental models of interaction. Such an ability would then be proposed as a significant factor that contributes toward younger adult's superior performance with contemporary products. If this is the case, designers should be made aware that such factors could also increase the usability and intuitive interaction of future products and designs targeted toward teenagers.

The over-arching aim of this chapter is to examine how humans learn and interact with products differently according to age and how best research practice can induce the best design output. Increasing our understanding of how learning and mental model development differs according to age and direct interaction with products, will help us design more effectively for the teenagers of today and also improve access to future technology for all.

8.2.1 Experimental Research Approach

30 individuals were recruited by advertising in regional publications and in local shops to maximise ecological validity within the constraints of the resources available, and were assigned to one of three groups according to age: 16–25 (10 participants), 26–59 (10 participants) and 60–80 (10 participants). This was on the premise that by the age of 25 the most significant physical and psychological changes have taken place (National Institute of Health 2011; Educational Informatics 2011) and stabilise until the age of approximately 60-plus, where natural cognitive degradation often occurs (Clark et al. 2006).

By separating the sample into these three groups the intention was to evaluate the results in terms of verifying if cognitive development and ability (having increased from birth and stabilised around the age of 25) may be an additional factor that contributes to those under the age of 25 being able to interact with modern technology products more effectively in comparison with those over the age of 25 in accordance with Docampo-Rama (2001) and Freudenthal (2001). Clark et al. (2006) proffer that the next phase of cognitive alteration – a decline in cognitive ability – generally occurs due to natural atrophy from the age of 60. This assertion justified the comparison between the younger, mid, and older adult age groups across a number of criteria, including verification of cognitive ability with the application of the Cantabeclipse Cognitive Assessment Tool (Cambridge Cognition 2011).

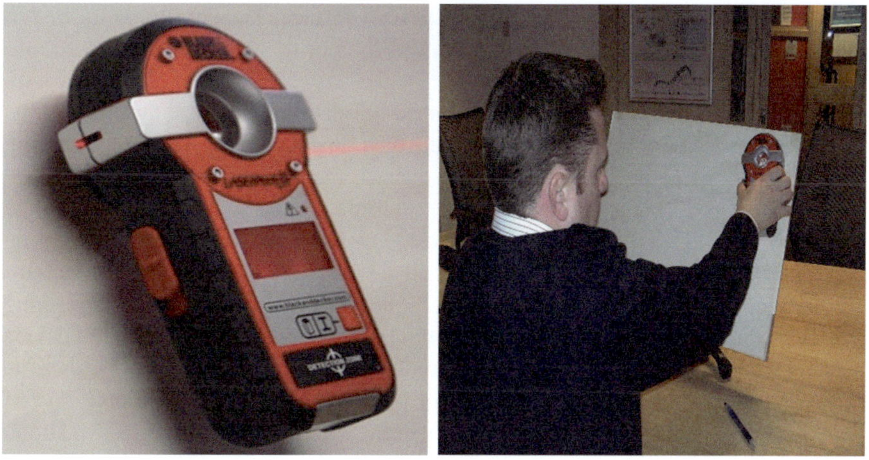

Fig. 8.3 Black and Decker laser level

Fig. 8.4 Icon sheet

8.2.2 Experimental Apparatus and Equipment

The Black and Decker laser-level is a multifunctional device contained within a unique design that emits a laser level line and is also capable of detecting wooden and metallic studs or pipes and electricity cables obscured behind fascia's (Fig. 8.3). Users must set the device to detect wooden studs indicated by a wooden block icon, or metal pipes indicated by an icon of a beam representing a metallic object, by pressing a red toggle switch on the front of the device (Fig. 8.4). The device is calibrated by pressing and holding down a button on the right of the device. Once calibrated the device emits an audible 'beep' and requires the button remain depressed whilst the user passes the device across the wall surface. The detector is located in the 'Detector Zone' and for accuracy it is this area of the device that must be considered during operations of detection.

As it passes over a stud, vertical lines on the display converge and an audible 'beep' occurs when directly above the stud. The display reflects this by presenting converging lines coming together. Once passed, the beep ceases and the vertical lines retract. The procedure of electrical cable detection is identical, without the need to 'set' the device. The feedback provided is similar with an additional warning LED illuminating when the device detects live electricity. The laser-level functionality is accessed by inserting a hanging tool into the rear of the device and pushing the slider button on the left to the 'Laser On' position (Fig. 8.3). Whilst the device may be limited, the level of conceptual understanding required, isn't. Further, its novel nature ensures the likelihood of prior product experience is minimal.

An icon identification sheet was developed, replicating the icons displayed upon the product and its packaging (Fig. 8.4). Participants were asked at the beginning of the experiment what they understood the images to mean, then reviewed their contributions after product exposure, and in this way it was possible to observe learning and increased understanding through interaction.

Participants were presented with the device and asked to explain what the design of the product expressed about its potential use, what they understood about the product, and to indicate any design features observed. Observations of features were recorded on a feature identification sheet allowing subsequent post-experimentation comparison (Fig. 8.5). A total of 34 product features were identified to which participants' pre- and post- experimentation scores could be compared.

8.2.3 Experimental Design

A Between-subjects design was employed, assigning 30 participants to one of three groups according to age: 16–25 (10), 26–59 (10) and 60–80 (10).

Independent Variable: Age: 3 levels: 16–25, 26–59, 60–80.

Dependent Variables: Cantabeclipse reaction time and memory span performance, task performance/interaction time, icon recognition pre/post exposure, feature recognition pre/post exposure, prompted product recall, Technological Familiarity Questionnaire (TFQ) performance.

8.2.4 Experimental Procedure

A user interaction laboratory and experimental protocol were developed to ensure experimental consistency in terms of ambient space, lighting and temperature and to minimise the encroachment of extraneous variables.

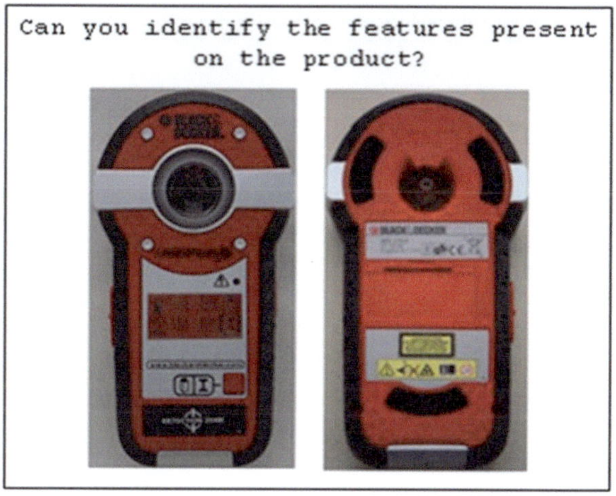

Fig. 8.5 Feature recognition sheet

The Cantabeclipse Cognitive Assessment Tool (Cambridge Cognition 2011) was used to assess reaction times, short-term memory span, coordination and motor skills, and afforded further post experimentation analysis of differences between age groups that ensured that any age-related differences in performance were not limited to the interaction experiment alone.

Participants were initially asked to explain what they understood the icons and warning images displayed upon the product's packaging, and interactional features employed within the product itself to mean via images presented on paper (Fig. 8.4). They were then asked to review their contributions after product exposure, to permit the observation of learning and increasing understanding through product interaction.

Participants were then presented with the new-to-market product and having been asked to discuss their design pre-conceptions of it, they were then asked to perform six interactive tasks whilst being recorded. These tasks represented the full range of activities the device was designed to facilitate and were randomised to minimise any foreseeable order effects.

In conclusion, each participant completed a Technological Familiarity Questionnaire (Wilkinson 2011) to verify their level of prior experience with various forms of technological equipment, and how frequently they interacted with contemporary technology. The questionnaire posed two questions regarding a list of contemporary products: "How often do you use the following products?" and "When using the products, how many features of the product are you familiar with and do you use?". Responses were then rated according to Blackler's (2006) protocol which provided individual Question TFQ Scores and an overall combined TFQ score.

Table 8.1 Mean data per age group (n=30)

Means per age group	16–25	26–59	60–80
Cantabeclipse reaction time (s)	49.2	52.1	52.8
Cantabeclipse memory span (number of items)	7	6	5
Product task performance/interaction time (s)	38	51	79
Warning icon recognition (pre-exposure)	4.6	5.5	4.1
Warning icon recognition (post-exposure)	8.4	8.3	6.2
Product feature recognition (pre-exposure)	8.7	10.8	6.4
Product feature recognition (post-exposure)	16.4	15.7	11.7
Number of similar products referenced	3.0	2.7	1.1
TFQ question 1 score	28	16	28
TFQ question 2 score	41	20	16
Overall TFQ score	69	36	44

8.2.5 *Experimental Protocol*

- Brief participant upon study expectations, emphasise freedom to decline at any point without recourse or redress, and acquire informed consent
- Administer cognitive assessment using Cantabeclipse assessment tool
- Administer initial assessment of warning icon recognition
- Record initial product exposure, understanding, and feature recognition
- Record task performance with verbalisation:

  Fit battery, find wooden stud, find metal pipe, find electric cable, fit hanging tool, hang and operate laser level

- Reassess participant understanding of product and interaction
- Assess post exposure icon recognition
- Assess post exposure feature recognition
- Administer Technological Familiarity Questionnaire (TFQ)
- Debrief and thank participant for their participation in the study

8.3 Results

The Cantabeclipse reaction-time test that screens for vision, hearing, movement and comprehension impairment, highlighted no neuropsychological issues across the sample but did indicate differences in task completion times between age groups (Table 8.1).

Although a 1-way analysis of variance (ANOVA) showed no significant effect of age on reaction time ($F (2, 27) = 0.594$ $p > 0.05$), there was a moderate positive correlation between the two variables with a higher level of age associated with a higher level of reaction time ($r = 0.317$ (30), $p < 0.05$). This correlation indicates that the younger generation's interaction is somehow enhanced as they perform more rapidly than their older counterparts.

A 1-way analysis of variance showed a significant effect of age on memory span: F (2, 27)=5.205, $p<0.05$. Tukey HSD post-hoc analysis indicated that the mean score for the 60–80 age group (M=4.9, SD=1.19) was significantly different than the 16–25 age group (M=6.9, SD=1.44). However, the 26–59 age group results (M=6.4, SD=1.64) did not significantly differ from either of the remaining groups.

The relationship between age and memory span was investigated using a Pearson product–moment correlation coefficient and indicated a moderate negative correlation between the two variables with a higher level of age associated with a smaller memory span ($r=-0.664$ (30), $p<0.01$). This suggests that age is a factor in memory capability, and that the younger generation possess a greater ability to store and recall information.

A multivariate analysis of variance showed a significant effect of age on task interaction time: F (2, 27)=8.146 $p<0.05$. Tukey HSD post-hoc analysis indicated that the mean score for the 60–80 age group (M=1.71, SD=0.30) was significantly different than the 16–25 age group (M=1.37, SD=0.33). However, the 26–59 age group results (M=1.49, SD=0.32) did not significantly differ from the remaining groups.

The relationship between age and task completion time was investigated using Pearson product–moment correlation coefficient on each of the tasks and the mean. Although there were no other significant correlations, in five instances there was a moderate positive correlation between the two variables with a lower age associated with a lower task completion time (fitting the battery, finding the wooden stud, finding the electric cable, hanging and operating the laser level, and the average task completion time). The results suggest that age is a factor in the speed with which the tasks were completed and that as age increased so did the time taken to complete these tasks.

Multivariate analysis of variance indicated a significant effect of time of assessment and age group on the number of icons identified: F (2, 27)=415.969, $p<0.01$ Analysis indicated no significant difference between the age groups at the pre-experiment exposure stage, but a significant difference between the 60–80 age group (M=6.20, SD=2.34) and the 26–59 age group (M=8.20, SD=1.93) and between the 60–80 age group (M=6.20, SD=2.34) and the 16–25 age group (M=8.40, SD=0.84) post-experiment.

The relationship between age and icon identification was investigated using Pearson product–moment correlation coefficient. There was a strong negative correlation between Age and pre-experiment icon identification ($r=-0.335$ (30), $p<0.05$), Age and post-experiment icon identification ($r=-0.613$ (30), $p<0.01$), and Age and difference between pre and post-experiment icon identification ($r=-0.394$ (30), $p<0.05$). Although initially age was not a significant factor in icon identification, it appeared to be a factor in the amount of iconic knowledge gained during interaction and exposure, and implies that the younger generations are optimally positioned to recognise, understand, and acquire iconic information.

Multivariate analysis of variance indicated a significant effect of time of assessment and age group on the number of features identified (F (2, 27)=268.518 $p<0.01$). In the pre-experiment exposure stage, analysis indicated that there was a significant difference between the 60–80 age group (M=6.40, SD=3.50) and the 26–59 age group (M=10.80, SD=5.18). The 16–25 age group results (M=8.70, SD=3.09) did not significantly differ from either of the remaining groups. However, in the post-experiment exposure stage, analysis indicated a significant difference between the 60–80 age group (M=11.70, SD=3.19) and the 26–59 age group (M=15.70, SD=6.05) and between the 60–80 age group (M=11.70, SD=3.19) and the 16–25 age group (M=16.40, SD=2.91). In both stages age was a significant factor in feature identification.

There was also a strong negative correlation between age and pre-experiment feature identification ($r=-0.384$ (30), $p<0.05$), age and post-experiment feature identification ($r=-0.544$ (30), $p<0.01$), and age and difference between pre and post-experiment feature identification ($r=-0.394$ (30), $p<0.05$).

Increases in age correlate to a significant decrease in feature recognition at the pre and post-product exposure stage. Increases in age also correlate to decreases in the ability to acquire product feature knowledge. In both these instances, then, the younger generation were able to acquire knowledge and accurately determine more features of the product used, and therefore appeared advantageously placed to interact more effectively with this example of contemporary technology.

A 1-way ANOVA showed no significant effect of age on the mean number of products recalled during exposure (F (2, 27)=2.965, $p>0.05$) although there was a moderate negative correlation between the two variables with a higher level of age associated with a lower level of recalled products ($r=-0.383$ (30), $p<0.05$). In terms of the number of similar products participants referenced, although differences between groups were not significant, increases in age did correlate to a significant decrease in prompted product recall. This reinforces the existence of a generational effect – that our ability to recall products is negatively correlated to increases in age and may contribute to the notion that increasing age equates to a reduction in the regularity of interaction with modern products. This may be a key factor causing the younger generation to exhibit enhanced performance in terms of icon and feature recognition as they are more familiar and interact more regularly with contemporary technologies that utilise such aesthetics.

The Technological Familiarity Questionnaire (TFQ) results confirmed the above finding. Although a 1-way analysis of variance showed no significant effect of age on TFQ Q1 Score (frequency of product interaction): F (2, 27)=0.890, $p>0.05$, a 1-way analysis of variance showed a significant effect of age on TFQ Q2 Score (awareness and use of product features): F (2, 27)=4.973, $p<0.05$. Tukey HSD post-hoc analysis indicated that the mean score for the 60–80 age group (M=25.4, SD=11.21) was significantly different to the 16–25 age group (M=50.1, SD=17.12). However, the results for the 26–59 age group (M=43.0, SD=23.58) were not significantly different from either of the remaining groups. A 1-way ANOVA showed a significant effect of age on Overall TFQ Score: F (2, 27)=3.470, $p<0.05$. Tukey HSD post-hoc analysis indicated that the mean score for the 60–80 age group

(M = 64.8, SD = 22.36) was significantly different to the 16–25 age group (M = 97.3, SD = 16.32). However, the results for the 26–59 age group (M = 85.6, SD = 39.69) were not significantly different from the remaining groups.

There was no significant difference between the frequency of interaction with the products identified upon the questionnaire according to age, but there was an effect of age upon the awareness and use of product features. Post-hoc Tukey analysis indicated that there was a significant difference between the older age group and the younger age group, implying that older individuals were significantly less aware or use fewer features of the examples of the technological products presented upon the TFQ questionnaire than the younger age group (see Wilkinson 2011, for an overview).

The relationship between age and technological familiarity was investigated using Pearson product–moment correlation coefficient and this showed a strong negative correlation between Age and TFQ Q2 ($r = -0.509$ (30), $p < 0.01$) and Age and TFQ Total Score ($r = -0.462$ (30), $p < 0.05$).

Increases in age were significantly correlated to decreases in the frequency with which participants interacted with the technology identified in the Technological Familiarity Questionnaire, and to a decrease in the use and awareness of product features. This indicates a strong generational effect; that in this instance the younger generation are more aware of product features and engage with a larger variety of technology than older individuals.

8.4 SRK Analysis of Interaction

Rasmussen's (1993) SRK model of behaviour accounted for fluctuations in the level of consciousness required during interaction based on the assumption that individuals operate at a level appropriate to the familiarity of the situation (Thomas and van Leeuwen 1999). In this instance, SRK Analysis (Wilkinson 2011) is used to classify human behaviour during interaction and simultaneously assess the extent of interactional complexity users experience as a consequence of product design. It is also used to investigate and observe how individuals learn to operate technological products through experience, and to identify where product design may enhance or impede this process. Here the qualitative data consists of the complete video-footage of each individual's experience of interacting with the product within the experiment. The footage was observed, recorded, and then coded in transcript form. The actions of each individual were subsequently interpreted with regard to which category of SRK behaviour the participants' behaviour was most indicative of (see Chi 1997, p.8 for the formal procedure for assessing and interpreting qualitative data).

To ease discrimination, each of the three categories were assigned a different colour and participants responses highlighted accordingly; Skill-based, automatic, behaviour (Green), Rule-based behaviour (Blue), and Knowledge-based, slow, conscious-processing, behaviour (Red).

Table 8.2 Example of SRK classification (Participant within the 16–25 age group)

Time	Observed behaviour	Participant verbalisation	SRK Decision rationale	Knowledge Acquisition or Learning component
39.33	Device picked up in right hand and turned over, cover facing up		Skill-based motor action	
39.37	Battery cover removed with left hand		Skill-based motor action	
39.39	Polarity checked – scan of terminals in product and on battery		Application of rule regarding battery fitment	
39.41	Device checked consciously and in greater detail for battery polarity instructions		No prior experience / search for knowledge or information	New knowledge of interaction is learned or imparted
39.47	Battery inserted		Application of rule regarding battery fitment	
39.49	Cover replaced		Skill-based motor action	
39.50	End			

The following example (Table 8.2) focuses upon the insertion of the battery into the novel product (Task 1) by a single participant that involved locating and removing the battery compartment cover, determining the correct orientation of the battery, correctly fitting the battery and replacing the cover. The time taken to insert the battery is 17 s. The behaviours are swift and automatic – grasping the device and removing the battery compartment cover on the rear of the device. These behaviours are demarcated in Green following the definition of Skill-based behaviour discussed previously.

In total, 180 individual data sets were classified accordingly and the following data were also recorded;

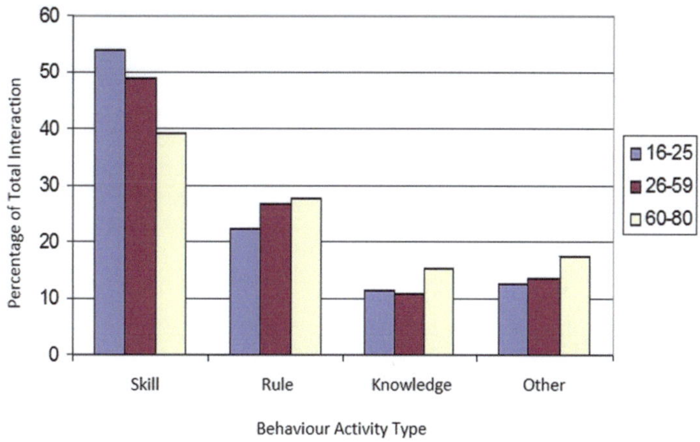

Fig. 8.6 Behaviour activity type according to age group membership (n=30)

- The timings of interaction
- The visual and auditory feedback produced by the device during interaction (omitted in the above example)
- The individual verbalisations and actions of participants
- The skill, rule or knowledge-based classification decision
- The knowledge acquired, sought or affirmed during interaction

A full record of the experimental data obtained, including the individual transcripts and their SRK and thematic analysis are permanently available online at the following url: https://www.academia.edu/7053308/User_Experiences of Product Interaction

Evident from Fig. 8.6 is that the overall predominant behaviour type participants engaged in was skill-based in nature. Rule-based behaviour was the second most commonly occurring activity type with both knowledge-based and other activity showing comparatively minute differences in terms of overall percentages of behaviour participants engaged in. Differences according to age group membership are also apparent: the 16–25 age group engaged in greater amounts of skill-based interaction (54 %) than either of the 26–59 age group (49 %) or the 60–80 age group (39 %) who indulged in higher rates of rule and knowledge-based activity.

Conducting SRK Analysis also permitted the examination of the type of knowledge sought by users when interacting with the product. Reflected within instances of interactional complexity, Fig. 8.7 indicates when users were reduced to a knowledge-based level of interaction. These are key points when knowledge was both required and acquired to continue interaction with the product. Thus, this approach identifies what, when, and where, within interaction, knowledge is sought and learned, as well as identifies the specific issues causing users the greatest interactional complexity.

The features causing the most challenge and greatest interruption to operation at a skill, or rule-based level of interaction, revolve around determining Battery Polarity and the location of the Battery Compartment Cover. The next most fre-

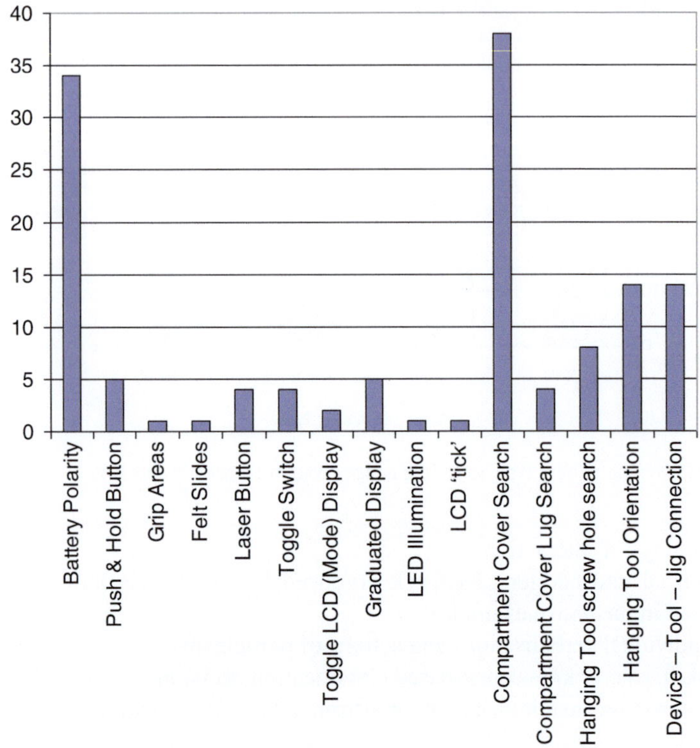

Fig. 8.7 Instances where interaction was reduced to a knowledge-based level, indicating the features of interaction and areas of learning involved (n = 30)

quently occurring design implications centre upon the use of the Hanging Tool attached when operating the laser-level function. With regard to learning and ease of knowledge acquisition, this analysis indicates that further consideration of how the information regarding battery polarity and battery insertion (and battery compartment cover location and removal) is conveyed to users would be well justified.

8.5 Discussion

It is appropriate at this juncture to recap the study's original research aims and address them in summary. To recall, the main research aims were:

1. To investigate the existence of age-effects regarding prior experience and any associated effects upon interaction with a novel contemporary household product, chosen at random for its newness to market.

2. To investigate if young people, based on their experience of contemporary technology, are able to create more accurate mental models of engagement that facilitate superior interaction with novel products.
3. To investigate the efficacy of framing interaction in terms of Rasmussen's (1993) Skill, Rule and Knowledge-based Model of behaviour and thereby determine how knowledge acquisition is facilitated and identify instances of interactional complexity that could be overcome by better design with input from real users.

Framing interaction in terms of SRK behaviour assisted the identification of interactional design and complexity issues, as well as assisted the analysis of the learning activity that contributes to mental model development and understanding. Increases in age were found to correlate to a significant decrease in memory span, and icon recognition at the pre and post-product-exposure stages and also correlated to decreases in iconic information acquisition during exposure. Increases in age correlated to significant decreases in feature recognition at pre and post-product-exposure stages, and to decreases in the ability to acquire product feature knowledge. This provides further evidence for the existence of generational effects – that as we age our ability to acquire new knowledge and learn from interaction decreases, and the knowledge we bring to interaction is also reduced.

The content and creation of mental models appears adversely affected with age; older individuals not only possessed less accurate prior experience and information for effective interaction, but their ability to acquire and consolidate relevant information, also declined with age. The overall conclusion is that products should ideally be designed to facilitate user-interaction at a skill-based level for successful operation and accurate mental model development. This research highlights specifically how and when learning occurs during interaction, and revealed precisely what information is required and learned. If this is considered within the design process, it may be possible to reduce the interactional complexity experienced by users regardless of age, making products more usable and accessible to a wider proportion of the population. The findings provide further evidence for differences in terms of knowledge of and engagement with contemporary technology but, further, indicate that those of a younger disposition are more capable of developing accurate mental models and effective learning strategies when presented with novel products.

8.5.1 Why Might Young People Be Better at Product Interaction?

The findings indicate that the younger generation are more adept at accommodating new interaction styles and apply more flexible approaches to novel problem solving, but why might this be the case? Well, for a start, young people are exposed to technology at an increasingly younger age than ever before. Consider how quickly and easily babies and young children mimic their parent's interaction with toy (and often real) mobile telephones. A source of great amusement until a call goes through to a random number or important files or photographs are accidentally deleted.

Young adults are born into a world of technology and are encased by it. This concept isn't new but it does seem more pervasive. Mark Weiser is widely acknowledged for coining the phrase *ubiquitous computing* in 1988 (Want 2000) but perhaps 'ubiquitous connectedness' may be more representative of today's environment with concepts such as the Internet of Things and Big Data.

In the past there was widespread anecdotal evidence of parents asking young people – usually their offspring – to program the VCR (Video Cassette Recorder), and this rang true for a whole generation. Today young people are engaged and engaging with a wider variety of connected technologies; technologies that often leave the older generation nonplussed and as evidenced by this research, often disadvantaged.

Why is this? One reason may be that both government and industry have understood that young people are the driving force of tomorrow's technology, and that to be competitive, an environment where young people can become skilled in this field from an early age needed to be fostered.

Accordingly, education has changed dramatically, with greater emphasis upon *computational thinking* (Department of Education 2015). This has become an integral part of the curriculum taught to children from the age of seven upward in response to the fact that although computer literacy had increased, the number of young people entering the programming industry was falling and one solution was deemed to be early exposure and development of programming skills. Indeed, this increased emphasis upon the importance of programming as an essential skill is reflected by the increasing availability of open-access, online courses that are subsequently engaging with a wider audience. Online materials and tools are designed to encourage children (Scratch, Tynker.com, Code.org), university students, and independent adult learners. Amateur programmers also benefit from a wealth of online resources (CodeAcademy, W3Schools, Lynda.com; MOOCs, e.g. Coursera, edX, IDEO Design Kit). In schools, children from the age of seven are introduced to "Beebots" – programmable floor robots – to be taught control, directional language and programming. Further, the notion of computational thinking is applied more universally in terms of classification keys to help children identify and categorise objects in a more object-oriented manner, which resonates with the approaches required for programming. The cross-curriculum use of Beebots has:

> "…really helped with their questioning skills. It has also made it far easier for them to link the dots… [the kids] are far more interested in finding out why something is doing what it's doing, rather than just accepting that it does it…they can hypothesise without embarrassment, give reasons for their conjecture, and convince with their results"
>
> (Anonymous (2015): Teacher of 7–8 year old Year 3 students)

Undoubtedly these and other factors will contribute significantly to future generation's involvement in technology development, and it is apt that the design community and designers themselves realise this, as this generation will be, and often are already, the designers of tomorrow.

8.5.2 *How Can We Involve Young People in Research Activities?*

Just as young people's approaches to technology are flexible and innovative, similarly innovative approaches are required to involve young people in research activities. In 2013, the National Centre for Product Design and Development Research in Cardiff, hosted a HACK event specifically aimed at engaging younger people. The two-day, 'SPIDER-HACK' (2013) saw teams of young people, local businesses, third sector organisations, and Cardiff City Council work together with the support of in-house developers to design better ways for young people to organise, manage, and plan for their future careers. This event was orchestrated under the guise of Supporting Public Service Innovation using Design in European Regions – SPIDER (2013) (http://www.thespiderproject.eu/), and aimed to investigate how mobile and web technologies could be developed to assist 16–19 years olds make informed decisions about their future careers and lives.

In order to maximise the involvement of potential users and benefit from a participatory design approach, a range of young people were also interviewed to allow the design teams to discover exactly what issues matter most to this demographic, prior to the event itself. This informed the design process and ensured that every mobile or web-based app prototyped, reflected or responded to a genuine need of the actual and intended users.

8.6 Conclusion

The content and creation of mental models of interaction were found to be adversely affected with age. The models and prior experience that younger individuals possessed, contained more relevant information to drive effective interaction, and their ability to acquire and consolidate *new* relevant information was also superior. In particular, increases in age correlated to a significant decrease in icon and feature recognition at pre and post- product exposure stages. In addition, the 16–25 age group engaged in greater amounts of skill-based interaction than either the 26–59 age group or the 60–80 age group who indulged in greater rates of rule and knowledge-based activity. Skill-based activity notably decreased task completion times for the younger age groups and, accordingly, these factors in combination, are seen to have culminated in enhancing intuitive interaction with the product for this group. The results of this investigation pose significant implications for technology development for a younger audience and emphasise the importance of involving them within research. With the younger generation becoming the designers of tomorrow, the community needs to ensure they have the knowledge and expertise to design intuitively and inclusively for all our tomorrows.

8.6.1 *Considerations When Involving Young People in Research Activities*

There are no unique approaches that need to be adopted when involving teenagers, specifically, in research. That is to say, the same rigourous approaches that should be used when conducting any research, apply equally to any subset of the sample population. Being Disclosure and Barring Service checked in the United Kingdom to work with any population, including older and vulnerable people and children, is advisable from an ethical standpoint and, depending upon user group, mandatory (Disclosure and Barring Service 2015). Indeed, consideration should be given to the ethical, legal, and safety implications of performing research with any user group, regardless of age, at the earliest opportunity.

In terms of participant recruitment, caveats that may appear normal to experimental psychologists or user-centred designers, are worthy of emphasis. For example, the sourcing of a representative sample from which to generalise should be paramount, and the success of this intention should be verified. This should include utilising participants from a broad spectrum of educational backgrounds, geographical locations, physical and psychological abilities, and effort should be invested in avoiding unnecessary bias or the introduction of extraneous variables that may affect individual performance.

An experimental protocol should be developed to ensure consistency of implementation across and between participants, and must be rigorously followed to ensure that any differences in performance cannot be attributed to experimenter deviation, irregularity, or other variables.

Informed consent must be obtained prior to any interaction session. The consent form should detail the title of the project and what it is attempting to investigate and explicitly state what the participant is being asked to do. It should also state the expected outcomes and benefits of research participation, along with stressing that participation is entirely voluntary, that confidentiality will be maintained, all data anonymised, and that the participant's integrity in terms of data protection will not be compromised, and that they are free to leave at any time without redress or recourse. It is also accepted practice to provide participants with a contact point for future reference.

Figure 8.8 attempts to draw these themes of consideration together in a simple schematic. Although not exhaustive, it does place the user (or participant) at the centre of consideration. It highlights some of the approaches and techniques that are available and that have been referred to in this text, and finally, from an experimental design perspective, it reminds us of the overall considerations that must be made when conducting scientific investigations involving human participants.

As emphasised in Fig. 8.8, prior to all experimentation, a comprehensive Hazard Analysis and Risk Assessment should be performed to ensure no one is placed in an unsafe environment or situation, and ethical approval obtained in advance of any investigation. Further, it is advisable a sensitive and person-centred approach to the research is adopted as this form of research involves issues that affect individuals

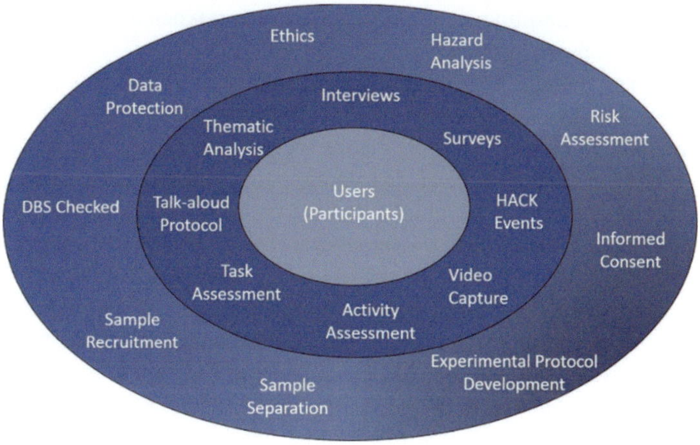

Fig. 8.8 Considerations for user involvement in research

from a myriad of backgrounds, possessing different capabilities, experiences, and expectations. Whilst it is important to determine the abilities of individuals, it should not be pursued at a cost to their personal well-being or to the detriment of their self-belief.

8.7 Reflections

If time and resources presented no obstacle to research, it would be rewarding to repeat the investigation using a more granular age separation; perhaps separating the sample from 16–80 in approximately 10 year intervals. This may elucidate more specific findings and a specific age range within which interactional ability is optimum.

The thematic analysis of the main investigation was conducted solely by the author, and although this coding independence was intentional, if time and resource were no object, it would clearly be preferable to have such activities performed by a number of independent coders and to investigate the consistency of the results to minimise any subjective effects (see Tinsley and Weiss 2000, for the importance of inter-coder or inter-rater reliability). However, commercially, this is not always practical and some realistic compromises do have to be made. In this study much time and effort was consumed ensuring the definitions of Skill, Rule, and Knowledge-based activity used were thorough, clear, and unequivocal – to make it transparently clear exactly how the approach was applied and to make it easily repeatable.

It is worthy of note that transcription and coding are often labour-intensive and this study was no exception; the data collection and analysis consisted of 30×1 h records that were transcribed and coded in their entirety. On average this assumed a 1:3 ratio. One hour of raw material taking 3 h to transcribe and at a later point in time code. Such a commitment should be born in mind when designing any experiments or interaction sessions.

This study and chapter has, however, successfully identified how and why conducting research with a teenage population is important. Due to the differences that exist in terms of age-effects regarding prior experience and their effect upon interaction with novel products, it is clear that young people based on their experience of contemporary technology, are able to create more accurate mental models of engagement that facilitate superior interaction. Thus, to design truly engaging products that resonate with such a unique sector and demographic, we must find ways to involve them closely in and throughout design research. This chapter provides examples of how this might successfully be achieved by focussing upon how to better include, motivate, and involve a broader subset of the population – and particularly teenagers – within empirical and commercial research activity.

Today's teenagers will be tomorrow's older generation, and it is also true that today's teenagers face and interact with a greater wealth and diversity of technologies and products than ever before. If the intricacies of interactional complexity outlined are considered within the design process, it may be possible to reduce the complexity experienced by users of any age, making products even more usable, applicable, and accessible to a wider proportion of the population now and in the future.

References

Alario E-X, Ferrand L (1999) A set of 400 pictures standardized for French: norms for name agreement, image agreement, familiarity, visual complexity, image variability, and age of acquisition. Behav Res Methods, Instrum Comput 31(3):531–552

Anonymous (2015) Observations on teaching. [Letter]. (Personal Communication, 5 April, 2015).

Blackler A (2006) Intuitive interaction with complex artefacts. Ph.D. Queensland University of Technology, Australia

Cambridge Cognition (2011) Cantabeclipse cognitive assessment tool. [online] Available at: http://www.camcog.com/science

Chan C, Wong A, Lee T, Chi I (2009) Modified automatic teller machine prototype for older adults: a case study of participative approach to inclusive design. Appl Ergon 40(2):151–160

Chi M (1997) Quantifying qualitative analyses of verbal data: a practical guide. J Learn Sci 6(3):271–315

Clark C, Paul R, Williams L, Arns M, Fallahpour K, Handmerc C, Gordon E (2006) Standardized assessment of cognitive functioning during development and aging using an automated touchscreen battery. Arch Clin Neuropsychol 21:449–467

Crilly N, Maier A, Clarkson P (2008) Representing artefacts as media: modelling the relationship between designer intent and consumer experience. Int J Des 2(3):15–27

Department of Education (2015) National curriculum key stages. [online] Available at: https://www.gov.uk/government/collections/national-curriculum#curriculum-by-key-stages

Design Council (2008) Inclusive design education resource [online] Available at: http://www.designcouncil.info/inclusivedesignresource

Design Council (2010) Design industry research report. [online] Available at: https://www.designcouncil.org.uk/knowledge-resources/design-industry-research-2010

Disclosure Barring Service (2015) [online] Available at: https://www.gov.uk/disclosure-barring-service-check/overview
Docampo-Rama M (2001) Technology generations handling complex user interfaces. Ph.D. TU: Eindhoven
Dong H, Bobjer O, McBride P, Clarkson J (2006) Inclusive product design: industrial case studies from the UK and Sweden. In: Bust P (ed) Contemporary ergonomics. Taylor and Francis, Great Britain, pp 338–342
Education Informatics (2011) Brain development and education for the information age. [online] Available at: http://www.edinformatics.com/news/teenage_brains.htm
Embrey D (2003) Understanding human behaviour and error. [online] Available at: www.human-reliability.com/articles/Understanding%20Human%20Behaviour%20and%20Error.pdf
Freudenthal D (2001) Age differences in the performance of information retrieval tasks. Behav Inform Technol 20(1):9–22
Grudin J (1991) Obstacles to user involvement in software development, with implications for CSCW. Int J Man–mac Stud 34:435–452
Hansen J, Percival J, Aldred H, Brownsell S, Hawley M (2007) Attitudes to telecare among older people, professional care workers and informal carers: a preventative strategy or crisis management? Univ Access Inf Soc 6(2):193–205
Howard J, Howard D (1997) Learning and memory. In: Rogers A (ed) Handbook of human factors and the older adult. Academic, San Diego, pp 7–26
Inclusive Design Group (2011) Inclusive design: countering design exclusion. [online] Available at: http://www-edc.eng.cam.ac.uk/research/inclusivedesign
Keates S, Clarkson J (2003) Countering design exclusion – An introduction to inclusive design. Springer, London
Langdon P, Lewis T, Clarkson P (2010) Prior experience in the use of domestic product interfaces. Univ Access Inf Soc 9(3):209–225
Lewis T, Langdon P, Clarkson J (2006) Investigating the role of experience in the use of consumer products. In: Designing accessible technology. Springer-Verlag, London, pp 189–98
Lim CSC (2010) Designing inclusive ICT products for older users: taking into account the technology generation effect. J Eng Des 21(2–3):189–206
Lindgaard G, Dillon R, Trbovich P, White R, Fernandes G, Lundah S (2006) User needs analysis and requirements engineering: theory and practice. Interact Comput 18(1):47–70
Mayhew DJ (1999) The usability engineering lifecycle. Morgan Kaufmann Publishers, California
Muller M (2002) Participatory design: the third space in HCI. In: Jacko J, Sears A (eds) The human computer interaction handbook: fundamentals, evolving technologies and emerging applications. Lawrence Erlbaum, Mahwah
National Institute of Health (2011) Report on brain immaturity. Washington post. [online] Available at: http://www.washingtonpost.com/wp-dyn/articles/A52687-2005Jan31.html
Nichols TA, Rogers WA, Fisk AD (2006) Design for aging. In: Salvendy G (ed) Handbook of human factors and ergonomics, 3rd edn. John Wiley & Sons, Hoboken, pp 1418–1445
Nielsen J (1993) Usability engineering. Academic, California
Pullin G (2011) Design meets disability. MIT Press, Cambridge
Rasmussen J (1993) Deciding and doing: decision making in natural contexts. Ablex, Norwood
Rabbitt P (1993) Does it all go together when it goes? The nineteenth Bartlett memorial lecture. Q J Exp Psychol 46A(3):385–434
Reason J (1990) Human error. Cambridge University Press, New York
Sanders E (2002) From user-centered to participatory design approaches. In: Frascara J (ed) Design and the social sciences. Taylor and Francis, London, pp 1–9
Sharma V, Simpson R, LoPresti E, Mostowy C, Olson J, Puhlman J, Hayashi S, Cooper R (2008) Participatory design in the development of the wheelchair convoy system. J NeuroEng Rehabil 5:1–10
Sicart M (2008) International journal of computer game research: defining game mechanics. [online] Available at: http://gamestudies.org/0802/articles/sicart

SPIDER HACK Event (2013) [online] Available at: http://www.theservicedesignprogramme.org/2013/08/spider-hack-event-with-cardiff-council/

SPIDER - Supporting Public Service Innovation using Design in European Regions (2013) [online] Available at: (http://www.thespiderproject.eu/),

Tarakanov-Plaz A (2005) Design concept for ATM machine, accessible for the elderly users in Israel. J Int Soc Gerontechnol 3(2):107–110

Thomas B, van Leeuwen M (1999) The user interface design of the fizz and spark GSM telephones. Taylor and Francis, London

Tinsley H, Weiss D (2000) Interrater reliability and agreement. In: Tinsley HEA, Brown SD (eds) Handbook of applied multivariate statistics and mathematical modeling. Academic, San Diego, pp 95–124

Want R (2000) Remembering mark weiser: chief technologist, Xerox PARC. IEEE Personal Commun 7(1):8–10

Weiss S (2002) Handheld usability. John Wiley & Sons, Chichester

Wickens C, Hollands JG (2000) Engineering psychology and human performance, 3rd edn. Prentice Hall, Upper Saddle River

Wickens C, Gordon S, Liu Y (1998) An introduction to human factors engineering. Addison-Wesley Educational Publishers Inc., New York

Wilkinson C (2011) Evaluating the role of prior experience in inclusive design. PhD thesis, University of Cambridge. (Also available online)

Wilkinson C, De Angeli A (2014) Applying user centred and participatory design approaches to commercial product development. J Des Stud. Elsevier, United Kingdom, pp 614–631

Wilkinson C, Gandhi D (2015) Future proofing tomorrows technology: UX for an ageing population. User Experience Magazine, UXPA 15.1. Available at: http://uxpamagazine.org/future-proofing-tomorrows-technology/

Wilkinson C, Langdon P, Clarkson J (2011) Evaluating the design, use and learnability of household products for older individuals. In: Proceedings of the 24th HCI international conference, Orlando, United States, pp. 250–259

Wilkinson C, Langdon P, Clarkson J (2013) Exploring prior experience and the effects of age on product interaction and learning. In: Proceedings of the human computer interaction international (HCII2013), Las Vegas, United States, pp 457–466

Wirstad J (1988) On knowledge structures for process operators. In: Goodstein L, Andersen H, Olsen S (eds) Tasks, errors, and mental models. Taylor and Francis, London, pp 50–69

Wogalter M (2006) Handbook of warnings. Lawrence Erlbaum Associates, New Jersey

Zitkus E, Langdon P, Clarkson J (2011).Accessibility evaluation: assistive tools for design activity in product development. In: Proceedings of the 1st international conference on sustainable intelligent manufacturing (1) pp 659–670

Chapter 9
Designing Teenage Emotions with a Life of Their Own

Neil Winterburn, Peggy Gregory, and Daniel Fitton

Abstract In this chapter, two participatory design activities are described in which teenagers create lo-fi designs describing emotions and explain the rationale for their design choices. Designs annotating and describing emotions are categorised as anthropomorphic, abstract, object based, or biomorphic. The chapter concludes: (i) teenagers use a variety of visual metaphors to describe emotions, (ii) teenagers use anthropomorphic visual metaphors most often to describe emotions and (iii) teenagers make more use of abstract and biomorphic visual metaphors to describe 'negative' emotions. The effect of materials on designs is analysed, suggesting that teenagers are more likely to create designs describing emotions featuring anthropomorphic visual metaphors when using malleable three-dimensional materials. Suggestions are made for the use of externalisation and personification as part of interactive emotion displays within affective systems. A focus group evaluation of a prototype mobile app is described, which suggests that teenagers place more importance on an affective systems ability to support social relationships than they do its ability to support psychological development. This research will be of value to interaction designers and Child-Computer Interaction researchers seeking to understand how teenagers use different visual metaphors to describe different emotions

9.1 Introduction

In this chapter, we describe an empirical study designed to capture teenagers' lo-fi designs describing emotions and an evaluation of a prototype mobile app. The goal of this work is to explore how teenagers represent and reason about emotion, in

N. Winterburn (✉)
Child-Computer Interaction Group, University of Central Lancashire, PR1 2HE Preston, UK
e-mail: n.winterburn@uclan.ac.uk

P. Gregory
School of Physical Sciences and Computing, University of Central Lancashire, Computing and Technology Building, PR1 2HE Preston, UK

D. Fitton
Child-Computer Interaction Group, School of Physical Sciences and Computing, University of Central Lancashire, PR1 2HE, Preston, UK

© Springer International Publishing Switzerland 2016

L. Little et al. (eds.), *Perspectives on HCI Research with Teenagers*,
Human–Computer Interaction Series, DOI 10.1007/978-3-319-33450-9_9

Fig. 9.1 Play-Doh designs representing different emotions experienced by the Teen Persona 'Gary'

order to design applications allowing teenagers to externalise and personify their emotions. This work grew out of creative workshops with young people organised as part of earlier projects exploring approaches to visualising thoughts and feelings with digital technology. Understanding how teenagers use visual metaphors to describe different emotions is important to interaction designers, TeenCI researchers creating technologies involving emotions, and individuals' working with teens more broadly (e.g. psychologists, teachers) (Fig. 9.1).

The participatory design of affective systems for teenagers is a new area of research that covers many domains. It combines the multidisciplinary field of Child-Computer Interaction (CCI), which incorporates 'psychology, and especially developmental psychology, learning sciences, product and interaction design, computer science, media studies, and game design' (Read and Markopoulos 2013). It also incorporates the multidisciplinary field of Affective Computing, which includes Computer Science and in particular artificial intelligence, cognitive science, also emotion theory, art and entertainment, health and wellbeing.

Fonagy et al. (2004) have stated that the ability to describe and find meaning in emotions is of vital importance to teenage development and mental health. The popularity of mobile apps and games among teenagers provide a useful platform for designers seeking to support teenage emotional and psychological development outside of formal school and therapy settings. The participatory design activities described in this study were devised to give voice to teenagers in the design process and to support their emotional and psychological development.

In line with Bang et al.'s (2012) taxonomy of motivations for constructive design research, the motivational context for this study is a mixture of a practice based/artistically inclined approach and an empirical or technological provoked approach. The practice-based motivation for this research was to further explore observations made about the design contributions shared by teenagers participating (Bishop 2005) in a previous art project known as Flunstellas (Froggett 2011), which aimed to engage teenagers in producing creative visualisations of ideas, emotions and memories.

During adolescence teenagers are undergoing intense development and change, including a quest for identity. Fonagy et al. (2004) state that these changes provide them with 'a far more complicated set of thoughts about his own and others' feelings and motivations.' These 'new ways of thinking and feeling about people's feelings and behaviour, as well as about his own feelings and behaviour, can be overwhelming, and the adolescent needs to absorb the implications' (Fonagy et al. 2004).

In response to these challenges faced by teenagers, the applied context for this chapter was the development of a novel mobile app. The app was intended to support teenagers in describing and interpreting complicated and mixed emotions by externalising and personifying them as virtual autonomous agents (Reynolds 1999). Users interact with these emotions as they move around an environment, competing and interacting with one another. The mobile app has two purposes, the first is to support teenagers in better describing and understanding how they and other people experience mixed emotional states, and the second is to share these descriptions and understandings with others. Resnick's (1997) motivation to develop StarLogo was to enable children to explore decentralised systems found in the natural world by building their own simulations. Similarly the motivation for this work was to develop new empirically-grounded, conceptual and computational tools that support teenagers to explore decentralised models of cognition and affect (Velásquez 1997). The complex and abstracted nature of decentralised models of emotion raises complex and new design challenges. Specifically, which kind of visualisation methods can be used to display emotions as autonomous agents in a way that is accessible and meaningful to teenagers? To address this design problem it is important to understand both the kinds of visual metaphors that teenagers use to describe emotions and the most effective methods for discovering them. The two studies described in this chapter were designed to explore the following research questions:

RQ1. Which kinds of visual metaphors do teenagers use to describe emotions?
RQ2. How does the use of different materials affect teenage designs of affective displays?

9.1.1 *Related Work*

This section gives an overview of affective computing and the involvement of teenagers as design partners in the field of TeenCI. It goes on to review emotion theory, the development of teenage theories of mind and techniques to externalise and personify emotions from family therapy.

9.1.1.1 Affective Computing

Affective computing is the study of computing systems that recognise, interpret and simulate human emotions. Picard (1995) defines the research of emotion in Computer Science as 'computing that relates to, arises from, or influences emotions.' Highly influenced by Sentics (Clynes and Menuhin 1977), Picard focused particularly on the use of computers to sense, reproduce and transmit emotions. She cites a range of applications for emotionally intelligent, wearable and ambient systems to be used in education, entertainment and the workplace. Boehner et al. (2007) challenged the dominant model of affective computing in which emotion is considered to be a discrete form of objective data. Instead they emphasise the socially constructed discourse within which emotion is produced. They suggest that instead of being designed only to measure and transmit our emotions, affective systems should also be designed to support the negotiation of subjective interpretations of emotion. The success of such a system would be measured by 'whether users find the system's responses useful for interpreting, reflecting on, and experiencing their emotion' (Boehner et al. 2007). As this research aims to develop tools to support teenagers describe emotions and negotiate their meaning, it operates within the Boehner's emotions as an interaction paradigm.

9.1.1.2 Child Computer Interaction

One of the dominant themes in CCI literature is research seeking to better understand children's involvement in the design of technology (Mazzone et al. 2008). In their discussion about the distinction between CCI and Human Computer Interaction (HCI), Read and Bekker (2011) note the lack of control that children often have when they engage with technologies and their discretionary use of technologies. Furthermore, Read and Markopoulos (2013) identify research into the participation of children in the design of new technologies as an important challenge for the future. Guha et al. (2004) argued that as technology is becoming an increasing part of children's lives, then children should be actively involved in its design. It has also been argued that participation also benefits designers (Guha et al. 2005). In response to her frustrations with levels of control and authorship offered to children in participatory design studies, Druin (1999) pioneered the cooperative design method. By emphasizing small numbers of children having high levels of participation over long periods of time, this method places children alongside other specialists in a multidisciplinary team.

Given the practical and time-based constraints of many CCI projects and the desire to engage with large groups of children, Read et al. (2006) developed the MESS (Mad Evaluation Sessions with Schoolchildren) day format. At MESS days groups of around 5 children rotate around a carousel of design and evaluation activities, participating in a wide range of activities in a short space of time. In the literature a variety of processes have been proposed for analysing children's designs of interactive systems after participatory design sessions. Xu et al. (2009) describe a method for analysing the component parts of children's drawings of their experience of tangible media. Aspects of drawings were categorised according to user experience metrics and statistical analysis was then applied, to ensure that meaningful results were achieved. Read et al. (2013b) conducted a design study to test the effect that materials had on children's design contributions for organic interfaces. Designs were categorised as being driven either by the affordance of the materials, or by a particular design idea. The study found that materials had an effect on designs created for organic interfaces, with over half of the designs categorised as being driven by the materials. This chapter describes new techniques to analyse teenage designs of affective displays that are informed by the methods of Xu et al. (2009) and Read et al. (2013b). Affective learning (Picard et al. 2004) sets out a framework for children's engagement with affective technologies within constructionist pedagogy (Papert and Harel 1991). The affective learning framework focuses on children's right to participate in the building of emotion sensing systems, rather than how emotions might be used, displayed and interpreted. Our chapter not only includes teens in the design process, but also stands in contrast to it because we focus on the ways in which they describe and relate to emotions using psychological techniques.

9.1.1.3 Teenagers as Design Partners

Teenagers are generally defined as young people between the ages of 13 and 19. For the purposes of understanding teenagers as participants in Interaction Design, Fitton et al. (2013) identified the following key traits including.

- Desire for independence and autonomy.
- Desire to develop/maintain individual identity.
- Desire for association with peers.
- High susceptibility to peer influence.
- Willingness to take risks.

Teenagers have been identified as being of particular interest as participants in design and evaluation studies. Read et al. (2013a, b) stated that their child like tendencies coupled with their increased cognitive capacities can mean that 'In many situations, and given the right tools, teenagers may be the best evaluators of technologies, and with their imaginative risk taking minds, the best designers of products. TeenCI researchers designing with teenagers have used a variety of different methods and techniques. Horton et al. (2012) describe the use of teen personas to facilitate their work with a group of teenagers on the meaning of 'cool'. Amin et al. (2005) worked with a group of teenagers to design an interface to give affective context to SMS texting. Findings suggested that teenagers would value the use of facial expressions, avatars, decorative text and location awareness to contextualise SMS texts. The COOL project (Mazzone 2012) worked with teenagers from a Pupil Referral Unit to design a computer game that supports the development of emotional intelligence (Salovey and Mayer 1990). Design activities included devising a scoring system for different emotions and matching emotional terms to simplified facial expressions. The game produced made use of facial expressions to support players to learn how to recognise distinct emotional states in others. The COOL project is a good example of design research that benefits both the researchers and participants. Researchers gained new insights into how teenagers perceive and choose to describe emotions and the teenagers took part in creative activities that supported them to develop the ability to express and reason about emotions. This research builds on the methods developed for the COOL project, it also aims to gain new understanding of teen emotion whilst supporting the psychological development of participants, but differs to the COOL project due to its focus on the description and interpretation of complicated and mixed emotions.

Fitton and Bell (2014) identify Teen Computer Interaction as a new area within HCI, distinct from CCI. They give an overview of the current state of developmental psychology and HCI research involving teenagers and address a set of key challenges for Teen Computer Interaction. The research in this chapter responds to Fitton and Bell's question of "What are the appropriate methodologies for engaging teenagers in HCI research?" by investigating which participatory design methods are appropriate to engage teenagers in the design of affective systems. The findings respond to the question "How can we gain insights into unknown teen populations?" by demonstrating that teenage design contributions can reveal new insights into their perceptions, attitudes and preferences towards subjects as personal as emotions and how emotions can be represented.

9.1.1.4 Emotion Research

Since Picard (Picard 1995) defined the field, affective computing has taken its theoretical grounding from emotion theory within cognitive science. Prinz (2012) gives an overview of how emotion theory has moved away from a purely cognitivist understanding of emotion, to one that also investigates non-cognitive emotion processing, socio-cognitive appraisals and diverse cultural practices. Hoffman (1986) belonged to a group of researchers who began to limit the processes that could be described as cognitive, by positioning non-cognitive and embodied modes of information processing as fundamental to our understanding emotion. Lutz's (Lutz 1988) anthropological study of emotions as a part of everyday life on a south Pacific atoll, suggest that emotion is meaningful only within a particular social context. 'To experience a feeling as, say, anger, love, happiness, lust, or frustration, one must be grounded in a cultural context that makes anger, love, happiness, lust, or frustration meaningful' (Lutz 1988). This study has developed a scheme to categorise teenage designs informed by theoretical debates between cognitivist, embodied and cultural understandings of emotion.

9.1.1.5 Teenage Development and Emotion

Theory of Mind (TOM) is a term used to describe our ability to understand our own thoughts and feelings and those of other people. The ability to apply TOM to describe and find meaning in emotions is of vital importance to teenage development and mental health (Fonagy et al. 2004). Modern developmental psychology suggests that our ability to access our own mental states and to infer those of others is constructed slowly over time. Astington et al. (1990), describe children's initial development of a theory of mind, between the age of two and four, as a new developmental phase. By understanding themselves and others as 'things that think' children are able to make distinctions for the first time between objects in the world and mental representations of these objects. Chandler et al. (1988) argue that a mature understanding of theory of mind does not occur until adolescence. At this time the relativist implications of earlier developmental stages of theory of mind are applied to everyday social situations. Fonagy et al. (2004) state that the key task of adolescence is the development of the psychological self, as a distinct entity from the main parents or carers. Due to neurological changes taking place, many adolescents risk being overwhelmed by greater access to information about their own and other people's mental and emotional states. 'Thus we believe that one thing that drives - but can also derail – the achievement of separateness is freshly enhanced cognitive complexity, which means that the adolescent is faced with the task of integrating a far more complicated set of thoughts about his own and others' feelings and motivations' (Fonagy et al. 2004). Fonagy et al. use the term mentalisation to describe the application of TOM. The ability to mentalise is key to teenage affect regulation, which itself is vital to the development of a sense of agency and self. 'The concept of mentalized affectivity marks a mature capacity of the regulation of affect and denotes the capacity to discover subjective meaning in one's own affective states' (Fonagy et al. 2004). Fitton and Bell (2014) argued that 'researchers have an ethical and moral responsibility to appreciate these developmental issues when working with teenage user group.' The research in this chapter seeks to develop interactive digital tools to support teenagers to engage in both mentalisation and mentalised affectivity. Participatory design activities used in this process were devised to support teenagers to use visual design and movement to describe and find personal meaning in their emotions, a key step in personal development.

9.1.1.6 Externalisation and Personification

Externalising is a narrative therapy practice, first introduced to family therapy by Michael White in the early 80's (White 2006). Carey & Russell 2002), explain the ethos of externalisation as an understanding that 'the person is not the problem, the problem is the problem.' When working with teenagers, this can be combined with personification, the practice of attributing objects or animals with human characteristics: for example, literature for children often includes animals that can talk. Klein (1929) notes that personification is a common feature of young and older children's play. It is used as a mechanism to externalise psychodynamic conflict and make sense of family issues by transferring them into the behaviour of fantasy characters. Butler et al. (2009) used puppetry within narrative therapy to support children to personify their problems and construct stories about problems in their lives. They concluded that the use of the puppet supported the children to objectify their problem and create a critical distance between themselves and it. The studies we discuss in this chapter, draw on these ideas and make use of lo-fi design activities to explore what teenagers' emotions may look like if they were to be visualised using digital technologies. This research aims to combine the use of externalisation and personification, with technological features known to appeal to teenagers, such as interaction, gameplay and networked collaboration, to describe and make sense of their emotions. The categorisation scheme developed in this study is drawn from externalisation and personification theories and techniques in the research cited. Responding to Fitton and Bell's (2014) question of 'What theory should be considered in work with teenagers?'. This chapter aims to explore if theories from family and developmental psychology are useful when designing affective displays for and with teenagers.

9.2 Study One

The first study was an exploratory participatory design activity. The EGG model (Marti and Rizzo 2003) is a framework that can be used by designers to categorise the context of their design activity (as reactive, proactive or emergent) in order to help decide the techniques that would be most appropriate to employ. This activity was situated in the Emergent phase of the EGG model, which is typically conducted during the brainstorming or early design phases of a project. To support innovative design thinking the activity was framed using a fantasy narrative in which emotions are externalised as things with a life of their own, visible to other people. To ground this narrative in a real world use context, two other techniques were used, a set of teen personas and a scenario featuring a classic teen dilemma, 'What to do with an empty house?'(i.e. parents not at home).

9.2.1 Design Objectives

The design activity had two main design objectives:

- Gain insight into existing practice: To understand whether teenagers can create visual, verbal and kinaesthetic metaphors to describe emotions.
- Concept generation: Elicit emergent interaction design ideas for the display of emotions as autonomous agents.

9.2.2 Method

The design study was run at a MESS day (Read et al. 2006) at the University of Central Lancashire and carried out by a convenience sample of 10 mixed groups of 55 young people from Years 8 and 9 (aged 12 to 14), from two Secondary Schools in the North West of England. Each group spent 25 min on the activity. Given time constraints and the variation in theory of mind found within this age group, teen personas, a scenario and a fantasy narrative (Iversen and Dindler 2008), were used to scaffold the activity. To encourage fun Play-Doh was used as a design material with an open design task that involved aspects of imaginative play.

9.2.3 Design Activity

The ten groups of 4–7 young people each carried out the same design activity with the same materials and structure. The group was introduced to the idea that in the future we may have technology that allows us to see each other's thoughts and feelings. They were told that the activity aimed to explore what this kind of technology might look like. Next they were introduced to a set of teen personas (Horton et al. 2012) and asked to choose one to be used by the whole group (personas convey imaginary individuals representative of a target user population). Teen personas were used to support participants to talk about emotions without worrying about divulging personal information that could leave them vulnerable. Each group was introduced to the same scenario in which their persona faced the choice between babysitting for their younger brother or having a wild party at their house. Participants were told that their teen persona was confused about the situation and was experiencing mixed emotions. Finally the narrative took a turn towards fantasy. The group was told that due to an unexplained phenomenon it was possible for other people to see the teen personas emotions floating around them. They were told that the personas emotions took on different shapes and colours and that they moved as if they had a life of their own. The group was introduced to a set of 6 plastic tokens featuring textual statements from the perspective of the persona. Each token featured an appraisal of an emotion. To describe a range of emotions, the statements

Table 9.1 Table of affective appraisal statements for the big 5 personality types

Personality Type	Statement
Openness to experience	'I feel excited thinking about a party at my house.'
Conscientiousness	'My Mum looks sad when I disappoint her.'
Extraversion	'I feel relaxed with my mates around.'
Agreeableness	'I feel happy when my mates make me laugh.'
Neuroticism	'I feel tense when my mates moan about me.'

were informed by the big 5 personality types identified within personality psychology (Eysenck 1991), the prepared statements shown in Table 9.1 were used, each mapping on to a different personality type, in order to lower the number of variables within the study.

Taking a token each, the young people were instructed to imagine what the persona's emotion might look like if it were visible and to build a Play-Doh model around the token. Each young person within the group worked individually with their own box of multi-coloured Play-Doh and a time limit of 7 min to sculpt a model. The duration of the design activity was defined by time restrictions imposed by the MESS day format. After this time, the Play-Doh shapes were brought together and each participant was asked to describe their design and explain the rationale behind it. Data was collected by taking photos of the designs and by making audio recordings of the participants describing their designs.

9.2.4 Results

The designs were reviewed and the participants' verbal descriptions were annotated. Then the designs were coded into four categories by the first author according to the participants' verbal descriptions. Despite instructions to create shapes to represent emotions, the vast majority of designs were representational. Because of this the following categories were based on the subject matter of designs, using terms drawn from art and design theory (Botar and Wünsche 2011).

- Anthropomorphic: Designs using embodied visual metaphor.
- Biomorphic: Designs that personify emotions as living things.
- Abstract: Designs that externalise emotions in nonrepresentational forms.
- Object: Designs that externalise emotions as non-living things.

Of the 56 designs made by the children 25 (44.6%) featured visual representations of the body, 15 (26.8%) featured objects, 8 (14.3%) featured living things and 8 (14.3%) were abstract, (Fig. 9.2).
Participants were able to justify design decisions made for 54 of the 56 designs made

Participant 1 'They are all bright colours, I was going to finish it with it being a person and they're (the coloured balls) all in the stomach, all the excited feelings.' (Fig. 9.3)

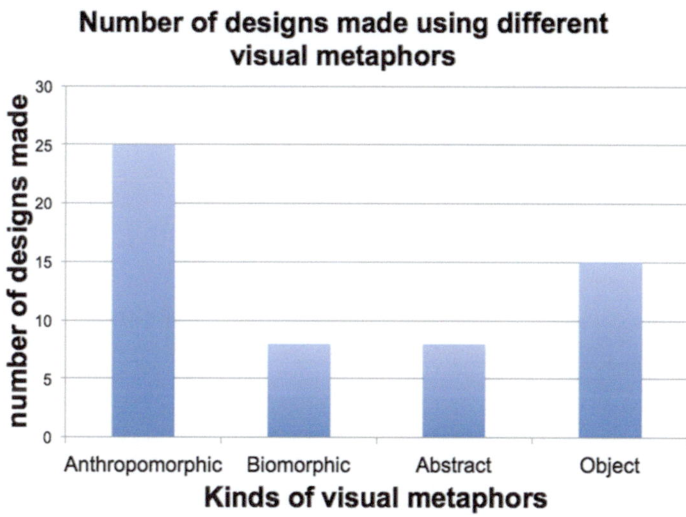

Fig. 9.2 Number of models made using each visual metaphor style

Fig. 9.3 An Anthropomorphic design of an excited emotion

Fig. 9.4 An Object-based design of a happy emotion

Participant 2	'When I think of these things I think mostly of blobby spaceships.' (Fig. 9.4)
Participant 3	'It's just different coloured wavy lines because that's how you feel when you're relaxed…it moves like a squid.' (Fig. 9.5)
Participant 4	'Triangles are the strongest structure.' (Fig. 9.6)

Participants were asked to enact movements to describe emotions by playing with the models that they had created. They were able to verbally describe and justify movements for 67 % of the designs that were created. Below is a transcript of an excerpt of a conversation between the first author and a teenage participant, discussing how the model shown in Fig. 9.5 might behave and interact with other emotions.

Researcher	"How would this one move?"
Participant 1	"Have you ever seen a squid move, it's like you have these things, tendrils, they just suck up and push forwards."
Researcher	"If this one, came across this one (a pyramid representing a tense emotion) what would it do?"
Participant 1	"It would try and wrap itself around it, to mask the tense, underneath a relaxed exterior."
Researcher	"What would happen to the triangle one?"

Fig. 9.5 A Biomorphic design of a relaxed emotion

Fig. 9.6 An Abstract design of a tense emotion

Participant 1 "It would slowly start getting smaller until it disappeared, like it's getting eaten."

Researcher "Ok so it comes across the excited one? How might they effect each other?"

Participant 1 "Well excited is a more powerful feeling than relaxed, so it would take over more, the relaxed feeling would try and stay out of its way."

9.2.5 Analysis

Analysis of the results of this study suggests that teenagers use a variety of visual metaphors to describe emotions. Although the most popular choice of visual metaphor was anthropomorphic, which accounted for 45 % of the designs made, the other three categories were also well used, with object metaphors at 27 %, biomorphic accounting for 14 % and abstract for 14 % (Fig. 9.7). In response to research question one, 47% of the shapes designed represented the body in some way. The high use of anthropomorphic metaphors is in line with much contemporary research on emotion that places non-cognitive physiological responses, sensations and physical behaviours as being a key part of emotion (Prinz 2012). 29 % of the designs made use of objects as a visual metaphor. There was a wide variation amongst these designs, from skateboards, to rockets, to chairs. Although fewer young people used biomorphic forms, those who did were able to explain why they had chosen certain colours, shapes and visual metaphors. The anthropomorphised designs were codified further, into representations of facial features, bodily action, embodied sensation and human figures. This coding revealed that a large number of designs made

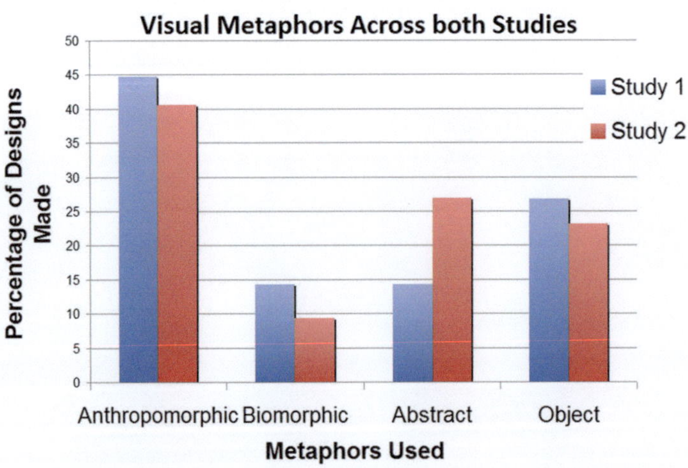

Fig. 9.7 Percentage of models made using different visual metaphor styles during studies 1 and 2

use of facial expressions to convey emotion. 16 out of 28 designs related to the body making use of facial features, 2 representing embodied action such as flexing of muscles, 3 representing bodily sensation such as a bubbling stomach and 7 representing human figures. That 67 % of participants were able to invent and justify movements and behaviours for their designs suggests that personification may be a useful visualisation technique for the display of mixed and complicated emotional states for teenagers. More work would be needed to understand which kinds of movements and behaviours teenagers use to describe the interaction of different emotions.

9.3 Study Two

The second study was designed to expand on the findings of the first study that teenagers use a variety of visual metaphors to describe emotions.

9.3.1 Design Objectives

The design objectives of the second study were:

- Expand on the findings of the first study: Check that teenagers can create visual metaphors to describe emotions.
- Explore the effects of materials: Discover if using 2D or 3D materials affects the visual metaphors that teenagers use to describe emotions.

9.3.2 Method

This study took place in a classroom at a Secondary School in the North West of England. Participants were a convenience sample of 38 teenage pupils selected by a teacher. The participants were aged between 12 and 15, studying in years 7, 8 and 9. Of the sample, 26 were girls and 12 were boys.

9.3.3 Design Activity

The study was a between subjects design, with two sets of independent variables, the use of 2D (coloured card) or 3D (Play-Doh) materials and the use of two different sets of emotional terms as stimuli. The dependent variables were the designs created by the participants and the terms they wrote to describe them. A list of terms for emotions, devised for the COOL project (Mazzone 2012) were reused in this study, because they had been shown to be accessible and useful to teenagers to describe and interpret emotions. The study was split into 4 blocks, A, B, C & D with each block offering a different combination of the two sets of dependent variables. As part of a MESS day event, the time limit for the activity was defined as 25 min to ensure the study aligned with scheduled classes. For each activity, the participants were split into 2 groups, either A & B or C & D. During each activity one group was equipped with Play-Doh and sculpting tools, the other group used coloured card and scissors. Both groups were given a design worksheet and within the groups participants worked individually. The worksheet featured 4 rectangular frames. Each frame was titled with one of the 4 emotion terms. Groups A and B used the terms, love, pride, nervous and angry. Groups C and D used the terms sad, guilty, happy and scared. Participants were asked to use the materials to create a shape to describe each of the 4 emotions and place each shape on the relevant frame. The participants were also instructed to write a textual description of what they had made in their own words, in a text box provided below their model. They were provided a space to work by themselves and given a 7 min time limit to complete the task.

9.3.4 Results

The first author analysed the text data generated by the participants to describe their own designs and categorised the designs using the coding strategy described in Study One. From a total of 160 designs created, 65 (41 %) featured anthropomorphic visual metaphors, 15 (9 %) were categorised as biomorphic, 43 (27 %) were categorised as abstract and 37 (23 %) were categorised as object metaphors, (Table 9.2). 30 anthropomorphic designs were created using 2D materials compared to 35 using 3D (Table 9.3). There were 8 biomorphic designs created using 2D materials compared to 7 using 3D. 29 abstract designs were created using 2D materials compared to 14 using 3D and 27 object designs were created using 2D materials compared to 10 from 3D materials.

Table 9.2 Categorisation of visual metaphors used by teenagers to describe emotions

	Anthropomorphic	Biomorphic	Abstract	Object
Happy	7	4	2	9
Sad	12	2	6	2
Scared	6	4	6	5
Angry	6	0	9	4
Nervous	3	1	10	3
Guilty	3	4	7	7
Love	21	0	0	1
Pride	7	0	3	6
Total	**65**	**15**	**43**	**37**

Table 9.3 Categorisation of metaphors used by teenagers to describe different emotions 2D compared to 3D materials

	Anthropomorphic	Biomorphic	Abstract	Object
2D	30	8	29	27
3D	35	7	14	10

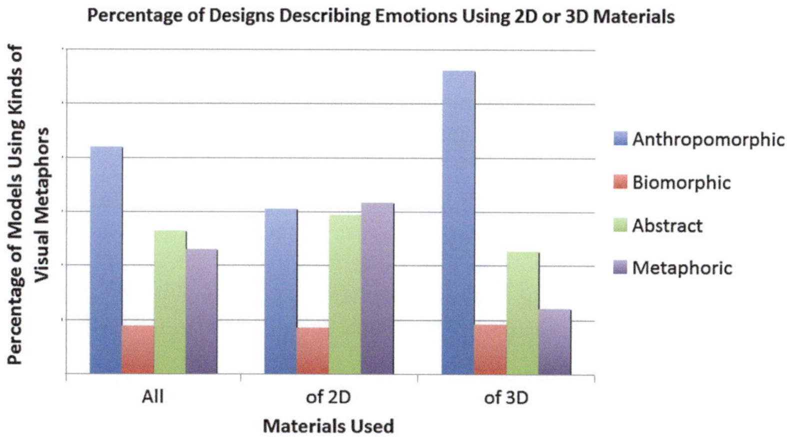

Fig. 9.8 Percentage of designs describing emotions using 2D or 3D materials, featuring different visual metaphor styles

9.3.5 *Analysis*

The percentages of designs that were categorised as either anthropomorphic or object based are largely consistent with the results of the first study (Fig. 9.7). There was a slight reduction in the percentage of anthropomorphic designs created from 45 % to 41 %. Similarly there was a slight reduction in object-based designs, from 27 % in the first study to 23 % in the second. Biomorphic design creation decreased from 24 % in study 1 to 9 % in the second study, with a 15 increase in abstract designs from 14 % in study one to 27 % in study two.

The emotional terms in this study can be categorised as positive or negative. In this basic scheme, sad, scared, angry, nervous and guilty are categorised as negative and happy, love and pride are categorised as positive. The images created to describe negative emotions featured more abstract and biomorphic visual metaphors than those created to describe emotions categorised as positive (Table 9.2).

An analysis of the designs produced by participants using 2D or 3D materials revealed that participants using the 3D material (Play-Doh), created more designs using anthropomorphic visual metaphors than those using coloured card, see Fig. 9.8.

9.4 Study Three

Informed by the findings of this research, a prototype app was designed to display mixed and complex teenage emotions. The app transferred ideas explored in this study into the digital realm and allowed for the integration of knowledge gained here, with new explorations of the use of interactive movement behaviours to describe the interaction of different emotions. The app allowed users to select and interact with externalised and personified emotions, visualised as autonomous agents. Users control which emotions are brought to life onscreen, selecting different visual designs and controlling movement behaviours with a set of sliders.

A third study was conducted to investigate the use of early evaluations of prototypes to stimulate discussion on possible use contexts for mobile affective displays and any ethical issues that the prototype raised. The second evaluation study was run at FACT, the Foundation for Art and Creative Technology in Liverpool as part of a creative summer school. This evaluation activity was carried out by 1 mixed gender and mixed age group from a convenient sample of 7 young people from Liverpool, aged 11 to 18. The participants were recruited through their involvement with the summer school.

9.4.1 Design Objectives

The study was a formative, exploratory evaluation conducted in order to gain an understanding of teenage attitudes and perceptions towards affective displays and their social use.

9.4.2 Design Activity

The participants were given information about the development of the project and its aims. To avoid the risk of satisficing (giving superficial responses that are perceived to be acceptable) the young people were told that the app (Fig. 9.9) had been designed by another member of the research team (i.e. not the researcher conducting the study). Participants were introduced to a set of two teen personas, adapted from those in (Horton et al. 2012) for the purposes of this study, and asked to select one each. The set of personas included one male and one female teenager. The personas both featured the same scenario, in which the persona was lead protagonist. In this scenario, the persona had taken advantage of their parents being away and opened their house to a wild party. The party had started well, but now it was full of strangers and their persona is experiencing mixed feelings about the whole situation. Participants were given an Android tablet each, and were instructed to use the app. They were told that their task was to use the app to control the movement and

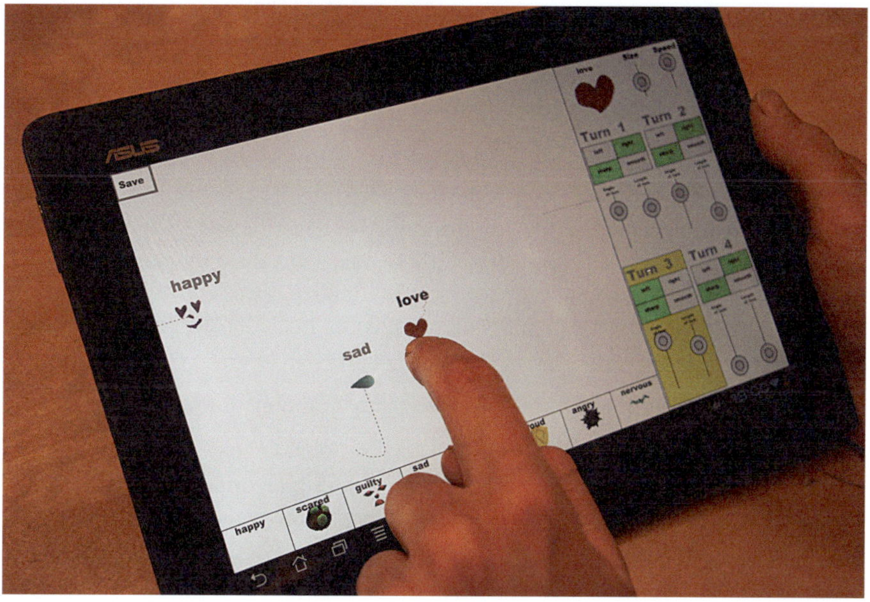

Fig. 9.9 Screenshot of the prototype mobile app Empath

appearance of emotions to describe how their teen persona would be feeling at this point in the scenario. Participants were allowed 5 min to use the application individually before participating in a focus group discussion to evaluate the application, in which participants were asked to imagine how the teen persona would feel about the app.

9.4.3 *Results*

The discussion transcript was analysed by the first author and participants' comments about the app were coded into three categories, personal development, relationships and privacy (Table 9.4). These categories were selected in response to the issues that participants raised during the discussion and the value judgements that were perceived to underpin their comments. Each monologue contributed by a participant was treated as a separate comment and pseudonyms are used instead of real names in the following discussion. Of the 20 comments in the transcript, 6 focused on how the use of mobile emotion displays could affect teenagers relationships with others, echoing Fitton et al. (2013) inclusion of the 'desire for association with peers' as a key characteristic of teenagers.

Ethan "If people would be able to view your emotions, you would be more self-conscious about how you were feeling, if people could see that you were angry then people could stay away from you."

Table 9.4 Number of comments raised by teenagers in focus group discussion

	Relationships	Privacy	Personal Development
Benefits	1	0	5
Neural	0	2	2
Concerns	5	5	0

The need for teenagers to develop the ability to describe and reason about their emotions, emphasized by Fonagy et al (2004) was also valued by participants who made seven comments discussing how mobile affective displays could support personal development. Seven of the twenty comments made by the group concerned how affective systems like these might affect teenager's right to privacy.

Danny "That's why I would prefer to keep my emotions in me, just to be sure, because anything can get hacked now."

The comments were also coded by sentiment and categorised as either benefits, neutral or concerns in order to gain some more general evaluative insights within the three categories.

Of the six comments about how the app could affect relationships, one described a benefit and five described concerns. Of the seven comments relating to privacy, five raised concerns and two were neutral, whereas of the seven comments on how the app could affect personal development five described benefits and two were neutral. A transcript of the focus group discussion is included in the Appendix at the end of this chapter.

9.4.4 Analysis

When asked to consider how a teen persona might feel about the mobile app, teenagers taking part in the evaluation raised twice as many issues relating to relationships and privacy as they did to personal development. The issues raised about privacy and how use could affect relationships were overwhelmingly negative, whereas comments about the apps potential effect on personal development were largely positive. This suggests that for these teenagers the value of affective displays is judged not only in terms of personal development, but that the teenagers are also considering the wider contexts of use and associated implications (such as the possible consequences of inadequate privacy).

9.5 Discussion

Much of the CCI research exploring the design of emotion displays has worked within the emotion as information paradigm. Both the COOL (Mazzone 2012) project and the SenseMS (Amin et al. 2005) project, found that teenagers preferred to use designs featuring facial expressions when asked to describe emotions accurately. Both these projects designed systems that aimed to communicate emotional information as unambiguously as possible using one display method to describe a range of emotions. The present study also found that teenagers use anthropomorphic visual metaphors the most to describe emotions. This emphasis on non-cognitive (Hoffman 1986) and embodied (Prinz 2012) interpretations of emotion fits well with contemporary theories of emotion.

The studies described in this chapter also discovered that teenagers have a more complex approach to the design of emotion displays than has been previously thought. A fine-grained approach was taken to understand the different ways that teenagers use visual metaphor's to describe different emotions. Although teenagers taking part in this study created anthropomorphised designs the most, they used a range of visual metaphor styles to describe emotions. This suggests that while anthropomorphised visual metaphors remain central to teenager's representation of emotion, a variety of visual metaphor styles should be considered when designing affective systems for and with this group. This would both echo existing practice amongst teenagers as captured in this study and encourage the collaborative interpretation of the meaning of emotions amongst peers as encouraged by Boehner et al. (2007). Interaction designers developing affective systems to support the teenage development of mentalised affectivity (Fonagy et al. 2004), should offer the affordance of 'many paths, many styles' (Resnick and Silverman 2005) for the display of emotions. As Fonagy et al (2004) have stated, the ability to describe and find meaning in emotions is of vital importance to teenage development and mental health. Teenagers participating in this study made more use of abstract and biomorphic designs to describe 'negative' emotions such as scared, angry, nervous and guilty. That teenagers use different visual metaphors to describe negative emotions is a new finding and has implications for interaction design with this group. Abstraction and biomorphism are already used as techniques within art and narrative therapy to externalise and personify negative emotions. It seems likely that their ambiguity and their lack of relation to the body make these kinds of designs useful to teenagers to separate themselves from problematic emotions and think critically about them. That teenagers have used these visual metaphors and techniques whilst designing an interactive system, suggests that they are transferrable from therapy settings to the design of affective displays.

Participants of this study created more designs describing emotions featuring anthropomorphic visual metaphors when they were using Play-Doh. This suggests that choice of materials has an effect on teenage design contributions for affective displays. The results of this study do not identify whether the key factor here is the difference between 2D and 3D materials or hard and soft materials.

9.5.1 Reflections

Findings from this work support the view that it is particularly important that teenagers participate in the design of affective systems, because adults simply do not have the insights and understandings teenagers themselves can provide. The activities were designed to be accessible and meaningful to teenagers, using techniques that have been shown to work with this age group and ethical guidelines set out by the ChiCI group.

By asking teenagers to actively design their own emotion displays, instead of categorising simplified diagrams of facial expressions as with the COOL project, the design activities allowed participants more freedom to explore different kinds of visual metaphors. Although participants still used anthropomorphised visual metaphors the most, the use of 2D and 3D materials has revealed a more nuanced picture of how teens prefer to visualise emotion and suggested new ways to describe difficult emotions. This decision to reject established visualisation methods as a default starting point could be applied to different visualisation and design activities involving teenagers in the context of mobile apps, web sites etc.

The context of app design, a design space that many teenagers are interested in, acted as an effective motivator for engagement in creative activities that have already been shown to be of benefit to teenage development. By creating visual metaphors to describe different kinds of emotions, participants constructed their own visual language to describe and make sense of their own and other people's emotions. As one participant said when evaluating the mobile app.

Josh "It might help people explain their emotions, if they have difficulty communicating them, they could show them in a visual way."

Activities in the first and the third study, exploring the use of personification and externalisation to describe the behaviour of emotions as digital autonomous agents, offered teenagers a new way of describing mixed emotions. In the first study, teenagers were able to easily invent interactive behaviours for emotions, of the kinds often seen in computer games. For example one participant described movements they were enacting with models of emotions. "It would slowly start getting smaller until it disappeared, like it's getting eaten." As many teenagers are used to encountering the interaction of agents in dynamic decentralised systems whilst playing computer games, it is likely that this design activity builds on their existing implicit knowledge of these systems. This application of using a 'decentralised systems' way of thinking in art-therapy techniques such as externalization and personification is valuable because it offers teenagers new ways to describe complicated and mixed emotions in a language that makes sense to them.

The first two studies in this research we conducted as part of MESS days. This format enables researchers to access to a large number of teenagers in a short space of time and is an effective way to involve difficult to reach teenagers, who might not otherwise access participatory design activities through engagement with arts or other community provisions. MESS days are experienced by participants as part of school activities, the behavioural expectations and social norms in school are likely to affect design contributions, particularly when designs are describing the private subject of teenage emotions. It is possible that participants in this study self-censored design contributions that they may otherwise have shared in another setting. The effect of social context on the teenage design of affective systems could be researched carrying out the same activities across formal educational and informal social settings. The use of MESS days also placed constraints of the time allowed for study activities and demands on the researchers to ensure everything was reset and prepared quickly as groups of participants moved between activities, these practical organisational issues need to be considered carefully for other researchers wishing to use a similar approach with success.

The description of emotions is a highly subjective task for all ages. This is particularly the case for teenagers both due to the social pressures of adolescence and the different rates that teenagers develop theory of mind and social skills. For these studies it was important that the design stimulus was both accessible, engaging and consistent across the study group. In response to Fitton and Bell's (2014) research question of "What are the appropriate methodologies for engaging teenagers in HCI research?", we found that combining teen personas with a fantasy narrative, was an effective way to frame a lo-fi design activity aiming to stimulate innovative design thinking whilst dealing with a potentially sensitive topic for teenagers, emotion. Participants were able to quickly understand the design space, the visual display of emotion and intended use context. The pseudonymity that personas offer are particularly useful to support teenagers to share visual and verbal descriptions of emotions. The methods used in this study also addressed the question of "How can we gain insights into unknown teen populations?" by demonstrating that teenage design contributions can reveal new insights, in this case into teenage preferences for the display of emotion. It is likely that this combination of teen personas and fantasy narrative as stimulus for lo fi design activities will prove useful to those looking to engage emergent teenage brains with innovative design thinking across a range of spaces and technologies. It is also likely that with fine grained analysis, these design contributions will reveal new and fascinating things about teenage experiences of technology.

The use of role play with models created by the participants was an effective and intuitive way for teenagers to demonstrate the personification of emotions. This is demonstrated by the ease with which 66 % of participants were able to invent distinct movements to represent the interactions of different emotions. Although this helped the researcher gain an understanding of which kinds of movements these teenagers might find useful to describe emotions as autonomous agents, this was not captured quantitatively. In future studies this data could be captured by filming or otherwise tracking the movement of models as participants played with them.

An important limitation of this research is the difference in design between studies one and two. Study one made use of teen personas and narrative framing for design stimulus, whereas study two used basic text descriptions of emotions. All of the participants in study one worked with Play-Doh, but half of the participants in study two created drawings. Participants in study one were asked to elaborate verbally on their results, whilst in study two they were asked to write text descriptions, which due to the natural variance in literacy skills, could differ greatly between the age groups. Because of these inconsistencies, it is not possible to claim that the second study validates the first one. Researchers conducting similar studies should attempt to replicate the same design activity, in order to validate findings or make one of the changes described here, to understand its effect.

The design of affective displays for teenagers is a new area of research within HCI. The design of affective systems for adults is already a complex challenge, combining this with the developmental needs of adolescents and the lack of understanding we have of teen computer interaction can make this feel like a leap into the unknown. As this generation of teenagers face the developmental challenges in a digital culture in which tastes, boundaries of privacy and behavioural norms are constantly moving, there is a greater risk that technologies designed to support teenage development, could not only fail to satisfy this aim, but actually cause harm. The focus group discussion was a useful way for researchers to gain an understanding of teenage perceptions and attitudes towards mobile emotion displays. The informality of the setting and the activity supported a relaxed discussion in which participants appeared to speak their minds, although the presence of peers is likely to have shaped their behaviour and the points they raised. The discussion suggested that these teenagers would rate the value of an affective display not just for the impact it has on their personal development, but also their relationships and right to privacy. Although this study has found that theory and techniques from therapeutic settings, such as the externalisation and personification of emotions can be transferred to the design of affective systems, it is important to understand key differences between the therapeutic context, with its emphasis on one to one private relationships and the complex networked social life of teenagers. Because of this, it is vital that teenagers are involved in the design of affective systems, both to ensure that emotion display methods are meaningful to teenagers and that they don't make vulnerable teenagers more vulnerable. Ultimately, if technology is going to pervade the emotional life of teenagers, then it is ethically important that teenagers have a voice in how that technology is designed.

9.6 Conclusions and Further Work

This chapter explored the design of affective applications with teenagers and posed 2 key research questions of *which kinds of visual metaphors do teenagers use to describe emotions?* (RQ1) and *how does the use of different materials affect teenage designs of affective displays?* (RQ2). In response to research RQ1, this study has three key conclusions:

- C1. Teenagers use anthropomorphic visual metaphors the most to describe emotions.
- C2. Teenagers use a variety of visual metaphors to describe emotions.
- C3. Teenagers make more use of abstract and biomorphic designs to describe 'negative' emotions such as scared, angry, nervous and guilty.

In response to RQ2 this work found:

- C4. Teenagers are more likely to create designs describing emotions featuring anthropomorphic visual metaphors if they are using soft malleable and three dimensional materials.

While this chapter contributes a range of valuable insights and understandings around the visual metaphors that teenagers use to describe different emotions, there is still much to explore within this space. For example, more work needs to be done to explore whether the model developed by Read et al. (2013b), can be applied to understand exactly how the affordances of materials effect teenagers designs of affective displays.

Further work is planned to develop and evaluate interactive systems featuring teenage emotions visualized as autonomous agents, capable of interacting with their environment and one another. This work will aim to combine the benefits of externalisation and personification with the kinds of technological features that are known to appeal to teenagers such as interaction, gameplay and networked collaboration. It will be informed by the modelling and simulation approaches used by modelling toolkits (Resnick 1997) and serious games (Susi et al. 2007).

The importance of technologies ability to support vital peer relationships has been identified by Read and Markopoulos (2013) and Fitton and Bell (2014), but its importance to the design of affective systems to this group is new. Read and Beale (2011) have offered useful methods to capture teenage perceptions of safety and privacy in cloud computing. The challenge of designing affective systems that support teenagers to develop the ability to describe, reason about and share emotions and respond to their need for tighter social relationships with peers whilst maintaining their right to privacy is new to HCI. This research challenge will require affective systems to be designed and evaluated from a perspective of social use and privacy as well as just individual personal development. The overall contribution of this work to the field of TeenCI is a categorisation of the visual metaphors teenagers use to describe different emotions along with the associated methods that were successfully used to engage teenagers exploring and representing emotions. It is hoped that these findings be useful to interaction designers and researchers developing affective systems for and with teenagers.

Appendix: Interview Transcript

Transcript of interview in Study 3, from chapter 'Designing Teenage Emotions with a Life of their Own'.

Researcher "How do you think teenagers like Ian or Amanda would feel about using something like this?"

Ella "I think it would be quite helpful to them, because teenagers are meant to be in a time of struggle and you're just realizing who you are and who you want to be, so therefore, using something like that to gather your emotions might be helpful, instead of having to talk to someone about it, you could just collect them all in there."

Michael "But some people don't like interactive things like that do they, some people are just quiet and don't show their emotions until later on, or some people just show their emotions at the moment."

Danny "Some people might not want to put their emotions into something that other people might see."

Researcher "How do you think that teenagers like Ian or Amanda would feel about sharing something that they did using something like this, with other people? How would that work? What would be the positives and negatives with it?"

Danny "You could stick in a thing to help them, so if they stick a certain thing in, then it might say 'try to do something to calm yourself down.' or 'try to do something to make yourself happy.' It could say, 'Try take a bath to make yourself happy.'"

Kate "It might help people explain their emotions, if they have difficulty communicating them, they could show them in a visual way."

Researcher "What are the risks with people putting their emotions out there?"

Ella "If someone knows you and they go on to your tablet and find out that you were angry or whatever, then they then know what you felt angry over and what you did that day, therefore they could start making you feel angry again."

Ethan "I had another positive, for people with Asperger's who might find it hard to find emotions, this could be really helpful, and it could be an easy way."

Researcher "Why?"

Ethan "Because it's more visual."

Danny "It might not help that much though, because it's still just sliding things up or down."

Researcher "If we were to imagine the 100 years from now and think about the technologies that we might be having then, if the sky is the limit and we are thinking these slider things don't give you that much control, and they aren't that much fun, then what could we have instead?"

Jacob "In a hundred years, they could actually, allow human minds to get access to the internet, via virtual replicas of ourselves we could make games of our own."

Researcher "Would anyone fancy that?"

Kate "Yes."

Ethan "Yes."

Michael "I don't know what he said, but yes."

Researcher "So is this what you are saying, that there could be virtual versions of yourselves, so your thoughts could be on the internet."

Jacob "Well technically you would be on the in the internet, not on, but in."

Researcher "If your emotions are in the internet, then what are the positives and negatives of that in your everyday life?"

Kate "They are very public, but that might be a good thing if people were more frank with each other, it would change society though. You would have to try it out on a community of people and see how it would change their behaviour."

Researcher "Any more thoughts on if the sky was the limit how those ideas might work?"

Ethan "If people would be able to view your emotions, you would be more self-conscious about how you were feeling, if people could see that you were angry then people could stay away from you."

Ella "You might actually be able to program something to read your emo tions, just be reading your thoughts and your face, similar to what he was saying, so it might be better because you wouldn't have to put in your emotions, it would just automatically know."

Researcher "So you wouldn't have to go through a screen?"

Researcher "So we were talking about the risk as to people being able to see if you were angry."

Danny "People might rather than actually show their true emotions, they might want to mask their true emotions and do something different, so not actually show what their emotions are, when other people are looking at it."

Ella "There should be a privacy setting, so that people can only see half of the emotions that you want them to see, so that you are able to explore all of your emotions in to make you feel better, but then people can't see all of them. But the problem with that is the people who need to know, like all of your emotions like your parents or whatever, won't know because of the private settings, so they wouldn't be able to find out. Therefore you could just put 'Happy' and 'Cheerful' when actually you are just depressed."

Researcher "So possibly we are just reproducing the same problems that we have in the real world. Any thoughts on how you could get around that?"

Danny "You could have it like on Facebook, so that when you post something only certain people see it, only the people that need to know."

Researcher "Thinking of the people you know, the organizations in your life, businesses, and governments, people that you know in your social life, who would and who wouldn't you trust?"

Danny "I wouldn't trust nearly anyone really. If you think of everything now, it's all gone public, Facebook and twitter, everyone can see it, so I think your emotions now are the only thing that you've got that are private. So if you make that public, then you've not got anything to hold onto."

Ethan "If you were in street just walking about, you wouldn't want everyone to know your emotions. Maybe if you could say why you were angry, then people could avoid that, and not just say 'I'm Angry.'"

Nadine "You could have more emotions, hungry, jealousy stuff like that."

Ella "If someone is out to get you angry, then they would automatically know what they need to do to make you upset and you would just get it every single day, I mean people would know how to make you happy as well so that may help, but if people know how to make you upset, then you are going to end up being so bullied and so miserable that your school life or your work life or whatever, I think it could also increase the amount of suicides because people, are just being upset constantly, so they might just end up killing themselves."

Ethan "There should be a way to block them."

Researcher "There are loads of risks."

Ethan "There are risks with everything though, it's like social network, YouTube, there's always a risk, so it wouldn't just be with that, it would be everything."

Danny "That's why I would prefer to keep my emotions in me, just to be sure, because anything can get hacked now."

References

Amin AK, Kersten BTA, Kulyk OA, Pelgrim PH, Wang CM, Markopoulos P (2005) SenseMS: a user-centered approach to enrich the messaging experience for teens by non-verbal means. In: Proceedings of the 7th international conference on human computer interaction with mobile devices & services. ACM, New York, pp 161–166

Astington JW, Harris PL, Olson DR (1990) Developing theories of mind. Cambridge University Press.

Bang A, Krogh P, Ludvigsen M, Markussen T (2012) The role of hypothesis in constructive design research. In: Proceedings of the Art of Research Iv.

Bishop C (2005) The social turn: collaboration and its discontents. Artforum 44(6):178

Boehner K, DePaula R, Doursh P, Sengers P (2007) How emotion is made and measured. Int Hum-Comput Stud 65(4):275–291

Botar OAI, Wünsche I (2011) Biocentrism and modernism. Ashgate Publishing, Ltd, Farnham

Butler S, Guterman JT, Rudes J (2009) Using puppets with children in narrative therapy to externalize the problem. J Ment Health Couns 31(3):225–233

Carey M, Russell S (2002) Externalising – commonly asked questions. Int J Narrat Ther Commun Work 2002(2):76
Chandler M, Astington JW, Harris PL, Olson DR (1988) Doubt and developing theories of mind. Dev Theor Mind 1: 387–414
Clynes M, Menuhin Y (1977) Sentics: the touch of emotions. Anchor Press, Garden City
Druin A (1999) Developing cooperative new technologies inquiry: for children with children, In Proceedings of the SIGCHI conference on human factors in computing systems, ACM, pp 592–599
Eysenck H (1991) Dimensions of personality: 16, 5 or 3? – criteria for a taxonomic paradigm. Personal Individ Differ 12(8):773–790
Fitton D, Bell BT (2014) Working with teenagers within HCI research: understanding teen-computer interaction. In: Proceedings of the 28th international BCS human computer interaction conference on HCI 2014 – Sand, Sea and Sky – Holiday HCI (BCS-HCI '14). BCS, UK, pp 201–206
Fitton D, Read JCC, Horton M (2013) The challenge of working with teens as participants in interaction design. In: CHI'13 Extended abstracts on human factors in computing systems. ACM, New York, pp 205–210
Fonagy P, Gergely G, Jurist EL (2004) Affect regulation, mentalization and the development of the self. Karnac Books, London
Froggett L (2011) New model visual arts organisations & Social engagement, Psychosocial Research Unit, University of Central Lancashire. Available at: www.artsandhealth.ie/wp-content/uploads/2013/02/New-Model-Visual-Arts-Organisations-and-Social-Engagement.pdf. Accessed Mar 2014
Guha M, Druin A, Chipman G (2005) Working with young children as technology design partners. Commun ACM 48(1):39–42
Guha ML, Druin A, Chipman G, Fails JA, Simms S, Farber A (2004) Mixing ideas: a new technique for working with young children as design partners. In: Proceeding of the 2004 conference on interaction design and children building a community, ACM, pp 35–42
Hoffman ML (1986) Affect, cognition, and motivation: foundations of social behavior, 1, pp 244–280.
Horton M, Read J, Fitton D, Little L, Toth N (2012) Too cool at school-understanding cool teenagers. PsychNology J 10(2):73–91
Iversen O, Dindler C (2008) Pursuing aesthetic inquiry in participatory design. In: Proceedings of the tenth anniversary conference on participatory design 2008. Indiana University, pp 138–145
Klein M (1929) Personification in the play of children. Int J Psycho-Anal 10:193
Lutz C (1988) Unnatural emotions: everyday sentiments on a micronesian atoll and their challenge to western theory. University of Chicago Press.
Marti P, Rizzo A (2003) Levels of design: from usability to experience. In: HCI International 2003, 10th international conference on human-computer interaction
Mazzone E (2012) Designing with children : reflections on effective involvement of children in the interaction design process. Doctoral dissertation, University of Central Lancashire
Mazzone E, Read J, Beale R (2008) Understanding children's contributions during informant design. In: Proceedings of the 22nd British HCI group annual conference on people and computers: culture, creativity, interaction, vol 2. British Computer Society, pp 61–64
Papert S, Harel I (1991) Situating constructionism. Constructionism 36:1–11
Picard RW (1995) Affective computing
Picard RW, Papert S, Bender W, Blumberg B, Breazeal C, Cavallo D, Machover T, Resnick M, Roy D, Strohecker C (2004) Affective learning—a manifesto. BT Technol J 22(4):253–269
Prinz J (2012) Emotion. In: Calvo P, Gomila T (eds) The Cambridge handbook of cognitive science. Cambridge University Press.
Read JC, Bekker M (2011) The nature of child computer interaction. In: Proceedings of the 25th BCS conference on human-computer interaction, British Computer Society, pp 163–170

Read JC, Beale R (2011) What teenagers think about when they think about safety in the cloud. ACM SIGCHI Workshop, Vancouver

Read JC, Horton M, Iversen O, Fitton D, Little L (2013a) Methods of working with teenagers in interaction design. In: CHI'13 Extended abstracts on human factors in computing systems. ACM, New York, pp 3243–3246

Read JC, Fitton D, Horton M (2013b) Theatre, playDoh and comic strips: designing organic user interfaces with young adolescent and teenage participants. Interact Comput 25(2):183–198

Read JC, Markopoulos P (2013) Child–computer interaction. 2013. Int J Child-Comput Interact.

Read J, MacFarlane S, Kelly S (2006) The ChiCI group. In CHI'06 extended abstracts on human factors in computing systems, ACM, pp 295–298

Resnick M (1997) Turtles, termites, and traffic jams: explorations in massively parallel microworlds. MIT Press.

Resnick M, Silverman B (2005) Some reflections on designing construction kits for kids. In: Proceedings of the 2005 conference on Interaction design and children, ACM, pp 117–122

Reynolds CW (1999) Steering behaviors for autonomous characters. In: Game developers conference, vol 1999, pp 763–782

Salovey P, Mayer JD (1990) Emotional intelligence. Imagin Cogn Pers 9(3):185–211

Susi T, Johannesson M, Backlund P (2007) Serious games: an overview. University of Skövde, Sweden

Velásquez J (1997) Modeling emotions and other motivations in synthetic agents. In: AAAI/IAAI, pp 10–15

White M (2006) Narrative practice with families with children: externalising conversations revisited. In: White M, Morgan A (eds). Narrative therapy with children and their families.

Xu D, Read J, Sim G, McManus B (2009) Experience it, draw it, rate it: capture children's experiences with their drawings. In: Proceedings of the 8th international conference on interaction design and children, ACM, pp 266–270

Chapter 10
Working with Teenagers in HCI Research: A Reflection on Techniques Used in the Taking on the Teenagers Project

Daniel Fitton, Beth T. Bell, Linda Little, Matthew Horton, Janet C. Read, Michelle Rouse, and Nicola Toth

Abstract Engaging participants and choosing an appropriate technique in the research process are vitally important in developing successful products, devices and interventions. HCI researchers need to choose techniques that are suitable and appropriate for the user population being considered. In this chapter techniques used within HCI research activities with teenagers during the Taking on the Teenagers research project are considered, providing a brief case study example of each. The key features of each technique are then summarised, in order to allow comparison between techniques and assist both researchers and practitioners when selecting techniques. Second, the authors reflect critically upon their practical experiences working with teens and the lessons they have learned, in order to formulate nine guidelines that inform best practice when working with teenaged user populations.

10.1 Introduction

Involving participants in the research process is now recognised as an important part of any project (McDonagh and Bateman 2012). Including participants at any stage from developing the research question to dissemination activities is purported

D. Fitton (✉) • M. Horton • J.C. Read
Child-Computer Interaction Group, School of Physical Sciences and Computing, University of Central Lancashire, PR1 2HE, Preston, UK
e-mail: DBFitton@uclan.ac.uk

B.T. Bell
Faculty of Health and Life Sciences, York St John University, York YO31 7EX, UK

L. Little • N. Toth
PaCT Lab, Department of Psychology, Faculty of Health and Life Sciences, Northumbria University, Newcastle NE1 8ST, UK

M. Rouse
Macmillan Cancer Support, 89 Albert Embankment, Vauxhall, SE1 7UQ London, UK

© Springer International Publishing Switzerland 2016

L. Little et al. (eds.), *Perspectives on HCI Research with Teenagers*, Human–Computer Interaction Series, DOI 10.1007/978-3-319-33450-9_10

to enhance the quality of the research (Royal College of Pediatrics and Child Health 2010). One particular target group who increasingly participate in HCI research projects are teenagers. Teenagers are now actively encouraged to express their opinions and contribute in the decision making process especially about services, developments, interventions and research that will impact them (Matthews 2001; Lambert and Glacken 2011). However, as Lang et al. (2012) state teenagers are often treated like short adults or tall children and not as a unique population.

Researchers (adults) are unlikely to have sufficient understanding and be too far removed from their own adolescent experience to fully be able to empathise with teenagers (Aitken 1994). Cognitive abilities develop and change rapidly throughout childhood (Berk 2013; Feldman and Bishop 2003) and these cognitive differences are reflected in the way youths think, feel and behave in today's technology driven world (Druin 1999; Read et al. 2011). Engaging youths directly in the HCI research and design process enables understanding and appreciation of these differences (Druin 1999; Read et al. 2011; Walsh et al. 2013). It furthermore prevents adults making false assumptions about young populations on the basis that they were once youths themselves. Each generation has its own unique culture, norms, values and shared understandings and researchers need to comprehend this, rather than impose their own experiences and knowledge upon it (Fitton et al. 2011). However, we need to acknowledge the majority of this research has focused on designing for children aged seven to eleven, and little attention has been paid to developing techniques that are suitable for use with the teenage population. Yet there are strong theoretical reasons for assuming that researchers should approach working with this population differently to how they approach working with child and adult populations.

Throughout this chapter we have adopted a broad and inclusive definition of teenagers, which defines teenagers as all individuals aged from 11 to 19, in order to encompass the diverse range of complex changes that occur gradually during adolescence (although some theorists argue that the changes of adolescence persist beyond this timeframe into the early twenties and young adulthood—see Steinberg 2008, for discussion). However, due to the complexity of the changes that occur within this time frame, and the large individual differences in the rate at which these changes occur, it has been argued that teenagers are not a homogenous group. In particular, an approximate distinction has been made in the literature between younger (11–15) and older teens (16–19), in light of the immature cognitive and social functioning of younger teenagers, relative to older teenagers (Berk 2013; Steinberg 2005, 2008). Other researchers have sought to further distinguish between mid-adolescence (teenagers aged 15–16) from these groupings (e.g. Mäkinen et al. 2012). In adopting a broad and inclusive definition of teenagers, we do not mean to minimise the important differences that exist between teenagers of different ages. Instead, we have endeavoured to highlight the ages of the specific teenagers involved in our research, and also instances wherein our findings are particularly applicable to specific sub-groups of teenagers.

10.1.1 Teenage Development

The teenaged years are recognised as a unique period in human development, characterised by diverse biological, psychological and social change (Berk 2013; Lloyd 2001). In terms of biological changes, puberty transform a child into a reproductively functioning adult during the teen years, consequently creating marked changes in teenager' physical appearance and also an increased interest in sexual partners (Collins et al. 2009; Loomba-Albrecht and Styne 2009). As a consequence, teens express an increasing desire to socialize with and please members of the opposite sex (Furman et al. 1999) whereas during childhood, they would have preferred to socialize with, and, aim to please, children of the same sex (Maccoby 2002). A diverse range of cognitive developments occur during the teenage years, including an increase in memory function, speed of processing and the acquisition of abstract thought capabilities (Steinberg 2005), as the teenage brain approaches physical maturation. Advances in developmental neuroscience have enabled researchers to demonstrate how developing teen brains actually process information differently to both adults and children (Steinberg 2005, 2008). Importantly, teenagers display a heightened sensitivity to social-reward, and an increased propensity to take risk: both of which have been attributed to the unique functioning of the teen brain (Blakemore and Mills 2014; Blakemore and Robbins 2012).

Psychologically, the key developmental task faced by teens is that of identity formation wherein the teen must negotiate their own sense of personal identity from the range of possible identities modelled within the socio-cultural environment (Berk 2013; Lloyd 2001). As such, teens express a desire for individuality and independence—evidenced on both an individual and collective level—that is not apparent amongst child populations (Chittenden 2010; Moore 2009). For example, the historical rise of teen sub-cultures such as goth, mod and rocker movements are believed to have stemmed from an underlying teen desire for individuality (Moore 2009). Social concerns also heighten during the teen years, as adolescents seek peer approval and acceptance in order to validate their new emergent identity (Rubin et al. 2006; Steinberg and Morris 2001). Therefore peers become an increasingly salient influence on teenagers, replacing parents as the most potent influence in an individual's life (Rubin et al. 2006). Finally, the teenage years are also characterised by social transition, wherein individuals gradually become no longer seen as children, and are consequently afforded the rights and responsibilities of adults. In developed countries, this is typically a socially-prescribed and progressive process, wherein teenagers are gradually afforded legal rights as they pass age-related milestones.

10.1.2 Teens, Technology and HCI Research

In light of the complex biological, psychological and social changes that occur during the teen years, the technological needs and desires of teenagers may be very different to those of both adults and children. It has been proposed that some technology may play a unique role in adolescent development. For example, online blogging has been hypothesized to be popular amongst teens as it facilitates their need for self-expression (Chittenden 2010), whereas engaging with social networking sites such as Facebook may satisfy teen desires for social acceptance and approval (Boyd 2009). Teenagers also engage with media and technology more than any other age group and also tend to be early adopters of emergent technology, making the teen population a particularly lucrative and buoyant consumer market to target with gadgets and technological devices (Gram-Hanssen 2005; Walsh et al. 2013).

Engaging teens in the HCI research and design process may provide the only means of truly understanding their wants, desires and needs particularly in relation to technology. However, researchers interested in engaging teenagers in HCI research and design projects may need to adopt a different approach when working with this population. For example, a small, yet growing number of studies have examined the techniques that engage teens in the participatory design process (Danielsson and Wiberg 2006; Iversen and Smith 2012; Mazzone et al. 2008). Poole and Peyton (2013) offered practical advice to those wishing to work with adolescent user populations in a design context, based on existing research within the social and behavioural sciences. In their paper, a limited range of data collection techniques are discussed in terms of their possible advantages and disadvantages, including interviews, focus groups, observation and videography, and video collage. Poole and Peyton (2013) conclude with a call for more research that highlights the methodological challenges in this area. The need for further exploration of the methodological challenges involved when engaging teenagers in research also emerged as a key theme from recent international workshops focusing on this area. This importance of understanding and exploring methods for use with teenagers was a key theme identified at a workshop entitled 'Designing Technology for Teens' held at the NordiCHI conference in Copenhagen in 2012. Also a workshop titled 'Exploring methods of working with teenagers in interaction design' was held at the CHI conference in Paris in 2013, which focused on identifying which methods should be used to engage teens in research and participatory design.

This chapter is a direct response to the call for more research that highlights the methodological challenges involved when working with teenagers in HCI research projects and in interaction design made at international workshops on this theme and in published works (e.g. Poole and Peyton 2013.) It aims to contribute to the literature in two key ways. First it provides an overview of the techniques that the authors have used when working with teenagers in HCI research and design projects. Using a framework developed by Mazzone (2012), the key features of these techniques are highlighted, enabling useful comparisons to be made between them.

Second, by critically reflecting upon this experience with teenagers, the authors provide a set of nine empirically-driven guidelines to aid researchers when working with this unique user group, particularly those who may not have done this before.

10.2 Techniques

In this section, the authors outline a series of techniques that have been employed when working with teens in research projects. The projects have been carried out by the Psychology and Communication Technology Laboratory (PaCT Lab) at Northumbria University, and the Child Computer Interaction (ChiCI) Group at the University of Central Lancashire, UK. The techniques have been utilised by researchers working across several different projects, from two different academic disciplines, namely psychology and interaction design. PaCT and ChiCI have worked both independently and collaboratively on several of these projects using techniques that encompass a broad range of themes including: energy-use; organic material design; design for cool and online trust and persuasion. A diverse range of teenagers took part in the research, including teenagers of different gender, age and ethnicity, from a range of socio-economic backgrounds, geographical location and school type. As none of the techniques described were developed specifically for working with teenagers a brief rationale is provided as to why we believed these approaches would be particularly suitable for working with teenagers in research projects, based on our understanding of the existing social and behavioural science literature. In the following section, each technique used is summarised, and presented with a brief case study of its use.

It should be noted that the approaches detailed in this chapter and elsewhere in the book are not intended as an extensive list of all research techniques that can and have been utilised by researchers working with teenagers in HCI research projects. Other techniques have been employed with teenagers, such as videography, bodystorming, card-sorting, contextual enquiry, future workshops, role-play and technology immersion. However these have not yet been explored in detail with teenage participants by our team of researchers and the purpose of this chapter is to provide pragmatic guidance for working with teenagers that is embedded in both theory and our own practical experiences. Therefore the techniques described are only those that we have used ourselves with teens in our research projects. Furthermore, the following section aims to provide a generalised overview of each research technique along with an example of application for illustrative purposes only. Consistent with the existing literature (e.g. Nelson and Stolterman 2012; Stolterman 2008), we do not advocate that researchers identically reproduce these techniques without due thought or consideration to the specific needs or challenges of their own research project. Researchers cannot adopt a "one size fits all" approach when choosing an appropriate technique to use in projects. The research techniques that we have used to engage teens have been tailored appropriately, in order to meet the specific needs of the research question. Some suggestions of how individual techniques may be customised are provided in each of the following descriptions.

10.2.1 Diaries/Log Books

Diaries and log-books present a way of recording teens' thoughts, attitudes and behaviour over a prolonged period of time. For example, Whalen et al. (2001) used electronic diaries with teens to explore smoking and mood. Data recorded in diaries can enable researchers to understand the knowledge, feelings, beliefs and behaviours of participants. Diaries afford the opportunity for participants to record their lives, reflect on behaviour and provide evidence of using different products, artifacts or technologies. Findings, for example, can help identify appropriate technology-based solutions. Diaries can also be used to understand how teenagers feel about certain things e.g. particular technologies, and their response to technology-based interventions. Diaries may be particularly appropriate means for engaging teenagers in HCI research and design activities as documenting aspects of self-development and recording day-to-day activity is a popular pastime amongst teenagers (Nurmi 2004). Diary-keeping is also likely to be an activity that teenagers are very familiar with due to its popularisation in teen media (including TV shows aimed at teen audiences, such as My Mad Fat Diary and The Carrie Diaries). In our research, teens' diaries have been completed in different mediums (online or paper-based), in different social situations (individually or as a group), using different tools (photographs) and in different locations (home or school) (Table 10.1).

10.2.2 Story-Making Sessions

In story-making sessions, teens are encouraged to develop stories that document how, when and where they typically use artifacts, products or technology. For example, these sessions can provide researchers with situations and scenarios to

Table 10.1 Case study of a diary study (for full study details see Bell et al. 2015)

Aim	Monitor and understand teenagers' daily energy-saving behaviour following participation in an online energy-saving intervention
Materials	Online energy-saving diary completed individually using school computer
Participants	180 teenagers (13–15)
Location	Computer cluster of school in North-East England
Duration	Five days (5 minute completion each day)
Facilitation	Teachers supervised the daily completion of the diary
Outputs	180 energy-saving diaries allowing researchers to evaluate the effectiveness of the intervention in changing teenagers' energy-saving behaviour

Fig. 10.1 Example of story created during story-making session

Table 10.2 Case study of a story-making session (for full study details see Toth et al. 2013b)

Aims	To explore and understand teenagers' daily patterns of energy use
Materials	A range of materials including paper, glue, scissors, catalogues, pens, pencils and felt tips. A written brief was provided. Some teenagers used their paper diary, which they had previously completed, as a prompt for this activity
Participants	96 teenagers aged 10–19
Location	Schools and organisations within the North East of England
Duration	30–60 minutes per session
Facilitation	One researcher facilitated all sessions
Outputs	96 stories about teenagers' energy use were created. The researchers used these stories, along with diaries, to develop written scenarios about teenage energy use which were used as prompts within focus groups

help in the design of future technologies. Desjardins and Wakkary (2011) used a drawing and story-telling method to explore sustainability with children. Not all teens express themselves in the same way and so in story-writing activities that we have hosted teens have been encouraged to write, draw or use alternative methods (e.g. cut and paste images from magazines) to create their individual stories (see Fig. 10.1 for an example). We felt that story-making sessions would be appropriate for use with teenagers since they facilitate self-expression (similar to diary-based activities) and also afford opportunities for creativity (Table 10.2).

Table 10.3 Case study of mind mapping study

Aims	To explore and understand young adults awareness of information sources both online and offline
Materials	Blank paper and pens
Participants	39 young people aged 16–25, divided into small groups
Location	Schools and organisations within the North East of England
Duration	30 minutes
Facilitation	One researcher facilitated all sessions
Outputs	The mind maps informed researchers' understanding of how young people search for information, and think about topics of interest to them

10.2.3 Mind-Mapping

Mind maps allow teens to note down their thoughts in a visual manner and make connections within a diagram about a given subject. It can enable those who are more visual learners to portray their thoughts and is a useful tool in group work if the participants are not confident speaking in front of others. Previous research with teens, for example, Punch (2002) used mind maps as a group activity to explore teenagers' initial thoughts about a topic. In particular, we felt the group-working involved in this kind of task would be particularly suitable for teenagers due to their predilection for associating with peers (Table 10.3) (Rubin et al. 2006).

10.2.4 Paper Design Activities

Commonly used in participatory studies with children, the range and scope of paper design techniques ranges from providing an empty piece of paper to a participant, to the provision of pre-printed structured documents to which researchers add content. For example, Katterfeldt et al. (2012) used paper prototyping to obtain ideas from a group of teenagers in the design of a website for vocational learning by getting the teenagers to draw the website in a printed browser window. Allowing creativity and free thinking, the use of drawing in HCI research and design situations is sometimes criticised as it is often limited by the abilities of the participants, particularly with young children. However, as teenagers have more advanced cognitive abilities than younger children (Steinberg 2005) using this technique with older children significantly alleviates this problem. From the teenagers' design ideas it is possible to understand themes and also take away specific concepts for eventual interactive prototypes. For an example see Fig. 10.2 (Table 10.4).

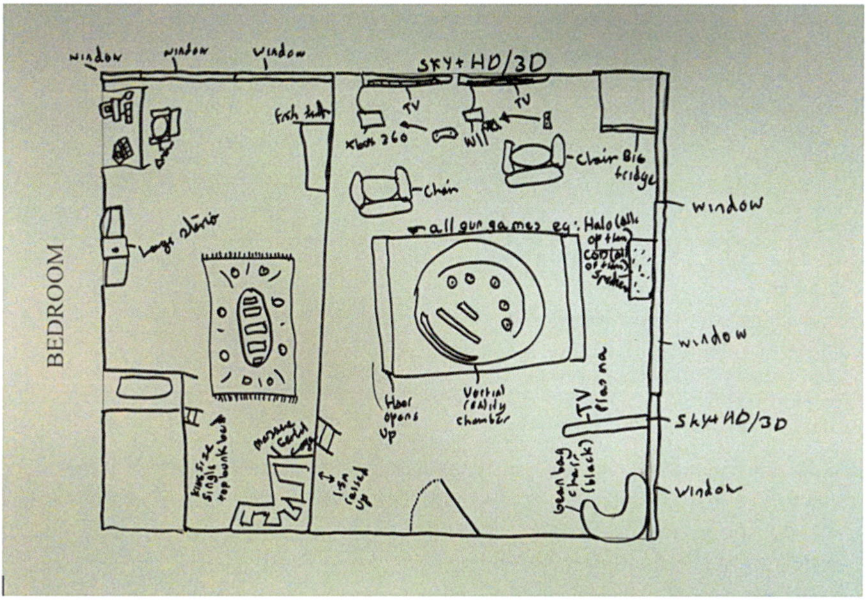

Fig. 10.2 Example of paper bedroom design

Table 10.4 Case study of a paper-based design activity (for full study detail see Read et al. 2011)

Aims	To explore and understand what teenagers would find cool things to have in their bedrooms and provide insights into cool behaviours
Materials	Large sheets of papers and pens
Participants	50 teenagers aged 11–15
Location	Secondary school in the North West of England
Duration	Approximately 1 h
Facilitation	The teenagers worked in same sex pairs determined by their school teacher. All instructions were given by the research team prior to the activity commencing
Outputs	25 bedrooms designed by the pairs of teenagers. These were analysed by the research team against the categories of cool previously identified looking into both gender and age differences

10.2.5 Recorded Internet Search

Recorded internet searches have been used to understand and explore teen online behaviour. The searches made by teenagers can also help to understand how this group thinks about certain topics (Guinee et al. 2003). Allowing the teenagers to actively search online, following their natural behaviour, provides an insight into their normal everyday activities. The free reign and minimum supervision of the

Table 10.5 Case study of recorded internet search study

Aims	To explore and understand the natural online searching behaviours of marginalised and un-marginalised teenagers
Materials	Computers with Internet Explorer History Viewer software installed were used for the search activity. Paper log-books were provided so that participants could also note down what they thought of the sites they were visiting
Participants	39 participants aged 16–25, divided into small groups
Location	Schools and organisations within the North East of England
Duration	30 minutes
Facilitation	One researcher facilitated all sessions
Outputs	Teenagers' internet searching activities were evaluated and group comparisons were made

task further encourages natural searching habits to be displayed. We used this technique to explore any differences in search habit between marginalised and unmarginalised young adults. However, recorded internet searches work well with all populations due to the covert and unobtrusive nature of the technique (Table 10.5).

10.2.6 Focus Groups

The purpose of the focus groups was to understand the thoughts, feelings, attitudes and behaviours in relation to the aims of the project and in particular the research question. Focus groups are frequently used with children and teenagers, for example, Arteaga et al. (2010) carried out focus groups with teenagers to inform the design of a prototype for teenagers about physical activity. Focus groups are believed to work better with teenagers than one-on-one interview techniques since the group environment eases teenagers' self-consciousness, and the presence of other teens helps stimulate discussion (Peterson-Sweeney 2005). We have extensively utilised focus groups with teens at various stages in projects, particularly during the design process, including at the start to generate ideas and at the end to evaluate ideas, techniques and designs. Focus groups have often been used to expand on ideas and themes stimulated through other research techniques, and also to inform the development of future research activities, such as questionnaires. Prompts, including device prototype (either actual device or a video/image of), diary excerpts, situations or scenarios, photographs, internet searches and mind maps, were used in focus groups to stimulate debate and discussion. Often the prompts had been created by the teens themselves in previous work enabling a "teen-centric" approach wherein teen experiences were used to stimulate teen discussion. The sizes, duration and subject matter of the focus groups varied across projects and topics (Table 10.6).

Table 10.6 Case study of a focus group (for full study details see Toth et al. 2013b)

Aims	To explore and understand energy use with teenagers
Materials	Written scenarios were used as prompts. An interview schedule was used to guide the discussion
Participants	40 teenagers: 7 focus groups with 5–8 teenagers per group
Location	Schools and organisations within the North East of England
Duration	25–60 minutes per session
Facilitation	One researcher facilitated all focus groups
Outputs	The data analysis resulted in six themes emerged about teenagers and energy use

Fig. 10.3 Photograph taken at the energy-awareness engagement event hosted by Northumbria University in July 2012

10.2.7 Engagement Event

Engagement events involve teens spending a whole or half-day participating in multiple research activities related to the overall project aims, such as interactive prototype demonstrations, questionnaire completion or story creation (see Fig. 10.3). Teen experiences, thoughts, feelings, attitudes and behaviour relevant to the project aims are captured on the day in photographs, videos, diaries, activity-worksheets, questionnaires and focus groups. For example, Fawcett et al. (2013) describe the

Table 10.7 Case study of an engagement event

Aims	To engage teenagers with the research project and gather data to help understand teen energy use
Materials	Several interactive activities including a poster/newspaper competition and prototype demonstrations
Participants	102 teenagers from four schools within the North East of England
Location	University in the North East of England
Duration	One day event (although follow-up activities lasted 3 months after this)
Facilitation	Several members of the research team along with student volunteers
Outputs	Data was collected from several activities during the engagement day. The event also served an additional purpose in that 102 teenagers engaged with the research project and the topic of energy

use of "teen design days", daylong events employing multiple research techniques, to engage ethnic minority youths in design-related activities. Researchers may also choose to engage in further follow-up activities, such as interviews or focus groups, days or weeks later, allowing teens the opportunity to reflect upon their experience. We also created a 'video style booth' where the teenagers could give feedback during the engagement event. Though labour intensive, engagement events provide an effective way of collecting a diverse range of data from a large sample (Table 10.7).

10.2.8 Obstructed Theatre

Fully described in (Read et al. 2010), obstructed theatre describes the requirements of an interactive product through the use of a dramatic narrative that focusses what is needed without exposing a potential technological solution. The participants then design solutions to fit the requirements conveyed in the narrative. The narrative conveys requirements through a realistic scenario of use and the product being used is obstructed (i.e. not visible) to avoid giving the participants ideas that may influence the design solutions participants create. The potential of this technique when used with teenagers is to create a narrative with which they can easily identify which potentially enables participants to produce a design which fits well with their own individual requirements. The theatre provides an opportunity to engage teen participants using a media more appealing than a presentation given by a researcher or a textual instruction sheet. The key challenge in this technique is the production of the obstructed theatre, in the following case study this was created by a teen informant (as simple cartoon animation—see Fig. 10.4). Obstructed theatre was chosen to convey requirements for a design activity; participants were given a paper booklet in which to record their designs using pens, paper and other design materials (Table 10.8).

Fig. 10.4 Screen shot from obstructed theatre video

Table 10.8 Case study of obstructed theatre (for full study see Read et al. 2013a)

Aims	To explore the design of organic user interface designs for a device to enable teenagers to be aware of their own energy use
Materials	Animated obstructed theatre cartoon (created in Adobe Flash with a voice-over), instruction booklet for participants
Participants	50 teenagers aged between 13 and 15
Location	Schools within the North West of England
Duration	50 minutes per session
Facilitation	Researchers introduced the study and obstructed theatre video then ensured tasks were followed by participants
Outputs	A wide variety of innovative ideas providing energy usage information were produced, these designs were recorded as photographs

10.2.9 Questionnaires

Questionnaires have been used to measure and increase understanding of teen thoughts, attitudes and behaviours in a structured way, and can be administered on a large scale, through a variety of different mediums (online vs. paper-based). For example, Livingstone and Helsper (2010) used online questionnaires to understand teenagers' approach to online risk. Questionnaires may be used to assess whether the findings of smaller exploratory studies involving teens (such as focus groups)

Table 10.9 Case study of a questionnaire study (Toth et al. 2014)

Aims	To explore and understand teenage attitudes and behaviours surrounding energy use
Materials	An online questionnaire about energy use developed by the researchers
Participants	286 teenagers aged 13–19 years completed the questionnaire
Location	Participants completed the questionnaire online in a variety of locations (e.g. home, school)
Duration	Approximately 30 minutes
Facilitation	Teenagers completed the questionnaire individually and all instructions were included within the questionnaire
Outputs	Insights into teenage energy use

Table 10.10 Case study of Mission to Mars (for full study details see Read et al. 2013b)

Aims	To further understand the attributes of cool that are important to teenagers
Materials	A set of questions on paper to help create a guide for an alien visiting their school and a tape recorder to record their guide once finished
Participants	60 teenagers aged 11–16
Location	Secondary school in the North West of England
Duration	Approximately 1 h
Facilitation	The teenagers worked in groups or 2 or 3 and were provided with instruction from the research team prior to commencing the activity
Outputs	12 guides were recorded along with 12 completed sets of question answers for analysis of cool attributes

may be applied to larger populations of teens. Though researchers have voiced concerns about using questionnaires with youth populations, we believe this technique is appropriate for teenagers due to their advanced cognitive abilities comparative to children (Steinberg 2005), so long as the language was tailored for this age group (Table 10.9) (Hill 2006).

10.2.10 Mission from Mars

This technique was originally intended for use with young children and involves an individual or group making a narrative to an alien about the products they have, or the activities they do. Dindler and Iversen (2007) created the technique as a way of involving children in the design of an electronic school bag. The technique is designed to capture a full understanding of the concepts by virtue of the need to describe things very literally to the alien listener. As an example if a teenager was describing "slouching", he or she would have to explain what this term meant. This technique adds considerable context to research project and design studies with unfamiliar (to the researchers) user groups (Table 10.10).

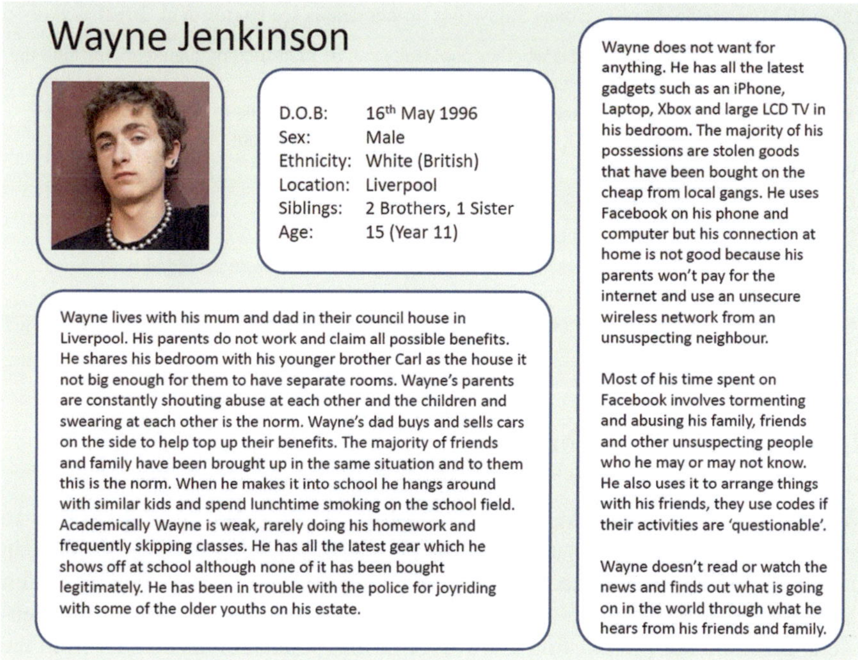

Fig. 10.5 Example of teen persona

10.2.11 Personas

A persona is a fictitious person, described as being a realistic representation or a stereotype, and is often used as a technique to help HCI research and design teams focus on pseudo-users (see Fig. 10.5). Personas can be used in research in many different ways. In participatory activities, personas are used to prompt discussion amongst teens and also to explore the extent to which the research team have understood them. Personas of children and teenagers have been used in studies with children (Antle 2006) in the design of a mentoring application, and in interaction design fore-health applications (Bredies 2008). A set of personas can be developed that aim to represent the characteristics and behaviours of a group that can subsequently be presented to teenagers for discussion and validation. This technique was selected as it allows adults to consider designing for teenagers and also can also be used to help teenagers envision, understand and design for other teenagers (Table 10.11).

Table 10.11 Case Study of Personas Study (For further details see Horton et al. 2012)

Aims	To understand whether cool traits can be identified by teenagers through the use of personas
Materials	A set of 10 teenage personas on paper with a table to identify what each personal had, or did, that was either cool or uncool
Participants	63 teenagers aged 16–17
Location	Secondary school in the North West of England
Duration	30 minutes per session
Facilitation	The teenagers worked in groups or 2 or 3 and were provided with instruction from the research team prior to commencing the activity
Outputs	27 sets of personas with the cool and uncool traits of each persona identified for analysis

10.3 Choosing a Technique

While many techniques have been developed and used, there is little advice to researchers and practitioners assisting them in selecting an appropriate technique in their work. In the previous section we have provided an explanation of why we felt that the individual techniques that we chose would be appropriate for use with teenagers, based on our pre-existing knowledge of that population as derived from the social and behavioural sciences. However, researchers must consider more than just "who" they are working with and for when selecting a research technique to use. For example, within the field of Child-Computer Interaction Mazzone (2012) has developed the Chi-Co-S (Children Co-design Session) Framework which provides a set of steps to inform five aspects of creating and running a co-design session (Why, Who, Where, When, How) based on studies carried out with mainly younger children. The "Why" aspect of the Chi-Co-S framework provides a matrix to help researchers and designers reason about the underlying motivation and scope for their design activity. The work described here was in the context of a research project where a key aim was co-design of technologies but where understanding of users was also crucial, we therefore added an 'Understanding Users' element to the Chi-Co-S framework matrix for the "Why" aspect (Fig. 10.6). We see this understanding as crucial when working with a user group such as teenagers that are often challenging for adult academics to understand, and as being important for all design scopes and design session objectives. In the interdisciplinary work presented here, psychologists generated insights into teenagers and their relationship with energy use that fed into the 'Understanding Users' aspect, these insights helped inform the following co-design activities. Additionally, the primary aim of many of the activities described previously was specifically to explore areas that needed to be more clearly understood by the design team. Typically the understandings gathered from these session were used to inform a later design activity, compounding the importance of the 'understanding users' aspect shown in Fig. 10.6.

Mazzone (2012) also provides a table of design techniques used with children, along with a suggested design phase (Exploration, Generation, and Evaluation) that

WHY	Design Scope			
Session's Objectives	**Understanding Users**	**Improving** (Re-design of existing products)	**Supporting** (Design a new way to support a well-known activity/sole and existing problem)	**Envisioning** (Envision novel situations of use and future technology)
	Context Exploration (Retrieve information on context of use)	Investigate the use of existing technology.	Explore and understanding context of use and related activities	Reflect on context and values
	Concept Generation (Generate concepts or ideas)	Re-design technology	Generate novel solutions for defined requirements	Define possible concept scenarios
	Evaluate (Test and Validate earlier solutions)	Evaluate improved usability	Evaluate satisfaction of users needs and design requirements	Evaluate high level/abstract concepts

Fig. 10.6 Adapted matrix of "why" aspects from the co-design process (taken from Mazzone 2012)

allows it to be used in conjunction with the matrix shown in Fig. 10.6 above. While we do not wish to emulate the work of Mazzone directly, a similar approach is valuable in allowing comparison to inform selection of appropriate techniques for teens. For each technique described in the previous section Table 10.12 includes:

- *Suggested research phases:* Which research objective the technique aligns with.
- *Outputs created:* The materials/media generated by the participants in the session.
- *Preparation required:* It is assumed that in any research project the investigator will create information sheets describing any tasks for participants and any proforma required to data, designs etc. This column captures any additional preparation required in order to use the technique.
- *Specific resources required:* It is assumed that in any research project the investigator will create information sheets describing the tasks for participants and any proforma required to gather data, designs etc. This column captures any additional resources that need to be created.
- *Facilitation required:* Here we give an indication of the level of facilitation we found necessary in order to use the techniques as described in the previous case studies.
- *Number of participants:* This column captures the number of participants that can be engaged in a single session.

Table 10.12 Overview and key features of techniques for working with teenagers in interaction design

Technique	Description	Suggested design phase(s)	Outputs created	Preparation required	Specific resource required	Facilitation required	Number of participants
Diaries/Log Books	Recording of teenage activities, thoughts, attitudes and behaviours	Exploration	Completed diaries (individually or in groups)	Creation of empty diaries (paper based or electronic)	Dependent on delivery technique	Initial instructions for completion and possible reminders for completion	1–500
Story-making	Creating visual representations of scenarios	Generation	Completed stories (individually or in groups)	Preparation of story making kits for participants	Variety of materials (e.g. paper, glue, scissors, pens, etc)	A researcher present during the session to give instruction	1–30 (per facilitator)
Mind-mapping	Visual representation of teenagers needs	Generation	Completed individual mind-maps	–	Blank paper and pens/pencils	A researcher present during the session to give demonstration	1–30 (per facilitator)
Paper designs	Creating visual designs and ideas	Generation	Design ideas on paper	Preparation of kits and any printing on design sheets	Variety of materials (e.g. paper, glue, scissors, pens, etc)	A researcher present during the session to provide support	1–30 (per session)
Recorded internet searches	Recording teenagers online search behaviours	Exploration	Log of search	Install search recording software on computer	Search recording software installed on computer	A researcher present during the session to give instruction	1–30 (per session)
Focus groups	Understand teenager collective opinions	Exploration, Generation, Evaluation	Recordings of discussion for further analysis	Preparation of topic guide, questions, and prompts	Recording equipment	At least one researcher to facilitate the focus group	4–7 (per session)

Engagement events	Whole day of multiple research activity sessions	Exploration, generation, evaluation	Multiple data-sets from assorted activities	Preparation of all activities and organisation of event	Dependent on activities	Multiple researchers to supervise activities and teenagers	30–150
Obstructed theatre	Design activity hiding potential solution ideas	Generation	Design ideas on paper	Creation of obstructed theater video	AV equipment	A researcher to provide clear instruction/ensure designs are unambiguous	1–30 (per session)
Questionnaires	Gathering specific information	Exploration, evaluation	Completed questionnaires	Creation of the questionnaires (paper- based or electronic)	Dependent on delivery technique	Dependent on delivery technique, location, and number of participants	As many as possible (no maximum)
Mission from Mars	Providing narrative of ideas, products or activities to an alien	Generation	Completed dialogues between teenagers and an alien	Creation of questions to be used in the dialogue	Recording equipment to capture dialog	A researcher present during the session	1–30 (per session)
Personas	Use of fictitious people/users to consider ideas	Exploration, generation, evaluation	Designs, evaluations, or other depending on activity	Creation of personas, design of use in study and supporting materials	Dependent on type of study to be carried out	A researcher present during the session	1–50 (per session)

Drawing on the authors' experiences from the successful case studies described in the techniques section, Table 10.12 summarises the salient aspects of each technique and is intended to inform the selection of an appropriate ways for working with teenagers. We must emphasise that the parameters that we have used to categorise each of the techniques contained within Table 10.12 are for guidance only and should not be perceived as fixed. Techniques may be used in innovative ways that go beyond the categorisations we have made, in order to meet the demands of a specific research challenge, we recommend researchers exercise creativity in the use of these techniques. It must also be iterated that the table is not exhaustive and other techniques for working with teenagers in research exist, but these have not yet been explored in detail with teenage participants by our team of researchers.

10.4 Analysis

For each of the eleven techniques described in the Techniques and Choosing a Technique section, the authors individually reflected critically upon the occasions wherein they had used the technique with the teenage population. In particular, team members were encouraged to reflect upon four key themes: (1) how well we felt that the technique had worked with teenagers (in terms of how well teenagers had engaged with the technique and the outputs that it produced) and why (2) any problematic issues encountered and why, (3) any specific considerations that needed to be made, and (4) whether any differences emerged between using that technique with teenagers in comparison to adult and child population. Individual reflections were developed into guidelines using a procedure analogous to grounded theory (Corbin and Strauss 1990). Initial group phone discussions were held to collectively discuss individual critical reflections and organise them into common themes and observations (known as concepts), and also identify any apparent contradictions in these concepts. These concepts were then organised into categories by two members of the research team which represented connected concepts and these categories then formed the content of the nine guidelines that we set out in the following section. Grounded theory was chosen as a template for the present analysis since it does not impose a pre-existing theoretical framework upon the dataset (i.e. the critical reflections), and this was deemed to be important given the lack of research techniques literature that particularly focuses on the teenage population.

Once the guidelines had been developed, they were refined by all research team members in an iterative manner to ensure that all individual reflections had been accounted for. In addition to developing the nine guidelines, there appeared to be three central observations/themes that overarched all of the guidelines. These three superordinate observations are outlined below:

- *Teenagers were very willing research participants* and appeared happy to engage in all research activities. All team members unanimously reported experiencing this apparent contradiction to the urban myth that the teenage population is dif-

ficult to work with. Furthermore, the willingness of teenagers to engage in projects makes a strong case for increasing the engagement of researchers with this group in research activities. The enthusiasm spanned relatively mundane activities, such as story writing, to more innovative and novel activities, such as Mission from Mars.
- *Teenagers are both serious and playful.* In addition to enjoying the activities, there was also evidence that in all instances teenagers took the task seriously, whether this was the development of a mind map or the creation of a PlayDoh prototype, confirmatory questions asked by the teenagers during the studies evidenced a desire to "get it right". Playfulness featured in some of the techniques (Obstructed Theatre, Mission from Mars), and the teenagers embraced this, however they were well aware of the differences when using more serious techniques and were able to switch from one to another. We also tended to use more playful techniques when engaging with younger teens, e.g. Mission to Mars, than when engaging with older teens.
- *Teenagers show advanced cognitive abilities (compared to children).* While there is extensive evidence from the social and behavioural sciences to support this, the research team felt it was important to describe how these advanced cognitive abilities may manifest themselves in research activities. In the stories and the personas, teenagers demonstrated that they could reflect on, and design for, teenagers who were not exactly like themselves—this ability to abstract is much less evident in younger groups. When compared with children, in both focus groups and engagement events, teenagers were seen to be critical in their considerations of solutions and technologies. They proposed, and were able to articulate, new ideas that were grounded on a good understanding of the limitations and constraints particularly related to design of artifacts and technologies. In techniques engaging drawing, teenagers were much more able to annotate their drawings and to be specific in their ideas than younger children.

10.5 Pragmatic Suggestions for Working with Teenagers

In this section, we present nine pragmatic suggestions for working with teenagers in research contexts, based on our own critical reflections of using the techniques described previously. The guidelines, along with the specific reflections and experiences that led to their creation, are as follows:

10.5.1 Consider Group Dynamics

Based on existing research and recommendations (e.g. Hennessy and Heary 2005), we encouraged group work amongst teens where possible, since the presence of other teens seems to provide a "buffer" between the teen and the researcher, making teens feel more comfortable voicing their opinions. However, we found that group dynamics can affect the quality of the data yielded from group-work activities. In particular, the following factors should be considered when facilitating group work amongst teens:

Age Conversations with teachers indicated that younger teens may feel intimidated and inhibited by the presence of older teens in group work situations. Therefore in all our research, teens were separated into age-based groupings: junior teens (aged 14 or younger) and senior teens (aged 15 or older). While these categorisations were based on the recommendations of the teachers, the distinction is similar to the distinction between younger and older teens that is made in the behavioural and social sciences, recognising that important bio-psycho-social differences exist between early and late adolescence.

Gender Amongst younger teens, working in mixed-gender groupings did not affect the quality of the data yielded. However with older teens this was a major issue. For example, focus groups held as part of the energy project with same-sex participants yielded fewer topic-relevant extracts than mixed-gender groups (for full study details see Toth et al. 2013a, b). It is likely that using mixed-gender groupings would exert a more inhibitory influence over group discussions if the topic matter was particularly sensitive.

Group Size For group work that involved working in close collaboration with peers (e.g. focus groups, group diary production), it was found that working in groups of 4-7, generally yielded more detailed data, avoided cross-talk and transcription difficulties, and prevented shyer teens from not engaging in the group discussions. This is contrary to the advice set out by Poole and Peyton (2013) who advised that focus groups with teenage participants worked better with larger numbers (up to twelve participants). However, this advice may have been misleading, since it was provided on the basis of a single study investigating a highly sensitive topic: sexual health (Hyde et al. 2005), and may not be representative.

Friendship Groups Where teenagers needed to be especially creative, for example Mission from Mars, allocation to friendship groups appeared to be beneficial.

10.5.2 Use Mixed Research Media

Increasingly, researchers are motivated—often due to financial pressures—to deliver HCI research and design activities online rather than through traditional paper-based or face-to-face mediums. In our research practice, we delivered some techniques online, such as diary based studies and questionnaires which provided interactivity, engaging graphics and as such would typically be expected to suit this user group. However, paper based techniques were also used (personas, diary studies etc.) as well as physical prototyping in Obstructed Theatre. There was no evidence that any one medium was especially deficit in terms of the HCI research and design facilitation, and as such choice of research media is likely to be influenced by practical considerations such as cost, location and number of research participants.

10.5.3 Remember Teenagers Are Not Children

Many researchers working with teen participants may also have experience working with younger children. However, we have found teenagers to be a very different user group, able to work much more independently, faster, and more critically than children, consistent with their more advanced stage of bio-psycho-social development (Steinberg and Morris 2001). In interpreting data and ideas it is essential that the research team understand this as the inexperienced researcher may respond inappropriately to the teenagers by, for example, not respecting their maturity and failing to provide enough activities to fill a research activity session.

10.5.4 Remember Teenagers Are Not Adults

It is important to remember that in the eyes of the law, and in terms of ethical participation, teenagers still represent a vulnerable user group. In all the studies outlined in this paper, consent for participation was gathered from both the schools (and/or parents) and the teens. Furthermore, while teenagers are more developed than children in many ways, they still do not possess the full maturity of adults. Ensuring all instructions are clear is very important, that teenagers understand what they are required to do, and researchers should be prepared to provide more instructions and answer all questions.

10.5.5 Embrace Playfulness and Seriousness

Following the theme of teenagers as neither children and nor adults, we found that teenagers engaged with both playful and serious activities, reflecting how both playfulness and seriousness feature in their educational and social experiences. In our research, it was refreshing to note that teenagers were able to switch between playful and serious tasks, and were able to differentiate between these without the need for formal instruction. In the Obstructed Theatre technique teenagers have the opportunity to play with materials from their childhood; in Mission from Mars, they were able to communicate in a fantasy scenario and thus remove themselves from some of their present reality. However, not all teenagers found such playful approaches easy, perhaps reflecting individual differences in personality, thus "safer" activities that are familiar to them and that fit into some of the expectations of school life, like written tasks and questionnaire completion, may be more appropriate for some.

10.5.6 Appreciate Teen Differences

It is also important when working with teenagers to understand the context of their educational development—although a group may all be the same age they may differ significantly both in terms of their educational ability and their ability to focus and remain on task. Particular attention should be paid to working with teenagers from marginalised groups (e.g., older teens who are neither in study nor in work) as researchers may need to further adapt their research techniques for them. The importance of this may be highlighted in our investigation into online trust and persuasion, wherein we worked with groups of both un-marginalised teens and marginalised teens to produce mind-maps of their typical online search activities. Findings from this task provided a striking visual representation of the differences between marginalised and un-marginalised young adults, with the un-marginalised group developing more complex mind maps when compared to the marginalised groups. This can be seen in Figs. 10.7 and 10.8 below.

In order to manage this difference, we advise that researchers should prepare a range of instructions including written, verbal and pictorial diagrams to enhance understanding within vulnerable teens. Research facilitators should also ensure that they can readily expand upon any instruction or question asked, offering clear and concise explanations and prompts to assist the teenagers in expressing the experiences and beliefs.

10.5.7 Make It Rewarding

In many cases the reward for teenagers is simply taking part. The more engaging the activity the easier we have found it to recruit teenagers. The engagement event, as an example, was attended by more than 100 teenagers and the obstructed theatre studies attracted over 50 teens from two schools. Techniques for recruiting teens, include approaching schools, adverts on social networking sites and distributing flyers at teen events. In general, we found that working with schools or other institutions (such as youth clubs and employment centres) to recruit teen research participants, and offering rewards to that institution for their help, was the most successful technique of teen recruitment. The offer of individual rewards, such as entry into a prize draw for vouchers, can also be effective in recruiting and motivating teens to engage in research. Marginalised teens may be more difficult to recruit regardless of the reward offered (though not impossible), especially if these teen are not in

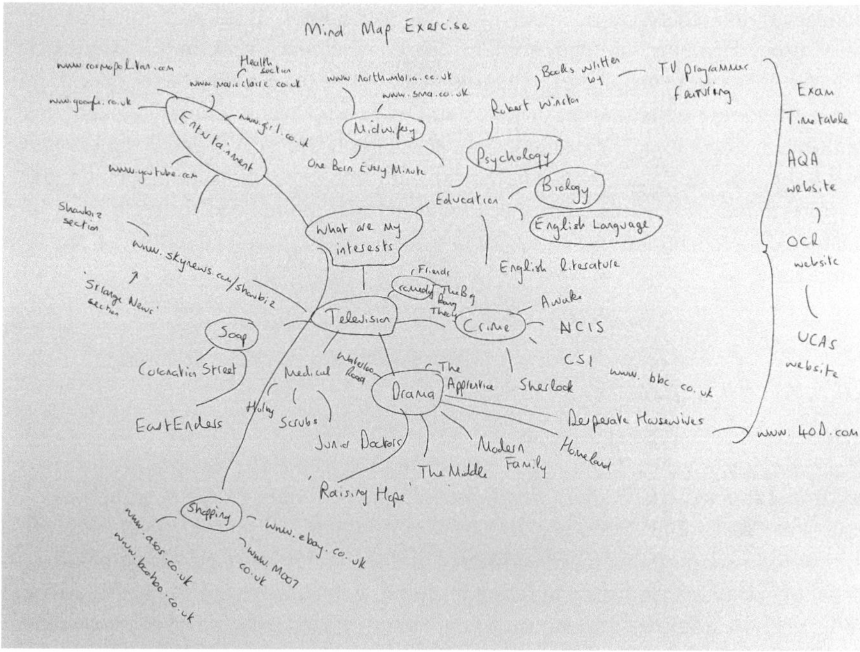

Fig. 10.7 Mind-map of online searching behaviour produced by an un marginalised teen

Fig. 10.8 Mind-map of online searching behaviour produced by a marginalised teen

full-time mainstream education. For example, see Hansen and Iversen (2013) for a more in depth discussion of factors influencing teen motivation to participate in interaction design research.

10.5.8 Use a Range of Techniques

Within a single session, where at all possible, a range of techniques should be deployed. This avoids potential boredom and caters for different learning styles as well as gathering different attitudes and perspectives. As an example, teens grew bored of the recorded internet search activity after 15–20 minutes and focus group conversations generally fell quiet after 20–30 minutes, if no additional prompts were used. However, as evidenced in our engagement event, and in Obstructed Theatre, teens were capable of engaging in activities for a much longer period, provided they were either varied or perceived to be fun. We therefore advocate using multiple methodologies, if needed, throughout the HCI research and design process. Not only does such an approach help to sustain teen interest, meaning that the quality of the data yielded through these techniques is maintained throughout, it also enables data triangulation and as such, a more holistic understanding of the teen population.

10.5.9 Be Reflective

Reflecting on our own experiences when working with teens and writing this paper we found this to be extremely useful; enabling a self-audit of our existing research practices. We would encourage researchers to adopt a similar critically reflective approach towards evaluating the efficacy of the activities that they have utilised, in order to optimise their utility in future research. In addition to encouraging personal reflection we would also recommend encouraging teen research-partners to reflect critically upon their experiences in the research process by gathering either written or verbal feedback through follow-up questionnaires or interviews. Determine the extent to which teens enjoyed the research activities, whether they felt able to fully express their opinions and offer feedback of how the activity could be improved. In our experience, teens responded well to being asked such questions since it provided them with an additional opportunity to self-express and feel personally valued.

10.6 Reflections

Within the Child-Computer Interaction community there has been growing interest in exploring how to work with teenage participants in HCI research and design contexts. This chapter contributes to the understanding of working with and for teenagers in two key areas. Firstly, the chapter summarises the main techniques that our team have used when working with teenagers in HCI research and design contexts. In total, eleven techniques are described with demonstrative case studies, encompassing the traditional approaches from psychology and social sciences, as well as the more innovative approaches that have been specifically designed for interaction design exploration. The salient aspects of each technique were highlighted, using a framework developed by Mazzone (2012), in order to enable comparisons between these techniques. We believe this will be of assistance to future researchers and practitioners working with teens by facilitating the technique-selection decision-making process.

However, a key limitation of the present chapter is that only the techniques that have been used with teen populations by the authors have been described, and it must be iterated that other techniques for working with teens exist. The techniques discussed in this paper were originally developed for engaging either adult or child populations in HCI research and design contexts, and then tailored for use with teenagers by the research team. As such, there is the potential for the development of unique and innovative techniques, which have been designed specifically for use with the teenage population, by considering the specific needs of this user group. In addition, there are a wide range of other existing techniques which may also be applied successfully with teenagers. The process through which techniques are tailored for use with different populations is also of interest. Within the work described here, the technique tailoring process included the alteration of instructions, task complexity, balance between seriousness/playfulness, and the group size/composition. It may be interesting to un-pack this customisation process in more detail in order to understand it more fully.

The second contribution of this chapter is the nine pragmatic guidelines for working with teenagers, which are embedded in the research team's own critical reflections of their experiences working with teenagers in HCI research and design contexts, as well as broader theory. The guidelines that are presented collectively highlight some of the unique, and seemingly contradictory aspects of working with teenagers, in comparison to other populations, i.e., that they are both child-like and adult like, both homogenous and different, and both playful and serious. These contradictions, evident in the guidelines we present, provide important insights into the unique challenge of working with teenagers as participants in HCI research and design approaches. We believe that the guidelines presented have diverse and wide-ranging applications and will be of use to those working in all aspects of teen HCI research and design contexts; particularly those who have not previously worked with this population.

Similarities do exist between our guidelines for working with teenagers in interaction design and those developed for working with other age-based populations. It could be argued that all guidelines proposed in this work (with the exception of guideline 3 and 4) may be applicable when engaging any user population in research. Issues such as group composition, appropriateness of reward and diversity in techniques and materials need to be considered in any design activity to some extent. However, we believe that the way in which these issues are applicable to the teenage population, and the subsequent implication of these guidelines for researchers working with teens, may be seen as unique. For example, group composition (Guideline 1. Consider Group Dynamics) must be considered when conducting group-work activities with all populations. However, for teenagers we found that working in groups with opposite-sex participants hindered group discussions with older teens but not with younger teens, possibly due to their growing awareness of, and attraction to, the opposite sex making them feel self-conscious and uncomfortable (Collins et al. 2009). Similarly, rewards (Guideline 8. Make it Rewarding) are important for motivating research participants of all ages to engage in research activities. Therefore though some of our guidance for working with teens may be universally applicable to all ages, the way in which the guidance applies to the teen population appears to be unique.

10.7 Conclusion

While the present chapter makes two useful contributions towards understanding the methodological issues and challenges associated with working with teenagers in HCI research and design, there is still much to be contributed to this space. First, there is much more to be understood about the benefits of engaging teenagers in research and design processes, in terms of the outcomes from the tasks and types of session and also the psychological/social benefits to the teens of having been actively engaged in such activities. Second, all of the techniques that we used with teenagers appeared to be successful in engaging the teen population and producing high quality HCI research and design outputs. It is unclear whether this is due to the customisation of the techniques that we made, or whether the three overarching observations that we discovered about teens (i.e. that teens are willing research participants, capable of embracing both playfulness and seriousness, with advanced cognitive capabilities) are responsible for this. We hope that others will build on this work with new techniques, findings, understandings and insights to ensure continued exploration and debate in this important area of involving teenagers as participants in research and design projects.

Acknowledgements We would like to acknowledge all the teenagers, and teachers, who have participated in the studies discussed in this paper. Part of this work was funded by RCUK/EPSRC research grants (EP/1000720/1; EP/I002251/1)

References

Aitken SC (1994) Putting children in their place. Association of American Geographers, Washington, DC

Antle AA (2006) Child personas: fact or fiction? In: Proceedings of the 6th conference on designing interactive systems DIS '06, 22–30, ACM, New York

Arteaga SM, Kudeki M, Woodworth A, Kurniawan S (2010) Mobile system to motivate teenagers' physical activity. In: Proceedings of IDC 2010. ACM, Barcelona

Bell BT, Toth N, Little L, Smith MA (2015) Planning to save the planet using an online intervention based on implementation intentions to change adolescent self-reported energy-saving behavior. Environ Behav.

Berk LE (2013) Child development. Pearson, Upper Saddle River

Blakemore S, Robbins TW (2012) Decision-making in the adolescent brain. Nat Neurosci 15(9):1184–1191

Blakemore SJ, Mills KL (2014) Is adolescence a sensitive period for sociocultural processing? Annu Rev Psychol 65:187–207

Boyd D (2009) Why youth (heart) social network sites: the role of networked publics in teenage social life. Retrieved 17th January 2013, from Northumbria University: http://papers.ssrn.com/sol3/papers.cfm?abstract_id=1518924
Bredies K (2008) Using system analysis and personas for e-health interaction design. In: Proceedings of design research society conference 2008 DRS '08, 16–19. DRS, Sheffield
Chittenden T (2010) Digital dressing up: modelling female teen identity in the discursive spaces of the fashion blogosphere. J Youth Stud 13(4):505–520
Collins WA, Welsh DP, Furman W (2009) Adolescent romantic relationships. Annu Rev Psychol 60:631–652
Corbin JM, Strauss A (1990) Grounded theory research: procedures, canons, and evaluative criteria. Qual Sociol 13(1):3–21
Danielsson K, Wiberg C (2006) Participatory design of learning media: designing educational computer games with and for teenagers. Interact Technol Smart Educ 3(4):275–291
Desjardins A, Wakkary R (2011) Children's drawing and telling of sustainability in the home. In: Proceedings of the 2011 annual conference extended abstracts on human factors in computing systems, ACM, Vancouver
Dindler C, Iversen O (2007) Fictional inquiry-design collaboration in a shared narrative space. J CoDesign 3(4):213–234
Druin A (1999) The design of children's technology. Morgan Kaufmann Publishers Inc., San Francisco
Fawcett P, Fisher KE, Bishop AP, Magassa L (2013) Using design thinking to empower ethnic minority immigrant youth in their roles as technology and information mediaries. In: CHI'13 extended abstracts on human factors in computing systems. ACM, Paris, pp 361–366
Feldman RS, Bishop J (2003) Development across the life span. Prentice Hall, Upper Saddle River
Fitton D, Horton M, Read JC (2011) Designing with teens. Digital engagement'11. Newcastle. Retrieved 17th January 2013, from Northumbria University: http://de2011.computing.dundee.ac.uk/wp-content/uploads/2011/10/Designing-with-Teens.pdf
Furman W, Brown B, Feiring C (eds) (1999) Contemporary perspectives on adolescent romantic relationships. Cambridge University Press, New York
Gram-Hanssen K (2005) Teenage consumption of information and communication technology. In: Proceedings of the 2005 European Council for an Energy Efficient Economy. Retrieved 10th January 2013:http://www.sbi.dk/miljo-og-energi/livsstil-og-adferd/miljoadferd-i-boligen-moderne-og-senmoderne-livsstilsbegrebers-forklaringskraft/teenage-consumption-of-information-and-communication-technology
Guinee K, Eagleton MB, Hall TE (2003) Adolescents" internet search strategies: drawing upon familiar cognitive paradigms when accessing electronic information sources. J Educ Comput Res 29:363–374
Hansen EIK, Iversen OS (2013) You are the real experts! Studying teenagers" motivation in participatory design. http://users-cs.au.dk/poulsen/sider13/129/0129-paper.pdf. Accessed 1 Aug 2013
Hennessy E, Heary CM (2005) The use of focus group interviews in pediatric health care research. J Pediatr Psychol 27:47–57
Hill M (2006) Children's voices on ways of having a voice children's and young people's perspectives on methods used in research and consultation. Childhood 13(1):69–89
Horton M, Read JC, Fitton D, Little L, Toth N (2012) Too cool at school-understanding cool teenagers. PsychNology 10(2):73–91
Hyde A, Howlett E, Brady D, Drennan J (2005) The focus group method: insights from focus group interviews on sexual health with adolescents. Soc Sci Med 61:2588–2599
Iversen OS, Smith RC (2012) Scandinavian participatory design: dialogic curation with teenagers. In: Proceedings of the 11th international conference on interaction design and children . ACM, New York, pp 106–115
Katterfeldt ES, Zeising A, Schelhowe H (2012) Designing digital media for teen¬aged apprentices: a participatory approach. In: Proceedings of the 11th international conference on interaction design and children. ACM, New York, pp 196–199

Lang AR, Martin JL, Sharples S, Crowe JA, Murphy E (2012) Not a minor problem: involving adolescents in medical device design research. Theor Issues Ergon Sci. http://dx.doi.org/10.1080/1463922X.2012.678910

Lambert V, Glacken M (2011) Engaging with children in research: theoretical and practical implications of negotiating informed consent/assent. Nurs Ethics 18(6):781–801. Published online 2011 June 6. doi: 10.1177/0969733011401122

Livingstone S, Helsper E (2010) Balancing opportunities and risks in teenagers' use of the internet: the role of online skills and internet self-efficacy. New Media Soc 12(2):309–329

Lloyd BT (2001) A conceptual framework for examining adolescent identity, media influence, and social development. Rev Gen Psychol 6(1):73–91

Loomba-Albrecht LA, Styne DM (2009) Effect of puberty on body composition. Curr Opin Endocrinol Diabetes Obes 16:10–15

Maccoby EE (2002) Gender and group process: a developmental perspective. Curr Dir Psychol Sci 11(2):54–58

Mäkinen M, Puukko-Viertomies LR, Lindberg N, Siimes MA, Aalberg V (2012) Body dissatisfaction and body mass in girls and boys transitioning from early to mid-adolescence: additional role of self-esteem and eating habits. BMC Psychiatry 12(1):35

Matthews MH (2001) Citizenship, youth councils and young people's participation. J Youth Stud 4(3):299–318, 1469–9680

Mazzone E (2012) Designing with children: reflections on effective involvement of children in the interaction design process. Ph.D. thesis, University of Central Lancashire

Mazzone E, Read JC, Beale R (2008) Design with and for disaffected teenagers. In: Proceedings of the 5th Nordic conference on human-computer interaction: building bridges. ACM, Lund, pp 290–297

McDonagh JE, Bateman B (2012) 'Nothing about us without us': considerations for research involving young people. Arch Dis Child Educ Pract Ed 97(2):55–60

Moore R (2009) Sells like teen spirit: music youth culture and social crisis. New York University Press, New York

Nelson HG, Stolterman E (2012) The design way: intentional change in a Nelson, H. G., & Stolterman, E. (2012). The design way: intentional change in an unpredictable world (p. 296).

Nurmi J-E (2004) Socialization and self-development: channeling, selection, adjustment and reflection. In: Lerner RM, Steinberg L (eds) Handbook of adolescent psychology, 2nd edn. Wiley, Upper Saddle River, pp 85–124

Peterson-Sweeney K (2005) The use of focus groups in pediatric and adolescent research. J Pediatr Health Care 19(2):104–110

Poole ES, Peyton T (2013, June). Interaction design research with adolescents: Methodological challenges and best practices. In: Proceeding of IDC 2013. ACM, New York

Punch S (2002) Interviewing strategies with young people: the 'secret box', stimulus material and task-based activities. Child Soc 16:45–56

Read JC, Fitton D, Mazzone E (2010, April) Using obstructed theatre with child designers to convey requirements. In: CHI'10 extended abstracts on human factors in computing systems. ACM, pp 4063–4068

Read J, Fitton D, Cowan B, Beale R, Guo Y, Horton M (2011) Understanding and designing cool technologies for teenagers. In: Proceedings of the 2011 annual conference extended abstracts on human factors in computing systems. ACM Press, Vancouver, pp 1567–1572

Read JC, Fitton D, Horton M (2013a) Theatre, playdoh and comic strips: designing organic user interfaces with young adolescent and teenage participants. Interact Comput 25(2):183–198

Read JC, Horton M, Fitton D, Little L, Beale R, Toth N (2013b) On being cool – exploring interaction design for teenagers. In: Proceedings of BCS HCI 2013: the internet of things.

Royal College of Paediatrics and Child Health (2010) Young persons health special interest group. Not just a phase – a guide to the participation of children and young people in health services. RCPCH, London

Rubin KH, Bukowski WM, Parker JG (2006) Peer interactions, relationships, and groups. In: Eisenberg N, Damon W, Lerner RM (eds) Handbook of child psychology: Vol 3. Emotional and personality development. Wiley, Hoboken.

Steinberg L (2005) Cognitive and affective development in adolescence. Trends Cogn Sci 9(2):69–74

Steinberg L (2008) A social neuroscience perspective on adolescent risk-taking. Dev Rev 28(1):78–106

Steinberg L, Morris AS (2001) Adolescent development. Annu Rev Psychol 52:83–110

Stolterman E (2008) The nature of design practice and implications for interaction design research. Int J Des 2(1):55–65

Toth N, Bell B, Rulton K, Horton M, Little L (2013a) Engaging teens: case study of an engagement event with teenagers. Manuscript submitted for publication.

Toth N, Little L, Read JC, Fitton D, Horton M (2013b) Understanding teen attitudes towards energy consumption. J Environ Psychol 34:36–44

Toth N, Bell BT, Avramides K, Rulton K, Little L (2014) Is the next generation prepared? Understanding barriers to teenage energy conservation. In Energy consumption: impacts of human activity, current and future challenges, environmental and socio-economic effects

Walsh G, Foss E, Yip J, Druin A (2013) Octoract: an eight-dimensional framework for intergenerational participatory design techniques. Retrieved 11th January 2013 from: http://www.bigyipper.com/wp-content/uploads/2010/11/CHI2013-tech-report.pdf

Whalen CK, Jamner LD, Henker B, Delfino RJ (2001) Smoking and moods in adolescents with depressive and aggressive dispositions: evidence from surveys and electronic diaries. Health Psychol 20(2):99–111

Chapter 11
Future Directions for Quality TeenCI Research

Janet C. Read and Matthew Horton

Abstract TeenCI is a new area for study and, as has been shown in this book, there are many challenges that need to be overcome. These challenges include access to teenagers, understanding the ethics around research, methods to engage with teenagers in research, as well as adjusting research for specialist settings such as healthcare. This chapter contributes a reflective understanding in regard to how best to choose methods and interpret results when working with teenagers. It presents a point of examination of the quality of research when mapped against the specifics of teenage autonomy and research positionality. The mapping is framed against an exploration of teenage culture as it impacts on research studies in TeenCI. Three studies are explored each, of which shed light on problems inherent in exploring teenage moods, preferences, likes and dislikes in HCI research. Some general guidelines are included for improving the quality of TeenCI research and two models are provided to assist in the framing of research in order that others examining the findings can make an informed decision as to the strength of any validity that is claimed from the research.

11.1 Introduction: Teen-Computer Interaction

As has been shown in the studies described in this book, teenagers are interesting to study in HCI. Not only are they an interesting sub-culture, they are also a group known to be early adopters, and users, of technology and so can shed light on technologies in unique ways. More than any other user group, teenagers have the freedom and the means to use technology for their own ends; unconstrained by work systems and work demands, financially mobile and technologically savvy, their use of technology is interesting and dynamic. Each 'generation' of teenagers adopts a new technology and uses it in their own way to fit with their own needs; it might be Blackberry Messenger, it might be Facebook, it might be YikYak, it might be

J.C. Read (✉) • M. Horton
Child-Computer Interaction Group, School of Physical Sciences and Computing, University of Central Lancashire, PR1 2HE, Preston, UK
e-mail: jcread@uclan.ac.uk

© Springer International Publishing Switzerland 2016

L. Little et al. (eds.), *Perspectives on HCI Research with Teenagers*,
Human–Computer Interaction Series, DOI 10.1007/978-3-319-33450-9_11

UToePA. Teenagers are also interesting, as their behaviours can be considered semi-tribal (Demant and Østergaard 2007). They move in groups, they have group identities and group values and they are highly protective and supportive of their own kind to the apparent disregard of others.

Researchers and developers in HCI have certainly been slow to move into the specific study of the design of technology for teenagers. There are logistic and pragmatic reasons for this such as difficulties with access and the perception that teenagers are quite challenging to work with as participants. This late attention to teenagers as a group worthy of consideration has inevitably highlighted that the methods used in HCI and in CCI might need adapting and changing – thus the very reason for this edited set of works as an opener on this space.

This chapter challenges the reader to think about where research might take us in the community as we seek to study methods for working with teenagers in HCI contexts. The intention is to challenge researchers working in this field to think considerably harder in order to do 'better' research. To provoke this discussion, two models on which to position TeenCI research work are presented along with guidelines for teen engagement.

11.2 Teenagers and Adults, Culture and Communication

Teenage culture has been studied in considerable depth by social scientists; much of the literature in this book comes from such study. Approaches have considered the cultural associations of groups of teenagers as well as the individual behaviours of isolated teens and the relationships within families of teenagers when interacting with non-teens. It is widely reported that teenagers inhabit a cultural space that is some distance from that inhabited by adults; it is also the case that groups of teenagers separately form cultural groups that can be quite distinct from one another. Aside from the teenage culture, the teenager is himself or herself situated in a national, ethical or local culture associated with his or her birth situation. It is known that in Western cultures, for example, the teenage culture is quite distant from the adult culture and the teenagers in these cultures tend to live quite separate from the adults; in other cultures, adults and teenagers are much closer. This is referred to as a divergence in the norms of adolescent and adult subcultures and this divergence characterises Western cultures (Schlegel &Barry 1991). The segregation of teens from adult society enables a teenage peer culture to flourish but at the same time this creates conditions in which the communication paths between the adult and teenager become problematic. At the same time, the teenager inhabiting a space some distance from adult culture may have increased autonomy due to his or her independence from the adult sub culture.

11.2.1 The Teen Reflection/Autonomy Landscape

In TeenCI research, an important consideration is therefore to examine the segregation of the teenage culture from the adult culture and be aware that this can be quite variable. This consideration needs to be made early in the research design; at the point of 'data creation' – ie when data is gathered. It is important to understand how much autonomy the teenagers might have in order to determine to what extent they are 'conforming' to adult views and adult images of the world. This autonomy is most important where a task that is associated with the data creation requires a great deal of reflection on the part of the teenager. A teenager with low autonomy, required to be very reflective, may contribute data that is not representative of his/her views. The relationship between the openness of the data being gathered and the autonomy of the teenager is shown in Fig. 11.1 – the TRALa (Teenage Reflection/Autonomy Landscape) model.

In the case of a research study, quadrant A represents where the teenager has a high degree of autonomy and where the data to be gathered is relatively easy to formulate by the teenager. In this instance there will naturally be a reasonable robustness to the data collected. Quadrant B represents where the teenagers have high autonomy but where the data requires deeper reflection – the quality of the data gathered here is more likely to be dependent on other aspects of the teenager's culture and on maybe the educational maturity and life experiences of the teenager. Such data will need to be treated with a lens of caution. Quadrant C also represents data that will need caution. Here, where teenagers have low autonomy, the data, whilst reasonably straight forward will perhaps have some power skews. The data should be looked at in terms of to what extent the teenagers felt free to express their views.

Quadrant D is the worst place to be in this matrix. The teenagers here have low autonomy and a complex task to complete; bringing together the difficulties associated with both situations. The caveats around life experience and education play into this along with any power skews. Researchers clearly need to be very careful about doing work in this area.

11.3 Better Research Design

The amount of autonomy that teenagers have in a study is partially cultural but it can also be about the design of the research. Techniques used in HCI that can be used to shrink power distances include the use, for example, of Obstructed Theatre (Read et al. 2010), a technique that describes a design problem without exposing any preconceived adult ideas so that the teenagers are not over influenced in what they design. Other techniques include paying close attention to relationships within power heavy locations, for example, the influence of teachers in school settings (Read and Mazzone 2008).

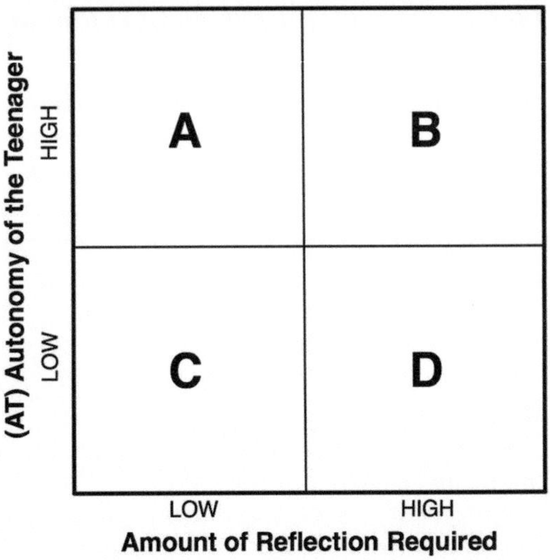

Fig. 11.1 TRALa – Teen Reflection/Autonomy Landscape

The research may need reflection on the part of teenagers in order to better understand what is being studied or seen. One way to reduce potential problems, where high levels of reflection are coupled with low autonomy, is to limit the use of open ended questions in surveys, provide guidance and scaffolding in interview situations and use props and tools to help teenagers express complex ideas. The trick for researchers is to be mindful of the two axes and to be cautious about working in the more problematic quadrants (like D).

11.3.1 The Researcher Interpretation/Distance Landscape

In all instances, teenagers inhabit different sub cultures than adults; it is the distance between these cultures that varies as opposed to the existence of them being called into question. In social science, the terms ingroup/outgroup or insider/outsider are used to frame how groups of people observing others might be affected by their different cultures, belief systems and values (Tajfel and Turner 1979). Insiders are thought to be better able to understand cultural subtleties when observing a group but outsiders are thought to be able to better see negative and positive aspects (Shope 2006). With insiders it is reported that they almost might know a culture so well that in interviews they are 'completing the sentences' of the individuals they are working with – this closeness can create almost a tunnel vision of observation whilst also an empathy for meaning (Kanuha 2000); thus it might be highly desirable for interpretation of signs and symbols but might be less effective for examining more direct research findings being less open to seeing things that are 'against' a personal belief.

Mullings (1999) writes that the division of onlookers into two tribes – viz. insiders and outsiders is problematic as there is more realistically a continuum where

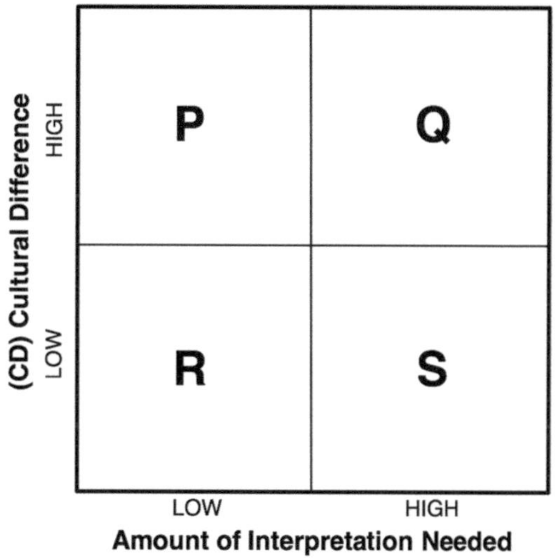

Fig. 11.2 RIDLa – Researcher Interpretation/ Distance Landscape

people are insiders or outsiders to a degree; further he suggests that it might be possible for a researcher to 'play' as an insider to some extent, or to 'play' as an outsider to some extent even if he or she would be traditionally seen as an outsider or an insider. The ability of a researcher to 'play' a different role is a key factor in situations where there is a large cultural difference between the adult and the teenager.

In TeenCI research, the positionality (as it is referred to by Visser (2001)), of the researcher is critically important when findings are being interpreted and analysed. The position of the researcher is therefore very important at the data analysis stage (typically more so than at the data creation stage where the position is less likely to affect interpretation and more likely to affect the choice of research designs); clearly the positionality of the researcher is most important where data needs to be strongly interpreted as opposed to simply being tabulated.

Figure 11.2 shows the RIDLa (Research Interpretation. Distance Landscape) model of researcher position and data interpretation and positions where research studies might situate. As in TRALa, the RIDLa model helps in the interpretation of 'difficult' positions in terms of data interpretation. In quadrant P in this model, the researcher is taking an outsider position on the data (large cultural distance) but the data is requiring minimal interpretation. This is a fairly safe place for analysis; any outsidedness of the researcher should not be so much of a problem. However, in quadrant Q, outsidedness becomes a potential concern for the reasons outlined earlier. Here, there is an outsider needing to interpret the meaning of teenage data. Without the context and knowledge of the teenage culture this interpretation might be questionable.

Quadrant R on this model has the insider as an interpreter of non-complex data. There has to be some caution in so far as this person may be seeking for confirmation of ideas but again, the lack of complexity in the data leaves this as a not too concerning arrangement. Quadrant S is the most problematic in this representation as the insider may both be very good at interpreting the data or may be very polarized and either of these positions, from the insider, could result in different meaning from the data. The advice for research teams might be to both be aware of one's own position when doing interpretation but also to consider making up teams of analysts who are not all standing at the same position.

11.4 Doing Better Research

As suggested in the literature, it may be possible to 'play' as an insider or outsider and thus bring new perspectives to the interpretation of data. A rather better solution is to become more familiar with teenage culture in order to be an informed insider. Where a problem in data interpretation is predicted, for example the work situating in quadrant S the researchers should seek to manipulate their position on the CD scale if at all possible and if that is not possible then it could be argued that the team should go back to the drawing board and redesign the study so that less interpretation is needed. An alternative in this case is to delegate interpretation to teens themselves, as seen in qualitative psychology (see Vaterlaus et al. 2015).

11.5 Application of TRALa and RIDLa to Cases

To illustrate these concepts and to bring the ideas into life, three cases are described here of HCI studies with teenagers. Each of these studies was carried out without consideration of any of the aspects outlined above; they are brought here to retrospectively reflect on positionality of researchers and teenage autonomy.

11.5.1 UThink

The UThink project was funded by the Esmee Fairburn foundation in the UK and sought to create an interactive product that could be used with teenagers to examine their emotional intelligence. The context behind the study was that there already existed a paper intervention that was used with psychologists and teenagers, in case settings, to discuss and explore responses to, and attitudes around conflict situations. The funding sought to create a game-like interface, to be also used in dialogue sessions, with a caseworker, in order that the activities around behaviour exploration would be more engaging. The HCI aspects of this project were around gathering design ideas for the new interactive product. A team of five researchers worked on this project, two were psychology graduate students, educated in the UK in an area local to the study, three were HCI researchers; one of these was from continental Europe and two had been educated in the UK. In terms of autonomy, the teenagers in this project were selected from a pupil referral unit, a school like institution where teenagers were 'held' having been excluded from at least two state schools. The pupil referral unit was therefore a place almost of correction and the attitudes within the location were of hostility to authority but also around controlling behaviours.

The data gathered in this project included plasticine cameos, shot with still cameras aka. Wallace and Gromitt, showing conflict scenarios, it included images of emotions for use in feedback and it included rich data. Thus there was data that needed considerable reflection to construct (eg what is a conflict scenario), interpretation was relatively straightforward as most of the data gathering activities were quite structured (Mazzone et al. 2008). On the TRALa model, most of the data collection in this study was in the D quadrant, but the problematic nature of this was reduced by making the tasks playful hence increasing autonomy; on the RIDLa model, most was somewhere between P and R but the inclusion of UK educated individuals in the research team tended this towards R.

11.5.2 ColourMe

The ColourMe project is a PhD study looking to see how colour might be used alongside mood as a means to allow teenagers to communicate with one another (Balta and Read 2014). Within this project, one of the research activities was to discover what teenagers thought about a range of colours and to examine whether or not these colours could be mapped to, or could represent, certain moods. For this examination teenagers were recruited from four countries (the UK, Denmark, Romania and the US). These teenagers completed a questionnaire online that was around 70 % simple questions (with answers chosen from a pre-given selection), and around 30 % reflective questions. These latter questions included things like *'Describe the colours in a room that you like'*.

In this study the researchers looking at the data were all from HCI. One was a young researcher who had been a teenager herself not so long ago in Romania, thus she would have been relatively close to the Romanian data; the other two were older, one had had several teenage children in the UK system in recent times, the other had not been near a school for over 40 years and had few encounters with teenagers. In the analysis of the data in this study, there was conflict across the team as to how literally each answer could be taken. The easy to interpret data was not a problem; the problem was a little more evident with the written answers. It was observed that none of the team had experience of the US school system – the students from that school were high achievers working in a school that encouraged innovation and free thinking as part of its identity therefore it was assumed that they would have high levels of autonomy. These were different from those from Romania for example although no attempts were made in the study to quantify these differences. In this study therefore, we would position the data gathering mainly in A, where students had high autonomy and little complexity; but for interpretation, there was certainly a mix of cultural distances, pushing interpretation towards Q. This was mitigated against by having a group doing the interpretation.

11.5.3 Cool

The third example is from a 3-year research project funded by RCUK that is referred to in Chap. 10 of this book in more detail. This project sought to design technologies for teenagers for energy reduction. The study in focus here was carried out early in this project and aimed to examine how best to design for teenagers. A study was designed to explore the concept of 'cool' as it attributed to teenage design. The research question was - could cool be captured and described as a design requirement for technology for teens? The study in this case took place in two UK schools with a team of four HCI researchers all of whom had been educated in the UK with two of them having children of an age similar to those being studied. Teenagers made data that was reflective in nature – they designed a bedroom of the future that would have in it all they could desire.

These designs were drawn on large sheets of paper and then analysed by the team in terms of what components were evident. The two schools were quite different. One had mainly high achieving pupils, one had mainly low achieving pupils, the regions of the city from which the two groups were recruited were quite different, one was largely middle class home owner parents in salaried employment, the other was primarily social housing, high levels of unemployment and temporary work contracts. These two groups clearly demonstrated different abilities to imagine (reflect) and convey but these were less about autonomy and more about ability to express themselves using the chosen tools, thus on the TRALa model, this work would be positioned between quadrants A and B. In examining the data, the team had to bring a lot of interpretation; for example, was the fish tank around the bed there for its novelty or for its retro-ness;? was the proliferation of TV products to do with wanting expensive items or to do with wanting non-personal entertainment?; this positioned the analysis in quadrants S and Q. There was some evidence of insider style confirmation behaviour where those with teenage children applied local beliefs to analysis (Read et al. 2011).

11.6 Discussion

This chapter has highlighted the need to consider the positionality of the researcher and the cultural positioning of the teenager in terms of its effect on HCI studies. It has suggested that, depending on the data being gathered and the extent to which it needs interpretation; there can be varying confidence in the results associated with the researcher's position and the teenager's autonomy. In bringing this book to its close, where readers have met a myriad of research ideas and have seen a collection of methods and cases, it is pertinent to consider what challenges the community needs to address as this research field matures. Clearly the research needs to take account of ethics, especially where studies are working with teenagers in health settings and in situations where their autonomy is reduced. There is a need to design novel and imaginative design and research methods that engage teenagers, speaking to their cultures, and there is a need to gather case studies of work with teenagers showing robust and effective ways to interpret data from teenagers. For researchers starting out on their careers, models like the two presented in this chapter may assist in avoiding some of the traps that exist in this research field. The practical examination of a research plan, coupled with extensive reading of the works of researchers publishing in this area will ensure that studies are carried out in as robust a way as possible.

For researchers working in TeenCI; the following suggestions are made:

1. Examine the autonomy of teenagers, ahead of research studies in terms of their freedom to express ideas and any parental influence (and teacher influence) on their contributions. Where autonomy is expected to be low – design the data capture with this in mind, or find ways to increase autonomy. In the study with enactments in Chap. 9, for example, the teenagers gain autonomy by virtue of the research design; similarly in the work in Chap. 5, the features of the participatory design are intended to bring autonomy to an otherwise constrained setting.
2. Researchers should examine their own position, along an insider/outsider scale and determine, given the amount of interpretation needed, whether this is a problematic position to be in. As a strong insider is the researcher seeking only to confirm his or her own beliefs, as a strong outsider are the wrong interpretations being made? If there is a problem, bring in other views or seek to 'play' a different position. Interpretation could have been a problem in the study in Chap. 6 with the rich pictures but this was mitigated against by using multiple coders. In Chap. 4, the researchers included the voices of teenagers to help make sense of the data. In Chap. 8, the data analysis was constrained in order to limit the amount of interpretation needed and hence minimize the risk of poor interpretation.
3. Seek to be clear, as is exemplified here in Chap. 5, about studies and the landscapes when reporting work. Be clear for the readers about the teenagers, the context, the culture and the adult influence.

Working with teenagers in HCI research is challenging and rewarding. There are pressing problems in the world and in teenagers' worlds, that need innovative solutions. Teenagers have hugely creative minds, known to be more so than other populations, so are well placed to contribute to solutions. They are easy adopters of technology and they have still the playfulness of children, making them an engaging group for innovative design installations. For HCI research with teenagers to become more than just a series of case studies, the community needs to further its thinking on methods and research design in order to create a body of reusable knowledge. In doing that it needs also to be mindful that the teenager is a shape shifter, how the teenager behaves from 1 year to the next is not predictable. For this reason, more than any other, researchers working with teenagers in HCI need to constantly be on the alert in order to understand cultural changes, power distances and flaws/shadows of interpretation.

These are exciting times for HCI as it embarks on a new adventure with teenage participants. These young minds have so much to bring to the design of interactive technology, even if they are sometimes unaware of this themselves. This is summed up rather splendidly by Mignon McLaughlin, who writes:

'How strange that the young should always think the world is against them – when in fact that is the only time it is *for* them. ~Mignon McLaughlin, *The Neurotic's Notebook*, 1960'

References

Balta A, Read JC (2014) Colour preference in teenage boys' bedrooms. In: Proceedings of the 28th international BCS human computer interaction conference on HCI 2014-Sand, Sea and Sky-Holiday HCI, BCS

Demant J, Østergaard J (2007) Partying as everyday life: investigations of teenagers' leisure life. J Youth Stud 10(5):517–537

Kanuha VK (2000) "Being 'native versus' going native": conducting social work research as an insider. Soc Work 45:439–447

Mazzone E, Read JC, Beale R (2008) Design with and for disaffected teenagers. Nordichi 2008, ACM Press, Lund, Sweden.

Mullings B (1999) Insider and outsider; both or neither; some dilemmas of interviewing in a cross-cultural setting. Geoforum 90(4):337–350

Read JC, Mazzone E (2008) "MESS days". Interfaces 71

Read JC, Fitton D, Mazzone E (2010) Using obstructed theatre with child designers to convey requirements. CHI2010, ACM Press, Atlanta

Read JC, Fitton D, Cowan B, Beale R, Guo Y, Horton M (2011) Understanding and designing cool technologies for teenagers. CHI2011, ACM Press, Vancouver

Schlegel A, Barry H (1991) Adolescence: an anthropological inquiry. NY Free Press, New York

Shope JH (2006) You can't cross a river without getting wet\A feminist standpoint on the dilemmas of cross cultural research. Qual Inq 12:163–184

Tajfel H, Turner JC (1979) An integrative theory of intergroup conflict. The social psychology of intergroup relations?, 33, 47

Vaterlaus JM, Patten EV, Roche C, Young JA (2015) # Gettinghealthy: the perceived influence of social media on young adult health behaviors. Comput Human Behav 45:151–157

Visser G (2001) On the politics of time and place in transforming South African research environment: new challenges for research students. S Afr Geogr J 83(1):233–239

MIX
Papier aus verantwortungsvollen Quellen
Paper from responsible sources
FSC® C105338

If you have any concerns about our products,
you can contact us on
ProductSafety@springernature.com

In case Publisher is established outside the EU,
the EU authorized representative is:
Springer Nature Customer Service Center GmbH
Europaplatz 3, 69115 Heidelberg, Germany

Printed by Libri Plureos GmbH
in Hamburg, Germany